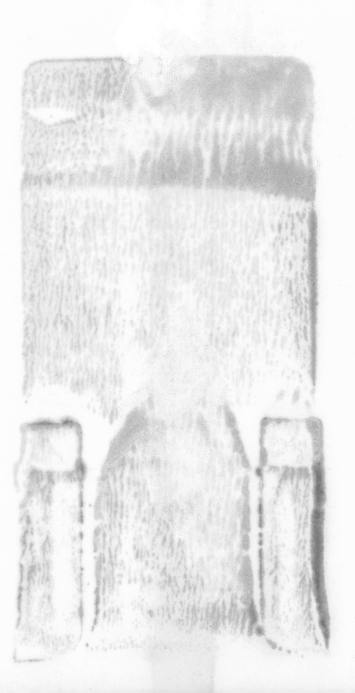

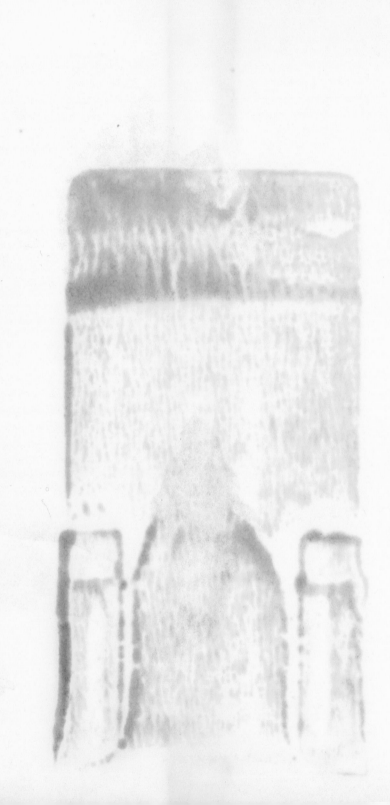

LOGIC
AND
REALITY

LOGIC
AND
REALITY

Gustav Bergmann

THE UNIVERSITY OF WISCONSIN PRESS

MADISON 1964

Published by the University of Wisconsin Press
430 Sterling Court, Madison 6, Wisconsin

COPYRIGHT © 1964 BY THE REGENTS OF
THE UNIVERSITY OF WISCONSIN

PRINTED IN THE UNITED STATES OF AMERICA BY THE
GEORGE BANTA COMPANY, INC., MENASHA, WISCONSIN

Library of Congress Catalog Card Number 64-10261

To Leola

Preface

SOME philosophers never change their minds. Those who do are of
two kinds. One kind vacillates, often abruptly, between two
extremes such as, say, phenomenalism and materialism. With
the other kind the changes are gradual and show a direction. I belong
to the latter kind.

This is my third book in first philosophy. In *The Metaphysics of Logical Positivism* (1954) the major concern is with epistemology; the
implicit ontology is a reluctant phenomenalism. Since the act is recognized, the phenomenalism is atypical. Recognition, though, is not
enough; it merely opens the way. The task is to find a dialectically adequate ontological assay of the act. If this decisive step has been made,
then, structurally, realism has been achieved. In *Meaning and Existence*
(1960) ontology has come to the fore; structurally, realism is achieved;
much of the phenomenalist debris is cleared away. In this book the
realism is explicit and fully articulated. In the concluding essay the
last piece of debris is buried. That leaves no doubt about the direction
of the several changes. They took me over twenty years. The reprieve,
even if only conditional, is welcome.

One who has struck out on his own, either ignoring or challenging the
fashions of the day, will not, if he is sober, be certain that everything
he has gradually come to believe is true. I am very sober. Yet there is
one belief I have come to hold very firmly. One cannot arrive at a dialectically adequate realism without recognizing that the world's form
exists. Logic is but a reflection of the world's form. Hence, one cannot
fully articulate one's realism without ontologizing logic. That accounts
for the title of this book and, more importantly, for its thematic unity.
The belief I so firmly hold is the theme. The fourteen essays are
fourteen variations on it.

Essays XIII and XIV, which were written last, have not been published before. Essays VII and XI appear here for the first time in English. Essays IV, VIII, XI, and XII are *pièces d'occasion*, lectures I was invited to deliver before academic audiences in Scandinavia and Italy during the academic year 1961/62, while enjoying the hospitality of the four Swedish universities. I was, however, allowed to choose my topics and I chose them so single-mindedly that I can only hope they fitted the occasions as well as my purpose of furthering the completion of this book.

Edwin B. Allaire, May Brodbeck, Reinhardt Grossmann, and Herbert Hochberg have been as indispensable to me as ever. More specific acknowledgments of what I have learned from them, either by talking or by reading what they have written, will be found throughout the volume.

Aside from a few editorial changes the nine pieces which were originally published in English are reprinted as they originally appeared. Essays I, VII, and XI are the originals of translations which appeared in Italian journals. A table indicating where each of these twelve pieces has been published will be found at the end of the volume. The necessary permissions by editors and publishers have been granted and are gratefully acknowledged.

May Brodbeck has once more helped the reader by spending much time and effort on making an index which is both detailed and accurate.

My wife skillfully and faithfully read the proof.

G. B.

Iowa City, Iowa
March, 1963.

Contents

LOGIC

AND

REALITY

Acts*

*Quand je voyais un objet extérieur, la conscience que je
le voyais restait entre moi et lui, le bordait d'un mince
liséré spirituel qui m'empêchait de jamais toucher
directement sa matière.*

Proust

LORD KEYNES tells us that "Moore had a nightmare once in which he could not distinguish propositions from tables." The manifest content of a bad dream often crystallizes around a traumatic experience during the day. In its manifest content Moore's was a philosopher's nightmare. I can think of a philosophical trauma that may have precipitated it.

A philosopher is one who has a certain "store" of articulate beliefs and argument patterns which he has acquired in trying to answer some philosophical questions. These questions usually form a "group" in the sense that the answers to them depend in several ways on each other. To work out answers to such a group which are thorough enough to be worthwhile and, above all, to secure them dialectically takes many years of hard labor. Sometimes it is therefore good strategy either to ignore or to touch but lightly even questions one knows to be related to his group. Eventually, though, such questions have a way of imposing themselves. When they do, the philosopher must provide reasoned answers, preferably drawing only on the store he has gathered, or, if he must add to it, taking care that the additions fit with what has been gathered before.

Moore at the time of his nightmare had already gathered a considerable store by thinking long and deeply about a group of questions the answers to which divided the realists, with whom he sided, from the

* This essay appeared first in Italian translation in Rivista di Filosofia, 51, 1960, 3–51. Subsequently the English original was published in The Indian Journal of Philosophy, 2, 1960, 1–30 and 96–117. Reprinted by permission.

3

idealists of his day, whom he hoped to refute. It could be, therefore, that during the day before the bad dream he had suddenly been impressed by one of those questions (such as the distinction between facts and propositions) with which idealists try to perplex realists and which he could not, or at least could not immediately, answer by drawing on his store. This, I imagine, was his trauma.

I have for quite some years and with ever increasing absorption labored on a group of philosophical questions about minds. Recently Reinhardt Grossmann, a younger friend who has joined me in these labors, asked me how, by drawing only on the store thus gathered, I could distinguish seeing something, say a tree, from either imagining it or thinking about it. The question was one I had strategically brushed aside before. This time, when I could not immediately give an answer sufficiently thorough to be worthwhile, I was impressed; perhaps because I have come to feel that the work on my original group has reached some sort of provisional closure. Though I was impressed, I had no nightmares. I just thought hard for a few days. Then I found what I believe is the answer. If it is, the strategy of temporary neglect has paid off once more. If it isn't, it will at least have helped me to solve a problem of a very different kind.

Some time ago the editors of this journal most graciously asked me for a contribution. I accepted the invitation with alacrity, not only because Italy has been *la patrie de mon coeur* ever since long long ago I first set foot on her sacred soil, but also because I am fascinated by the post-war renaissance of Italian philosophy. Nor is this the first time I enjoy the hospitality of an Italian philosophical journal. But the papers I have published in Italy so far all appeared in English, either with or without translation. Also, they all presuppose a measure of acquaintance with mathematical logic. That sort of thing does not have many readers, either in Italy or, for that matter, elsewhere. The editors suggested therefore that I do a piece, to appear in Italian only, that might reach a larger public. A synoptic exposition of my method and beliefs would be welcome. So would an essay on a specific topic, provided only it exemplify the method and be characteristic of the beliefs. Nor did they suggest that I use no symbols. No one could have asked for more leeway. Yet I was perplexed. To write a mere synopsis seemed tedious, no matter how useful it may be in the case of an author who publishes mostly essays.[1] Some specific topics I wouldn't know how to treat with-

---

[1] The most detailed exposition is to be found in *The Metaphysics of Logical Positivism* (Longmans, Green and Co., 1954) and *Meaning and Existence* (The University of Wisconsin Press, 1960). I shall refer to them as MLP and ME, respectively; with a numeral indicating the number of the essay. *Philosophy of*

out using symbols. Quite a few others could not, from where I stand, be so treated economically. And I did want to avoid the apparatus of symbolic logic. More seriously, if one is systematically as deeply involved and committed as I am, his treatment of most any specific topic, no matter how characteristic it may be, to some extent presupposes his "system." That is why, eager as I was, I was also perplexed. So I postponed and postponed. Grossmann's question solved my problem.

How do you distinguish your seeing a tree from either imagining it or thinking about it? It seems odd that one who claims to have spent many years on the philosophy of mind was not ready with an answer. The reason that in this case it really isn't is that during all these years my main concern was with one thing and one thing only: to secure the ontological status of mind within a pattern of analysis whose greatest weakness, as I had come to believe, was that it did not make an adequate place for mind. To speak as before, this concern determined my group. As I now clearly see, what happened was that, even though I spoke often of mind in general, I actually limited myself, with one exception, to the analysis of sensing. (The exception is my recent analysis of memory.[2]) Since only minds can sense, since sensing is a species of direct acquaintance, since I insisted that we are directly acquainted not only with what we sense but also with the act of sensing, and since in general the distinction between an "act" and its "content" is indeed the key to an adequate philosophy of mind, the limitation, severe as it may seem, did no harm as far as my original group was concerned. But now the time has come to get rid of it. That is what I propose to do in this paper which is thus about the specific question that puzzled me for a while. Since it is a philosophical question, I must first make clear what precisely it is about. This I shall do by first presenting as a background what an Italian philosopher might call *la problematica* of my original group. The presentation, in the nature of things, will be somewhat synoptic. But since it is done for a purpose, it may be selective and need not be too technical, which should help to avoid some of the tedium of a synopsis and will at any rate permit me to get along without symbols. The question itself is such that I can, not too uneconomically, answer it without using symbols. Thus, happily, there will not be a symbol in the body of this paper.

Mentioning symbols brings up the idea of method. A philosopher's

Science (The University of Wisconsin Press, 1957) is not primarily a book about first philosophy. But some relevant material may be found there, too.

[2] ME14.

method determines and is determined by his idea of the philosophical enterprise. Thus it is fundamental. My method is fundamentally linguistic. It also uses a symbolic scheme of the kind called an ideal language. *Relatively speaking*, that is a technicality. So I shall first of all, without mentioning ideal languages, say something about what I believe to be the right method and conception of philosophy. Later on, I shall indicate once or twice where, when things are to be done more thoroughly, the technique becomes indispensable.

From the tradition I know many philosophical questions. But I also know that most of the traditional answers as well as many of the questions themselves are either paradoxical or absurd. One philosopher tells us in all seriousness that bodies do not "exist"; another, that minds don't. A third, while telling us something, adds in the same breath as an essential part of his teaching that what he is just telling cannot be told (is "ineffable"). Clearly, that is paradoxical. What is to be done? At Vienna a generation ago, as at Oxford now, they took the nihilistic way out. We mistake for a philosophical question one that is either scientific or grammatical or, perhaps, a mixture of both. The mistake, or illusion, is the product of linguistic confusion. Such nihilism I emphatically reject. Instead, I distinguish between philosophical and commonsensical uses (of words). In each of the three examples I gave, at least one word is used philosophically, 'exist' in the first two, 'ineffable' in the third. Philosophical uses (I shall always mark them by double quotes) must be explicated or, as one also says, reconstructed by talking about them commonsensically; hence the tag, reconstructionism. The reconstructed question, typically, is neither scientific nor grammatical. Nor does it disappear. In answering it, one must again speak commonsensically, that is, to repeat, without using any word philosophically. The distinction between the two uses, philosophical and commonsensical, is one of the two fundamental ideas of the method. If anything, it is the more fundamental. So I shall, before turning to the second, consider an objection.

By what "criterium" do you distinguish the two kinds of use? How do you "define" common sense? Unless you do, what you shall say hangs in the air. Thus runs the objection. Assume that I fall into the trap and try to answer. If the answer be systematic, I shall be told that it "presupposes" my system; if commonsensical, that, as I should know from the tradition, common sense is anything but philosophically unproblematic. Assume, though, that unwarily I produce an answer which my original objector accepts as a "justification" of my method. If so, then another, either more tenacious or more familiar with familiar dialectical patterns, may ask me for a justification of the justification. What I would actually say, wary as I am, is not at all in the desired sense an answer. I would say, with unabashed circularity, that the philosophical uses are those which lead, in the familiar way, to either paradox or absurdity. The point is, first, that a method can only be judged by its results, that is, after it has been put to work. The demand that one must "justify" it before one may use it makes even less sense than the demand for "justification" usually does. (Notice the double quotes.) The point is, second, that what we do know from the tradition is not that either common sense or for that matter its long arm, science, is "problematic," which in an obvious sense it isn't, but rather, that with a little dialectical skill it can be made to yield the philosophical questions. But then, this very skill consists, among other things, in the unnoticed substitution of philosophical for common-sensical uses. Historically, the objection is but another version of the idealistic demand for a philosophy without "presuppositions." Unlike my first teachers, the logical positivists, I hardly ever use 'nonsensical'. So I shall merely say that philosophical questions containing the relevant use of 'presuppositionless' are among that atypical minority which upon reconstruction disappears.

Language has been called a picture of the world. The phrase is metaphorical and has been used philosophically. But it has a common sense core. If one knows the rules by which, literally, pictures of a certain kind are made, one can by studying such a picture find out a good deal about what it depicts. Similarly, if one knows the construction and interpretation rules of a language that can be spoken about the world, one can by studying them find out a good deal about the world. (I add "and interpretation," because these rules involve more than just grammar or, as one says, syntax.) This is the common sense core of the metaphor. The second fundamental idea of the method is that one always can and often must philosophize by talking about (the structure and interpretation of) a language in which everything commonsensical can be said. That one can do so is obvious. But the roundabout seems contrived. The question, therefore, is why often one must. The answer has two parts.

Language, like the thoughts it serves to express, is literally a part of the world. So it can itself be spoken about. This brings up the distinction between speaking and speaking about speaking. The two sentences 'Rome is beautiful' and 'Rome is the name of a city' illustrate it. Failure to observe it leads to ambiguity which in turn may lead to either absurdity or paradox. Analysis shows that such failure, in certain subtle contexts, is at the root of much philosophical talk, i.e., of talk in which words are used philosophically. More precisely, if such talk is reconstructed by the method, then it turns out that its peculiar flavor, of either paradox or absurdity or at any rate obscurity, has disappeared because in reconstructing it we have been aware of the distinction. The linguistic turn guarantees such awareness. This is the first part of the answer. The second goes deeper.

Any language of necessity *shows* certain features of the world which philosophers want to talk about but which cannot without futility be *expressed* in this language. Making use of a dialectical pattern Bradley invented, I recently showed that in considerable detail.[3] Here I shall only try to make it plausible. Consider 'Peter is blond'. Assume it to be true; that merely brushes aside what does not matter. The noun and the adjective name an individual and a property respectively. The sentence, by saying what it says, shows, without saying it, that the former exemplifies the latter. The copula, everyone knows, is expendable. 'Peter blond' would do. Some languages otherwise very similar to ours work that way. In this case one may say that the juxtaposition of the two names to form a sentence shows that the individual exemplifies the property. Consider now '(The individual) Peter exemplifies (the property) being-blond'. After a fashion, this longer sentence expresses (says) what the shorter one merely shows. However, it manages to do that only by showing, through the way in which its words are strung together, that the individual and the property jointly exemplify (relational) exemplification. In this obvious sense the longer sentence is futile. Anyone familiar with Bradley's regress knows that its peculiar futility has been a source of philosophical paradox. At this point, as so often in philosophy, it should help to grasp what has been said if attention is called to what hasn't. I shall make three such comments. First. One may object to the longer sentence on the ground that by "naming" Peter, the color of his hair, and exemplification, it suggests that these three entities enjoy the same ontological status. (I use 'entity' without ontological commitment.) I believe that the objection is well taken. Only, this is not what I have been talking about. Second. The longer sentence may be and in fact sometimes is used commonsensically as a somewhat stilted synonym of the shorter one. In this case it does not express what philosophers wish to talk about when mentioning exemplification. This marks it as a dweller on the critical boundary between philosophical and commonsensical uses. Third. I have not said that exemplification is "ineffable." Quite to the contrary. I suggested a safe way of talking about it.

What exists? That is the fundamental question of ontology. In both question and answer ontologists used 'exist' philosophically. Of course,

[3] "Ineffability, Ontology, and Method," *The Philosophical Review*, 69, 1960, 18–40, and pp. 45–63 of this book.

'exist' also has a commonsensical use. Commonsensically, 'Chairs exist' is synonymous with 'There are chairs'. A phenomenalist, for instance, does not therefore contradict himself by holding that while chairs exist (there are chairs), they yet do not "exist." Exploring ontological talk about "existents" (i.e., entities which "exist"), one soon discovers that it is governed by two ideas. First, every "existent" is a "simple." Second, all other entities "consist" of "simples." These uses of 'simple' and 'consist' are themselves philosophical. In explicating them one is forced into the linguistic turn. Take 'brown' and 'the color of my daughter's eyes'. The first refers to a certain color directly; the second, indirectly. A name, in the strict sense of 'name' and 'naming', is a word that tells us nothing about the entity to which it refers. It is, as one says, a mere label. The relevant notion of simplicity has several strands. One is unmistakable. An entity is a "simple" if and only if the only way of directly referring to it, in any conceivable language, is to name (label) it. To an entity which is not simple one can directly refer by an expression containing no other referential words than the names of certain simples. Of these latter the entity "consists."

Some ontologists hold that the world's simples are "things"; some others, that they are "facts." This is the deepest split. Among thing ontologists, the nominalists hold that "individuals" are the only existents. Others hold that "characters" (both properties and relations) also "exist." Still others add "quasicharacters." These uses of 'fact', 'thing', 'individual', 'character', and 'quasicharacter' are all philosophical. To explicate them in a dialectically safe manner one must again resort to the method. But I shall not tarry beyond mentioning, since the word is of my own coinage, that a quasicharacter is what is expressed by certain words connecting sentences, such as the 'because' in 'this is such-and-such because that is so-and-so'. Or, according to the way I speak, one who counts quasicharacters among the world's existents believes that some such words are names. As to my own views, if they are to be stated in traditional terms, I am a thing ontologist, I am not a nominalist, and I do not believe that quasicharacters "exist."

When I look at a red spot, I know not only that it is just that but also that the spot itself is an individual, that the color is a character (universal), and that the former exemplifies the latter. How do I come to know that? Or, what amounts to the same, what do 'individuality', 'universality', and 'exemplification' express? There are three types of answer. What is expressed is contributed by the mind. That is the idealistic answer. What is expressed is, literally, nothing. It seems to me that one who gives this answer has set his feet on a path which will eventually lead him to materialism. Wittgenstein certainly, in what now appears to me as a series of inevitable steps,[4] moved from the doctrine of the *Tractatus* that "logical form" is nothing (and "ineffable"!) to the implicit materialism (philosophical behaviorism) of the *Investigations*. The third answer, I believe, is the right one. "Logical form" has ontological status. This status, while radically different from that of "existents," does not depend on minds. Notice the double quotes around 'logical form'. Again, I shall not tarry to explicate this use. Instead, I throw in another traditional word in order to provide, by means of a traditional formula, a rough idea of my view. The world's "form" does not "exist," yet it "subsists." Some truths, e.g., the ones obtained from 'S or not-S' by substituting any sentence for the letter, express features of the world's "form." Such truths are called "analytic." The explication of this use of 'analytic' is a very major problem. For its solution, symbols (ideal languages) are indispensable. As to terminology, I use *logical*, both for the word and the thing, when I speak about features of the world's "form." Speaking about what either exists or "exists," I use, again for both word and thing, *descriptive*. As to the expository strategy of this essay, remember that I used exemplification as an example before. I did that to prepare the ground for what has just been said. And I am now preparing the ground or planting a signpost for one of the fundamental ideas of my analysis of mind. A world in which there are minds contains not only characteristic "existents" but also a characteristic logical constituent. This constituent is expressed by 'means', whenever it is used in such sentences as '(The thought that) Peter is blond means that Peter is blond'.

Since I have begun planting strategic signposts, let me go on for a moment doing just that. To do it most efficiently, it will be best to indicate first how I shall use certain crucial words. To mark them as crucial, I shall italicize the first occurrence of each. I shall not, however, surround them by double quotes. For the uses I shall make of them are all commonsensical, just as the sentences of the next paragraph in which they occur are all truths, and even truisms, of common sense. But perhaps I should mention that in this case, as in so many others, common sense includes certain elementary data of phenomenology and analytic introspection, which latter two are indeed two things and not one. Of this later.

A thing is either *physical* or *phenomenal* and never both. Nor is there any intelligible sense of 'physical', 'phenomenal', and 'consist' in which a thing consisting of physical things could be called phenomenal or,

---

[4] Edwin B. Allaire is now engaged in a detailed analytical study of this transition. See his "Tractus 6.3751," *Analysis*, 19, 1959, 100–105.

conversely, one consisting of phenomenal ones, physical. Call this the first great dualism of our world. I dislike 'dualism'; would rather say that in this fundamental respect ours is a two-level world. But I cannot quite resist the convenience of the shorter expression. A chair, its shape, and its color are physical. So is a nerve cell. A visual sensum, its (phenomenal) color, a memory image, a sensing, a seeing, a remembering are phenomenal. The two levels are, as one says, mind and body. 'Mental' is often used as I here use 'phenomenal'. For reasons of my own I reserve 'mental' for a more restricted use. That has something to do with the other great dualism. The first directly divides all things into two mutually exclusive kinds. The second rests on the distinction between an *act* and its *intention*. Sensing, perceiving, thinking, remembering, imagining are kinds of acts. What is sensed, perceived, thought of, and so on, is the intention of an act. This distinction is more complex than the first. I sense a colored spot. In this case not only the sensing, which is the act, but also the colored spot, which is its intention, is phenomenal. I perceive a chair. The act, of course, is again phenomenal. Its intention, though, is physical. The distinction is thus not just one among phenomenal entities. On the other hand, while there are many things which never were and never will be intentions of acts, one act often is the intention of another. The distinction thus does not directly divide all phenomenal things into two mutually exclusive kinds. Yet it leads to such a division. For there are phenomenal things which are neither acts nor ingredients (not: intentions!) of acts. To have a name for this kind of thing I shall call them *primary*. Sensa and the characters they exemplify are primary things. (They are not the only ones.) The acts which intend them are of course sensings. Sensing is merely a species of being (directly) *acquainted*. For we are sometimes directly acquainted with some of our acts though we do of course not sense them. (Whether sensing itself is a genus does not matter for my purpose.) Finally, every phenomenal thing is either primary or (the ingredient of) an act. I express this by saying that just as our world is a two-level world (every thing is either physical or "mental"), so our minds are two-level minds (every "mental" thing is either primary or ((the ingredient of)) an act). The use I just made of 'mental' is quite common as well as commonsensical. I surrounded it with double quotes merely because in this essay I shall consistently avoid it, using 'phenomenal' instead and calling *mental* those and only those phenomenal things which are not primary. Arbitrary as it may seem, this choice of words will not only prove convenient; it will also appear that it makes structural (and historical) sense.

That much for the crucial words and some important truisms. Now for four comments. The first states still another truism which I shall need. The remaining three are minor signposts. Then I shall be ready for the major signpost I want to plant.

First. There is still another dichotomy among phenomenal entities. Some "contents" can be decomposed by *analytical introspection.* Those which can't are called *introspective simples.* This division overlaps the other. Pitches, taken phenomenally, are instances of introspectively simple primary characters. Remembering, as I have analyzed it, is an introspectively simple mental character. Right now, I shall merely say that the two notions are commonsensical. Later on, we shall have to explore what goes on when we introspect.

Second. I gave two examples of intentions, a colored spot, taken phenomenally, and a chair. A colored spot, or, rather, a spot being colored is a fact, not a thing. A chair, as we ordinarily speak and think of it, is a thing. I hold that, strictly speaking, every intention is a fact (i.e., what is expressed by a sentence). Or, as I have put it, all awareness is propositional. In some contexts the matter is of great importance. Nothing untoward will happen, though, if in this essay I do not press the point.

Third. Some sentences in the next to the last paragraph would be less labored had I not deliberately avoided calling acts things. The parenthetical mention of their ingredients served the same purpose. As will transpire, I hold acts to be facts, not things. That is indeed one of the two fundamental ideas of my analysis of mind. (The other is the logical constituent expressed by 'means'.) But I did not want to anticipate it; nor of course did I want to say anything that seems to contradict it; hence the circumstantiality.

Fourth. Traditionally, what an act intends is called either its content or its intention. In my earlier writings I used 'content'. Henceforth I shall avoid 'content' completely, use 'intention' instead. The main reason for the change is this. On the one hand, 'content' is often so used that it carries the connotation of something phenomenal. In the first comment I quite deliberately provided an example of this use. (That is why I there surrounded the word with double quotes.) On the other hand, intentions are either physical or phenomenal. There is thus the danger of a blur. In my earlier writings, since I dealt in detail only with phenomenal intentions, no harm was done. Now it seems better to avoid the danger. Nor is this the only reason for the change in words. In the tradition, 'content' has also been so used that an act's content is not its intention but, rather, what provisionally I called one of its ingredients.[5] Of this later.

---

[5] This has been impressed upon me by Reinhardt Grossmann, who combines an accurate grasp of the issues with a thorough knowledge of the act tradition.

In philosophy as elsewhere, the most attention is not always given to the most profound. Ontology, during the last three hundred years or so, is a case in point. Little as I could say about it, I managed to give quite a list of ontological questions. They are, I am convinced, the most formidable as well as the most profound. The realism issue is not even on my list. Yet during all this time it received what I have come to believe is an undue amount of attention. The *realism issue* is a short name for the familiar group of questions debated between the classical realists on the one hand and the classical phenomenalists and idealists on the other. The realism group overlaps with another, centering around the first dualism and traditionally known as the mind-body problem. Because of this overlap, the realism and mind-body problems are inseparable. The connection between the two groups centering around the two great dualisms is of a different kind. Closely related as they are, there are yet in each group some questions the answers to which do not depend on the answers to some in the other group. What may happen if that is not clearly seen is what I believe did happen. Some classical philosophers, intent on dialectically securing the "existence" of physical things, thought it necessary to deny that acts "exist." Quite a few of these ended up as materialists, also denying, either explicitly or implicitly (like the later Wittgenstein), that primary phenomenal things "exist." Some others, equally intent on dialectically securing the "existence" of acts, found it necessary to deny that physical things "exist." Some extremists among them even denied that primary phenomenal things "exist." (Italian philosophers will at this point think of Gentile.[6]) Both sides were deceived. One is not dialectically forced to the denials of either the moderates or the extremists (materialists, absolute idealists) among them in order to assert what they wanted to assert. The diagnosis, if correct, is important. So I built my expository strategy around it. My specific topic is a question in the philosophy of mind, one of the group centering around the second dualism. I promised to expound it against a background. I shall keep

---

He is now engaged in writing a book on it. Intriguingly, he also tells me that my views are closest to Twardowski's. I know Twardowski's name, of course; but I have never read a line of his.

[6] To mention Gentile in this way is not to imply that, had I been faced with the same unfortunate choice which the Italian philosophers had to face for so long and had I not been able to think of an alternative, I would not have sided with Gentile against Croce. No one who has ever felt the fascination of first philosophy could do anything else. The many important and delightful cultural pursuits that go traditionally by the name of philosophy are one thing. So are political allegiances. First philosophy is another thing. I am about to say, in the text, that the epistemological turn can and has been overdone. But to reject it entirely or not to appreciate it is to reject or not to appreciate first philosophy.

the promise by showing what does and what doesn't depend on what in the two groups centering around the two dualisms, as well as how what doesn't has come to be mistaken for what does.

A philosopher, pointing at a chair, asserts that it is a chair. Or he asserts that physical objects exist. Another asks him on what ground he makes these assertions. He answers. Thereupon the other repeats the question. And so on. This question and answer game has always been a discernible strand of the dialectic. At the beginning of the modern period it became dominant, or very nearly so. Call this the epistemological turn. As philosophy took it, the realism issue came to the fore. To understand the connection, consider that the question and answer game cannot go on indefinitely. Both parties therefore must agree on a rule for breaking it off. "Every statement (assertion) must be analyzed down to what we are acquainted with." On this rule everyone agreed, either explicitly or implicitly, except perhaps some radical sceptics whom I leave to their doubts. Call it the Principle of Acquaintance (PA). 'Acquainted' and 'analyzed down' are the operative word and phrase. I shall first unpack the phrase, then the word. A statement, S, has been analyzed down when one has arrived at a second, S', such that, first, S and S' are either both true or both false, and, second, the referential words in S' are all names of what we are acquainted with. 'Acquainted' has two uses. Having more or less thoroughly inspected a physical thing, we may say, quite naturally, that we are acquainted with it. This is the broad use. In the narrow use, the only things we are acquainted with are phenomenal. Both uses are commonsensical, though the narrow one is of course a bit esoteric. Sometimes it is marked by an adverb ('directly acquainted'). For my purposes it will be better to mark the broad use. So I stipulate that in this essay 'acquaintance' without qualification refers to direct acquaintance. That also goes for PA.

A classical phenomenalist may reasonably be taken to hold that only phenomenal things "exist." That is his formula. How does he arrive at it? How does he use 'exist'? I shall answer in three steps. The answer will both clarify and confirm what has been said so far. First. The transition from phenomenal things to introspective simples is an easy one. The only direct way of referring to introspective simples, in any conceivable language, is to name them. So I modify the formula to assert that only introspective simples exist. It follows that the phenomenalist's "existents" are simples in two commonsensical meanings of the word. That confirms my diagnosis that ontologists search for "simples" as well as, in one important case, my explication of the philosophical use of 'exist'. Second. "We cannot know anything to exist or, if it exists, what it is like unless we are acquainted either with it or with a part of it or, wholly or in part, with a thing of its sort."

Call this proposition K. How is 'know' used in it? Either it is used commonsensically. In this case K is patently false. Or it is used philosophically, so that 'knowing', with some qualifications suggested by K
itself, is synonymous with 'being acquainted with'. In this case K is
tautological. Third. All phenomenalists accept PA as well as, more or
less explicitly, the use of 'knowing' which makes K tautological. But
from PA and K their formula follows. Hence the agonizing stalemate
between the classical phenomenalists and those classical realists who,
as many of them do, accept PA. It was a stalemate rather than a phenomenalist victory because as long as the two uses of words are not
distinguished, common sense inevitably rebels. The distinction is indeed
the only way out, or, rather, it is the first step on this way. The classical
philosophers, we know, did not make the distinction. G. E. Moore,
though, the great master who recently left us, did make it, after a
fashion. So did a group of philosophers known as the linguistic phenomenalists. Moore failed. The linguistic phenomenalists remained
under suspicion, not unjustly I think, of being implicit phenomenalists.
Again, it will help if I explore what went wrong in these two cases.

Moore insisted that philosophers must speak commonsensically.
That is one of his two great merits. He accepted PA. Unhappily, he also
accepted as commonsensical or, at least, as in some sense appropriate
the use of 'knowing' that makes K tautological. His way out, or, if you
please, his formula was to hold that a physical thing is a spatio-temporal
congeries of primary phenomenal things. Everyone knows, though,
how cautious he was. So it might be more cautious to say that this
would have been his favorite way out. That alone makes it worth our
while to grasp clearly why it is a dead end. If 'physical' and 'phenomenal' are to be taken commonsensically, and I merely follow Moore's
teaching when I insist that I wouldn't know how else to take them, a
physical thing simply isn't a congeries of phenomenal ones. Or, to say
the same thing differently, Moore did not in his formula observe his
admirable injunction that we must always speak commonsensically.
That alone suffices to dismiss the formula.[7] But I shall add three comments. First. I spoke of a spatio-temporal congeries. (That provides a

---

[7] The same goes for William James's "neutral monism." Only, James adds still
another absurdity. His simples, like Moore's, are phenomenal things. Yet he tells
us that to be a phenomenal thing is to be, or perhaps to be in, a certain kind of
congeries. His awareness of the act problem, unlike Moore's, is dim at best.
Russell, in his Jamesian phase, was more keenly aware of it. See especially his
1924 piece, "On Propositions: what they are and how they mean," reprinted
in *Logic and Knowledge* (R. C. Marsh, ed., Macmillan, 1956). Since then, though,
he has steadily moved down the slope toward that dismal materialism (identity
of mind and brain) which now he so loudly proclaims. It is deeply sad that this
may be the last word of one who is nevertheless the dominant figure of the century.

commonsensical meaning for the ontologist's 'consist'.) In the large body of literature following these lines there is a tendency, to say the least, to take 'spatio-temporal' physically in this context rather than phenomenally. That clearly begs the question. Second. Immersing one's self into this literature, one is overcome by a feeling of futility and frustration. Something, one feels, has gone radically wrong. What is wrong, I submit, is that it simply isn't the philosopher's business to tell us what physical things, be they chairs or electrons, consist of, in any conceivable commonsensical sense of 'consist'. That is the business of the scientists. I stand forever vigilant to repel their intrusions into philosophy. But I am equally prepared to restrain transgressions in the opposite direction. Third. Moore emphasized the second dualism; as he sometimes put it, the distinction between seeing and what is seen, their being two things and not one, as well as our being acquainted with both. This emphasis, at a time when it was badly needed, is his other great merit. Interestingly in this context, he called only acts mental. That alone does not make primary phenomenal things into plausible constituents of physical ones. Nothing is further from my mind than to accuse Moore of either so crude an error or of a verbal trick. Yet I cannot but feel that the remark is somehow to the point.

Unlike Moore, who erred by commission, the linguistic phenomenalists failed through omission. Remember the way I unpacked 'analyzing down'. It shows how at this point the linguistic turn quite naturally suggests itself. The linguistic phenomenalists, as their name indicates, took this turn. For every sentence S mentioning physical things there is another, S', such that, first, S and S' are either both true or both false and, second, the referential words in S' are all names of what we are acquainted with. That is the main thesis of these philosophers. More or less implicitly, they also accepted K. They did not say, however, that introspective simples (or, perhaps, phenomenal things) were the only "existents." Their critics put it to them that whether or not they actually said it, what they did say implied just that. The linguistic phenomenalists replied that either to assert or to deny that only phenomenal things "exist" is to talk ontologically; that philosophical talk in general and ontological talk in particular makes no sense; and that they themselves therefore studiedly abstained from such talk. The reply is so woefully incomplete that the critics were more nearly right than wrong. What were the crucial omissions?

In answering this question I shall change tactics. So far I have spoken analytically. Now I shall show my hand. I accept PA. Why, then, shouldn't I, too, be found guilty of implicit phenomenalism? The charge is grave. So I beg to be accorded the time—I have the breath—

for a careful defense. I shall first indicate an argument I shall not use, then explain the two crucial omissions.

Even though I tried not to tip my hand, the reader will have guessed, correctly, that I emphatically reject K. If 'knowing' is used common-sensically, K is patently false. Or else the proposition introduces a special use of 'knowing'. This use not only serves no purpose but almost inevitably spawns confusion. That is why I reject K. If, however, I rested my case there, I would merely appeal to common sense in order to dodge the dialectic of the realism issue. This is the wrong kind of appeal to common sense. Nothing is further from my mind. I merely reject an opening move which is transparently inept. This is fundamental. That in entering this or any other dialectic I insist on unravelling it by the method is, relatively speaking, a matter of detail. This shows in what sense I am and in what sense I am not a "common sense philosopher." (The label has been pinned on me, with all sorts of sociological overtones, by one of my Italian critics.)

The method enjoins us to abstain from philosophical talk. This, though, is merely its negative moment. If, by means of it, we are to do what the classical philosophers tried to do, two more things are required. We must explicate the philosophical uses. I proposed what I believe to be an adequate explication of the philosophical use of 'exist'. But again, by this explication alone the linguistic phenomenalists could not have refuted their critics. Rather, it would have made them see how well founded the criticism really is. To meet it successfully, one must also do the other thing which the method requires.

Physical things "exist." They do not "exist." The classical positions clash. The clash seems irreconcilable. Yet, each classical position has a commonsense core. The method reveals these cores and permits us to state them so that they no longer clash with each other. This is the second thing that needs to be done. Since it is also the heart of the enterprise, I want to say a bit more about it. First, though, let us take leave of the linguistic phenomenalists. As far as it goes, what they said is not wrong. But we understand now how far short it falls from what needs to be said. All that these philosophers did, or rather, tried to do, for they did not always succeed in not speaking philosophically, was to state once more the commonsense core of phenomenalism! Thus they could not hope to escape the charge of implicit phenomenalism.

I just spoke of *the* commonsense core of a classical answer or position. That sounds as if there were one such core, to be uncovered once and for all by a mechanical application of the method. Things are not that simple. Is it then better to speak of several cores which can and therefore must be distinguished? Yes and No. It will do as long as one keeps in mind that these several cores are dialectically connected in many ways and in such a manner that some of them may be said, quite intelligibly, to lie deeper than some others. The recovery of this dialectic is the heart of the enterprise. Nor need the search in depth ever come to an end. Its only limits are the limits of our ingenuity. To reconstruct and reconcile the classical positions is to pursue that search. But there is something peculiar about such reconstruction. Otherwise there could be no reconciliation. To explain the peculiarity, I shall venture a comparison.

At the beginning of the century a new style in painting emerged. Its name, cubism, alludes only to a part of the novelty. The other part is this. We are told that we are looking at a picture of a guitar, or of a woman's face. At first glance, with an untutored eye, we see nothing of the kind. Looking more closely, we discern "elements"; different perspectives of the object in question in what seems an arbitrary scatter; or perspectives of the several different parts of the object; or, perhaps, merely a scatter of characteristic lines. Looking still more closely, we discover that the apparent scatter is a very deliberate pattern which in its own way justifies the claim that we are looking at a picture of either a guitar or a woman's face. Yet there is nowhere a representational image. The reconstructionist's several cores are like the painter's "elements." His deliberate pattern is produced by the method. As in the painter's case, elements and patterns are equally essential. Finally, just as there is nowhere on the canvas a representational image, so the reconstructionist never speaks philosophically. It may help the reader and it will at any rate help me to plant another signpost if I illustrate the last point.

At the very beginning I averred that to secure the ontological status of mind has long been my major concern. But I also refuse to speak ontologically. How can these two things be reconciled? I so analyze the act that its ingredients become introspective simples of the kind I call mental. I also hold, as the phenomenalists did, though without making the mistakes they made, that *in principle* and for certain purposes every statement mentioning physical objects can be replaced by another one in which all the referential words name introspective simples of the kind I call primary. *Hence, if I were to speak philosophically, as I do not, I would have to say that minds "exist" in exactly the same sense in which bodies do.* Thus I secure locally the ontological status of minds. I say locally because, since there is nowhere a representational image, success ultimately depends on the pattern as a whole as much as on the local "element." Some will not like all this subtlety, finding it excessive and even devious. I merely observe, with a smile, that whatever method a philosopher may adopt, he needs indeed *l'esprit subtil*. Nor can he do without *l'esprit géometrique*. For that need I am on record as a user of artificial languages (formalisms) though not, I hope, as a "formalist." (This label, too, has been bestowed on me by an Italian critic.)

The realistic position has quite a few commonsense cores. Since I have not in this essay made it my business to do justice to all of them, I shall introduce but two, the one which is the deepest and the one which I think is the most obvious and shallow. The latter I mention because, even though it is obvious and shallow, it has been the source of much quibbling, and because, since it is so obvious and shallow, the quibbles can be dismissed rather casually. There is nothing casual about the former. One very good reason for calling it the deepest is that one must grasp it accurately in order to understand the connections (and the lack of such) between the groups of the two great dualisms.

Return to the sentence in the next to the last paragraph in which I underlined the phrase 'in principle'. Use S and S' as before. There is no sentence S', or, perhaps better, it is for more than one reason quite beyond our power to construct a sentence S' which could for all purposes serve as S does. As one usually says, the "phenomenalistic reconstruction" is schematic or a reconstruction in principle only. That is why I underlined the phrase. The obvious core at which this circumstance points is rather well expressed by those who insist that while sensa are transparent, thin, and fleeting, physical reality is opaque, thick, and enduring. Of course. No reasonable man will disagree. The shallow argument holds that PA may be rejected on this ground alone. It is properly refuted by pointing out that "phenomenalistic reconstruction" has one and one purpose only, namely, to serve as a tool for philosophical analysis, and that, even though merely schematic, it serves this purpose exceedingly well.

A thing is what it is irrespective of whether or not either you or I or any one else perceives it, remembers it, thinks of it, and so on. This is the deepest core. Notice that I said thing, not just physical thing, thus including phenomenal ones. That alone shows how deeply the issue cuts. Commonsensically, the proposition is a truism. I, for one, am as intent as the most embattled classical realist on securing it dialectically. The phenomenalists, since they either ignore or explicitly deny that acts "exist," cannot even begin to do that. The idealists, as consistently they should, dialectically undermine the truism. The nexus between an act and its intention is not only unique (*sui generis*) but also so close that they must be counted as one "existent" rather than as two (or more). This is the gist of their contention. Nor is it hard to find the commonsense core on which it rests. Phenomenally, the nexus is close indeed. When the medievals said that an act's intention "inexists" in it, they acknowledged this closeness and uniqueness by coining a new word. As will transpire, I agree that the nexus in question is *sui generis*. (I use 'nexus' rather than the more idiomatic 'relation' whenever I do not wish to prejudge whether the "nexus" is a relation, or a quasirelation or, perhaps, something else. Technically, it will be remembered, relations obtain among things; quasirelations either among facts or among facts and things).

Clearly, we stand here at the point where the two great dualisms hang together. Moore saw that. Otherwise he wouldn't have begun his refutation of idealism by arguing so painstakingly that the notion of an unsensed sensum is not a contradiction in terms. Problematic as it may seem, I agree that it isn't. Moore, we saw, slipped when he tried to build a bridge from this defensible premiss to the indefensible conclusion that a physical thing is a congeries of sensa.

Just as clearly, everything depends on an adequate analysis of the act, in the case its intention is phenomenal, which as I now clearly see is all I have done so far, as well as in the case it is physical, which is the specific topic of this essay. To be adequate, the analysis must satisfy two conditions. First, it must, together with others, lead to the solution of all philosophical problems. (As always, the "pattern" is as important as the "local element." I once expressed that by the formula, which has been much misunderstood, that the method must solve all philosophical problems "simultaneously.") The analysis must, second, jibe with common sense. Common sense, we just saw, in this case includes some stark facts of phenomenology. Specifically, the analysis must do justice to that commonsense core of the idealistic position, the closeness of the nexus between an act and its intention. But common sense in this case also includes its long arm, science. Specifically, the analysis must jibe with the thesis of psychophysiological parallelism. I shall next say what needs to be said about that thesis.

Psychophysical parallelism is the name of a philosophical position. That is why I avoided the phrase. Psychophysiological parallelism is a scientific thesis. Science deals with facts and with facts only and it deals with them commonsensically, not dialectically. A scientific thesis is a very broad or sweeping factual statement, of the sort called a frame of reference, in which the known facts and laws fit and those as yet unknown are with good reason expected to fit. Since it is so sweeping, a thesis always remains open to doubt; it is a "guess" in the peculiar sense in which the Humeans use 'guess'. Why then need we bother with it? In a manner of speaking which is as easily understood as, alas, it is misunderstood, the philosopher in his own peculiar way suited to his own peculiar purpose describes the world. His purpose is dialectical clarification. Thus he better make sure that what he clarifies or analyzes is the world we actually live in. Among the best relevant information available are the theses of science. This is just a piece of common sense *about* philosophy and surely a far cry from the stultifying scientism of the logical positivists. One who objects to it on the ground that science changes and therefore a thesis at best remains forever open, conceives of the philosophical enterprise as a search for certainty in some elusive sense of 'certain' which I do not even understand. This is just another piece of common sense about philosophy, the one to which the pragmatists herostratically sacrificed everything else. As to "certainty," the task is not to establish it but, rather, to explicate the several philosophical uses of 'certain'.

What happens when Jones perceives a chair? The scientists' account has two parts.

First. A complicated physical process has occurred. At the end of it Jones's brain is in a state in which it would not be if it were not for the presence and the physical properties of the chair. This is not to say that what this state actually is depends only on the chair. It also depends on the state of Jones's body, including his brain, when the process began. And there are still other factors. Yet we say, perfectly intelligibly, that the chair is the cause of the brain state.

Second. Whenever Jones's brain is in a certain state, he himself is in a certain conscious state. (One often says, and I would rather say so myself, that he has a certain mental content. 'Conscious', as will appear, is even a bit misleading. But I have in this essay reserved 'mental' for another use and altogether forsworn 'content'.) The conscious state and the brain state that go together are of course two things and not one. A scientist who insists that they are one no longer speaks as a scientist or, for that matter, commonsensically, but embraces the absurd philosophical position of materialism. He remains within his province when he tells us that the nexus between the two states is not one of cause and effect in either direction. Whenever there is the one, there is the other, and conversely. That is all. Or, perhaps, the nexus is many-one in the direction from body to mind. This is a matter of scientific detail, just as that the relevant bodily state is in the brain and not in the left little toe. This is the scientists' account of perception. It will pay to add another piece of their frame of reference.

Third. The physical universe is comprehensively lawful and causally closed.[8] Hence, the only way in which a conscious state, whether perceptual or volitional or anything else, can interact with any part of the physical universe is through its parallel brain state. To interact here means, of course, to make a difference for the ensuing part of the physical process. With this piece of scientific common sense the dialectic of "freedom" must be made to jibe. That, though, is another task I have not undertaken in this essay. I turn to what does and what does not follow for what I did undertake.

Jones's conscious state, when perceiving the chair, may be just a percept. (I use this very loose term, percept, only provisionally.) Or it may be just an act of perceiving. Or it may be (contain) both, percept as well as act. The three alternatives are equally compatible with the scientists' account. That is crucial. The mistaken belief, held either explicitly or implicitly, that in order to safeguard the scientific account one must purge the act pervades and vitiates much of the tradition. *This is one way in which the groups of the two dualisms do not hang together.* But, of course, so widespread a belief must rest on grounds which are at least *prima facie* plausible. These grounds will become clear as we proceed.

Assume, then, that the conscious state is (or contains) an act of perceiving. The act's intention is the physical thing, in our example, the chair. How about the nexus between the two, that nexus which is so uniquely intimate? One may try to discover it within the scientific account. As I shall presently show, what one finds there is not sufficiently close or intimate. That creates a dialectical problem. *This is one way in which the groups of the two dualisms do hang together.* One may of course on this ground reject the scientific account. That is merely quixotic. Really to solve the problem, one must discover outside of the scientific account a nexus which is compatible with it and, at the same time, close enough to do justice to the commonsense core of idealism. As will eventually transpire, my solution is of that kind. Next I shall show why what the scientists tell us will not do.

The nexus between the act and the chair in the scientific account has two links. One, call it causal, connects the chair with the physiological state. The other, call it parallelistic, connects the latter with the act. 'There is something which is a such-and-such if and only if there is something else which is a so-and-so'. All details apart, this is the schema of the parallelistic link. Notice, first, that it is synthetic. Notice, second, that while 'such-and-such' and 'so-and-so' mark the places of descriptive words referring to phenomenal and physical (physiological) charac-

---

[8] For an analysis of these two notions, see *Philosophy of Science*.

ters respectively, all other words in it are logical. Notice, third, that these logical words all express features that would subsist in a world otherwise like ours but without minds. (Remember what was said at the beginning about the ontological status of logic.) I express this by calling the parallelistic link synthetic, logical, and nonspecific (with respect to mind). Call such a link correlational; the nexus between an act and its intention, intentional. Any explication which makes the intentional link correlational does not do justice to its peculiarity. No chain is stronger than its weakest link. For our immediate purpose, therefore, we need not even examine the causal link. The intentional nexus is not to be found in the scientific account. But a little digression here will smooth the exposition.

Scientists merely try to discover what is the cause of what, are not concerned with the dialectic of "cause," use 'cause' commonsensically. So, therefore, in epitomizing their account, did I. Now the dialectic looms. The causal nexus is correlational. This is the gist of Hume's analysis. Those who object to it (and its modern derivatives) do so on the ground that it makes the causal tie not strong and close enough. (As it happens, rather irrelevantly for this essay, my own views on causation are of the Humean type, like the logical positivists'. Ironically, though, some of their latter-day disciples, toying with "dispositional concepts," "reduction chains," and modal logic, have become unwitting Aristotelians.[9]) What are the alternatives available for strengthening the causal tie? To make it analytic, thus blurring together the uses of 'cause' and 'reason', leads to the extremism of the idealists. To make the causal tie both synthetic and descriptive (so that it may "exist" and not merely "subsist") would seem more moderate. This is indeed the gist of many "realistic" views on causation. It also provides the cue which I wanted this digression to yield.

The intentional tie is not just correlational, i.e., synthetic, logical, and nonspecific. Thus it, too, or, rather, its explication must be strengthened. My solution, as will be seen, makes it analytic, logical, and specific. Another alternative, it would seem, is to make it synthetic and descriptive. I shall next sketch a position which takes this gambit. Exactly as I shall sketch it, it may not have been held by any classical philosopher. So I shall not ask for trouble by ascribing it to one. There are nonetheless two good reasons for considering it briefly. Wholly or in part, explicitly or implicitly, its dialectic has been very influential in the tradition. That is one good reason. Eventually the gambit fails.

[9] See MLP15, *Philosophy of Science*, and "The Philosophical Significance of Modal Logic," *Mind*, 69, 1960, 468–85.

Understanding accurately why it fails yields further insight into how the several questions in the groups of the two dualisms hang together. That is an even better reason.

Jones (or his mind) and the chair are both substances or, at least, continuants. Whenever he perceives the chair, or imagines it, remembers it, thinks of it, or what not, the two continuants jointly and, of course, asymmetrically exemplify a descriptive relation. Or, perhaps, they exemplify a quasirelation. Over that distinction, important as in some contexts it is, I promised not to fuss. With this proviso, then, acts are descriptive relational characters (universals) and thus in all fundamental ontological respects on a par with, say, spatial and temporal relations. This is the heart of the position. I shall offer five comments. The first and the second briefly indicate a connection and a difficulty which I shall not pursue. The last three elucidate difficulties which affect my main theme.

First. Commonsensically, there are of course continuants and even substances. Dialectically, the two notions are very difficult. If one wants substances or even continuants to "exist," the difficulties become formidable.[10] Many philosophers held, either explicitly or implicitly, that if acts (or their ingredients) are to "exist," so must substances or, at least, continuants. This belief, I submit, was one of the major causes for the decline of the act in recent philosophy, especially among the so-called empiricists. (I have long wondered what, if anything, this label still means.) Upon my analysis an act has an ingredient which is a phenomenal individual. (Presently I shall call such individuals awarenesses.) Since it is such an individual, if I spoke philosophically, I would have to say that it "exists." But these individuals are "momentary." As it happens, I do not believe that substances or even continuants "exist." This may or may not be so. The point is that, whether or not it is so, I have shown one way in which two fundamental groups, that of substance and that of the second great dualism, do not dialectically hang together.

Second. The position is of the kind which, with a reference to the first great dualism, is known as presentative or direct realism. It is also the position Moore would have liked to secure. The difficulties it encounters in the area of perception I take to be familiar. Anyone familiar with the British literature of the last half century or so also knows that they are unconquerable. Trying to conquer them, Moore, we saw, was forced into the absurdity of making a physical thing a congeries of phenomenal ones. Unconquerable as it is, this difficulty is not central to my theme. So I merely mention it lest I be misunderstood.

---

[10] See ME11, ME14.

Third. Every known descriptive relation is causally effective. This is merely a formula. Let me unpack it. The sheet on which I now write lies on my desk. Sheet and desk thus jointly exemplify a descriptive relation. The circumstance does not as such or directly affect the future fate of the paper. This would not be so if the sheet lay instead on a heated stove. Generally, I know of no descriptive relation which does not, given the appropriate additional circumstances, directly affect the future fate of the things that exemplify it. This is the point. If an act is a descriptive relation between a mental and, say, a physical thing, then the fate of physical things should at least sometimes be directly affected by their being the intentions of acts. That clashes with the thesis of psychophysiological parallelism. I call it a clash rather than an outright contradiction because verbally there is a way out. One may set acts aside as the one kind of descriptive relation which is not causally effective. But then, I ask, if one does that, does one really do more than attach an honorific label to the parallelistic nexus? Remember, finally, that a while ago I promised to identify the intellectual motive of those who purged the act in order to safeguard the scientific account. The clash I just described is this motive. It presupposes the conception, either explicit or implicit, of the act as a descriptive relation.

Fourth. For a (binary) relation to be exemplified, its terms must both exist. There are no centaurs. Yet I now think of one. If the intentional nexus is descriptively relational, what in this case corresponds to the existing chair which I perceive? There is no need to bring in centaurs. I mention them merely because, like Meinong's golden mountains, they are spectacular. Ordinary perceptual error will do; so will false beliefs. The difficulty is serious, particularly if, however covertly, one is a fact ontologist and if one does not distinguish between the two uses of 'exist'. One way out which many took was to crowd the ontological inventory with such entities as "false facts" which merely "subsist." The revulsion from such overcrowding was another cause for the decline of the act in recent philosophy.

Fifth. Is the nexus between two things jointly exemplifying a descriptive relation, say, two chairs, one to the left of the other, really as intimate and close as the intentional nexus? The answer depends on the view one takes of relations. If all relations are internal, as the idealists claim, then the answer is Yes. Naturally; since in the idealists' world all things are dialectically "one." One may believe, as I do, that the things of our world hang together in many ways, causally as well as logically, without at the same time believing, as I don't, that the idealists' answer answers anything, if only because, as the Americans say, at night all cows are black anyway. If one so believes, the answer is No. The chair to the left does not "inexist" in the one to the right, or conversely, as its intention does in the act. The descriptively relational nexus is thus not strong enough. Seen in this light, the gambit seems futile from the outset. As we saw, some things can nevertheless be learned from it. Let us now learn one more. Acts, every one agrees, are mental, not just in the broad sense of being phenomenal but in the narrow one in which I here use the term. That leads one to expect that what is "in the mind" or "inexists" in it is also mental and not just phenomenal. For, what would otherwise be expressed by the two words and the phrase ('mental', 'inexist', 'in the mind')? An act's intention should therefore always be mental. Yet a chair is not even a primary phenomenal thing; it is physical. The impasse seems without issue. In the Aristotelian-Thomistic pattern, with its fundamental form-matter dichotomy, there is a way out. What happens upon this account when I perceive the chair, in the relevant sense of 'perceive', is, all details apart, that (the matter of) my mind temporarily takes the form of the chair. This way is of course not open to me. Nor was it really to Malebranche.[11] Yet he took a cue from it when he taught that a mind knows only what is "in it" and that for anything to be in the mind it must be a property of the mind. Now, the nexus into which form and matter, neither of which "exists," enter in forming an "existent," is of course not the nexus of exemplification between a (nonaristotelian) individual and one of its properties; particularly if one insists, as, not being a nominalist, I would, if I were to speak philosophically, that the individual and its (simple) property both "exist." That is why I said that Malebranche merely took a cue from that old pattern. Presently it will appear that in a sense I also took this cue. I say in a sense because literally it is not true. For one, I do not work this way. For another, I am not very learned. More often than not these things are pointed out to me by my younger collaborators, some of whom are very learned. So perhaps I should say instead that the analysis of the act which I believe to be adequate is rather deeply rooted in the tradition.

An act's intention may be phenomenal. As I mentioned, this is the only case that I have so far treated in detail. Fortunately, it contains all the essential features of the general solution. So I shall take it up first. Then I shall turn to the general case. Or, what virtually amounts to the same, I shall answer the specific question from which I started, namely, how to distinguish perceiving a chair from thinking of it,

---

[11] About Malebranche, see ME12. It seems to me that neither his greatness nor the very crucial place he has in the tradition are nowadays fully appreciated. That is why I mention him.

imagining it, and so on. In both cases the argument rests on some phenomenological material. I shall begin with this material, then make some comments on what I believe is the right way of using it dialectically.

Sensa, which are individuals, and the simple characters they exemplify, or, as I shall briefly say, sense data are a kind of primary phenomenal things. Conspicuous as they are, Oxford now wants to convince us that they are but myths. It's one way of bullying us into a naïve sort of realism and materialism (metaphysical behaviorism). I cannot be convinced. But I am as always interested in the commonsense core of the excess. When we see (perceive) a chair, we do not see sense data. That is the core. In fact, we never "see" sense data. Sense data can only be sensed. (The truism, by the way, is synthetic, not analytic. This is one of the points I here neglect.[12]) Sensing is a species of acquaintance. Yet the psychologists tell us that a "percept" can be "introspectively decomposed" into sense data. There seems to be a little roughness. It is more apparent than real. What happens in introspection is what psychologists call a change of set. The act of perceiving is supplanted by one of acquaintance. We thus become acquainted with what psychologists call the "sensory core" of the "percept." Then we describe the "sensory core." Also, perception is relatively stable, while the introspective attitude is notoriously hard to maintain. This is the connection of sensing with perceiving or, for that matter, with any other act in which in this indirect manner sense data are or may be involved. Perhaps H. H. Price had it in mind when he spoke of "perceptual acceptance." But then, the phrase may mislead. One cannot accept what literally is not there.

Consider a conscious state consisting of a green sensum and nothing else. It would be more natural to say that all I am at the moment aware of is a green sensum, but I reserve 'awareness' for another use. Some may object to the paradigm on the ground that no conscious state is that simple or, if you please, so impoverished. I shall deal with the objection presently. First I want to establish the following "schema." 1. *Whenever there is a conscious state, there is an act.* That is the very nature of consciousness. In the paradigm, the act is a sensing; the conscious state is its intention. The intention of an act of perceiving is, say, a chair, which is a physical object and not a conscious state. And there is, as we shall see, still another complication. But it should be clear already why I avoid 'content', using instead once 'conscious state', once 'intention'. 2. *The act which must be there if there is to be a*

[12] See ME1.

conscious state is never itself a part of that state. We may of course become conscious of the act. In this case the original conscious state has been supplanted by another. There is then a further act which in turn is no part of the new conscious state, though we may become conscious of it, too, by a third act; and so on. 3. *We are often acquainted with our acts.* This is indeed the other fundamental kind of acquaintance. I am ready for a string of three comments.

First. The introspective attitude is hard to maintain even through one specious present. About the specious present, its role in phenomenological description, and the dialectic of 'instantaneous' and 'momentary' much needs to be said which I cannot here repeat.[13] The notion itself is familiar. The psychologists speak, however roughly, of a span of attention. What actually happens in the paradigm case can be described schematically as follows. The set may and often does shift several times within one specious present. Nor does it only shift between the green sensum and the "percept" to whose "sensory core" it belongs. More importantly for what I am about, it also shifts between acquaintance with the green spot on the one hand and acquaintance with this acquaintance on the other. The same holds for all conscious states. The set may and often does shift within one specious present between a conscious state and the act by virtue of which it is one. Nor, again, is this the only such shift that occurs. I just used 'schematically'; a while ago I used 'schema', even put it between double quotes. The word is the hook on which I want to hang what I have to say about the way the phenomenological material ought to be used in philosophical analysis. Return to the paradigm. What actually happens is simpler than I described it in one sense, less simple in another. One is tempted to say that the several acts "fuse." Brentano spoke of *eigentuemliche Verflechtung.* The description of all these subtleties is the job of phenomenology. The ones who are best at it are certain poets and novelists, also some religious writers and moralists, in spite of the fact, or perhaps because of it, that their descriptions are for the most part metaphorical or otherwise indirect. These documents, precious as they are, are one thing. Philosophical analysis is another thing. It is *not* phenomenological description, even though it *rests* on it as much as on any other piece of common sense. One who wants to use the phenomenological material dialectically, must have the power and the courage to "schematize" it. (Remember how ruthlessly I condensed the scientific account of perception; for the scientific detail is just as irrelevant.) But then, how can

[13] See ME14 and, especially, "Duration and the Specious Present," *Philosophy of Science,* 27, 1960, 39–47, and pp. 98–107 of this book.

I be sure that my schema does not either omit or distort what is essential? There is no advance guarantee, any more than there is advance "justification" of the method. By their fruits you shall know them.

Second. The second proposition of the schema asserts that there is an act (of mine) at exactly those moments at which I am not conscious of it. If an act were a physical entity, the assertion would be fully justified by what was said about the rapidly shifting sets. But an act is phenomenal. Some may therefore think that there is a difficulty. So I shall take the trouble to dispel the impression. A phenomenal entity actually is what it "appears" to be. This is indeed part of its nature. Less succinctly, any one who tries to define the notion otherwise will soon discover that, to whatever his definition may or may not apply, it will not serve the purpose for which he meant it. On the other hand, it is not part of the notion that for one of "my" phenomenal things to exist, it is necessary that I am conscious of it while it exists. The point is the one Moore made when he argued that the notion of an unsensed sensum is not absurd. This particular point is much more simply and more convincingly made by means of a formalism. What it amounts to is this. Provided that I am acquainted with what the character 'so-and-so' refers to, it makes perfect sense in any language to assert 'There is something which is a so-and-so' even if while asserting it I am not presented with that "something." It therefore also makes sense in a language whose "somethings" are phenomenal individuals.[14]

Third. Consider once more the second proposition of the schema. Poetically, one may say that an act can never catch up with itself. As soon as it does, it is another act. The pattern is anything but new. It is touched upon, for instance, in Hobbes' comment to Descartes' *Meditations* as well as in the latter's reply.[15] It is also similar to that dialectic of *en-soi* and *pour-soi* which plays such a large role in the existentialist literature. I have long been aware of the similarity. Only, I saw no particular point in calling attention to it. In a paper of this sort there perhaps is some point. But then, let me also point at a decisive difference. The several acts which cannot catch up with themselves succeed each other in time. According to that literature this

[14] With respect to our knowledge of the past and not only there, the so-called verificationists among the linguistic phenomenalists managed to miss the point. See ME14.

[15] To be familiar with *some* passages of *some* of the *major* documents of one's own tradition is not to be very learned. There is a difference between being learned and not being illiterate. Those who ignore the tradition to the extent it has been ignored in Vienna and, at least until very recently, in Oxford, are in danger of being illiterate.

"explains" the "origin of time." Or, perhaps, this is the way "the Self creates time." From where I stand, the "explanation" is but a cosmological myth or, perhaps more accurately, the beginning of one. I do not even know what it could possibly mean to explain the origin of time. The analytical philosopher, I said earlier, describes the world, in his own particular way suited to his own particular purpose. Now I add that, in the relevant sense, he does not "explain" anything. (Husserl, I think, would agree.) Notice that I spoke of the analytical philosopher, or of philosophical analysis, not just of "philosophy." I have no desire to monopolize the label. Nor do I wish to belittle either the merit or the cultural impact of myth-making that is properly refined. The existentialists' gloom strikes indeed a chord in my heart. Only, for me it is part of the gloom of the human condition that the overwhelming majority engaged in pursuits which traditionally go by the name of philosophy are so often prone to belittle, to ridicule, to denounce as culturally insensitive or even dangerous the exiguous minority of those who, like myself, are committed to first philosophy. *Sapienti sat*, particularly in Italy, which I so deeply love.

The analysis of the act which I believe to be adequate has two crucial features. Both are clear and distinct in the special case, where the intention is phenomenal. Neither requires modification in the general case. So I shall for a while stay with the special case and, also, with my paradigm, the green spot. The act in this case is an instance of being acquainted, or, as I briefly say, *an* acquaintance, just as quite deliberately I speak of *a* seeing, *a* remembering, and so on. The intention is the phenomenal fact expressed by the sentence 'This is green'. 'This' and 'green', that is, are taken to name introspective simples; the first the individual which is the sensum; the second, its color. A fact of course always has ingredients (constituents). Thus it is never a "simple" in the sense in which a thing may be one. The fact which is the intention of our paradigm is nevertheless, if I may so put it, as "simple" as a fact can be. The psychologists express that by saying, very loosely yet quite intelligibly and essentially correctly, that this particular fact is introspectively simple.

An act is not a thing but a fact. This is the first crucial feature of the proposed analysis. Specifically, an act is an individual exemplifying two simple nonrelational characters. ('Simple' without double quotes now always means 'introspectively simple'.) All individuals are simples. Thus the three (phenomenal) things which are the ingredients (constituents) of an act are all simples and the act itself, therefore, is a very simple fact. Since I am not a fact ontologist, I would not, even if I spoke philosophically, say that acts "exist"; but I would have to say

that their ingredients do. The ingredients are of the kind I called
mental. Hence, if I spoke philosophically, I would have to say that
mental things, or, a bit broadly, that minds "exist." Thus I secure the
ontological status of mind. This was mentioned earlier.

It will be convenient to have a general name for mental individuals.
I call them *awarenesses*. (For this use I have reserved the word.) To
understand what that does and does not imply consider how in a
phenomenological description one would use the general name 'tone'.
There is nothing in a primary phenomenal individual as such that makes
it a tone. We call it a tone because it exemplifies certain primary characters, say, *a* pitch and *a* loudness; 'pitch' and 'loudness' themselves,
without the indefinite article, being dispensable but convenient general
names (of kinds of characters).[16] As for tones so for awarenesses. What
makes an individual an awareness is that it exemplifies one each of
two kinds of characters. Like all phenomenal individuals, an awareness
is not a continuant but momentary. Perhaps it would be more accurate,
at least in some cases, to call it temporary. But I said before that I
would not enter into the dialectic of 'momentary'. Contrast this with
the corresponding feature of the relational analysis which has moulded
so much of the tradition. Upon this latter analysis a mind is a continuant or even a substance. An act occurs when, jointly with the act's
intention, the continuant temporarily exemplifies a descriptive relation. Upon my analysis an awareness is a temporary individual exemplifying two nonrelational characters. Thus I disentangle the two
groups of substance and of the second dualism. This, too, was mentioned
earlier.

An act is either an acquaintance, or a doubting, or a remembering,
and so on. What makes it just that? An awareness is a doubting because
it exemplifies a simple character which accordingly I call 'doubting';
it is an acquaintance because it exemplifies a simple character which
accordingly I call 'being acquainted'; and so on. If I am asked how I
know all that, I answer as Locke might have: Go and look into yourself! If asked, in the same vein, how I know that these characters are
simple, I answer: Go and look once more! Those who are still uneasy I
remind of what has been said about the schema. A single specious present may contain quite a number of acts, either with more or less the
same or with widely differing intentions, which also differ in the respect
now under consideration. I first doubt whether this is a square tower;
I entertain the thought of its being one; then I believe it. There is no

[16] Here my antinominalism and antisubstantialism show. What is assumed
thus requires much argument. The argument pervades my whole work. But see,
in particular, ME4 and ME10–14.

need for further or more elaborate examples. The variety one can thus produce with a rather small number of simple characters surely suffices to account schematically for the large number of "flavors" which detailed phenomenological description discerns. This, then, is one of the two kinds of characters every awareness exemplifies. Call it the *species* of the awareness.

I do not perceive without perceiving something. I do not remember without remembering something. And so on. Every act has an intention. The second kind of nonrelational character every awareness exemplifies corresponds to the intention. Notice what I do and do not say. I say that this character corresponds to the intention. I do not say that it is the intention, which would be sheer nonsense. In the paradigm the intention is the fact expressed by 'This is green'. The corresponding character I call 'the proposition this is green'; and I use *proposition* as a general name for this kind of character. The name is not really satisfactory. For one, it may give the impression that what in this special use I call a proposition is a linguistic thing, which of course it is not. It is a phenomenal character, in this respect exactly like, say, a phenomenal color, just as an awareness is a phenomenal individual and in this respect exactly like, say, a sensum. For another, 'proposition' has had a peculiar meaning in the tradition. It was used to refer to some very problematic *non*phenomenal entities, such as the merely subsisting "false facts" I mentioned, with which quite a few philosophers crowded their ontology in order to secure for each act an intention which at least subsists. Again, my propositions are not "propositions" in this very problematic sense. To avoid 'proposition', I have sometimes used 'thought'. But this is not very satisfactory either, specially not for what I am about in this essay. For to think of something rather than, say, imagining it or perceiving it, is a species of awareness. The sad fact is that I just haven't been able to find a good name. So I stick with 'proposition'.

All propositions are simple. Some may again object. Again, I shall entertain the objection later. Right now I want to take stock so that we may see where we stand; and I want to do that under the assumption that all propositional characters are simple. If they are, then the only way of referring to them directly is to name them. A name, in this strict sense, tells nothing about what it names. The phrase I used, 'the proposition this is green', refers indirectly. And, indeed, it tells a lot. It tells us—or should I say: it gives away?—the connection between the proposition and the intention which, as I so loosely said, correspond to each other. The idea that guides me is of course that an act has the intention it has by virtue of the fact that the awareness, which is one of its ingredients, exemplifies the propositional character, which is another. But then, this nexus must be ontologically grounded. Thus, were I to stop here, I would have failed miserably.

The nexus between an act's intention and the proposition which is one of its ingredients is logical, analytic, and specific. This is the second crucial feature of the proposed analysis. Consider the sentence 'The proposition this is green means this is green'. Call it M. M is analytic. That is what I mean by calling the nexus analytic. M expresses a quasi-relation between a character (the proposition) and a fact (the intention). This quasirelation is logical. That is what I mean by calling the nexus logical. The subsisting logical feature is expressed by 'means', when used as in M. This logical feature of our world, unlike all others, occurs in a world otherwise like ours only if there are in it minds like ours. That is what I mean by calling the nexus specific (with respect to mind).

The last paragraph sounds very peremptory. So I must do what I can to dispel that impression. 'Logical' and 'analytic', as I used them, are not just honorific labels. Both words have very important uses in the tradition. Thus they both need explication. (I say explication rather than explications because the two are inseparable.) The explication is long and laborious. The job has been done; it is one of the achievements of the last half century or so. All that remained to do was to put the pieces together.[17] But it requires a further argument to show that the way I apply 'logical' and 'analytic' to 'means' and M respectively is consonant with the explication of the traditional uses. This argument I have made elsewhere.[18] It, too, is rather elaborate. Moreover, it requires the use of formalisms. Naturally so, since, as the method reveals, the commonsense core of "analyticity" is a mathematical notion. Another question concerning what has been said in the last paragraph is more easily answered. As I analyze the intentional nexus, it is logical and analytic. Thus it merely subsists. Some may wonder whether a tie that merely subsists is close and intimate enough. Let those who wonder consider the tie between premiss and conclusion in any valid argument. It, too, is logical and analytic. Thus it, too, merely subsists. Yet it is as close and intimate as any I can think of.

I am ready for another string of comments. The first three hold for all acts, whatever their intention. In the last, by way of transition, are gathered some questions that do not arise in the case of phenomenal intentions.

First. The logical tie is not the only one that connects an act with its intention. There is also the factual tie, the one the scientists tell us

---

[17] See ME3.
[18] See ME1.

about. As I account for the former, it is compatible with the latter. Provided the account is otherwise adequate, that is one of its strengths. It will be instructive to compare the two ties. The factual one has two links. One is correlational. The other is causal and therefore either itself correlational or, if one is not a Humean, stronger. But, as I put it before, no chain is stronger than its weakest link. The intentional tie connects the intention with the propositional character. Upon our analysis, however, the act is complex. The chain that connects the intention with the awareness has again two links. Both links are logical. One is the intentional nexus. The other is the nexus of exemplification between the awareness, which is an individual, and the proposition, which is one of its characters. The nexus of exemplification is close and intimate indeed. (The desire to secure its closeness and intimacy dialectically is one of the major intellectual motives of all substance philosophies. Both links thus are very strong. So therefore is the chain.)

Second. A few pages back, when mentioning the Aristotelian-Thomistic pattern and Malebranche, I took a quick glance at that strand of the tradition which might not inappropriately be called the nonrelational conception of the act. The strand is recognizable by two verbal cues. The mind can only know what is "in it"; and the only things which are in it are its properties. This is one cue. An act's intention "inexists" in it or is its "content." This is the other cue. To combine the two, thus bringing out their implicit "logic," one merely has to remember that an individual's properties not implausibly may be called, and in fact have been called, its "content." This shows that, by making the proposition a property of the awareness, our analysis realizes the guiding idea of the nonrelational view. More accurately, one half of our analysis realizes it. The other half is of course our account of the nexus between the proposition and the intention. Thus we unscramble the two, proposition and intention, so that the latter, whether it be physical or phenomenal, need no longer be considered as mental or in the mind. The traditional nonrelational view does not know how to account for this second half, or, at least, not outside of the Aristotelian-Thomistic pattern. That is its fundamental weakness. This is also the right place to dissect, officially as it were, that three-fold ambiguity of 'content' to which I have repeatedly alluded. 1. 'Content' is used synonymously with 'intention'. 2. 'Content' is used as I use 'conscious state'. 3. A (mental) content is a property; either, classically, of a substantial mind, or, in my account, of an awareness. These are the three relevant uses. It is clear by now, I trust, what dangers one incurs if one does not distinguish among them. That is why I foreswore 'content'.

Third. In providing a background against which to appreciate the proposed analysis of the act, I have made it my task to show how the groups of the two great dualisms do and do not hang together. I am now ready to put the last touch on this job; and I shall do that in two ways. Both ways further illuminate what I meant when I said that the realism issue does not really loom as large in first philosophy as it seemed during the last three hundred years or so. (a) Physical objects "exist." They don't "exist." These are the classical positions. Assume for the sake of the argument that they both make sense and that, therefore, one is right. If the realists are right, then an act's intention is either physical or phenomenal. If the phenomenalists are right, then, all intentions being phenomenal, the first dualism collapses. Yet, as long as primary phenomenal objects are taken to "exist," i.e., as long as one does not embrace absolute idealism, the second dualism is not affected. Nor, therefore, is the intentional nexus. And this nexus is indeed the hallmark of minds. (b) Assume that minds and bodies both "exist" but that acts don't; i.e., that all "mental" things, as I don't here use 'mental', are primary, as I here use 'primary'. In such a world the intentional tie would be missing. The only nexus between its truncated "minds" and its bodies would be correlational. And this nexus is indeed the hallmark of bodies. (On causality I am a Humean.)

Fourth. (a) I asserted that all propositional characters are simple. In the case of the character I called 'the proposition this is green' that is plausible, if only because the fact expressed by 'This is green' is simple. In the case of an intention as complex as the one expressed by 'This is a chair'—and there are many which are much, much more complex— it is not *prima facie* plausible. In the general case, therefore, the objection whose consideration I postponed gains its full strength. That is why I postponed it. (b) A phenomenal thing actually is what it appears to be. Or, to use a rather barbarous term of the tradition, acquaintance is veridical. That is indeed its nature. It follows that in the special case of phenomenal intentions there are no such things as perceptual error, false beliefs, or, if you please, "false facts." In the general case there are. So we shall have to account for them. (c) Remember the first proposition of the schema: whenever there is a conscious state there is an act. In the special case the converse also holds. Moreover, in this case the conscious state is the intention of the act. In the general case that is of course impossible, since a chair simply isn't a conscious state. Yet there remains the question whether or not there is a conscious state, different from the one which is the act of perceiving, which, so to speak, represents the chair. We shall see.

How do I distinguish my perceiving something from thinking of it, imagining it, and so on? More precisely, since, of course, we all know how to make these distinctions, how do I account for them within my pattern? This is the question from which I started. As so often happens in philosophy, the answer will not take as long as one might expect from the time required to provide the background and make specific preparations. Again, I shall divide the task, staying for a while with perception; say, Jones's perceiving a chair. Is perceiving a simple species? If not, I should instead consider seeing, touching, and so on. Phenomenologically, there may be a question. Dialectically, I am convinced, the answer makes no difference. So I shall stay with "perceiving."

What happens when Jones perceives a chair? There is an act of perceiving. In other words, there is an awareness exemplifying two characters, namely, the species perceiving and the propositional character which I call 'the proposition this is a chair'. That much is forced upon us by the pattern. But it is not yet sufficiently precise. When perceiving something, I am conscious of my perceiving it and not, say, either remembering or imaging it. The species, that is, is part of my conscious state. An act, however, according to the second proposition of the schema, is never a part of "its" conscious state. I resolve this apparent difficulty as follows. Jones's conscious state when perceiving the chair is (contains) the act I just described, i.e., an individual exemplifying both perceiving and the relevant propositional property. The act which makes this conscious state just that, namely, a conscious state but which is not itself contained in it, is an acquaintance. To say the same thing differently, Jones, when perceiving something, is acquainted not with what he perceives but, rather, with his perceiving it. Similarly for the other species. When he thinks of something or remembers it, he is acquainted with his thinking of it or his remembering it. (This, by the way, is the way I recently analyzed remembering.[19] Now I merely extend the idea to all conscious states which are not acquaintances.) The pattern is clear, I trust. This is my answer to Grossmann's question. Since I stated it so abruptly, I must now explore its implications and consider the major objections I can think of. Then, but for two concluding remarks, I shall be done. The two objections which I shall consider first are of a kind I would call phenomenological.

Interposing the act of perceiving between the perceiver and the perceived, the account proposed does not do justice to the "immediacy" of perception. This is the first phenomenological objection. I am prepared to take it quite seriously. Proust apparently would not. Remember

---

[19] See ME14.

what he says, in the lovely passage I chose as an epigraph, about the *liséré* that prevents him from ever reaching the physical object. In these matters everyone can only speak for himself. Proust's claim may be true or more nearly true for some species of awareness. In perception, though, I, for one, can and sometimes do so lose myself in the object that for brief moments at least I am not conscious of any *liséré*. So I must account for these cases. Schematically I can. The task of taking care of the shades and flavors I leave, consistently with my conception of the philosophical enterprise, to the masters of another craft, such as Proust and those who may disagree with his sweeping assertion. As to how I account in part for the "immediacy" of perception—I say in part because another part will be found in the next comment—remember what was said earlier about introspection. Acquaintance is immediate indeed. If it were not for it, we would not even have the idea of immediacy. (Or should I say the ideal?) In introspection the set shifts from whatever it has been to acquaintance. In perception, I submit schematically, whenever we lose ourself in the object, the set shifts for brief moments from perceiving to a fleeting acquaintance with the "sensory core," or part of the sensory core, with which we become acquainted, still fleetingly yet more stably, when we deliberately try to decompose introspectively the "percept." (I surround by double quotes the two words the psychologists use, rather inaccurately for our purpose. They may also speak of "fusions.")

The proposed account is too intellectualistic. This is the second phenomenological objection. If while I am hungry I perceive a fruit, my mouth may water, my hand may tend to reach for it. Even when I am not hungry, it may arouse my appetite. Should I perceive a tiger rushing at me, I probably would freeze with terror. Even perceiving him behind the bars of a cage, I might feel some apprehension. There is thus more to perceiving and to distinguish it from, say, imagining or thinking, than the specificity of a purely "intellectual" act. This, I take it, is the objection. If my purpose were what it is not, namely, to produce an acceptable psychological account of perception, the objection would be unanswerable. Even for my purpose, I am prepared to take it seriously. There are many "additional" things which occur, typically, when I perceive something but not when, say, I either remember it or think of it. Typically again, I am conscious of these additional things, often more or less faintly, but at times not faintly at all. (The purely contemplative attitude, in which I am not conscious of them at all, is rather the exception.) "Feelings" and "kinaesthetic sensations," to speak once more as the psychologists do, are among these additional parts of the conscious state in perception. They are all primary phenomenal things, i.e., they belong to the sort of thing with which we are at times acquainted.[20] If they are present when I perceive something, my conscious state contains therefore in addition to an act of perceiving these primary things. Or, to say the same thing differently, I am, through a single act of acquaintance, acquainted not only with an act of perceiving but also with those primary things. However, no collection of such primary things, no matter how large and varied it may be, could ever by itself exhaust the conscious state I am in when perceiving something. This state contains as an essential part an act of perceiving. On this part the dialectic hinges. The rest is either psychology, which is a science among sciences; or it is phenomenology, which is not philosophy but, rather, part of the commonsense basis on which all science and all philosophy rests. That is why I feel justified in representing perception schematically by (acquaintance with) an act of perceiving.

In the last comment on the case of the green spot I gathered three questions, (a), (b), and (c) which arise, or arise more poignantly, in the general case. I next turn to these questions.

(a) Is the propositional character corresponding to a complex intention itself complex? I shall now examine the objection which maintains the affirmative. When I remember Vienna or brood over a star-crossed love, the intention is complex indeed; much more so than the one expressed by 'This is a chair'. Yet, for my purpose the latter is more than complex enough. Remember that I accept PA. One must always be prepared to replace any sentence S, by another, S', which is for many dialectical purposes equivalent to it yet contains no other referential words than the names of (phenomenal) simples. The S' corresponding to 'This is a chair' represents what is known as a "phenomenological reconstruction." This business, we saw, is so "complex" that it can only be carried out schematically. Elsewhere I presented an S' that will do for many purposes.[21] There is no need to present it here once more. We see already what is involved. 'The proposition this is a chair' is the natural indirect way of referring to the character whose simplicity is controversial. Write, generally, 'the proposition S'. Replacing in this phrase S by S', you obtain 'the proposition S''. Thus, since

---

[20] I need not on this occasion commit myself on volition. I am inclined to believe, though, that its core is always an act. The phenomenology of value is a related topic. See Herbert Hochberg, "Phenomena, Value, and Objectivity," *The Philosophical Quarterly*, 8, 1958, 208–25; May Brodbeck, "Toward a Naturalistic 'Non-Naturalistic' Ethic," *Philosophical Studies*, 2, 1951, 7–11; also MLP14.

[21] See ME2.

S' is very complex, the initial phrase, 'the proposition', must have a
"bracketing power," if I may so express myself, greater than seems
plausible at first sight. This is one way to state the objection. A second
way is to point out that a "percept" can in fact be "introspectively
decomposed." The first way is linguistic. The proper counter-argument
is therefore rather technical. So I shall omit it, particularly since the
argument against the second way is conclusive by itself. Its heart is contained in what was said earlier about introspection. "Having" a "percept," we do not even have the "sensory core"; to have the latter, the
set must switch from perceiving to acquaintance; after it has so
switched, we describe what we then have in terms of introspective
simples. (I used once more the jargon of the psychologists.) Thus we
do not literally "decompose" or "analyze" the percept. For that matter,
I do not even know what it could mean, literally, to decompose
introspectively or to "analyze" any conscious state. Take the extreme
case of a very "abstract" thought passing quickly and, as one says,
"vaguely" through our mind. We may try to "analyze" it, or so one
usually says, by a series of other thoughts. By a series of *other* thoughts.
That is just the point. Under certain circumstances into which we need
not inquire, we call this series an "analysis" of the original thought. If
the members of the series, or, rather, their intentions stand in certain
relations to each other and to the first thought, we call the latter
"vague." Existentially, though, or, as I would rather say, ontologically,
there is nothing either "vague" or "complex" about that original
thought. Like all phenomenal things it is actually what it "appears"
to be. And it is, while we are acquainted with it, completely and
exhaustively revealed to us. Thus it is, in the relevant sense, a simple.
This is how I meet the objection. The argument with which I meet it is
phenomenological. Yet I do not appeal to what I called shades and
flavors. Rather, I exploit dialectically an essential feature of all phenomenological description, no matter how schematic or detailed it
may be.

(b) Peter is not blond. Yet I believe, or remember, or imagine that
he is. The intention of my act is expressed by 'Peter is blond'. The fact,
or, synonymously, the state of affairs expressed does not exist. The
situation is among those which induced some philosophers to proclaim
the "existence" of "false facts." If one holds the descriptively relational
view of the act, it is not easy to see what else they could have done,
particularly since they did not distinguish between the ordinary and
the philosophical uses of 'fact' and 'exist'. How does our account cope
with the situation? I just said myself that the fact in question does not
exist. (I might have said, synonymously, that the state of affairs does

not obtain. But I chose deliberately the more jarring expression.) The point is that I used both 'fact' and 'exist' commonsensically. Speaking commonsensically, we say such things every day; and, as long as we do speak commonsensically, we do not get into any trouble. Trouble brews only when, speaking philosophically, we assert that "(simple) facts" are "existents."[22] Since I am not a fact ontologist, I would not, even if I spoke philosophically, say this. I say instead four things. 1. The sentence 'Peter is blond' can be accounted for by the PA. 2. It refers to a physical fact. 3. This fact does not exist. 4. The simple character 'the proposition Peter is blond', being exemplified by my awareness in the act or acts in question, does of course "exist"; or so at least I would have to say if I spoke philosophically. That is all. To grasp these four things accurately is to see that where some philosophers saw a problem, there really is none. To grasp that still more firmly, consider the corresponding M-sentence, 'The proposition Peter is blond means Peter is blond', which, we remember, is analytic. To wonder or worry "what it is about" in case Peter is not blond amounts to exactly the same thing as wondering or worrying what 'It is raining or it isn't' is about in case it rains.

(c) Schematically, when I perceive a chair, I am not acquainted with any of the sense data belonging to any of the sensory cores I may be acquainted with when the set shifts. Do such sense data nevertheless exist while I am perceiving the chair? Does our pattern suggest an answer to this question? Or, perhaps, does it force an answer upon us? The first is the substantive question. The other two are subsidiary. The important thing is not how we answer the substantive question but, rather, that we understand why it is not important which answer we give. There are several strands in this tangle; so I shall number them. 1. If we assert (assume) that some sense data are there, we run into the apparent paradox of unsensed sensa. That this is not really a paradox I have argued before. So we may, if we wish, say that some sense data are there. More precisely, we shall not run into dialectical difficulties by saying it as long as we are careful to add that, since we are not conscious of them, there is no act of acquaintance whose intention they are. 2. We did assert (assume) in a similar situation that whenever there is a conscious state, there is an act, even while we are not conscious of that act. This is indeed the first proposition of the scheme. The situation is similar because, just as the set can and often does switch, even within one specious present, from an act's intention to the act

---

[22] For a discussion of the difficulties of fact ontologies, see ME13 and "Ineffability, Ontology and Method."

itself, so in perception, it can and often does switch from perceiving a physical object to being acquainted with sense data. (Remember what was said, when I mentioned Proust, about losing one's self in the object perceived.) To this extent the "assumption" is suggested by the pattern. 3. The similarity just pointed out is "local." In the pattern as a whole, or dialectically, there is a difference. The schema unravels the traditional dialectic. Thus it is crucial. Either asserting or rejecting the suggested assumption that whenever we are perceiving something there are some sense data, is not crucial for anything. Those philosophers who for dialectical reasons thought it necessary to hold that whenever we are perceiving something we are actually acquainted with sense data got themselves into some well-known tangles. That is why I, for one, would rather not make the assumption. But again, that is unimportant. What is important dialectically is that one does not need to make it. 4. While I perceive the chair, *the* physiological correlate of a "sensory core" certainly exists in my body. Thus the parallelistic frame of reference forces us to assume that there are some sense data. This argument is fallacious. The fallacy is hidden behind the definite article which I italicized. When I perceive the chair there certainly is *a* corresponding physiological state. But this is a state corresponding to my perceiving it, not a state corresponding to a sensory core. For, if it were the latter, I would be acquainted with a sensory core and not, as in fact I do, perceive the chair.

During the last half century or so, the British (and some American) philosophers, in a huge literature to which I alluded, tried to produce an adequate account of perception. More precisely, they attempted to master the traditional dialectic of perception under two conditions. They embraced PA (as I do). And they were determined to arrive at one of the classical realistic positions (as I am not). In this inevitably they failed. But they succeeded in illuminating very thoroughly the traditional questions of the perception group, even thought up some new ones. This is the intrinsic value of that huge literature. The account of perception I propose is very traditional in that it permits us to take over everything that makes sense in that literature without, however, committing us to what doesn't. Naturally, I couldn't possibly now show that in detail. So I select two points of the utmost strategic importance.

I just spoke of an account of perception. What sort of account? The philosopher's account, as always, is descriptive. Specifically, I have attempted to describe my or some one else's conscious state *when* either he or I perceive something. *Under what conditions* either he or I perceive either this or that belongs to a causal account. The causal account, as always, is the job of the scientists. In attempting to give us such an account, they find it necessary to mention many things which I did not need to mention at all, such as my previous experiences; my present conditions, goals and desires; the physical and social state of the environment in which I and what I perceive find themselves; and so on. The matter is very complex indeed. Many who now distrust and belittle first philosophy, the Deweyan pragmatists and, I believe, some of their recent Italian admirers among them, do so because they feel that it either belittles or denies all these complexities. First philosophy does nothing of the kind. It merely assigns these matters to their proper context. Doing that, it attends to its own business of making dialectical distinctions.

Under what conditions is my perception veridical? For the British philosophers the question proved one of the big stumbling blocks. The reason is that, as C. D. Broad once put it (I do not recall his exact words), even if a percept is veridical, it does not in itself wear any mark or sign which tells that it is. The problem is of course the familiar one of perceptual error. What, then, do I have to say about it? Notice how I put the question. *Under what conditions* is the percept veridical? Both question and answer belong to the causal context. As a philosophical analyst, therefore, I have nothing to contribute. This, however, is merely the negative part of my answer. Positively, I shall illuminate it as follows. Assume that while suffering from a hallucination, I hallucinate seeing an elephant. While I hallucinate, I do of course not know that I do. (Once more, I leave the shades and flavors to those whom they concern even though I am as familiar as the next man with both nightmares and daydreams.) It follows that my conscious state while I hallucinated was one of perceiving the elephant. Later on, of course, I may say that I did not "really" perceive one. But, then, I merely infer that from my memory of my subsequent conscious states, from certain generalities I believe, and from some specific information, such as the reports of others, which I have gathered in the meantime. (This, incidentally, is one of the commonsense cores of Berkeleyan idealism.)

This is what I now have to say in direct support of the proposed account of perception and in rebuttal of the major objections I can think of. Now for two concluding remarks.

The exposition centered on perception. But once more, I trust, the pattern is clear. What goes for perception, *mutatis mutandis* goes for all other species, except acquaintance. When I think of the chair or imagine it (I may think of it without imagining it), the awareness in the case exemplifies the appropriate species, either thinking of or imagining.

This is the major difference. Thus the question from which I started is answered. That is not to say, though, that there are no other differences, or kinds of such. I shall mention three. *First*. The causal contexts are different. *Second*. Those "additional things," as I called them in the account of perception, which the conscious state may and often does contain will be different. *Third*. As always, there will be frequent shifts of set, even within one specious present. What the set shifts to will be different. The causal context I leave as always to those whom it concerns. Nor need I go into details with respect to the other two differences. These matters are familiar; so are the dialectical uses and abuses to which they have been put. Yet I wish to consider briefly an extreme case, in order to strengthen, or at least emphasize, a point made before. Take "abstract" thought; say, a mathematician thinking of, or entertaining, or doubting, a complicated algebraic truth (or falsehood). (I use 'abstract' commonsensically, as the psychologists do. The philosophical uses of 'abstract' and 'concrete' are very ambiguous and the source of many difficulties.) The case is extreme because in it the things mentioned in the second and the third difference massively obtrude. As one usually asks, what goes on in the mathematician's mind? We have all either experienced it or, at least, we are familiar with some interesting accounts by mathematicians and psychologists. The formula appears in inner speech or is heard by the mind's ear, i.e., in auditory imagery. Or it appears written down, in visual imagery. Or there are "representative" geometrical images. And so on. This is the additional material. As I said, it obtrudes. The psychologists express this fact, rather aptly for once, by saying that the abstract thought is "carried" by verbal and other imagery. The essential point I wish to strengthen is this. In the case of perception, I insisted, no amount of "additional" material the conscious state may contain will make it one of perceiving unless that state also contains an act of perceiving. As for perceiving, so for the extreme case of thought with an "abstract" intention. One may hear the formula with the mind's ear, one may see it written down before the mind's eye, and yet not "know" that what one thus "hears" or "sees" is anything but noises or geometrical designs without "meaning." (That in fact one doesn't is a causal matter.) If so, then how could a conscious state, or a series of conscious states which contain nothing else but these noises and designs ever amount to a believing, or an entertaining, or a doubting of what the formula means? I conclude that there is essentially in all this welter of obtruding material an act of thinking, or of doubting, and so on, and that the very "abstract" intention of this act is what the formula means. (I can also "reconstruct" the formula in my ideal language.)

Let us finally look at the inventory of phenomenal things. Or, using the term broadly for once, let us look at the ontological inventory of mind I have presented. All simple phenomenal things, i.e., those which, if 1 spoke philosophically, I would say "exist," are either individuals, e.g., sensa or awarenesses; or they are either properties of or relations among individuals, e.g., the spatial relations exemplified by visual sensa. But this is not the only division. All phenomenal things are either primary, e.g., sensa and the properties and relations they exemplify; or they are mental (in the narrower sense, as also below), i.e., they are either awarenesses or the characters exemplified by awarenesses. If I were to leave it there, I might leave the impression that the two realms, that of primary things and that of the mental, are more separate and disjoined than seems reasonable or, even, plausible. The two realms are not in fact thus separate or disjoined. Awarenesses of course have no color, taste, or pitch. Nor are they in space. But they are in time. Moreover, the temporal relations are the only ones which are exemplified either by two primary individuals or by two awarenesses or by one individual each of the two kinds. Time thus reveals itself once more as the great binder. As I once put it before, metaphorically, time is the true substance of the world.

Ineffability, Ontology, and Method*

THIS paper[1] has three parts. The first could very well stand by itself. "Ineffability" would be an appropriate title for it. The third part could almost stand alone, too. If it did, "Some Remarks on Ontology" would be an appropriate title; these remarks are not unconnected with what is said in the first part. The second part connects the other two by explicating some of the philosophical uses of 'form'. There is no part corresponding to the third noun in the title of the whole. What I believe to be the right method in philosophy distinguishes between the commonsensical and the philosophical uses of words, insisting that the latter all require commonsensical explication. Though by no means the whole of the method, which is a many-faceted thing, that is indeed one of its basic ideas. Also, it can be shown at work in relative isolation. As the paper proceeds, this idea comes gradually to the fore. Hence the third noun of the title.

I

Each of us is *acquainted* with some things and facts (states of affairs). Synonymously, these things and facts are *presented* to us. What one is acquainted with he knows. Each of us also knows much else. These things and facts, however, he knows only *by means of* what is, or has been, presented to him. A very large number of philosophers past and present either explicitly or implicitly accept these propositions. Some of those who now accept them explicitly call them a Principle of

* The Philosophical Review, *69, 1960, 18–40. Reprinted by permission.*

[1] Some of this material I presented first during the summer of 1958 at Northwestern University in a joint seminar with Herbert Hochberg, to whom I am indebted for many stimulating discussions. Since then I have benefited also from discussions with Edwin B. Allaire.

Acquaintance (PA). How are we to understand the italicized phrase in its last clause? That is a very large question or, rather, a group of questions. Proponents of a PA may still reasonably disagree on the answers to all or some of them. For what I am about, however, the last clause does not matter at all. So I shall ignore it. Notice next that I spoke of *a* rather than *the* PA. I did this in order to indicate that what I stated is merely a schema which one may reasonably call a principle only after he has specified what he takes himself to be acquainted with. Again, there is disagreement. In philosophical discussions some use their words so (and thereby choose their philosophical gambits) that they are, at some times, presented with (some) physical objects and some of the characters they exemplify. According to others, the things presented to us are all phenomenal, such as, say, color spots in a visual field, in such contexts also called sensa, and their colors, in such contexts also called phenomenal colors. For my purpose the disagreement does not matter. I shall take us to be acquainted with such things as colored spots in visual fields. In fact, I shall talk about no others. But I make this "choice" only because, without as far as I can see introducing any bias, it will simplify the exposition, and not because it happens to be the one I would make where it does matter.

Some hold that there are things so *simple* that if we want to speak about them directly, all we can do is name them—that is, attach words to them as mere labels. The qualification "directly" is meant to brush aside what is familiar as well as irrelevant for my purpose; for example, reference by definite description. The phrase "mere label" indicates that there is not and could not be anything about a linguistic expression serving as a name that provides a cue for what it is the label of. In so-called ideal languages (another controversial subject that I shall keep out, although a bit later I shall for convenience's sake use a few symbols and, still later, even the idea of an improved language) this shows itself in the circumstance that an expression serving as a name is (in the written case) a sign no (geometrical) part of which is itself a sign. It follows, or very nearly so, that one can name only what he is or has been presented with. All this is indeed part of the relevant notion of "simplicity," which I do not propose to examine in this paper. Whether this special use of 'simple' can be satisfactorily clarified may be controversial. Surely it is now again controversial whether there are in any language any expressions that are, in the sense specified, names. I shall proceed as if there were. What I want to say could be said even if there were not. But it might have to be said very differently. I shall therefore not claim that this "choice" of mine, the second I am making, merely simplifies the exposition. On the other hand, the simplification achieved by my first choice should by now be obvious. Everyone can agree that *if* it makes sense to speak about sensa and *if* there are things so simple that they can only be named, then sensa are among these things.

Notice that I said sensa are among those simple things and not, as might have been expected, sensa and some of their characters. Thereby hangs another controversy, the last one I must mention and show to be irrelevant, though only in a peculiar way, in order to clear the air and set the stage.

Consider a green spot. Call F the fact of its being green. It is as "simple" a fact as I can think of. Yet, being a fact, F, like any other fact, has constituents which are things. In this sense no fact is "simple." (The familiar difference thus revealed between the uses of 'simple' as applied to facts and to things, respectively, will play a role in the last part.) Which thing or things are the constituents of F? Some answer that they are two, namely, an *individual* (the spot) and a *character* (the spot's color). The answer seems obvious; to me it is obvious. But, then, it has not been and still is not obvious to many. Up to a point, of course, everyone agrees that in being presented with F he is presented with the color. Beyond that point, though, some try to make distinctions. They might claim, for instance, that the individual and the character are not presented in quite the same way, only the former but not the latter being "wholly presented." Objections against calling the character a thing, as well as against calling an expression directly referring to it a name, as either unusual or confusing, may be a linguistic symptom of this attempt to distinguish. An extreme and explicit variant of it is to insist that F has only one constituent (which is a thing) and that this constituent is neither the spot nor its color but, rather, the "colored spot." We have come upon the root of the realism-nominalism controversy, a disagreement so fundamental that one might expect it to be relevant to almost any question a philosopher is likely to raise. I shall take it for granted that F has two constituents which are things and which are presented to us whenever F is presented, namely, the individual and the character. But I shall also argue that F has three further constituents which *in some sense* are presented to us whenever F is. The accent in this paper is on these additional three—this excess, as it were, over either one or two constituents. This is the peculiar way in which, fundamental as it is, the difference between one and two, if I may so express myself, does not matter for my purpose.

When I know that this is a green spot, I know also that (1) the spot is an individual, (2) the color is a character, and (3) the former exemplifies the latter (and not, perhaps, the latter the former). How could I know all this if it were not, in some sense, presented to me? To grasp the idea more firmly, consider for a moment a visual field containing two spots, one red, one green. When this field is presented to me, I also know which spot exemplifies which color and, for that matter, also that no spot or color exemplifies the other spot or color. How, to repeat, could I know all these things if they were not presented to me? The three additional constituents of F are, accordingly, the two "properties" of (1) individuality and (2) universality, and the "nexus" of (3) exemplification.

Three brief comments before I continue should clear the air. First, I did not call exemplification a relation but, noncommittally, a "nexus." Unfortunately, I cannot think of an equally noncommittal word to take the place of 'property'. So I used the latter, with tongue in cheek, and on paper with quotation marks around it. Second, there is a sense in which the three additional constituents are not quite independent of each other. As we ordinarily think of it, the nexus of exemplification is asymmetrical. The distinction between individuality and universality introduces this asymmetry a second time. In the lower functional calculus (LFC) the dependence shows itself as follows. After we have distinguished between x- and f-variables (and the constants that can be substituted for them), the parentheses and the order in the conventional notation '$f(x)$' are redundant. '$.fx.$' and '$.xf.$', with the pair of dots indicating that the string is a sentence and without any attention paid to order, would do as well. (The case of relations is different, of course; but we need not bother with it.) Third, *if* the three additional constituents could be named, some (including myself) would insist that their names belong to a "type" different from that of either of the two names of the two constituents which are things. Whether or not this distinction is both sound and important makes no difference for my purpose. So, once more, we need not bother.

I refrained from calling the three crucial constituents things. Even so, some may feel that, merely by insisting on their being in some sense presented in F and therefore calling them constituents of F, I am opening the door to confusion by blurring a fundamental distinction. If I were to stop now, these critics would be right. The distinction they wish to defend is fundamental indeed. Nor is anything I have said or shall say meant to weaken it. Rather, I wish to make it more accurately, in order to avoid some confusions that may beset us if we do not make it accurately enough. For this purpose I turn to language. Specifically, I would say that I turn to the LFC. But if someone wants to think of what follows as a "language game," he may do so. In a "game" as limited as the one I shall play the difference makes no difference.

My calculus (or game) has two kinds of names or prospective names: lower-case letters ('a', 'b', $\cdots$) for individuals, upper-case letters

('G', 'H', $\cdots$) for characters. A sentence is a string consisting of one name of each kind. I shall continue to write it conventionally, for example, '$G(a)$'. Looking at a name of this game, I know, therefore—even if I do not know *which thing* it has been attached to as a label (or whether it has been attached at all)—the *kind of thing*, whether individual or character, to which it has been or could be attached. We have come upon a confusion lurking behind the phrase 'mere label'. In one obvious sense a name is a mere label. In another sense it is not. In this latter sense there are indeed no mere labels. Who sees that clearly also sees how the distinction between the two constituents of F which are things and the three further ones which are not appears in my game. The individual and the character are represented by "labels." Individuality and universality are represented by the shapes of these "labels," exemplification by two "labels" being strung together into a sentence.[1a]

The critic I just mentioned may grant that as long as I play this game the distinction he watches over is safe. But then what is to keep me from obliterating it by "labeling," in a different game, the three crucial constituents? He has a point. He adds that sooner or later I am even likely to play this different sort of game, since it is often part of the relevant use of "presented" that what is presented can be labeled. Again, he has a point. The proper way to meet it and, by meeting it, to safeguard the fundamental distinction is to show that any attempt at labeling the three additional constituents either leads to disaster or, at least, is futile. This I shall do next.

Let 'a', 'G', 'I', 'U', 'E' be the labels one may try to attach to the spot, its color, individuality, universality, and exemplification, respectively. What I controversially claim to be presented when F is presented would then be expressed by

(1) $I(a)$,   (2) $U(G)$,   (3) $E(G, a)$.

The roughness due to the fact that two capital letters occur in both (2) and (3) and altogether three letters in (3) I said before I would ignore. Notice, first, that in this game, too, the marks are of two kinds of shapes. For, if they were not, how would I know which go with

[1a] There is a blur here as obvious and, alas, as annoying as the failure to distinguish between *type* and *token*. Two tokens are two individuals exemplifying the same type. Juxtaposition, representing exemplification, is exemplified by the individuals in the tokens. All other representing features are constituents of the types. In Essay XII the blur has become a mistake, which has been pointed out to me by Mr. Douglas Lewis. But it has no untoward consequences whatsoever. See fn. 10b on p. 247. [Added in 1963.]

which to make a string that is a sentence? Notice, second, that in order
to understand (1), (2), and (3), I would therefore have to understand
first that exemplification and kind of object exemplifying or exemplified are represented by the juxtaposition of "labels" and the shapes of
the labels, respectively. This is the heart of the matter. It shows what I
meant by saying that any attempt to label the three crucial constituents is futile. I am also convinced that, if made uncritically, it sooner or
later will lead to disaster. This, however, I shall not show.[2]

'Ineffable' has been put to several philosophical uses. Philosophical
uses require commonsensical explications. A proposition is philosophical if it contains at least one word used philosophically. I offer what
has just been said about the futility of introducing 'I', 'U', and 'E' into
our game as the explication of the philosophical proposition, "Individuality, universality, and exemplification are ineffable." Clearly, one
may agree (as I do) that these three constituents of F are ineffable in this
sense without agreeing (as I do not) that they are ineffable in some
other sense, or that certain other things are also "ineffable," either in
this or in another unexplicated and philosophical sense. For that matter, one may wish to offer the claim that all philosophical uses require
commonsensical explications as the explication of the paradoxical
philosophical proposition that what philosophers try to say is "ineffable." If I may so explicate it, then I, for one, accept that proposition.
It is indeed one of the mainstays of my method. But, then, this is not
the way that paradoxical proposition was meant and used.

So far I have attended to the thing itself, without any mention,
except for a passing reference to the realism-nominalism controversy, of
the huge body of dialectical argument that has grown up around it.
Accordingly, I have not used any technical word, such as 'ontology'. I
even avoided the nontechnical words, such as 'form', which in these
arguments have been used philosophically. Nor have I mentioned any
names. One is on the lips of every likely reader. *Absentiā fulget*. I shall
not mention it, simply because I do not on this occasion wish to make
assertions about the proper reading of a notoriously difficult text and,
still less, about what was in the mind of its author when he wrote it.
One other name I shall mention. Much of what I have said is not new,

---

[2] Reinhardt Grossmann reminds me that, according to Meinong, who thought
about these things carefully and often profoundly, exemplification is the only
"real relation," while such relations as, say, being to the left of (i.e., the kind I
call descriptive) are merely "ideal." There is a general awareness that for some
such reasons Meinong, in spite of his care and profundity, bogged down. Grossmann is engaged upon a study designed to show accurately why and how
Meinong and some others who played similar gambits met their defeat.

of course. What is new, if anything, is the use I made of a certain argument pattern to explicate one philosophical use of 'ineffable' by demonstrating the "futility" of labeling, as we label some "things," the three crucial constituents of F. This pattern, though of course with a different twist, is that of a famous argument proposed by Bradley. Since his name is not now on everybody's lips, I think that I should mention it.

II

The key word of the dialectic is 'form'. 'Structure' is sometimes used synonymously, or very nearly so. I shall stay with 'form'. The key phrase is 'logical form'. 'The ontological status of logical form' or, briefly, 'the ontological status of logic' is the tag for the issue I am considering. My critic was apprehensive lest the line I took lead to the "reification of logical form." Had he used the phrase, he would have used 'form' philosophically. The thing to realize before tackling this use is that 'form' has three relevant commonsensical meanings. They are all syntactical. That is my cue for another effort to avoid controversy.

I promised to keep out the issue of ideal languages. I shall keep the promise. But I shall henceforth use the LFC (with the "label" constants I added to it) as an improved language, that is, as a calculus syntactically constructed and interpreted by interpreting its undefined signs only. Whether such a "language" is a suitable tool for philosophical analysis is now again controversial. But, again, the controversy does not affect us. For *if* I have committed myself to the "reification of logical form," then, *because* of the tool I use, the commitment should be even easier to spot in my argument than it would be if I did not use that tool. Thus, if a bias is introduced, it is one against the point I am arguing.

Form$_1$ refers to the shape of the signs and to the rules, based on their shapes and nothing else, by which they may be strung together into sentences. This is the first relevant commonsensical meaning of 'form'. If all sentences were atomic, my critic could be answered conclusively and exhaustively as follows. Signs are labels (though not mere labels) representing (simple) "things." Individuality, universality, and exemplification, the three "formal" or "logical" constituents of facts, cannot, except at the price of futility, be so represented. They are represented by form$_1$. The quotes I have put around 'formal' and 'logical' mark philosophical uses. The very sentence in which they occur explicates them. (About the philosophical use of 'thing' presently, in the third part.) Thus I safeguard the ontological distinction. Yet I need not, in order to safeguard it, deny that logical form (philosophical use) is like "things" *in one respect,* namely, that it, too, is presented to me. For indeed, if it were not presented, how could it be represented by form$_1$? And, if it were not presented, why do I use a language of just this form$_1$? Notice, too, that there is something ineffable, in the sense explicated, in any possible language, as long as by language we mean—and I do not know what else we could mean—something having signs and sentences as well as rules by which the former may be strung into the latter. I speak of possible languages rather than of possible worlds because the use of 'possible' in the latter phrase is patently philosophical, while in the former, as long as one thinks of an uninterpreted calculus, it is not.

In our language (LFC) not all primitive (undefined) signs are labels. Those which are not are called logical. What can be said about them, commonsensically, contributes to the explication of the philosophical use of 'form'. Instead of calling these signs logical—as for the most part I shall, in order not to strain the usage—I would therefore rather call them formal$_2$. Lest this seem artificial, consider that, to say the least, the unexplicated uses of 'formal' and 'logical' quite often blur into each other. We just came upon an instance in the synonymy of 'logical constituent' and 'formal constituent'. The synonymy of 'logical truth' and 'formal truth' is another. The only reason the redundance of 'logical form' is not more apparent is that the adjective serves to set off the philosophical context from such very different ones as those in which we speak of, say, the form of a symphony or a vase.

The logical signs are either variables or connectives or operators. A variable as such (that is, technically, a free variable) merely marks form$_1$. Since no more needs to be said about form$_1$, we are left with connectives and operators. For what I am about, though surely not otherwise, there is no difference between these two kinds. Thus nothing will be lost if for the sake of both brevity and simplicity I ignore operators and make my case for connectives.

Like form$_1$, the connectives (form$_2$) represent something which in some sense is presented to us. They represent an aspect of what some philosophers, using the word philosophically, call the world's "form." This is the gist of the argument. My critic at this point finds his worst fears exceeded. I began by claiming *some sort* of "ontological status" for exemplification and so on, which to him seemed bad enough. Now I am about to do the same for negation, disjunction, and so on, which to him seems even worse. Some of his dismay is due to the particular flavor of philosophical talk. The rest is properly dispelled by the commonsensical observations and distinctions that follow.

What form$_2$ represents is different from "things." This comes out in at least three ways. First, the nonlogical primitive signs, also called descriptive, are all labels; the connectives are not. Second, having constructed LFC syntactically, one may start its interpretation by attaching its descriptive primitives as labels to things. In principle, one must do that. Practically, one may instead make these signs "stand for" some words of our natural language, which, in an obvious sense, is the only one we speak and understand, just as a moment ago I made 'G' stand for 'green'. For the connectives the latter alternative is the only one available. We make '$\sim$', '$\vee$', and so on, stand for 'not', 'or', and so on. Third, the use of the connectives is completely and accurately regulated by the so-called truth tables, that is, by an algebraic machinery with two counters which can be made to stand for 'true' and 'false'. On this 'completely and accurately' hangs the current controversy about improved languages. *What form₂ represents is different from what is represented by form₁.* In the written case the difference appears, trivially, in the (geometrical) differences between form₁ and form₂. Much less trivially, it appears in the circumstance that while, as we saw, form₁ *cannot*, except at the price of futility, be represented by primitive signs of the language, form₂ *must* be so represented by at least one primitive logical sign. *Yet form₂ represents something.* Consider a calculus which is like LFC in being of the same form₁ but unlike it in that the algebraic machinery associated with its "connectives" has three counters instead of two. Technically, it is a lower functional calculus with a three-valued nonaristotelian logic. I do not know how to interpret this calculus so as to make an artificial language out of it. Nor does anyone else. And there is one and only one reason why this is so. We do not know how to interpret the "connectives." This shows that form represents something. Or, if you please, it shows what is meant by saying that it "represents" something (though of course not any "thing"), which is, in some sense, "presented" to us. Nor is that all. Still another very important point can and must be made in order to secure the distinctions and allay the fears. As I arranged the exposition, this point must wait for the third part.

Form₃ is a property of expressions. Take an expression, eliminate first all defined terms, then substitute appropriate variables for all descriptive primitives. Two expressions have the same form₃ if and only if this procedure, applied to both of them, either yields different tokens of the same type or can be made to yield them by applying to the variables of one the procedure known as "rewriting." This is the third relevant commonsensical use of 'form'. Notice in passing that it leads immediately to a fourth, which appears in the proposition that a sentence expresses a "formal" truth or falsehood (is analytic or contradictory) if and only if its truth or falsehood depends only on its form₃.

Form₃, too, represents something. After what has been said, this need not be argued separately. I have argued that form₁ and form₂ each represent something. Form₃ is compounded of form₁ and form₂. What it represents is correspondingly compounded of what is represented by form₁ and form₂. If someone pointed out that the use of 'compounded' in the preceding sentence is at least tinged with metaphor, I would not fuss. But I would observe that the unpacking of the rudimentary metaphor, after what has been said, is merely tedious. So I turn instead to three comments.

1. If the language contains *defined* signs, then the form₃ of expressions which are sentences may be given a representative (not, be represented) in the language. Take '$G(a) \lor H(a)$'. Substitution of variables for the (primitive) constants yields '$f(x) \lor g(x)$'. Write '$R(f, g, x)$' as an abbreviation for the latter expression. 'R' is a defined ternary predicate. (I continue to ignore types.) For every sentence a "corresponding" relation R can be defined. Two sentences are of the same form₃ if and only if the constituents which are things of the facts which they represent exemplify the same relation R. In this sense R is a representative of (not: represents) form₃. What it represents (or expresses, but not: is a representative of) is of course what is represented by form₃ (not: form₃).

2. 'Thing', it must have been noticed, I use so that a thing is what either is or by the rules of the language could be labeled. Defined signs are not labels. 'R' is a defined sign. Moreover, 'R' is a defined logical sign, that is, all the primitive signs in its definiens are logical and, therefore, not labels. These are two good reasons why introducing 'R' into the language is not a back-handed way of giving the wrong kind of ontological status to form₃. The fundamental distinctions are still safe.

3. Test what is being said now against what was said in the first part about exemplification by so defining 'Ex' that '$Ex(f, x)$' stands for '$f(x)$'. Notice that, unlike 'E', 'Ex' is a defined logical sign. Notice, too, that the possibility of introducing it does not in the least militate against what has been said about the futility of *labeling* exemplification. What one may wonder about is, rather, whether this futility does not infect all 'R'. In a sense it does. Only, if the expression is complex enough, then 'R' is of some technical use.

Those who distrust the distinction between the commonsensical and the philosophical uses of words more often than not want to be shown the exact point of transition. I would remind them of what James once said. One cannot light a candle so quickly that one sees what the dark is like. But I would add that in some cases one can do better than in some others. In the case of '(logical) form' one can do rather well. Sentences, it has been said, manage to express facts because they are "logical pictures" of the facts they express. In this context 'logical picture' is expendable. What is intended can be said without the phrase as follows. (S) *A sentence manages to express because, taken as a fact, it shares logical form with the fact it expresses.* Take once more our paradigm, F, and the sentence expressing it, '$G(a)$'. Here is what in this case I take (S) to mean: 'a' and 'G' represent the spot and the color, respectively; their shapes, the spot and the color being an individual and a character, respectively; their juxtaposition, the exemplification of the color by the spot. Generally, it seems, the idea of "shared logical form" is that of a one-one correspondence between the constituents of the fact expressed and geometrical features of the sentence expressing it, such that constituents of the same kind correspond to features of the same (geometrical) kind. If that is what (S) means, then I understand it. Of course I do, since it is exactly what I said myself. Only I said it without using 'logical form'. Thus I have shown, not surprisingly, that like all philosophically used words and phrases, the phrase is expendable. Now I shall show two more things; namely, first, that if the phrase is used as in (S) it leads to immediate catastrophe and, second, that in certain other contexts it invites confusion and makes falsehood seem plausible.

First, write '$G(a)$' without brackets, as I did before, and assume the two letters to be things. The assumption is in the spirit of the dialectic. Considered as a fact, a token of the sentence then consists of two things of different kinds standing in a certain (geometrical) relation. The constituents of this fact are, therefore, two individuals (the letters), two nonrelational (the letters' shapes) characters, and one relational (the letters' juxtaposition) character, and, if I may so express myself, individuality twice, universality three times, in addition, of course, to (relational) exemplification. Everything else apart, clearly they are too many for a one-one correspondence with the constituents of the fact expressed. It follows that if 'logical form' is explicated in the only way I can think of, the sentence and the fact do not "share" the same "logical form." Rather, we stand here at the beginning of an infinite regress. This is disaster indeed. The regress, by the way, though of course again with a different twist, is not unrelated to another part of Bradley's famous pattern.

What philosophers try to say is always ineffable. This, we remember, is the general ineffability thesis. As it was meant, though not as I suggested it might be explicated, it is vague and indefensible. Yet it has come to stand for quite a few things that are neither vague nor indefensible. The related distinctions between language as "part" and "picture" of the world and between speaking and speaking about speaking 'are two such things. Those who held the general thesis held it, in part, because they thought "logical form" to be "ineffable." That is why they used 'logical form' as they did in (S). As was shown in the last paragraph, the disaster that befell them is due to an implicit neglect of the two distinctions.

Second, form$_1$, form$_2$, and form$_3$, I argued, each represent something that in some sense is presented to us. What they represent I now call *logical form*. This explicates the use I shall henceforth make of the phrase. Nor am I the only one who, either implicitly or explicitly, uses the phrase in this way. That explains in turn the dismay of my critic. He takes me to assert that logical form "exists," which to him is absurd. So far I avoided 'exist', leaving it deliberately to the last part. At this point, though, I wish to say that had I cared to indulge, I could have borrowed a soothing word from the tradition. I might have said that logical form, though it does not "exist," yet "subsists." Of course, the tag merely dignifies the distinctions I made commonsensically and without using any tag, between the two kinds of "ontological status." But, then, sometimes tags are convenient. Right now I find this one handy for building a verbal bridge.

If logical form does not even "subsist," that is, if it has no ontological status whatsoever, then it is nought. Nought is nought, unchanged and unchangeably, in all "possible worlds." This is one pillar of the bridge. The occurrence of 'formal' in 'formal truth' provides the other. Remember that formal truths are also called logical; infer speciously that logical truths are nought; and you are in sight of the philosophical proposition the bridge leads to. (A) *The logic of our world is that of all possible worlds.* For example, '$p \lor \sim p$' is formally true in all possible worlds. The word used philosophically in (A) is 'possible'. One such use of 'possible' is easily explicated as follows. In our world a state of affairs is possible if and only if it is expressed by a sentence (of our language) that is not a formal falsehood (contradictory). Clearly this is not the way the word is used in (A). As it is used there, the phrase 'possible world' is inseparable. I find it difficult to explicate. Or, rather, in the one explication I can think of the phrase sounds rather inflated. One can, as we saw, construct calculi which are in some fundamental respects like and in some others unlike the calculus we can make into an improved language by interpreting it. Such calculi are possible (commonsensical use). The illustration I used was a three-valued lower functional calculus. If one wishes one may, with some bombast, speak of such a calculus as the language of a "possible world." If one does that, then (A) is patently false. I say patently because in the purely syntactical sense of 'formal truth'—and there is in this case no other—'$p \lor \sim p$' is not a formal truth, or, as in this case one says, rather, is not a theorem of the three-valued calculus. Thus I have kept my promise to show that in some contexts the unexplicated use of 'logical form' leads to confusion and falsehood. The context is that of (A). The confusion is that between the two suggested explications of 'possible'. The falsehood is (A) itself, which asserts what I call the *absolutist* conception of analyticity.

III

Ontology asks what "exists." This use of 'exist' is philosophical. I couldn't possibly here explicate it fully. I shall merely state two basic ideas, calling them basic because I believe that either explicitly or implicitly they have shaped the whole ontological enterprise. Then I shall point out a few of their implications. The connection with the first two parts is twofold. One of these ideas involves that of names or labels. For another, it will be remembered that, when discussing form$_2$, I promised an important further argument to allay the apprehensions aroused by its being given any sort of ontological status. This argument concludes the paper.

From now on, when I mention 'exist', I shall surround it with single quotes. When I report its philosophical uses, I shall surround it with double quotes. When I use it commonsensically, I shall not use quotes. And I shall presently treat 'thing' and 'fact' in the same way. The practice saves space and avoids tedium. But, of course, it should be kept in mind.

Ontologists do not just either catalogue or classify what exists. Rather, they search for "simples" of which everything that exists "consists." These simples, and nothing else, they hold to "exist," or to be the only existents. (I shall use 'existent' in no other way.) If, for instance, the tones in a symphony were simples, they would "exist"; the symphony, though of course it exists, would not "exist." This is the first basic idea. It amounts to an explication of the ontologists' philosophical use of 'exist'. Consider the classical phenomenalist. His tones are such things as sensa and, if he is not a nominalist, some of the characters they exemplify. His symphony is the physical object. And we know him to assert that physical objects do not "exist." That shows in one important case the adequacy of the explication. Notice, though, that it explicates one philosophical use ('exist') in terms of another ('simple'). Everything therefore still depends on whether an adequate explication can be found for this use of 'simple' (and of 'consist'). I do not propose to answer the questions that raises. I merely wish to state one idea which I believe to be a part of the philosophical idea of simplicity and which, therefore, no adequate explication of the latter can ignore. What is "simple" is so simple indeed that, in speaking about it (directly), the best or the most one can do, put it any way you wish, is to name it, that is, attach a label to it (though not necessarily, as we saw, a mere label). This is the second basic idea. It reveals a connection, not surprising from where I stand, between the ontological enterprise and language. The way I deliberately presented this connection shows that it does not at all depend on the idea of an improved, and still less of course on that of an ideal language. Once more, therefore, no vitiating bias is introduced if I avail myself of one of the advantages of improved languages. A name or label is simple in some linguistic sense of 'simple'. The idea of linguistic simplicity, though surely not philosophical, is yet not obvious. Thus it needs explanation. Improved languages, to say the least, provide us with models of what one might reasonably mean by 'linguistically simple'. This is the advantage of which I wish to avail myself.

Like all languages, our paradigm, the LFC with constants, contains signs (words) and sentences. That opens two possibilities; simple signs and simple sentences. (Perhaps it would be better to say simplest; but I shall stay with 'simple'.) A simple sign is one no (geometrical) part of which is a sign (for example, 'a', 'G', '∨'). A simple sentence is one no geometrical part of which is a sentence; for example, 'G(a)'. Such sentences are called atomic. But an atomic sentence contains at least two simple signs. In this sense not even an atomic sentence is simple. Thereby hangs a tale.

What sorts of entities (I must avoid 'thing') have been held to "exist"? The tradition has two streams. At times they intermingled. Also, one is so much broader that it may be called the main stream. Yet the two are clearly discernible. According to some philosophers all existents are "things"; according to some others they are all "facts." The former I call thing ontologists; the latter, fact ontologists. These uses of 'thing' and 'fact' are of course philosophical. But their explication seems by now obvious. A "thing" is what is named by a descriptive primitive sign; for example, 'a' and 'G', but not '∨'. A "fact" is what is referred to (I avoid 'named') by an atomic sentence. It is important to keep in mind how much narrower these (explicated philosophical) uses are than the commonsensical ones. We may and do call an entity a thing and say that it exists even though, in a certain ontology, it may not be a "thing" and therefore not "exist." As for 'thing', so for 'fact'. We naturally call what a sentence refers to a fact (state of affairs) and, if the sentence is true, say that it exists. But again, in a certain ontology it may not be a "fact" and therefore not "exist." An ontologist unaware of the ambiguity is likely to get into trouble. Of this presently; now for four brief comments.

First, in the first two parts I was concerned with securing *some* sort of ontological status for logical form, arguing that while it does not "exist," it yet "subsists." Naturally, therefore, I was not particularly concerned with what "exists." Yet one may infer from the way I proceeded and, in particular, from how I used 'name', that I am a thing ontologist and not a nominalist. The inference is correct.

Second, what I had in mind when I said that at times the two streams mingled are the several philosophies of substance. Every such philosophy is a heroic attempt to reconcile the irreconcilable. To grasp that firmly, consider the philosophical uses of 'substance'. They all share three features. First, "substances" are the only (independent) existents. Second, a "substance" is a "thing." Third, a "substance" is a thing that, by virtue of being this thing, has certain characters. But a thing having a certain character is expressed by a sentence; and sentences refer to facts!

Third, if the two ideas I singled out are basic, then fact ontologists would have to hold, either explicitly or implicitly, that some sentences at least are names. Many philosphers cannot make any sense out of the idea that a sentence may be the name of something. Thus they reject it as absurd; so do I. An analytical philosopher does not, however, just express his opinions but presents and examines arguments for and against all sorts of positions, including those he rejects. It is my next purpose to state correctly and accurately, which among other things also means as parsimoniously as possible, a difficulty on which any fact ontology must bog down.

Fourth, fact ontologies have been attractive to philosophers. Had they not been, why all the ingenious substance philosophies which, we just saw, try to have the best of both worlds? Whence the attraction? The clue—I planted it in the second comment—is a certain philosophical use of 'independent'. This idea of "independence" is also part of the idea of "existence." What truly exists ("exists"), exists "independently." None of us is ever presented either with an individual that is not qualified or with a character (quality) that is not exemplified by an individual. *In this sense*, "things" are not independent. An individual exemplifying a certain quality, on the other hand, or a certain quality being exemplified by an individual, which is the same, is a fact expressed by a sentence. This, I believe, is the deepest structural root of the attraction fact ontologies have had and perhaps still have for some philosophers.

I turn to the difficulty no fact ontology can overcome. To state it effectively, it will be best to state first two very general conditions. I speak of conditions rather than of principles or presuppositions because of the blur that has gathered around the latter notions. What I mean is that hardly any philosopher would consider his analysis adequate if it were pointed out to him that it fails to meet these "conditions."

Every sentence is about something. To separate what can be separated, consider for the moment only *true* sentences. To keep out what is irrelevant, consider only sentences not mentioning entities a philosopher may think problematic on grounds that have nothing to do with the issue. Translation into ontological talk of the commonsensical 'being about something' yields the condition that there must be some existents (at least one) such that since they (it) are there (exist) the sentence is true, while if they were not there, it would be false. This is the first condition. 'Meaning' has several meanings (uses). In one use, sentences are said to have meanings. What one calls the meaning of a sentence must not depend on whether the sentence is true or false. That is the second condition.

Return to F expressed by '$G(a)$'. Let '$\sim H(a)$' stand for the true sentence that the spot is not red. What is it about? The commonsensical answer is, of course, that it is about (expresses, refers to) the fact (not "fact"!) of the spot not being red. But, then, '$\sim H(a)$' is surely a sentence of the kind to which the first condition applies. Thus the fact ontologist must find an existent, that is, a "fact" the sentence is about. He presents us, as I believe he must, with the "negative fact" of the spot not being red. But, if this is a "fact," then he must by the rules of his own game be able to "name" it, that is, he must be able to produce an atomic sentence that refers to it. If he cannot, then he violates the second basic idea. '$\sim H(a)$' is not atomic. Nor ot course can he produce an atomic sentence that by any stretch of the imagination could be said to be about the fact in question. This most parsimonious way of stopping him in his tracks has not, as far as I know, been noticed in the huge literature about "negative facts." Failure to grasp explicitly the two basic ideas and, just as important, failure to distinguish between the two uses of 'fact' are three plausible reasons for this oversight.

In a fact ontology, what would *false* sentences be about? Once the barriers are down, the obvious answer is "false facts." The false atomic sentence '$H(a)$', for instance, would "name" the "false fact" of the spot being red. (The double quotes around 'name' mark my own reluctance, but I am playing someone else's game.) Some philosophers willing to put up with "negative facts" boggled at "false facts." At this point, something called a robust sense of reality is usually invoked. We must not have the world cluttered with such existents as the "false fact" expressed by 'The moon is made of green cheese'. Economy, in some such sense, does guide the ontological enterprise. This, however, is not the point I wish to make. The point is, rather, that the crowding or cluttering is not really as great as it might seem to one who fails to appreciate the distinction between the two uses of 'fact'. If, for instance, the sentence 'The moon is made of green cheese' upon analysis turns out not to be atomic, then even a fact ontologist would not have to put up with the fact it refers to as a "fact" of his world. He need merely count among his existents those "false facts" to which false atomic sentences refer. One may wonder whether, had this been clearly seen, those who swallowed "negative facts" would have strained at "false facts."

Consider for a moment a fact ontologist who holds fast to the second basic idea. In other words, he understands that by the rules of his game only atomic sentences can be "names." He has two alternatives. Either he accepts "false facts" or he holds that only true atomic sentences are "names." The second alternative is repugnant to him. The structural reason for this repugnance can be stated in four steps. 1. A true atomic sentence is a name. 2. A false atomic sentence, therefore, at least purports to be a name. 3. But a name that does not name anything is nonsense (has no meaning). 4. Yet false sentences have meaning. Notice that in 4 the second condition is operative. At this point our philosopher, unwilling to accept "false facts," thinks of another expedient. Reifying 'meaning', he makes sentences name "meanings." But what, then, becomes of "facts?" Obviously the "fact" of this being green cannot be identified with the meaning of 'this is green'. Otherwise, the difference between its being and its not being green, respectively, would be lost. The only way out is to reify 'true' and 'false' and make a "true" (or "false") fact a compound, in some obscure sense of 'compound', of "meaning" and "truth" (or "falsehood"). In this case, though, even a true atomic sentence refers no longer to a "simple" but to a "compound." Thus the first basic idea is lost.

The imaginary fact ontologist whose predicament I just exhibited reminds me of two important philosophers. Frege is close in both time and resemblance. Aquinas is more remote in both respects. Yet the resemblance to me is unmistakable. Frege modifies the pattern by means of his double semantic tie. A sentence expresses its meaning (he calls it sense) and refers (he uses the word technically) to one of the two existents 'True' and 'False'. In Aquinas' world, individual substances, which are the only existents, are created by God endowing "natures" with "being." That makes Being and Not-being correspond to True and False. *Ens, verum, res,* and *unum,* some will remember, are in a peculiar scholastic sense synonymous. *Unum,* I think, can here without strain be made to correspond to "simple."

I am ready to turn once more to that aspect of logical form which is represented by form₂. For reasons which I believe are obvious, the arguments have not centered on conjunction but, rather, on negation and disjunction. So I shall do two things. In the case of *negation* many thing ontologists thought they had come upon a difficulty of the kind one would call epistemological rather than ontological. I shall show that the supposed difficulty disappears if one grants that logical form is in some sense presented to us. In the case of *disjunction* I shall dissect and, by dissecting it, dispose of an objection against granting some kind of ontological status (in traditional terms, subsistence) to logical form.

Take a true negated atomic proposition, say, '$\sim H(a)$', asserted when F is presented. The "things" presented are the spot and its actual color (G). Those who think that there is a difficulty also seem to think that whenever we assert truly and in the presence of the best evidence available anything as "simple" as '$\sim H(a)$', what we assert should be presented to us. They solve their difficulty by concluding that we "deduce" '$\sim H(a)$' from '$G(a)$', which refers to what is presented to us, in conjunction with another proposition, of which we have knowledge of a special and privileged kind, to the effect that the two colors (G and H) are incompatible. The troubles this gambit leads to are notorious. To say the least, the price one pays for it is very high.[3] Fact ontologists of course may try to remove the alleged difficulty, consistently within their game, by introducing a "negative fact" as what is presented to us on such occasions. Perhaps that is one of the attractions of a fact ontology. On the other hand, I do not see the original difficulty. When I am presented with F, I am, among other things (not "things"), presented with the spot and its actual color. On some earlier occasions I have been presented with the color red. In some sense I am also presented with logical form. That is all that need be said about how I come to know that the spot is not red. In fact, it is part of what one may reasonably mean by saying that in some sense logical form is presented to us.

[3] See "On Nonperceptual Intuition," *Philosophy and Phenomenological Research*, 10, 1949, 263–64. A fact ontologist willing to pay the price might hope thereby also to get rid of "negative facts" by "analyzing," say, the fact of this being not red into the two "positive facts" of this being green and green being incompatible with red. The hope fails on the obvious ground that, of the two sentences 'This is not red' and 'This is green, and green is incompatible with red', the latter says more than the former. Ontologically, therefore, and this is the relevant context, I do not know what it means to "analyze" the fact expressed by the former into the latter. The reason for that not having always been obvious is probably that in certain discussions the ontological and epistemological contexts were improperly mixed.

Assume for the sake of the argument that 'This road leads to Oxford' and 'This road leads to Cambridge' are both atomic. The objection based on disjunction runs as follows. What exists is fully determinate. There is, therefore, or there may be, the fact that this road leads to Cambridge as well as the fact that this road leads to Oxford. For these are fully determinate. But there is in the world no such indeterminate *fact* as a road leading either to Cambridge or to Oxford. More dramatically, there is no "or" in the world. I have shown in the second part that one may grant some sort of ontological status to logical form, without thereby being committed to the belief that there is "or" in the world in the same sense in which there are "things." But I also promised on that occasion a further argument, which I am now ready to make. Return to the sentence in which the word 'fact' is italicized. Everything depends on whether it is taken commonsensically or philosophically. If it is taken commonsensically, then of course there are such facts. They exist. At least we say it every day and do not by saying it get into any trouble as long as we continue to speak commonsensically. If, on the other hand, that word in that sentence is taken philosophically (ontologically), then two things need to be said. First, a thing ontologist must not take it ontologically, for he knows no "facts." For him no fact, whether or not the sentence expressing it is atomic, is an existent. Nor, second, would a fact ontologist with a firm grasp of the two basic ideas have to worry about the indeterminateness of the fact expressed by a disjunction. In his world some "facts" do "exist." But these are all expressed by atomic sentences and are, therefore, determinate in the relevant sense. A disjunction, however, is not an atomic sentence. What it refers to, though a fact, for the fact ontologist as well as for anyone else, is therefore not even for him a "fact." Hence it need not be determinate. It may well be, by the way, that this determinateness of "atomic facts" is still another cause of the lure of fact ontologies. Perhaps such "determinateness" is an ingredient of "independence." However that may be, I conclude, first, that, irrespective of whether one is a thing or a fact ontologist, the objection collapses. This is as it should be. For whether or not logical form "subsists" *should not* depend on what kind of entities "exist." That, as I explicated the ideas, it actually *does not* should further blunt the suspicion that I unduly reify logical form. I conclude, second, that a thing ontologist, merely by raising the objection, accepts without noticing it the basic gambit of the fact ontologist. This, however, is the sort of thing a philosopher must not do without noticing it.

Generality and Existence*

*T*HE world's form has ontological status. That is the main thesis
of an earlier paper.[1] In arguing it, generality and existence were
deliberately ignored. This paper argues their case. Materially,
therefore, the two papers are but one. IOM contains quite a few preparatory moves. Such a move purports to show that a certain controversial question is or is not, as the case may be, being prejudged. Call
that a preparatory result. Since the two papers are materially one, the
preparatory moves of IOM need not be repeated. Since they are not
formally one, some preparatory as well as some main results will be
recalled in Section One.

I

The method distinguishes between the commonsensical and the
philosophical use of words. That is indeed its fundamental idea. Much
less fundamentally, it permits the use of so-called artificial languages
(interpreted calculi). In IOM the lower functional calculus (LFC)
proved very helpful. The use made of it was moderate, prejudging
much less than some now tend to fear. That was one preparatory result.
I shall continue, with the same moderation, to use LFC.

One key word was 'presented'. In one of its uses, some perceptual
(physical) entities are sometimes presented to us; in another, only phenomenal entities are. The first use undoubtedly is commonsensical. Is
the second philosophical or merely (as I hold) esoteric? Happily, we
need not decide. That was another preparatory result. Examples may
therefore be chosen by mere convenience, from either the perceptual or
the phenomenal realm, or without specifying to which of the two they
belong. The point is that we could not know what in fact we do know,
e.g., on certain occasions, what is expressed by 'This is a green spot',
unless certain entities were on these occasions in the acceptable sense

* Theoria, *28, 1962, 1–26. Reprinted by permission.*
[1] "Ineffability, Ontology, and Method," *The Philosophical Review*, 69, 1960,
18–40, and pp. 45–63 of this book; hereafter referred to as IOM.

presented to us. What is presented has "ontological status." That will recall how one crucial phrase of the opening formula has been explicated.[2]

Two other key words were 'simple' and 'name'. Some entities are so simple that the only way of directly referring to one of them in any conceivable language is by attaching a label to it. Only such labels are called names.[3] What are the world's simples? Happily once more, we need not stay for an answer. That, too, was a preparatory result.

The primitive signs of LFC are of two kinds or shapes, called descriptive and formal$_2$ respectively. Disregarding parentheses, the latter are either connectives or quantifiers. Only descriptive signs may be made to serve as names. They are of either the x-shape or the f-shape. The two shapes are formal$_1$ features of LFC. So is juxtaposition, say, of the x-shape 'a' and the f-shape 'F' in '$F(a)$'.

When presented with a spot's being green, I am presented not only with two simples, namely, an individual and a character, but also with individuality, universality, and exemplification. Unless I were presented with individuality and universality, I would not know that one simple was an individual, one a character, nor which was which. Unless I were also presented with exemplification, I would not know that the individual exemplifies the character. Hence, all five entities have ontological status.

Let the spot's being green be expressed by '$F(a)$'. The two letters represent, by naming them, the two simples. Individuality, universality, and exemplification are, in this order, represented, though not named, by the shapes of 'a' and 'F' and their juxtaposition, i.e., by the formal$_1$ features of '$F(a)$'. Representation is thus either by naming or without naming. The three nonthings in the example cannot without futility be named. The demonstration of this is a major part of IOM. It shows that the distinction between the two kinds of representation cuts deep. The connectives, which are part of form$_2$, also stand for (represent) something which must be presented and, therefore, have ontological status. That is another major part of IOM. Form$_1$ and the connectives represent part of the "world's form." That will recall how the other crucial phrase of the opening formula has been explicated. I say part of the world's form because the quantifiers also belong to form$_2$ and because of form$_3$.

---

[2] 'Entity' is again used neutrally. Except for an occasional formula, such as the opening sentence, philosophical uses are marked by double quotes. Once a philosophical use has been explicated, the double quotes are dropped. But see below concerning 'exist'. Formulae are italicized.

[3] For the dialectic that prejudges or ignores, see "Strawson's Ontology," *The Journal of Philosophy*, 57, 1960, 601–22, and pp. 171–92 of this book.

Replace all the descriptive primitives of a sentence (of LFC) by free variables. The result is a schema. Sentences which can be made to yield the same schema exemplify the same form$_3$. Form$_3$ is compounded of form$_1$ and form$_2$. Hence, if form$_1$ and form$_2$ stand for something that has ontological status, so does form$_3$. Like form$_1$ and form$_2$, form$_3$ is a geometrical (syntactical) feature. But the form$_3$ of a sentence, while exemplified by this sentence, is not literally exemplified by its schema. In this respect schemata are, not surprisingly, in the same boat with free variables. Take a free x-variable. Not only does it not name individuality, literally it does not even represent it as do the shapes of the descriptive primitives whose potential place in a schema it marks. As for variables, so for schemata. The idea is, simply enough, that even if one were willing to call an interpreted calculus a language, expressions containing free variables would not literally belong to it.[4] Connectives and, as I shall argue, operators do literally represent features of the world's form. This is a striking difference between form$_3$ on the one hand and form$_1$ and form$_2$ on the other.

Whether or not certain sentences are true depends only on their form$_3$. The truths or falsehoods such sentences express are called formal$_4$.

'Exist' and 'subsist' are key words in ontology. *Only the world's form subsists.* As I use 'subsist', the formula is true. Hence, since its subject has been explicated, it in turn explicates this use. The commonsensical use of 'exist' can always be avoided by means of circumlocutions containing 'there is (are)'. I shall make a point of avoiding it. The philosophical uses of 'exist' are many. Only one concerns us. *Only simples "exist."* The formula explicates this one use.[5] Even so, every instance of it will be surrounded by double quotes. This extra precaution is taken because commonsensical use will have to be made of 'existence'. The only alternative I can think of is 'there-is-ness', which is too barbarous even for my obstinacy.

II

The *particular quantifier* is the phrase 'there is (at least one)' as in 'There is a drugstore around the corner'. The *general quantifier* is the phrase 'for everything', as in 'For everything: if it is a dog then it is a

---

[4] In other words, it is merely logicians' jargon to call a schema a sentence or a variable a term. Jargon is often convenient. But it is harmless only in its proper place.

[5] A formula explicates a philosophical use if and only if that use makes it true. Such a formula I also call a pattern. Recently I listed eight patterns for 'exist'. See "Physics and Ontology," *Philosophy of Science*, 28, 1961, 1–14, and pp. 108–23 of this book.

mammal'. Whether or not the latter sentence and 'Every dog is a mammal' say the same thing may reasonably be questioned. It will be taken for granted that they do. Existential import so-called is merely a technicality. Nor does what remains after this technicality has been cleared up impinge on the dialectic to be displayed. If one disagrees, let him take notice of another prejudgment economy imposes. 'General' and 'particular' have been chosen instead of the more usual 'universal' and 'existential' in order to avoid in the one case the clash with 'universality' and, in the other, a dispensable derivative of 'exist'.

In IOM it has been argued that we could not know what in fact we do know unless individuality, universality, existence, conjunction, disjunction, and so on, were presented to us and that therefore, as 'subsist' is used, these entities all subsist. Also, some closely related matters were taken up. In this paper it will be argued that (as they will presently be called) generality and existence subsist. And, again, some further closely related matters will be taken up.

The quantifiers require some preparatory moves of their own. These will all be made in this section. Much, if perhaps not all, that must be said in making them has been said before, though perhaps not always in the way it will here be said.

"Nothing can be said about everything." The words intrigue. Are they the formula for a genuine piece of dialectic? If so, does the dialectic affect the general quantifier? 'Every dog is a mammal' makes sense. It is also true. Some uses of 'everything' could not possibly be affected by what does or does not lurk in the dialectical depths. One source of uneasiness may be the type difficulty. 'For everything' always may and sometimes must be replaced by some such phrase as 'for every individual', 'for every property'. That takes care of the difficulty. If some uneasiness still lingers on, I can think of only one source for it. 'Individual', 'property', and so on, have been used philosophically. To dry up this source, too, one merely has to distinguish between speaking and speaking about speaking. Since the use of calculi, or, better, their proper use keeps the distinction always before our minds, I turn at this point to the LFC.

'Individual variable' and 'individual constant' both refer to shapes. The former must be specified, e.g., 'x', 'y', 'z'. 'Individual constant' is merely a synonym for 'descriptive primitive of x-shape', suggested by the familiar rules for making certain designs (sentences) out of certain others. These are the only intelligible uses of those two phrases containing 'individual' adjectivally. Being both geometrical, they obviously are commonsensical.

Interpretation makes a calculus into an artificial language. It proceeds by rules which must be laid down beforehand. The LFC contains certain shapes called general operators. That is why it can be so interpreted that it transcribes[6] the general quantifier. To show accurately how that is done, three rule fragments will suffice. R1. Every individual constant may be attached as a name to one and only one physical object. Every physical object may be so named. R2. '*F*' is attached as a name to the color green. R3. '$(x)F(x)$' expresses that (a) *every physical object is green*. With this interpretation, we read '$(x)F(x)$' as (b) *every individual is green*. Taking them as one would at first sight, the two italicized sentences do not at all say the same thing. That causes but a moment's perplexity. 'Every physical object is green' is indeed the English sentence expressing what we would wish to express by '$(x)F(x)$' if *per impossibile* we spoke the artificial language. Clearly, this dissolution of the perplexity depends on the distinction between speaking, either English or *per impossibile* the artificial language, on the one hand, and speaking the former about the latter on the other. Usually one just says, with a blur which must now be obvious, that the individuals of the artificial language are physical objects. Once the blur is cleared up, the following five points also become obvious.

First. In stating R1 'every' is used as in 'Every dog is a mammal', quite harmlessly and not at all as in that intriguing string of words which may cause worry. *Second.* In stating R1, R2, and R3 'individual' has not been used at all, except adjectivally in 'individual constant'. Hence, no philosophical use could possibly have slipped in. *Third.* Since it occurs in the italicized sentence (b), 'individual' does occur in the interpreted LFC, at least after a fashion. There, though, its only use, as sometimes in English, is to express the type distinction, which in turn merely expresses what is presented to us, namely, individuality and universality. Hence this use, too, is commonsensical. *Fourth.* The operator symbols contain variables, e.g., '(x)'. One reason, we just saw, is the type distinction. Another is the variables' pronomial function, as exhibited by the design '$(x) \ldots x \ldots x \ldots$'. In sentences the variables are always bound, never free. Thus one may say that in English 'individual' and 'property' sometimes serve as bound but never as free variables. That fits well with Section One, where we saw that, literally, free variables do not occur even in artificial languages. *Fifth.* The individuals of the example are physical objects. They might just as well have been sensa, except that some now ques-

---

[6] An expression of an interpreted calculus is said to transcribe an English one if the former through the interpretation is made to express what is expressed by the latter.

tion whether 'sensum' has a commonsensical use. Otherwise, philosophical uses come in only when artificial languages are employed in explicating them.

That certain uneasiness about the general quantifier is disposed of. I know of no kindred one about the other. So I simply recall that '$(\exists x)F(x)$' is made to express that there is at least one individual which is green.

'f' goes with 'property' as 'x' goes with 'individual'. 'For every property' and 'There is at least one property' would thus have to be transcribed by '(f)' and '$(\exists f)$', respectively. These operators do of course not belong to LFC. A few of the arguments which follow involve them. But these can just as conveniently be made without symbols.

What can be said with the quantifiers cannot be said without them. The point is familiar; so are the arguments for it; yet they bear recalling. (a) Assume that there are N individuals in the world, N being either a huge integer or an infinite cardinal. For all we know, it may be the latter. But the argument loses none of its force if N is finite. So we may assume that it is. Assume also that each individual has been named. Let 'a_1', 'a_2', . . . , 'a_N' be their names (in LFC). The assumption is wildly unrealistic, to say the least. But again, the argument loses none of its force even if all individuals had been presented to us and we had named them. Let 'G' name a property not further specified and recall that 'P' implies 'C' if and only if 'If P then C' is a formal₄ truth.[7] Consider (1) '$(x)G(x)$' and (2) '$G(a_1). G(a_2) . . . G(a_N)$'. (1) implies (2). (2) does not imply (1). As one says, (1) is stronger than (2). Hence, even if (2) were actually available to us, as of course it is not, it could not do the job of (1). Yet, (2) is the most likely candidate for this job within the fragment of LFC that remains after the operators have been suppressed. (b) If (3) '$(\exists x)G(x)$' is false, no sentence of the fragment just mentioned could possibly say what it says. Strictly speaking, that alone is conclusive. But let us glance at what happens if (3) is true; $a_1, a_2, . . . , a_M$ being all the individuals that make it so. Since all sentences are of finite length, we may assume that M is an integer. The most likely candidate for the job of (3) is

$$(4) \qquad G(a_1) \lor G(a_2) \lor . . . \lor G(a_M).$$

(4) implies (3). (3) does not imply (4). As one says, (3) is weaker than (4). Comparing (a) and (b) brings out an important difference between the two operators. The statement with the general operator is stronger than the one without which, so to speak, comes closest. In the case of

---

[7] This is of course the narrow use of 'implies', not the wide one now also current.

the particular operator, the former is weaker than the latter. Many things we know, believe, doubt, entertain, and so on, can be expressed by statements like (1) but by none that are weaker; many others, by statements like (3) but by none that are stronger. It follows that the operators are indispensable.

III

Each quantifier represents something which is sometimes presented. Had it never been presented, we would not know what the quantifier meant. Of course, neither "something" is a *thing*. Assume for the sake of the argument that green and square are simples. The property of being green and square is compounded of them. A *thing* is either a simple or in this sense compounded of simples. The idiomatic use of 'thing' is much broader. This narrower one, always marked by italics, will save quite a few words. Let us save some more by picking a single one for each of the two "somethings," *generality* for the general quantifier and, for the particular one, *existence*. Sentences containing the general (particular) quantifier will be called general (particular) sentences.

Generality and existence subsist. That is the thesis. It rests on two arguments. As in IOM, each argument has two steps. In the first step one shows that the entity is sometimes presented; in the second, that it is not a thing. But there is also this difference that while in IOM the arguments were made *en bloc*, indeed had to be made *en bloc*, first for individuality, universality, and exemplification together, then for what all the connectives represent, generality and existence each requires an argument of its own.

It would be absurd to claim that generality is presented on *all* occasions one uses or could use, even for the best of reasons, a general sentence. I merely claim that (a) generality is presented on *some* such occasions, and (b) if it were not, we would not on *any* occasion know what the quantifier meant. To me (b) is obvious. Direct argument for it is beyond my present power of communication. Indirectly or dialectically, (b) is at the very center of the view that sees in ontology the center of the philosophical enterprise. For (a) everything depends on a good example. In the example I am about to give it does not even make sense to doubt either that all the *things* mentioned in the general sentence are presented or that we know what the sentence expresses. No example could be better. Nor need it be.

Some simples are sometimes presented. But an entity, to be presented, need not be a simple. Individuality, for instance, as was shown in IOM, is sometimes presented but is not a simple. That it is not a *thing* which is not a simple I took then and take now to be obvious.

But again, a *thing*, to be presented, need not be a simple. Take once more the character of being green and square. In the relevant sense, no one would call it a simple. Yet, when presented with a spot that is green and square, I am also presented with this character as well as with the fact of the spot's being green and square. Any doubt or hesitation some may feel at this point I shall allay later. The reason for making it now is that some characters presented in the example are not simple.

Presented with a single square inside a circle, I say (1) '*This* square is the *only* one inside *this* circle'. That is the example. Squares and circles,[8] we may safely assume, are individuals. Let '*a*', '*b*', '*F*' stand for this square, this circle, and the (relational) character of being *a* square inside *a* circle, respectively. The transcription of (1) is not of course '$F(a, b)$' alone but, rather, its conjunction with

$$(2) \qquad\qquad (x)\,[(x = a) \lor \sim F(x, b)].$$

(2) contains the general operator. I conclude that generality is *on this occasion* presented to me *in connection with* the fact $F(a, b)$. Instead of saying that it is (on this occasion) presented in connection with $F(a, b)$, one might as well say that it is (on this occasion) presented *in addition* to $F(a, b)$. That fits with what we saw before, namely, that the general statement is stronger than the molecular one which comes closest to it.

I am not the first to worry this bone. Russell worried it in *An Inquiry into Meaning and Truth*, where he experimented with an "empiricism" so narrow that we do not really "know" anything that cannot be expressed by a molecular sentence of LFC; the individuals of the interpretation being such things as sensa. Hence, even if the example is taken phenomenally, we do not really know that this is the *only* square inside this circle. That is perplexing. Russell discusses the perplexity at length. Yet he remains perplexed. The solution I propose, as so often in philosophy, is like the one Columbus fell upon when, challenged to stand an egg on its tip, he first cautiously flattened the tip. Generality and a chair—or, if you will have it, a sensum—are two entities very different from each other. But there is no difference in the way either is sometimes presented to us, with an immediacy, as one says, which is not only the mark of ontological status but indeed the ground of all knowing.

If generality were a *thing*, it would have to be either an individual or a character. That it is not an individual I take to be obvious. Nor of course is it a character of *a*. Thus it would have to be a character (of

---

[8] Not: being *a* square or *a* circle.

the second type) of either (a) F or (b) the character, referred to by the predicative expression in the bracket of (2), of being either this square or not a square in this circle. To exclude (a), let another square, c, appear inside the circle. Now F is presented twice, once in $F(a, b)$, once in $F(c, b)$. But there is no difference whatsoever in the way it is presented now in either fact and the way it was presented before in $F(a, b)$ alone. Hence, if F, as presented in $F(a, b)$, exemplified generality before, it would also exemplify it now. Yet, clearly, it doesn't. The argument excluding (b) proceeds *mutatis mutandis* as that for (a). A quasicharacter is an entity in all respects like a *thing* except that it is exemplified by facts. If there were quasicharacters (I do not believe that there are), generality might be, in the example, a quasicharacter exemplified by the fact $F(a, b)$. The argument excluding this third possibility proceeds again like that excluding (a).[9]

What is presented has ontological status. But to have ontological status is not the same as to be presented. To overlook that is to overlook the distinction between seeing and the seen, which G. E. Moore drove home so forcefully in the *Refutation*. Conversely, when we are presented with an entity, we are also presented with its having ontological status. 'Ontological status' is a clumsy phrase, invented by philosophers for philosophical uses.[10] Yet the use just made of it is commonsensical. To see that, replace the phrase, as henceforth I shall, by 'existence'. When presented with an entity, say, an individual, one is also presented with its (having) existence. That is commonsensical as well as obvious. Nor does it imply or even suggest that having existence is a character. That is why I avoid 'exist'.

Consider now the particular quantifier, or, rather,

(3) $(\exists x)G(x).$

If I know for which character 'G' stands I understand (3). *Without naming it or referring to it*, (3) *attributes existence to an entity exemplifying the character in question*. How, then, I ask once more, could I understand (3) if I were not sometimes presented with existence? Once more, I have reached the limits of communication. Two comments, though, may be of some use. *First*. As long as the sentence is very simple, '$G(\ \exists)$'

---

[9] One may wonder why instead of presenting these elaborate arguments I have not simply said that there is nothing "about" any individual or character to make it exemplify either generality or existence. In this context, the use of 'about' is not at all commonsensical but, however covertly, philosophical, since it presupposes a doctrine of "natures." That is the point. As it happens, I reject that doctrine. This, though, is beside the point.

[10] That is why I surrounded it with double quotes when explicating it in the Introduction. As we now see, that explication was but partial.

will do as well as (3). One merely has to add, once and for all, that the notation does not make '∃' into a name. Thus one must not be put off by the complexity of the current notation. As in the case of generality, one reason for it is that the variable in the operator marks the type distinction and has a pronomial function; another, that the position of the operator can be used to express what in English too is expressed by position. *Second.* One is never presented with an individual or any other entity without also being presented with its existence. An entity's existence is thus not, in the sense generality is, presented on some occasions in addition to the entity. That fits well with what we saw before, namely, that the particular sentence is weaker than any molecular candidate for its job.

An entity's existence is not one of its characters. If it were one, then it could, depending on whether or not it is also a simple, be either named or referred to be a predicative expression. I shall show that it cannot without futility be so named or referred to. Introduce *'exist'* into LFC as a predicate standing for existence. How, then, would one transcribe what without *'exist'* has been transcribed by (3)? The cue is the italicized sentence in the last paragraph which contains a common-sensical use of 'existence' though not, if only for precautionary reasons, of *'exist'*. The one and only way of bringing *'exist'* into play in transcribing (3) is to transcribe the italicized sentence. Its transcription is

$$(4) \qquad\qquad (\exists x)\,[exist(x) \cdot G(x)].$$

(4) contains the particular operator. Thus, what can be expressed without *'exist'* by the operator alone cannot even with *'exist'* be expressed without the operator. That is all I mean by calling the introduction of *'exist'* futile. Nor do I mean anything else by calling existence, since it is sometimes presented to me, a constituent of the world's form. But, there are still two possibilities to be excluded.

The existence of the individual with which I am presented when presented with $G(a)$ is not itself an individual. That I take to be obvious. Nor is it a character of a. That has just been shown. But it might conceivably be either a character of G or a quasicharacter of $G(a)$. These are the two possibilities left. Excluding them requires some preparations.

All individuals presented are qualitied; all characters presented are exemplified. *Things*, as one says, never stand alone. Or, as one also says, *things* are not independent, only facts are. (That explicates one of the several philosophical uses of 'dependent' and 'independent'.) Call this the independence feature. Is it a feature of all *things*, irrespective of whether or not they are presented to us? I cannot but believe that it is. Nor, if it were not, would we know that it is not. So I take for granted that it is.

If there is an individual there is a character it exemplifies; if there is a character there is an individual that exemplifies it; in either case, there is also the fact of the one exemplifying the other. That is the independence feature, stated once more, very simply. To say of anything that it is there is the simplest way of attributing existence to it. (Remember that I rejected 'there-is-ness' as a stand-in for 'existence' only because it is so barbarous.) Hence, a *thing* has existence, if and only if it is an ingredient of a fact that has existence. Are there then two kinds of *things*, those having and those not having existence? Or have I committed the fatal error of making one distinction too many?

What is presented has existence. Some characters, being sometimes presented, have existence. Lion is such a character. Hence, 'Lion has existence' is true. Some characters are not exemplified. Hence they do not have existence. Centaur is such a character. Hence, 'Centaur does not have existence' is true and I have not made one distinction too many. Centaur is not a simple. Nor is any other character not having existence. It will help if we check that against what (I believe) Moore once said in a very influential paper.[11] He, of course, used 'exist', not 'having existence'. So therefore shall I in the next paragraph, with italics.

Moore distinguished correctly between (a) 'Lion *exists*' and (b) 'Lions *exist*'. (b) he took to mean the same as (b') 'There is at least one thing that is a lion'. That too is correct. But he also said that (a) means the same as (b'). That was a mistake. The best way of showing that it was one is to examine three conscious or unconscious likely reasons or motives for making it. Whether or not Moore himself was swayed by any of them I neither know nor care.

Let (c) be a statement of the independence feature. (b) and (c) jointly imply (a). (a) and (c) jointly imply (b). Hence, if (c) is true, then (a) is true if and only if (b) is. (c) is true; but it is a statement of fact, however fundamental. To say that in view of this fact (a) and (b) are either both true or both false is one thing; to say that (a) and (b) have the same meaning is a very different thing. On the other hand, the independence feature is indeed so fundamental that it is easily overlooked or ignored or taken for granted, I do not quite know how to put it. That is one likely reason. In one important philosophical use of 'exist', only simples "exist." Lion is not a simple. Hence, (d) 'Lion "exists" ' is false. If one distinguishes between the commonsensical use

---

[11] "The Conception of Reality," reprinted in *Philosophical Studies*.

of the verb in (a) and its philosophical use in (d) then there is no difficulty. If one does not distinguish, one way out of the apparent difficulty is to make (a) mean what it doesn't mean. This is another likely reason. As nominalists philosophically use 'exist', only individuals "exist." This use, too, makes (d) false. There is thus the same apparent difficulty and the same tempting way out. This is the third likely reason.

Among the entities presented are characters which are not simple as well as facts. If they are presented they have existence. It does not follow that they also "exist." Failure to grasp that as accurately as we now do may cause those doubts and hesitations I mentioned when, before introducing the example for generality, I insisted that entities of these kinds are among those presented.

Return to $G(a)$. When presented with it, one is presented with the existence of two *things*, G and a, and of one fact, $G(a)$. One of the two possibilities still to be excluded is that the existence of a presents itself as a character of G. If it did, would the existence of G present itself as a character of a or as still another character of G? Both alternatives are absurd. The remaining possibility is that the existence of a presents itself as a quasicharacter of $G(a)$. If it did, would the existence of $G(a)$ present itself as a second quasicharacter of it or as a character of either a or G? Again all alternatives are absurd. Interchange 'a' and 'G' in what has been said so far in this paragraph and you will see that, if possible, the absurdity increases. Such absurdity, to be sure, is not contradiction. But is it not obvious that if *per impossibile* a *thing* were presented alone, its existence would also be presented? And is it therefore not also obvious that a *thing's* existence is not a character or quasicharacter of anything else?

I take it, then, that I have shown what I undertook to show. Generality and existence are sometimes presented to us. Yet they are not *things*. Hence they subsist.

IV

(A) In a *correct* language the occurrence of a *name* shows that the entity named has existence. (B) In a correct language existence cannot be represented by a predicate. The history of (B) is very long; that of (A), not very short. The meaning of 'correct' and 'name' were not always very clear. (A) and (B) are not only relevant to what has been said so far, they provide good starting points for what has to be said next. Thus I shall examine first (A), then (B). A correct language I take to be an artificial language and, in particular, the LFC, interpreted according to certain rules held to be correct. 'Name' in these contexts has two uses, one broad, one narrow. In the broad sense, a name is a descriptive primitive which has been attached as a label to a *thing*. In the narrow sense, the *thing* labeled must be a simple. (A) can be made good with the broad use. Nothing will be lost if we stay with the narrow one. Notice, though, that with this latter use the entities whose existence shows itself (if they have been named and (A) can be made good) also "exist." One who vacillates between the two uses may therefore be in danger of confusing existence and "existence."

Consider the following rule: A descriptive primitive of type zero (one) must not occur unless it has been attached as a label to an individual (simple character). One cannot label what is not there. That is in this context the import of 'label'. (No use is being made of the entity being simple.) Call an interpretation incorrect unless it proceeds by this rule. Obviously, (A) follows. Some closely related matters are less obvious.

For quite some time now 'linguistic truth' has been used philosophically. I shall distinguish three commonsensical uses, marking them by subscripts, as in the case of 'form'. A linguistic$_1$ truth is a statement about an (artificial) language implied by the rules for its interpretation *alone*. (A') An individual constant occurs in the LFC[12] if and only if there is an individual which it names. (A') restates one half of (A) without the metaphor or nearmetaphor of showing itself. (A'), we see, is a linguistic$_1$ truth.

Are there statements *of* LFC—not, like (A) or (A'), *about* LFC—which are true by virtue of the interpretation rules alone? I do not know of any. But it is instructive to grasp accurately why some are not. Consider (5) '$(\exists x)G(x)$' and (6) '$(\exists f)f(a)$', 'G' and 'a' being primitives.[13] By (A), there are two *things* named by 'a' and 'G'. Because of the independence feature there are therefore two other *things*, one exemplifying G, one exemplified by a. Hence, (5) and (6) are true. But they are not linguistic$_1$ truths, since the independence feature on which the argument rests is not itself such a truth. Nor of course is it a "linguistic" truth in any other intelligible sense of 'linguistic'.

Remember the truths called formal$_4$. A sentence (of LFC) expresses such a truth if any only if its truth depends only on its form$_3$, or, what amounts to the same, if and only if all instances of its schema are true. '$f(x) \lor \sim f(x)$' and (7) '$f(y) \supset (\exists x)f(x)$' are two such schemata. As the phrase has been used, philosophically, formal$_4$ truths are among "linguistic truths." That spots a second commonsensical meaning. A lin-

---

[12] More precisely: in the LFC *interpreted in accordance with the critical rule*. When there is no danger of confusion I henceforth suppress the italicized phrase.

[13] (6) does of course not belong to the LFC. But no harm is done.

guistic$_2$ truth and a formal$_4$ truth are one and the same thing. Replace in (7) 'y' and 'f' by 'a' and 'G', with 'G' standing for any character, either simple or otherwise, and you obtain the linguistic$_2$ truth '$G(a) \supset (\exists x)G(x)$'. To convince yourself that (5) and (6) are not linguistic$_2$ truths, replace 'G' in (5) and 'a' in (6) by (the transcriptions of) 'centaur' and a definite description that fails, e.g., 'the present king of France', respectively. The first two commonsensical meanings of 'linguistic truth' I distinguished are thus indeed two and not just one. Among other differences, linguistic$_1$ truths are truths about the LFC; linguistic$_2$ truths, truths of the LFC.

Turn now to (B). We saw in the last section that existence is not a *thing*. (B) follows from any set of "correct" rules requiring that *every* primitive predicate be attached to a *thing*. Without this stipulation, another statement can be made good, namely: (B') In a correct language a predicate of existence cannot be introduced without futility. That, too, we saw in the last Section. (B'), even though weaker than (B), is not uninteresting. It gains in interest if it can be shown that (C) while the introduction of '*exist*' has no untoward consequences, it does not in any way increase the expressive possibilities of LFC. That, too, has been shown, by two recent authors,[14] even though showing it was not the task they had set themselves. Rather, they attempted to show that (B) has no interesting core whatsoever. In this, if I am right, they failed.

The two authors proved (C), at least to my satisfaction, by showing that certain semischemata are (the semischemata of) formal$_4$ truths.[15] These are all conditionals; in all of them the antecedent is (9) '$(x)exist(x)$'. One, which will give the idea of them all, is

$$(10) \qquad (x)exist(x) \supset [(\exists x)f(x) \equiv (\exists x)(exist(x) \cdot f(x))].$$

As (10) shows, the calculus contains both operators. Notice, too, that the expression to the right of the equivalence sign in (10) is the schema of (4) in the last Section! I take it, then, that without being aware of it the authors have also shown that '*exist*' cannot be introduced without futility.

The authors call (9) a "semantic rule." This I understand only if I may take the phrase to mean that (9) is a linguistic$_1$ truth of (not: about) the LFC. In fact, even if the introduction of a predicate to

[14] G. Nakhnikian and W. C. Salmon, " 'Exists' as a Predicate," *The Philosophical Review*, 66, 1957, 535–42.

[15] A schema, it will be remembered, contains in addition to connectives and operators only free variables. A *semischema* contains in addition to connectives and operators at least one free variable as well as at least one individual or predicate constant.

express what is not a *thing* be "correct," (9) would be such a truth only
if definite descriptions are excluded from the artificial language.[16] At
one place the authors also tell us that (9) is not a "logical truth,"
though at another place, to say the least, they come very close to telling
us that it is one. As they use the phrase, a "logical truth" is a formal₄
(linguistic₂) truth. Nor can I think of any other plausible commonsensical meaning for that slippery phrase. (9) is of course not a linguistic₂
truth. To see that, just replace *'exist'* by (the transcription of) 'green'.

V

A puzzled reader inquires: "Why did you in Section Three present
two arguments, one for generality, one for existence? Don't you
remember

$$(11) \quad \text{'}(x)f(x) \equiv \sim (\exists x) \sim f(x)\text{'} \quad \text{and} \quad (12) \text{ '}(\exists x)f(x) \equiv \sim (x) \sim f(x)\text{'},$$

two schemata for truths of the kind you call formal₄ or linguistic₂? In
view of them, you might have chosen existence as a *simple* and used
(11) to *define* generality. Or you might have chosen generality as a
simple and used (12) to define existence. In the first case, the argument for existence alone would have done; in the second, that for generality alone." The two words I italicized spot two mistaken ideas, or
groups of ideas, which are likely causes of the puzzlement. It is essential
that they be accurately understood.

All definitions are stipulative. Any other use of the word, as, say, in
'reductive definition', must be carefully qualified. Let us stick with
calculi, discard trivialities. A definition creates a new sign by making
a certain shape into a sign of the calculus. The so-called definiendum is
a schema or semischema containing the new sign; the so-called definiens, a schema or semischema which doesn't contain it. The stipulation
is that corresponding instances of definiens and definiendum may stand
for each other. Hence, *if* the calculus is interpreted, corresponding
instances express the same thing. For an example, turn to the LFC;
assume that green and square are simples named by *'gr'* and *'squ'*,
respectively. Let *'grsqu'* be the new sign; (13) *'grsqu(x)'* and (14)
'gr(x)·squ(x)', definiendum and definiens, respectively. By virtue of
this definition *'grsqu'* refers to the character of being both green and
square, which is a *thing* but not a simple. The two sides of

$$(15) \qquad\qquad \text{'}grsqu(a) \equiv gr(a) \cdot squ(a)\text{'}$$

[16] One may object that *'exist* (. . .)' is not implied by (9), when '. . .' stands
for a definite description. A little reflection will show that the objection is beside
the point. Or, if you prefer it that way, the objector's argument makes use of (A).

being corresponding instances of (13) and (14), (15) is true, as are all other instances of the semischema

(16) $\qquad$ '$grsqu(x) \equiv gr(x) \cdot squ(x)$'.

All we need to know, in order to know that they are truths *of* LFC, is the definitional stipulation *about* LFC. Call truths of this kind linguistic₃. The standard reading of '$\equiv$' is *if and only if*. In linguistic₃ truths it may be read: *means by stipulation the same as*. No harm will be done as long as on the proper occasions one recalls that in so reading it one mixes speaking and speaking about speaking.

Interpretation rules, being rules, are stipulations. Yet they differ from definitional stipulations. Only the latter yield truths of the language; only the latter can be made about uninterpreted calculi; and so on. That makes it worth while to distinguish between linguistic₁ and linguistic₃. How about the differences, if any, between linguistic₃ and linguistic₂ (formal₄)? Two bad reasons may lead one to believe that there are none. For one, once the stipulation has been made, all instances of such schemata as (16) may be used *as if* they were linguistic₂ truths in the business of making proofs, i.e., in establishing what implies what. For another, the mathematicians have long been fascinated with the following question. Given an uninterpreted (!) calculus, can one after suppressing some of its primitive marks from the rest by means of definitions construct an isomorph (I do not stop to explain the word) of the original calculus? I appreciate the fascination. Yet, I have learned to use a long spoon when supping with the mathematicians. The best way of showing that these two reasons are bad reasons is to show that the distinction between linguistic₂ and linguistic₃ is not only worth while but of the essence.

Let (11') 'All if and only if not some not' stand as a rough English schema for (11). Or take (17) '$\sim(p \cdot q) \equiv \sim p \vee \sim q$' and (17') 'Not both if and only if either not the one or not the other'. Does it make sense to call the instances of (11), (12), (17) "linguistic" truths? Unlike those we called linguistic₁ and linguistic₃, they certainly do not rest on stipulation except in the obvious and pervasive sense that unless the calculus has been interpreted it is sheer nonsense to call any of its expressions either true or false. Nor do I know any other commonsensical meaning of 'linguistic' with which these truths are linguistic. The operator '(x)' has been made to stand for generality; '$\sim$', for negation; '$\vee$', for disjunction; and so on. Generality, negation, disjunction, and so on, being what they are, all instances of (11), (12), (17) are true. What is linguistic about that? A doubter may insist that after all in, say, (11') 'all' means the same thing as 'not some not'. Quite so. In (11), since it is a formal₄ truth, '≡' may be read *means the same as*. Again, no harm will be done as long as on the proper occasions one recalls that in so reading it one mixes speaking and speaking about speaking. Only, this is a different use of 'means', marking the sentence as a formal₄ truth, and not, as before, as the result of a definitional stipulation. That is why this time I write *means the same as* while before I wrote *means by stipulation the same as*.

Does it then make any sense to call formal₄ truths linguistic₂? Isn't the proposed synonym merely confusing? Of course it is. That is just the point. Nor did I propose it. I merely distinguish among the several commonsensical meanings which may be given and (I believe) have been given to a single phrase that is being used philosophically, which is best done by using that very phrase—with indices.

One of the two mistaken ideas is cleared up. For, we see now that, mathematics apart, it is simply a mistake to consider (11) as a definition, or potential definition, of generality in terms of negation and existence. As for (11), so for (12), (17) and all other formal₄ truths whose main connective is '≡'.

When '*A*' has been defined in terms of '*B*' and '*C*', *B* and *C* are said to be simpler than *A*. This commonsensical use of 'simple' enters into the philosophical one but is not its core. The core is that there are entities so "simple" that they cannot in any conceivable language be directly referred to except by labels. Let '*gr*' and '*squ*' name simples, '*grsqu*' be defined as before. Then the complex[17] *thing grsqu* is said to "consist" of the two simples *gr* and *squ*. That recalls how the two notions of simplicity jointly produce an ontological pattern: (S) *Entities are either simple or complex; the latter "consist" of the former*. Since (S) is familiar I merely recall it; since it is fundamental I shall sharpen it by showing two things. I shall show, first, that (S) is inextricably tied to the idea of *things*, or, if you please, since simple *things* are the only "existents," to the realm of "existence." I shall show, second, that for the world's form, or, if you please, in the realm of subsistence (S) does not even make sense.[18]

Does one ordinarily say that *grsqu* "consists" of *gr* and *squ*, or, even if 'stallion' has been introduced by the appropriate definition, that (being a) stallion "consists" of (being) male and (being a) horse? Surely

---

[17] Up to this point I deliberately avoided 'complex'.

[18] It has long seemed to me that certain passages of the *Tractatus* (5.4 and, *passim*, from 5.3 to 5.451) point in this direction. I am not at all concerned with the exegesis of that very difficult text. But I prefer acknowledging a debt which may be imaginary to ignoring one which may be real.

this use of 'consist' is not very common. It remains philosophical unless two points are explicitly understood. (a) All the word means in this use is that '*grsqu*' is the new sign in (13) and that '*gr*' and '*squ*', while not the only primitives, are all the descriptive primitives in (14). (b) A complex *thing* is not just a class of simples. The simples somehow hang together. Yet *things*, whether simple or complex, do not by themselves hang together with others. What makes them hang together is a fundamental tie, i.e., an entity which ties others together without in turn being tied to what it ties.[19] In a fact of the form$_3$ which is associated with the schema '$f(x)$', for instance, an individual and a character are made to hang together by the fundamental tie of exemplification. In *grsqu* the fundamental tie holding *gr* and *squ* together is conjunction, represented by the connective in (14). Thus, in a perfectly reasonable sense, which however is not the one I am explicating, *grsqu* could be said to "consist" not just of *gr* and *squ* but, rather, of *gr*, *squ*, and conjunction. To grasp that even better, let *grsqu*$_1$ be so defined that it refers to the character of being either green or square. *grsqu* and *grsqu*$_1$ are two things and not one. Yet, in the sense I am explicating, they both consist of the same two simples and nothing else.

This explicates (S) in the realm of *things*. Nor can I think of any other plausible explication. One may or may not wonder how useful (S) is. I merely undertook to show that for the world's form it makes no sense. It will be best if we attend first to what is represented by form$_1$ and form$_2$.

The constituents of the world's form represented by form$_1$ are individuality, universality, and exemplification; those represented by form$_2$, conjunction, disjunction, negation, and so on, as well as generality and existence. There are two good reasons why none can consistently be called a simple. *First.* A simple can only be labeled. By itself a label does not permit one to pick out the *thing* labeled. All we know, from the label's shape, is that the thing is either an individual or a character, as the case may be. Each connective and each operator represents, and by representing it picks out, a single and completely determinate feature of the world's form. *Second.* Nothing is in the same sense and in the same context both simple and complex. That is undoubtedly part of the idea, just as it is another part of it that the complex can be defined in terms of the simple. Thus, if we are to apply the idea, we must first mistake (11), (12), (17) for (linguistic$_3$ truths produced by)

[19] The notion of fundamental ties is implicit in the analysis of the Bradley paradox to be found in Section One of IOM. For a more detailed discussion, see "The Ontology of Edmund Husserl," *Methodos*, 12, 1960, 359–392, and pp. 193–224 of this book.

definitions. That is what at the beginning of this section the puzzled reader did. But then, having once made the mistake, he was quite right in reminding us that we have two alternatives, depending on whether we start from (11) or (12). In the one case, existence is simple; generality, complex. In the other case, generality is simple; existence, complex. Are they then both simples, or both complex, or is each both? What goes for the two operators goes for the connectives as represented by the sixteen truth tables. Is neither-nor simple or is not-both simple? Or are they both simple? And so on.

A form$_3$ is a geometrical character exemplified by sentences; the feature of the world's form it represents is shared (not: exemplified!) by the facts these sentences express. Each form$_3$ is associated with a schema. Each instance of the schema exemplifies the form$_3$. Take '$f(x)$', the simplest of all schemata. The form$_3$ with which it is associated is exemplified by '$G(a)$', '$F(b)$', and so on. The feature this form$_3$ represents is shared by all and only those facts which consist of an individual exemplifying a character. Form$_3$, being a geometrical character, consists, in the sense explicated, of form$_1$ and form$_2$. The form$_3$ associated with '$f(x)$', for instance, consists of the three simpler geometrical characters of having the shape of an individual constant, having the shape of a predicate constant, and being juxtaposed. It would be more than hasty to conclude that what a form$_3$ represents consists, in the same sense, of what is represented by form$_1$ and form$_2$.[20] To convince yourself that the supposed conclusion doesn't even make sense, turn once more to the form$_3$ associated with '$f(x)$'. It would have to consist of individuality, generality, and exemplification. If so, what ties the three together? Or does perhaps one of the three, exemplification, tie the remaining two? Exemplification ties individuals to characters. To say that it ties individuality to generality is simply nonsense. Hence, it is simply nonsense to say that what form$_3$ represents consists, in the sense explicated, of what is represented by form$_1$ and form$_2$. Nor can I think of any other meaning of 'consist' that makes sense out of this nonsense. I take it, then, that the pattern (S) makes indeed no sense in the realm of subsistence. It will pay if we test this conclusion on a rather important class of entities.

Let (18) '$Tr(f)$' and

(19) $$(x)(y)(z)\left[f(x, y)\cdot f(y, z) \supset f(x, z)\right]$$

[20] The "conclusion" is more than hasty because it jumps, without justification, from the sign to what it signifies. Section Two of IOM explains in detail how in one very important case this jump led to disaster.

be definiendum and definiens, respectively. 'Tr' stands for the familiar character of being transitive. (19), unlike (14), is a schema, not a semischema; hence, Tr, unlike $grsqu$, is not a thing. That is indicated by calling the entities of this class nondescriptive. Except for Leibnizian identity, all the interesting ones are characters, including relational ones of course, of the second or higher types. To be younger is a character. Younger being transitive is a fact. Ontological assay of the fact must yield "something" in addition to the character. Tr thus has some ontological status. What exactly is it? Consider the feature of the world's form which is shared by all instances of the form$_3$ associated with (19). To assert that being younger is transitive is to assert that it is an ingredient of a fact which shares this feature. As for being younger, so for being louder, taller, and so on.[21] That makes transitivity an "aspect" of this feature. If you dislike 'aspect', use 'constituent', 'component', or what have you. The truth is that I am running out of words. 'Aspect' is rather suitable, though, since in rewriting (19) as (18) we choose a certain way of looking at the feature. Again, it is this way of looking which makes transitivity a character exemplified by being younger, louder, taller, and so on. This is the state of affairs. I express it by saying that defined nondescriptive characters subsist as parts of the world's form and, in particular, as aspects of what is expressed by form$_3$.

Having distinguished between form$_1$, form$_2$, form$_3$, we have as it were distinguished three regions in the realm of subsistence, each containing what is expressed by one of the three geometrical (syntactical) "forms." Defined nondescriptive characters, we just saw, are not literally furniture of the third region. Why, then, not assign them to a fourth? Or, if they are to remain in the third, since they are merely aspects of its furniture, which subsists, why not assign them a special ontological status, saying, for instance, that while they don't subsist, they yet sub-subsist? To do either of these things would be against the spirit of the ontological enterprise as I conceive it.

What must be there so that we can know what in fact we do know? With this question the enterprise starts. The linguistic turn divides it into two questions. What do the signs and expressions of a suitable language stand for? What are the several ways, and the differences among them, by which the several kinds of signs and expressions manage to represent what they stand for? In the systematic part of the enterprise we try to provide the detailed commonsensical descriptions the two

[21] I avoid examples which are in fact not transitive, e.g., loving, in order to avoid the dialectic of "false facts," which has been attended to in the last Section of IOM.

questions ask for. In the exegetic part we use these descriptions to provide plausible and interesting explications of the philosophical uses to which the classical philosophers put the ontological vocabulary. To do that makes sense. To invent new philosophical uses either for old words or for new ones, such as the deliberately absurd 'sub-subsist', is merely gratuitous. For, once the method has been grasped and those detailed descriptions have been given, what else is there to be said?

These reflections also provide the answer to a final objection which runs as follows. "You claimed that 'ontological status' may stand, commonsensically, for what is sometimes presented to us. In this use, you replaced the compromised phrase by '(having) existence'. But you also claimed that existence itself has ontological status. Hence, existence itself has existence. Do you not then pile words upon words in a manner justly discredited? Or, at best, if that be the word, do you not tie knots for the sole purpose of untying them, which as you said is gratuitous?" My reply is as follows. Remember that I called the class of defined nondescriptive entities rather important. One reason is that according to some philosophers all arithmetical entities including the integers themselves are among its members. That is indeed the doctrine of *Principia Mathematica*. Accepting this doctrine, I would consistently have to say and do say that the integers subsist. Many more philosophers would agree that the integers are "something" even though, since they are not *things* either simple or complex, they do not of course belong to the realm of "existence." Consider now the obvious truth expressed by 'There is a prime number smaller than 3'. Written in symbols, the expression contains the particular operator. As long as one does not probe it dialectically, there is no difficulty. If one does, rather notoriously the knot becomes formidable. Nor of course is it of my making. The proposed analysis unties this knot. The particular operator attributes existence, i.e., ontological status. Whether the entity to which existence is attributed belongs to the realm of "existence" or that of subsistence depends on the context. Nor, as we saw, is that the only knot the proposed analysis unties. There is thus no reason for concern if some formulations of some of its consequences, such as existence having existence, at first sound a bit perplexing to some.

Like other specialists, philosophers are entitled to a few words, chapter-heading words as I like to call them, which they may use very broadly. Unlike others, philosophers must guard against using these words philosophically. 'Logic' is such a word. This essay is a study in the philosophy of logic. Yet, neither 'logic' nor 'logical' have been used in it. The lesson that lies in this abstinence need not, I trust, be spelled out once more.

*Meaning**

THE use of a word is philosophically important if its accurate description helps solving a philosophical problem. If the word has more than one such use, then of course accurate distinction among the several descriptions is of the essence.

'Meaning' has many uses. They are not all philosophically important. Yet several are. I could not speak profitably about all of these. So I shall organize my remarks around one. Eventually, there will be quite a few remarks about a second use. These remarks, though, will be even more fragmentary than what I shall say about the first.

There is nothing in or about philosophy of which I am as profoundly convinced as that its heart is ontology. This conviction, or insight, has long been lost, particularly though by no means only in the tradition from which I come. The loss has produced a peculiar situation. Since I must be succinct, I shall venture to describe it by borrowing two phrases from psychoanalysis. The "latent content" of many recent and current discussions is ontological; their "manifest content" is something else. Manifestly, a very large part of the current discussion is about language and therefore, inevitably, about "meaning."

The *meaning* of a word is what it refers to. As for words, so for sentences. The word *means* what it refers to. So does the sentence. This is the reference use of 'means' and 'meaning'. With it goes, in contemporary philosophy, the reference theory of meaning and the picture theory of language. Recently, both theories have been under heavy attack. The heart of the criticisms is ontological. One who sees that clearly can separate sense from nonsense in the two theories. Moreover, the case is very neat. The ontological core lies rather close to the surface. That is why I have chosen this use of 'meaning' as my first and main topic.

Since I must save time, let me call attention to the way I shall speak.

* *This is the first of two essays which appeared under the title "Meaning and Ontology" in* Inquiry, *5, 1962, 116–42. Reprinted by permission.*

1. I replace 'refer' by 'represent'. 2. I avoid 'name' and 'naming', reserving these words for one among several kinds of representation. 3. 'Exist' and 'having ontological status' will be used synonymously. 4. 'Entity' will be used so that whatever has ontological status is an entity.

The representation theory must meet four major criticisms. The three I shall take up first are variants of a common pattern. If the theory were true, every expression would represent an entity. But for some expressions there is no entity to represent. Or, what amounts to the same, the alleged entity does not exist. Hence the theory is false. This is the pattern. Clearly, it is ontological. The expression may be a word, a phrase, or a sentence. These are the three variants. Examining them in this order, word, phrase, sentence, will permit us in the discussion of the first to take for granted what will be considered as controversial in the discussion of the second, in which we shall again be able to take for granted what will be considered as controversial in the third. The examples I shall use for the first two criticisms are the word 'is', as used in 'This is green', and the phrase 'green and square'. For the third any false sentence will do.

Looking at a green spot, I say 'This is green'. In my ontology, the spot contains two entities of the kind I call *things*. Yes, of course, this is a rather special use of 'thing'. But it will pay if you permit me to postpone the specification. One of the two things is a bare individual, represented in the sentence by 'this'; the other, a universal represented by 'green'. This is *part* of my ontological assay of the spot. Again, it will pay if, for later clarification, you notice the emphasis on 'part'. Some will object on the ground that there are no universals; or that there are no bare individuals; or, perhaps, they countenance neither kind of entity. If so, these objectors will, either explicitly or implicitly, propose another ontology, in which the spot is assayed differently. Clearly, this is a legitimate disagreement. Equally clearly, it is a disagreement in ontology which can and must be separated from the controversies about the representation theory. The problems which I am about to examine and which are relevant for the theory arise upon any assay of the spot. Hence, I am not prejudging anything that matters for my purpose by assuming that my partial assay of the spot is uncontroversial. If so, then it is also uncontroversial that the sentence 'This is green' represents the spot while 'This' and 'green' represent the individual and the character, respectively. The issue is 'is'. What, if anything, does it represent?

I look at two pairs of spots, P and Q. One of the two spots in P is red and round; the other, green and square. Of the two spots in Q, one is red and square; the other, green and round. There is thus a difference between P and Q. In P red "goes with" round; in Q it "goes with" square; and so on. The difference must be ontologically grounded. There are two alternatives. Either the ground lies in me, the perceiver, or it lies in what I perceive. The first alternative is the structural root of idealism. So I shall here dismiss it out of hand. Upon the second alternative, the difference must appear as a difference between the ontological assays of P and Q.

Upon what has been said before, the partial assay of a green square spot yields three things, one individual and two universals, green and square. Accordingly, the assay of P yields altogether six things, two bare individuals and four universals, two shapes, round and square, and two colors, red and green. The assay of Q yields the same four universals and, of course, two different individuals. Neither assay shows what "goes with" what in what it purports to assay. Thus the difference in question remains ungrounded. The way out of this perplexity I propose is as follows.

Things, which are one kind of entity, form *complexes*, which are another kind. For two or more things to form a complex there must be an entity or entities that "tie them together." Otherwise, what would be the ontological ground for just these things here but not those things there forming a complex? Or, if you please, things do not "hang together" by themselves. That is indeed a large part of the promised specification of my use of 'thing'. The entities that make things hang together I call *fundamental ties*. Different ontologies have different fundamental ties. But each articulate one must acknowledge at least one such entity. In my ontology, the most pervasive fundamental tie is the one I call exemplification. If, as one says, an individual exemplifies a property, then they are held together by exemplification. You see now why I insisted that the assay of the single spot with which I began was partial. The spot contains at least three entities, the individual, the color, and exemplification. If you fear that I gratuitously *reify* exemplification, return to the perplexity about P and Q. But notice first, for later clarification, the emphasis on 'reify'.

P and Q each contain six things. If they contained no other entity, the perplexity would be irresoluble. In my ontology each contains also several occurrences of exemplification. These different occurrences tie the things differently. In P red and round are tied to the same individual; in Q they are tied to different individuals; and so on. Thus the perplexity is resolved. Nor do I know any other way of resolving it (or the corresponding ones in other ontologies). I conclude therefore that exemplification is an entity, exists, has ontological status. As far as the first objection to the representation theory is concerned, I conclude that the 'is' in 'This is green' does represent something, namely, exemplification. That disposes of the first criticism. Or, rather, it disposes of it in this case. I cannot, of course, on this occasion be exhaustive. But I shall add a few comments.

Anyone either familiar with Bradley's famous conundrum or clever enough to think of it himself will at this point raise an objection. If "entities" need others to tie them into complexes, what ties the ties to what they tie? I did not say that "entities" need ties; I said that "things" did; adding that this was indeed a large part of what in this context is meant by a thing, just as it is a large part of what is meant by calling an entity a fundamental tie that it needs no further tie to tie it to what it ties. Thus, even though I recognize the ontological status of exemplification, I do not "reify" it. For, to reify something, if it means anything precise, is to mistake it for a thing. Thereby hangs a point of cardinal importance.

Ontology is not a night in which all cows are black. More traditionally, there is more than one *mode* of existence, just as some modes have more than one kind. In 'This is green', as it was used before, at least three modes or kinds are involved. Two of the words represent "things"; the third, a "fundamental tie," the sentence itself, a complex of the kind called a "fact." As I here use the word (perfectly reasonably, as I have shown in the case of 'is'), all these entities exist. Some philosophers seem to have used it so that only things exist; some others so that only facts exist. What matters is not how one uses a word but, rather, that one knows how he uses it, thus avoiding purely verbal argument on the one hand and, on the other, the trouble into which one gets by using it unwittingly in different ways.

One may grant that exemplification exists and yet insist that its ontological status is lesser, not as good or not as full as that of a thing. These are metaphors. Metaphors that cannot be unpacked are in philosophy the greatest of all evils. As it happens, these particular metaphors can be unpacked. I, of course, must hurry on. The way I just distinguished between fundamental ties and things gives at least an idea of what can and must be done.

Availing myself of an old word, I call a fundamental tie a *subsistent*, make subsistence a mode of existence. Exemplification is not the only fundamental tie. Conjunction, disjunction, and so on, represented by the connectives, are others. Nor are all subsistents fundamental ties. Again, these are but a few glimpses at my ontology. Without them, the defense of the representation theory which I have undertaken would be unintelligible. With them, I hope to show that, *if* my ontology is defensible, then the representation theory is also defensible. Notice that I say if, not if and only if. I can think of several ontologies with which to defend the theory. Whether or not these ontologies fail elsewhere is a different matter.

Subsistents, if spoken about, are represented in what is said. Of course they are. How else could anything be spoken about. Some are represented by words, others in other ways. In some artificial languages, for instance, individuals and only individuals are represented by lower-case letters. The letter itself represents the thing, the letter's shape, i.e., its being lower-case, the thing's being an individual, or, as one says, individuality, which is a subsistent. Nor is this subsistent represented in any other way. This illustrates a characteristic feature of such languages. The several members of one mode or kind are all represented in the same way. It is this feature above all others that makes such languages a useful tool of ontological inquiry. This, though, is a different story. Nor are the critics of the representation theory interested in what is represented and how. They merely insist that some expressions do not represent anything at all. In the case of words I have done all I can do here by showing that one crucial word, which according to these critics does not represent anything, does represent a subsistent. So I turn next to a crucial phrase.

We know what a centaur is, even though there are none, only because we are familiar with the definition of the word, 'centaur'. To define a word is to replace it by a phrase. That makes the definiens of 'centaur' a crucial phrase. But I cannot resist the attraction of illustrations so simple that they illustrate nothing but the issue on hand. To provide myself with such an illustration, I assume, rather gratuitously, that there is nothing which is both green and square. That makes 'green and square' a crucial phrase. What, if anything, does it represent? That is the issue. It will be well if we first distinguish it from another.

If the phrase represents anything at all, then it represents a universal. That I take to be obvious. Philosophers disagree as to whether *any* universal exists. This, though a legitimate issue, is not the one at hand. I shall next show that I do not prejudge the latter by assuming that *some* universals exist, or, more precisely, that they have the ontological status of things. Assume in particular that green and square are things.

'Green' represents a thing of the kind called a universal, if and only if there is another thing, of the kind called an individual, which is green. This is not to say that for green to be a thing *means* that there is an individual which exemplifies it. Yet, this truth lies so deep that one cannot with impunity ignore it in ontology. Green is a thing. There are green individuals. Square is a thing. There are square individuals.

By assumption no individual is both green and square. It follows that 'green and square' does not represent a thing. What it seems to represent, conjunction being a fundamental tie between universals, is a complex thing. The issue, we now understand, is the ontological status, *if any*, of certain complexes.

'Green and square' is a phrase; 'green and or', another. The first is well-formed; the second is not. Whether or not a phrase is well-formed depends on our language. Our language is what it is because the world is what it is. There must therefore be something in the world which is the ontological ground of that striking difference between the two phrases. In this sense, the crucial phrase represents something. Nor do I mean anything else when I say, in the traditional language of ontology, that it represents a *possible* universal. That makes *possibility* a mode of existence. If you are startled or even shocked, part of the shock is due to the peculiar flavor of the traditional language. The thing to do is to make the required distinctions while speaking without that flavor. Right now I shall distinguish this use of 'possible' from three others. A later comment will also be relevant, showing that possibility is indeed the "lowest" ontological status. Or, rather, the comment will unpack the metaphor.[1]

We call possible what is represented by synthetic statements not contradicting known laws of nature. This is *one* use of 'possible'. We call possible what is not the negation of a truth of the kind called analytic or formal. This is a *second* use of 'possible'. The formal truths of our world are what they are because the subsistents of our world are what they are. A world whose subsistents are different from those of ours might be "three-valued" in the sense in which ours is "two-valued." (I use the two phrases as the logicians do.) If one says that such a world is possible, he uses the word in a *third* way. If one says, as I do, that 'green and square' represents a possible universal which as such has ontological status, he uses the word in a *fourth* way. To see how all this hangs together and makes sense, consider that the phrase

---

[1] The following also throws light on the status of possibility as a mode of existence. Let '*f*' be a predicate variable, '. . .' a predicative expression. The sentence '(∃*f*)(*f*(*x*) ≡ . . . *x* . . .)' is analytic, irrespective of whether the predicate expression represents a universal or a possible universal. Accordingly, the existential operator represents what I here represent by 'exist' (or, synonymously, 'having ontological status') without in any way specifying this status or mode. Nor is this surprising. 'There is' represents the same subsistent in 'There is a coffee house around the corner' as well as in 'There is a prime number between eleven and twelve'. Yet numbers and coffee houses do not belong to the same mode. See also note 2.

'green and not green' represents a possible universal (fourth use!) even though it is not possible (second use!) for anything to be green and not green.

Use 'simple' so that a thing is simple if and only if it is not a complex. Are there simple things? This is a very big question, which happily we need not answer. I mention it merely because it provides the opportunity for two remarks.

If there are simples, then there is a characteristic way of representing them by words called *names*. Or, rather, this is a specifiable use of 'name' and 'naming'. In some contexts this use is very helpful. Much less helpfully, some critics have argued that the representation theory is false because certain expressions do not name anything. If they mean that what (as I hold) such an expression represents is not a simple thing and can therefore not be represented in the way characteristic of names, then I quite agree. Only, if this is what is meant, then the argument has no force whatsoever. Nor do I see what else it could mean. This is the first remark.

A complex "consists" of several things and the fundamental ties tying them together. (I ignore, safely for my purpose, other subsistents.) This, to be sure, is a special use of 'consist'. But it is clear as it stands, just as this is the only clear idea we have of complex. Where there are complexes, there may be simples. As long as things are involved, the dichotomy simple-complex makes sense. Among subsistents alone it doesn't. Again, this is merely a glimpse, an assertion in need of support. All fundamental ties are subsistents. Take two of these entities. If they were tied together by a third, would the two still be fundamental ties? If all subsistents were fundamental ties, the reflection would be conclusive. Since some are not, it is not. Even so, it shows how plausible the assertion really is. Granting that it is also true, should we say that all subsistents are simples, or that all are complexes? I don't know what would be gained by saying either. But I do know how dangerous it is to apply arbitrarily one half of a dichotomy where the whole makes no sense. This is the second remark. I am ready to turn to the third major criticism.

There are two kinds of complexes. A complex is either a thing or a fact. A true sentence represents a fact. For a false sentence there is no fact to represent. The critics argue that it represents nothing. Quite probably you are able to anticipate my defense. The mode of possibility comprehends *possible facts* as well as possible things. The false sentence represents a possible fact (fourth use of 'possible'!). The argument is the same as before. Some expressions are well-formed, either as phrases or as sentences; some others are not. For sentences the possible facts are the ontological ground of this difference.[2]

All possible entities are complex. More precisely, they would be complexes if they were not mere possibilities. This is the cue for some comments on the so-called picture theory, or, more precisely, on the picture metaphor.

Language, it has been said, is a picture of the world. This is but a metaphor; so it must be unpacked. If it is unpacked into the representation theory then there is no difficulty. But there is also a specifiable sense in which language is not a picture of the world. If an expression represents either a complex or a possible complex put it into one class. Put all other expressions in a second class. That puts each (well-formed) expression into one of two classes. If the expression belongs to the first class you *cannot* without looking at the world tell whether what it represents is merely a possibility. If it belongs to the second, you *can*. You know that what it represents is not merely a possibility. The can and the can't are both of the essence of language. In a systematically constructed language one can, merely by looking at the expression itself, tell to which of the two classes it belongs. There is no such division among the features of a painting. (There is still another essential difference. One can say but one cannot paint that this chair is not green.) In *this* sense, language is not a picture of the world. In *another* sense, that of the metaphor as I unpacked it, it is. Some people who did not know how to unpack the metaphor were unnecessarily perplexed. This perplexity, too, has been turned into a weapon against the representation theory.

The fourth major criticism involves two issues, one weighty, one noisy. Are there bare individuals? This is the weighty issue. Are the schemata which, rather unfortunately, are called ideal languages, of any use in philosophizing? This is the noisy issue.

A bare individual cannot be recognized "as such." This is a truism. More precisely, it is what we mean by calling these simples bare. You recognize a man you have encountered before by recognizing a characteristic configuration of properties. A bare individual is merely the carrier (individuator) of its properties. Assume that a man "as such," minus all his properties, is a bare individual and you will appreciate the truism.

---

[2] Let '*P*' be a well-formed sentence; let '*M*' represent the intentional tie. The sentence '$(\exists f)fMP$' is true irrespective of whether P is a fact or merely a possible fact. The value that makes it true is of course the expression representing the-thought-that-P. Upon my explication of analyticity the sentence is also analytic. Thus the analogy with the sentence of note 1 is complete.

In Russell's ontology there are bare individuals. He also constructed an ideal language containing names for them. These he called *proper names*. Since we cannot as such tell one bare individual from another, proper names are of no use in a language one is to speak, either with others or, for that matter, with himself. In this sense, as well as in some others, ideal languages are not really languages. It does not follow that they are useless in philosophizing.

The fourth major criticism is for the most part a medley of arguments to the effect that there are no bare individuals and that those schemata are useless in philosophizing. One may well wonder where the theory comes in. The idea seems to be that it cannot be reconciled with what has just been said about proper names. I don't see why it can't.

Words spoken are sounds among sounds; words written, marks of chalk or ink. By themselves, they do not represent anything, don't refer to anything. We refer by means of them to what we have made them represent. What is there in or about these sounds or marks that makes it possible for us to put them to this use? The gist of the answer is very simple. There must be, and there is, an isomorphism between certain features of the representing entities and the entities represented. To learn a language is to learn the rules of this isomorphism.

I perceive now that this paper is white. The fact, this paper's being white, is the *intention* of this perceiving. We not only perceive facts, we imagine them, believe them, remember them, and so on. Call these the several species of *intending*. Intending is the connection between a mind and its intention. What exactly is this connection? The answer involves the intentional use of 'means' and 'meaning', to which I shall devote the rest of my time.

The mind is one thing; the intention is another; the sentence representing the intention is a third. Let P be the fact intended. Refer to the sentence representing it as the-sentence-P. (a) The mind intends P. (b) The-sentence-P represents P. (a) is one thing; (b) is another. I turn next to a peculiarity of intending which may well be responsible for this distinction not being as obvious to everybody as it should be.

(1) Caesar was murdered. (2) Caesar is Calpurnia's husband. (3) Calpurnia's husband was murdered. Smith knows (1) but neither (2) nor (3). Thus, of the two sentences (4) 'Smith knows that Caesar was murdered' and (5) 'Smith knows that Calpurnia's husband was murdered', the first is true, the second false. Yet, since (2) is true, (1) and (3) are *the same fact*. Smith both knows and does not know the same fact. That illustrates the peculiarity of intending. Nor is it just a peculiarity; it seems a perplexity. Presently I shall resolve it by distinguish-

ing among the uses of 'same'. First, though, let me connect it with the intentional use of 'means'.

(6) The-sentence-that-Caesar-was-murdered means that Caesar was murdered. (7) The-sentence-that-Caesar-was-murdered means that Calpurnia's husband was murdered. We all often use 'means' so that while (6) is true, (7) is false. This is the use of 'means' one calls intentional. Its peculiarities are exactly the same as those of intending.[3] That is, the range of substitution *salva veritate* after 'means' in sentences like (6) and (7) is exactly the same as that in sentences like (4) and (5) after 'knows' or any other expression representing a species of intending. This is not to say that 'means' in (6) or (7) represents such a species. Nor do I see how it possibly could, since, on the one hand, each of the two sentences mentions two physical facts, one of which is a sentence, while, on the other, only a mind can intend anything. As you see, the situation is very complex; so complex indeed that I could on this occasion barely raise all the questions. The key to all answers lies in the dissolution of the perplexity about intending. So I shall address myself to this task.

A relation is a thing, a kind of universal. To-the-left is a relation. If this individual is to the left of that, there are three things, two individuals and the relation, held together by (relational) exemplification, which is not a thing and hence not a relation, but a fundamental tie. If this is to be to the left of something, the something must be there. Possible entities cannot exemplify anything, either property or relation; otherwise they would not be mere possibilities. (This unpacks the earlier remark that the ontological status of possibilities is the lowest of all.)

Basically, there are two alternatives of assaying the situation in which a mind intends something. Upon the first, the mind and the

---

[3] There is one "exception." Let 'Peter' and 'Paul' be two names of one individual. Smith, knowing that Paul is blond, also knows that Peter is blond. Yet we would not say that the-sentence-Paul-is-blond means Peter is blond. The objection that if Smith does not know that Paul is also called Peter, he may know that Paul is blond without knowing that Peter is blond is without force. It rests on the confusion between the causal effects words perceived or imagined have on the occurrence of thoughts on the one hand and thoughts on the other. The-thought-that-Paul-is-blond is not verbal, not even in that weak sense in which the perceiving or imagining of the-sentence-Paul-is-blond may be called verbal. Those who use the word 'means' in investigating the causal effects of words and of words perceived, imagined, and so on, use it in a fourth way. This is the so-called causal or context use of 'means' and 'meaning'. With this use, lightning means thunder; the stimulus, or the stimulus perceived, the response. What has been said above about the objection corrects a flaw in my 1958 paper on "Sameness, Meaning, and Identity" (reprinted in *Meaning and Existence*).

species are both things and the species in particular a relation jointly exemplified by the mind and the fact intended. E.g., while I perceive that this paper is white, my mind and the fact, the paper's being white, jointly exemplify the universal perceiving. This alternative meets defeat in all cases in which the fact intended isn't there, doesn't exist, as in erroneous perception, false belief, imagining, and so on. Nor can the possible entities of my ontology save the alternative from a defeat that is inevitable indeed; for a mere possibility cannot sustain a relation. The second alternative conquers the difficulty by taking advantage of an essential difference between a fundamental tie and a relation.

Of the two sentences 'P' and 'not-P' one is true, one false. The one which is true represents a fact; the one which is false, merely a possible fact. The sentence 'P or not-P' is true. What it represents is there, is a fact, one of those formal facts (truths) which were mentioned earlier. In this fact, the constituent fact and the constituent possible fact are connected by disjunction. Disjunction is not a relation but a fundamental tie. That shows the idea. A fundamental tie can tie a mere possibility, thing or fact, to a thing or fact. The second alternative of assaying the situations in which a mind intends something takes advantage of this idea.

Upon this alternative, the one I have proposed, what is, as one says, in a mind, when the mind intends something, is a complex. One constituent of this complex is the species, i.e., it depends on whether the intending is a believing, a remembering, a perceiving, and so on. One other varies with the intention. This constituent I call the *thought;* if the intention is P, the-thought-that-P. P, being a fact, is a complex. The-thought-that-P is a simple thing, a nonrelational universal. So, by the way, is the species. *The connection between a mind and what it intends is not a relation but a fundamental tie between P and the-thought-that-P.* (That is the basic idea.) Representing the tie for a moment by the word 'means', we obtain the sentence (8) 'The-thought-that-P means P', which may be true and even a formal truth if 'P' represents a mere possibility. However controversial all this may be, it is not at all controversial that the range of substitution *salva veritate* after 'means' in (8) is exactly the same as in (4), (5), (6), (7). The idea is again simple; one thought, one fact. But then, what is "one fact"? Or, as before, what are the different uses of 'same' in speaking of *the same fact?*

There are three such uses. The second is stricter than the first; the third, stricter than the second. Upon the third, Smith may not both know and not know the same fact. Thus the perplexity disappears.

The use of 'same' is clear and unproblematic only in the case of simple things. "Two" simples, if they are the "same", are "one." The ambiguities arise when we say of "two" complexes that they are "one." So I shall henceforth assume that there are simples. (That merely saves many words saying very little.) A fact, of course, is a complex.

A paradigm for the *first use* of 'same fact' is provided by the story of Caesar and Calpurnia. Call the facts (1), (2), (3); P, D, Q, respectively. Call the three sentences representing them 'P', 'D', 'Q', respectively. That makes P the fact that Caesar was murdered, 'D' the sentence 'Caesar is Calpurnia's husband', and so on. Assume for the sake of the argument that Caesar and Calpurnia are simples. 'Q' is obtained from 'P' by replacing the name of a simple ('Caesar') by a successful definite description ('Calpurnia's husband'). Calling the description successful is but another way of saying that 'D' is true. This is the criterion for the first use. Upon this use, P and Q are the same fact if and only if one can be obtained from the other by replacing names with successful descriptions. Now let us look at the two complexes. Accepting, as I believe one must, Russell's account of definite descriptions, one sees immediately that while one of them, Q, contains Calpurnia, the other, P, doesn't. That shows how broad this use of 'same fact' really is. The two complexes said to be the same do not even contain the same things. I do not find it in the least perplexing that with this use one may both know and not know the same fact.

The *second use* calls P and Q the same fact if and only if the sentence 'P if and only if Q' is analytic. In this case, by the way, one also says that the sentences 'P' and 'Q' mean the same thing or have the same meaning, which is a third, perfectly good and sometimes very important use of 'mean' and 'meaning', the so-called logical use. That, though, is a different story. To continue with our own, let 'P' and 'Q' be (9) 'R and S' and (10) 'not-(not-R or not-S)', respectively. Obviously, (9) and (10) fulfill the condition. So let us again look at the complexes they represent. Looking hard enough, you will again see that there is a difference between them. Only, this time it does not lie in the things the two complexes contain but in the subsistents.

Remember what was said earlier. In the realm of subsistence there are no complexes and no simples. The dichotomy makes no sense. Conjunction, for instance, is not a complex compounded of disjunction and three negations. That pinpoints the difference between the two complexes represented by (9) and (10) respectively. In the first, R and S are tied by conjunction. In the second, R and S are affected by negation (I say affected because negation is not literally a tie), the resulting compounds are tied by disjunction, the result affected by negation. In this important way two complexes, which upon the second use are the same fact, differ. As to Smith, if someone wonders whether there really is a Smith who knows the one complex without knowing the other, I shall simply remind him that upon this use all arithmetical truths are the same fact. Some of us know some of them; but no one, I believe, knows all of them. Thus, once more, I do not find it in the least perplexing that with this use one may both know and not know the same fact.

Upon the *third* use two complexes are the same fact if and only if they agree not only in their simples but also in their subsistents and in the way the latter tie or otherwise affect the former. Upon this view, if the perplexity is to disappear, it should not be possible to both know (or otherwise intend) and not know the same fact. To see that this is indeed so, one merely has to check what this strictest of all criteria for the use of 'same fact' means for the range of substitution *salva veritate* after 'means' in (8) 'The-thought-that-P means P'. A moment's reflection will show that if the language contains no more than one name for each simple, then no range is left. Any change falsifies (8). Thus the idea "one fact, one thought" is realized and the perplexity has disappeared.

Duration and the Specious Present*

THE problem I shall discuss is specific, even minute. Yet, being philosophical, it arises and can be profitably discussed only in a context anything but minute, namely, that of a conception of philosophy and its proper method. I could not possibly unfold my conception once more for the sake of a minute problem. Nor do I believe that as things now stand this is necessary. I shall merely recall two propositions which are crucial in the context, and, in stating them, shall freely use its vocabulary. *The undefined descriptive terms of the ideal language all refer to phenomenal things wholly presented. These things all are either individuals or characters, and, if characters, either relational or nonrelational.* These are the two propositions. It may throw light on another crucial point not always well understood if I imagine someone to ask: Wholly presented to whom? The answer is: To the person to whose world the philosopher, who himself always speaks commonsensically, fits the ideal language.

Science is common sense elaborated. To speak scientifically, therefore, is to speak commonsensically. Thus I shall speak commonsensically, as by the rules of the context I must, if I avail myself of the time line of classical physics in stating next how I shall use 'duration' and 'instant'. An interval on the time line, however long or short, is a *duration*. A point on the time line is an *instant*. Instantaneous things are abstractions or fictions. The troubles into which one gets by using uncritically either 'abstraction' or 'fiction' are not now my concern. I merely use them to recall, with familiar words, that instantaneous things, if there be any, belong to elaborated common sense. Duration

* Philosophy of Science, *27, 1960, 39–47. Reprinted by permission. This paper is the result of a five-cornered discussion. Herbert Hochberg proposed the puzzle. Edwin B. Allaire, May Brodbeck, and Reinhardt Grossmann contributed with him to the solution. But it seemed pretentious to put five names to a short paper. So the four agreed to my writing it up. The responsibility, therefore, is mine alone.*

requires no such qualification. Return to the man to whose world the philosopher fits the ideal language. Assume that a green spot appeared in his visual field at time 0, persisted without interruption or change until time 2 (seconds), then disappeared. In the context, the spot *is* an individual. It *has* a duration. Notice, though, that it is the philosopher, speaking commonsensically, who just used the phrase 'having a duration' (and the word 'individual'), just as it is he who looked at his watch to time the spot. Note also what I shall mean by 'contained'. When the durations of, say, two individuals lie, in the time-line sense, inside a third, then I shall say that the two individuals as well as the qualities and relations they exemplify are *contained* in the third.

What is the "problem of time"? A philosopher's answer depends on his context. In mine it all hinges on the answer to one question. How are commonsensical statements containing either an explicit or an implicit reference to time, such as the statement that a certain individual has a certain duration, to be transcribed into, or, as one also says, reconstructed *in* the ideal language (IL)? The 'in' is crucial. (That is why I emphasized in the last paragraph that it was the philosopher who spoke and looked at his watch.) The question, though one in a sense, is yet so large that it can and must be divided into several smaller ones. Quite a few of these I have tried to answer, against the full background of the context, in a rather long study.[1] This time, I shall attend to one only. Even so, attention must be called to what in the context sets the style of all partial questions and answers.

'The specious present' is not a phrase in every one's mouth. Yet the notion is commonsensical. Those who elaborate it are the psychologists. A *specious present* is a duration. Specifically, it is what the psychologists call the (temporal) span of a man's attention. How long then is a specious present? What does its length depend on? What are the upper and lower limits? Wundt and his contemporaries worried such questions; quite legitimately, for they were psychologists. To us, both questions and answers are irrelevant. All that matters is that the notion, however to be elaborated, is commonsensical and is that of a duration. To see why this is so, turn to the two propositions from the context with which I began.

Time is part of the world's content, not of its (logical) form. Hence the undefined temporal terms of the IL are all descriptive. Furthermore, they all name relational characters exemplified by individuals and not either individuals or qualities of such.[2] That much I take from

---

[1] "Some Reflections on Time," in *Il Tempo* (Archivio di Filosofia, 1958), 49–82; reprinted in *Meaning and Existence;* hereafter cited as SRT.

[2] The limitation to relational things amounts to the rejection of absolute time. For details see SRT.

the context. The point is that for an undefined term to occur in the IL, the thing it names must be wholly presented. A necessary condition for a thing to be wholly presented is that it be contained in a specious present. Or, perhaps better, this is (part of) what in the context it means to be wholly presented. The task, therefore, is to "build time" (in the IL) from (the names of) temporal relations, each of which can be exemplified in a specious present. That is one of the two features which in the context set the style for all questions and answers about time. Let us look at the other.

Let 'a' and 'gr' be the names (in the IL) of the spot I mentioned and of its color. I assumed that it did not change. No individual can undergo any change whatsoever, either qualitative or relational, during its duration. That is the second feature. To see why this is so, assume that the spot did change color during its duration, began by being green, ended by being red. Since 'a' is its (unchanging) name, and since '$gr(a)$' is a well-formed sentence (of IL), '$gr(a)$' and '$\sim gr(a)$' would both be true. This, of course, is logical catastrophe.

It will help to drive home what has just been said as well as prepare the ground for what will be said presently, if I call attention to a possible ambiguity in the use of 'change'. Consider two sentences. (1) The world's individuals are unchanging. (2) There is no change in the world. Idiomatically, the transition from (1) to (2) is so slight that it hardly gives us pause. Yet there obviously is "change" in the world, since there is time in it. There is, and there must be, change possible in a specious present, since it is a duration. (Perhaps I should speak of the "world of the context," rather than of the "world." But the qualification is obvious; so I suppress it.) Imagine a specious present of duration [0, 5] containing two individuals, one green and of duration [1, 2], the other red and of duration [3, 4], and nothing else. The example shows the sense in which there is "change" in this world of unchanging individuals, or loosely, in this world without "change." This is the ambiguity in a certain use of 'change' I wanted to spot. The interval numbers I just used and shall continue to use are without any intrinsic significance. I use them merely to save tedious diagrams.

Next for four comments. They may seem a digression; yet they, too, prepare the ground. Moreover, they illustrate the method in connection with a minute point. Such illustration, I think, is always valuable. *First.* Are two individuals contained in one specious present simultaneous? Roughly, yes. For a specious present is so short that an even rougher notion of simultaneity will do quite well on many occasions. Consider then, for a moment, the definition of 'x is (roughly) simultaneous with y' by 'x and y are both contained in a (someone's) specious present'. Note that in trying on this odd definition we speak commonsensically and from without, as it were, that is, not within the world to which the IL is fitted. I put it so circumstantially because the IL is not really a language spoken by anyone. Having made the point, though, I shall not always be so accurate and, as is customary, speak about speaking (commonsensically) about and speaking in the IL. *Second.* Assume, for the sake of the argument and as will soon transpire contrary to fact, that the odd definiens is available in the IL as the name of a character exemplified by individuals. If it were, it wouldn't be of any help with the job of building time. This is the next point to be grasped. Consider the last example. The individuals of duration [1, 2] and [3, 4] respectively exemplify a (temporal) precedence relation, which beyond any doubt is sometimes wholly presented to us. Its name ('precedes' or 'earlier-later') rather obviously will be an undefined term indispensable for the building of time. Thus there would often be occasion to say of two individuals, in the IL, that they are (roughly) simultaneous as well as that one precedes the other. Rather obviously again, on this level of the reconstruction so rough a notion of simultaneity would be of no help. *Third.* The odd definiens is in fact not available on the lowest level of the reconstruction, where one deals only with (the names of) individuals and the characters they exemplify. On this level one is guided by what is usually called phenomenology. What psychologists call phenomenological reports is among the material from which they may eventually build their science. But phenomenology is not the science of psychology. Now consider three propositions. (*a*) 'Specious present', the crucial phrase of the spurious definiens, is a phrase of either common sense or the science of psychology (such as it now is). (*b*) Common sense and science lie in the reconstruction on a level or levels high above the lowest. (*c*) The job of building time must be begun at the very lowest level. For the level of common sense is being reached exactly when this job, together with some others, has been done. It follows from (*a*), (*b*), and (*c*) that the spurious definiens is not available at the lowest level. For the truth of (*a*), (*b*), and (*c*) I shall not argue on this occasion. But I grant, even insist, that the very phrase 'level of the reconstruction' requires unpacking. Once more, though, I believe that as things now stand such unpacking can be dispensed with in a paper of this sort. *Fourth.* Rules for the "interpretation" of the IL, i.e., what I have spoken of as fitting it to someone's world, are part of the full articulation of the method. By these rules, the conditions under which the names of individuals and of characters respectively may occur in the IL differ in one respect. Consider a relational statement (of the IL) referring to two things. If the two things are individuals, then both their names can occur in the statement only if there is a specious present in which they are both contained. (Otherwise at least one must be referred to by an existential clause.) The rule for the occurrence of predicates is less restrictive. This is the difference. It may be partly responsible for the confused idea that the psychological notion of a specious present enters in the wrong way into the building of time. To dispel the confusion, one must grasp the distinction between what may "show itself" and what can actually be said at any given level of the IL. The distinction is crucial; so crucial indeed that I believe it should be brought out again and again, in connection with all kinds of minute points.

Intervals on the time line either (1) lie outside of each other, e.g., [1, 2], [3, 4]; or, (2) they have an interval in common, e.g., [1, 3], [2, 4]; or, (3) one lies inside the other, e.g., [1, 4], [2, 3]. Combining (2) and (3), I shall say that in either of these cases the durations *overlap*. Individuals have durations. If their durations either lie outside of each other or overlap, I shall say that the individuals themselves do. If the durations of two individuals coincide, however, I shall say, not that they overlap, but that they are *synchronous*. The precedence relation mentioned before ('earlier-later') obtains between any two individuals if and only if they do not overlap.

The (partial) questions and answers about time are many. Quite a few of them, including very important ones, are not affected by the simplifying assumption that no two individuals overlap. One assumes, then, that two individuals are either synchronous or that one precedes the other. Or, what as far as these questions are concerned amounts to the same, one may assume that all individuals are instantaneous. Making either of these assumptions, one can build time from 'precedes' and 'synchronous'. If, as I shall, one drops the simplifying assumption, time must be built from 'precedes' and 'overlaps'. It is of course not my intention in this note to do the whole job. I merely propose to dissolve a puzzle, or solve a minute problem, one comes across at the very start.

Consider a specious present, SP, of duration [0, 2]. Its duration coincides with that of an individual, say, a green spot, called 'a' in IL. Another individual, called 'b' in IL, of duration [0, 1], is a red spot to the left ('lf') of the first. Speaking from without and commonsensically, that is, among other things, in a language containing temporal determinations without paradox, we may divide SP into two parts, refer to them by "at first" and "then," respectively. We can describe what I assume to be the whole content of SP by the following sentence: (S) At first the red spot was to the left of the green one, then it wasn't. There is thus no difficulty. But turn now to IL. Both spots are contained in SP. Hence, 'a' and 'b' are available "all through SP." To grasp that, one merely has to remember the fourth comment of the apparent digression. Now I give the word to the one who proposed the puzzle. In this situation, he says, one could in IL at first truly assert (S_1) '$lf(b, a)$'; then, equally truly, (S_2) '$\sim lf(b, a)$'. Conjoining the two sentences, you obtain (S_3) '$lf(b, a) \cdot \sim lf(b, a)$'. Thus we are in IL faced with contradiction, which is logical catastrophe.

This is the problem. In formulating it I planted the cue for a *first step* towards its solution. I spoke of asserting S_1, S_2, and S_3. Who does the asserting? The IL, I recalled, is not spoken by any one, not even by the person to whose world it is fitted. But disregard for a moment the reminder and assume that this person speaks the IL. I believe that in this way the first point can be made more forcefully. A visual field is the base of a cone. The beholder's eye is in its apex. Metaphorically, a specious present is the base of a narrow isosceles triangle. In its apex stands the "owner" of this specious present, who, as for the moment I assume, is also the "speaker" of the IL. From this point he surveys the whole duration of the specious present, say, SP. The point, though, is not itself located anywhere in this duration. Or, to say the same thing differently, whatever the speaker truly asserts may be asserted by him "all through SP." Only, we see now that, as I used it in stating the problem, the phrase 'all through SP' is itself problematic. But let me use it once more to point out that, as I interpret 'lf', '$lf(b, a)$' may be truly asserted all through SP, as may '$ov(a, b)$', where 'ov' stands for the transcription of 'overlap' into the IL. All this is obvious, I submit. In spite of the metaphor, as some now use 'logic', it merely states the logic or use of 'specious present'.

One may of course so interpret 'lf' that '$lf(c, d)$' is false unless the individuals named 'c' and 'd' are also synchronous. If so, then, in our case, '$\sim lf(b, a)$' is true and, if that need be added, may be asserted all through SP. For good reasons I have not so interpreted 'lf'. As I interpreted it, '$lf(b, a)$' is true, and, again, may be asserted by our "speaker" throughout SP. (I use the misleading wording once more in order to leave no doubt which it is in my power to remove.) It follows immediately that S_1, S_2, and S_3 cannot serve as transcriptions of S and its two conjunction terms, respectively. How, then, are they to be transcribed? I leave the answer to the fourth step. It will further illuminate the context and add to the interest of the problem, if I next show, in the *second step*, why a certain kind of answer won't do.

In a world of unchanging individuals, either synchronous or one preceding the other, there is change. This we saw before. That is one kind of change. What happens in our example at time 1, when the red spot disappears while the green one persists, is another kind; call it the second. Phenomenally, there is still a third, the kind that occurs when we say, commonsensically, that in a specious present a spot moves or that it changes (continually) either brightness or color. Phenomenally, part of the essence of the third kind is continuity. These, it seems to me, are the three "fundamental" kinds of change of which, in an obvious sense, all others are "composed." Presently it will appear that my argument is not affected if for the time being I ignore the third kind. Now consider duration. It is evident, or at least it is evident to me, that, aside from continuity, the second kind of change, that is, the one illustrated by the example, is the very essence of duration. The appeal to evidence, I submit, is not a sign of either fuzziness or sloth. Phenomenally the matter is fundamental. All one can do, therefore, is to make as clear as one can what one is talking about.

Those who propose the solution that won't do, if only because it is not completely thought through, assert that whenever a change of the second kind occurs, something mental occurs, too. One specious present comes to an end; another begins. Thus, in the example, SP is not really a specious present. There could be that close a tie between change in the world (without minds) and change in minds. Since in fact there isn't, the solution has a deceptively idealistic (subjectivistic) flavor. But, then, one need not be deceived. On the other hand, if one accepts the gambit, then, clearly, our problem disappears. That makes the matter at least worth considering. So I shall start on two strings of comments.

First. One may accept the gambit. What it amounts to, essentially, is to make one of the two simplifying assumptions that were mentioned. *Formally,* the (mathematical) continuum can be "constructed" from points on a line. *Phenomenally,* one narrows one's basis to what is presented in specious presents without either the second or the third kind of change. The price is high. I call it high because, e.g., the two spots of the example would no longer be individuals. Nor could they literally be named in the IL, i.e., they couldn't be referred to by undefined descriptive signs. Yet the price is not prohibitive. For, while the context requires that what is named be wholly presented, it does not require that what is so presented can also be named. Just think of the spot, mentioned at the beginning, which changes color in a specious present. As we saw, it cannot be an individual and cannot be named in my, or, for that matter, in any nonsubstantialist context.[3] And what holds for this spot, holds for any change of the third kind. About the alternative assumptions to which the gambit reduces I shall say this.

[3] For details, see SRT.

With things literally instantaneous I simply am not acquainted. That leaves the synchronous individuals. To start from them is to accept a "fundamental phenomenological quantisation of time." This I am reluctant to do, if only because it entails, or seems to entail, that something makes sense which to me doesn't, namely, the introduction of duration into a world without any change whatsoever. (This is also why I called change of the second kind the essence, apart from continuity, of duration.) I am not at all sure, though, that this is a conclusive argument. Probably, the best argument against the gambit is that it is not necessary.

Second. The proponents of the solution assert that no change of the second kind ever occurs in a specious present. That is patently false. In the preceding paragraph I have shown that one can propose their gambit without committing one's self to the falsehood. But the confusion likely to have spawned it is of some interest. Remember the metaphor of the narrow triangle. The confusion consists in considering a specious present as the content of a single act issuing from a mind located in the apex of the triangle. Ontologically this triangle is nowhere. That is the limit of the metaphor which thus, like all metaphors, has its dangers as well as its uses. Positively, an act, or, rather, what in the context corresponds to it, is itself an individual, called an awareness.[4] Thus it lives in the world and not, like the triangle and its apex, in a metaphor. Being an individual, moreover, it has itself a duration; and there is no reason why two or more such individuals should not, as in fact I find they sometimes are, be contained in the same specious present.

Executed in detail, the *third step* takes quite long. I shall take it very quickly. It amounts to the construction, in the IL, of the continuum of instants out of intervals (on a line) and the two relations of precedence and overlapping among them. Mathematicians know how to do that. So there is need for only one comment. If the construction is to succeed, some generalities containing the names of the two relations must be true. The mathematicians call such generalities axioms. Speaking commonsensically and therefore using some of the crucial words freely, the axioms assert such things as that, say, for any two intervals (individuals) which are neither contiguous nor overlap, there is a third preceding the one and preceded by the other. One may reasonably doubt whether these axioms are true. Or, perhaps better, one may wonder whether they do not go unreasonably far beyond what is ever

[4] See *Meaning and Existence,* specially the essay "Intentionality," but also SRT.

presented to us. On a different level, this is the question of how to introduce real numbers into measurement. Such doubts don't bother me; such questions don't preoccupy me. If necessary, the job may be done by resorting to the partial interpretation of a calculus.[5] Perhaps this is the place for a more general comment. The classical analysts, who flourished from the turn of the century to the beginning of the Second World War, and particularly the logical positivists among them, were greatly concerned with those doubts and questions. These things were at the very center of their interest. In these areas they made contributions which by now are uncontroversial—which doesn't mean, of course, that they were correct in all details or couldn't be otherwise improved upon. However that may be, I am more than willing to leave matters of this kind to the mathematical logicians. The difference in accent illustrates as well as any, I think, the difference between classical analysis and the kind of analytical philosophy some of us now practice.

We are ready for the *fourth step*, the solution of our problem. The third step yields a defined arithmetical functor of the first type, write it 'du' and call it 'duration', such that '$du(a) = [0, 2]$' and '$du(b) = [0, 1]$' transcribe what so far we could only say commonsensically, from without, about the two spots of the example. It remains to transcribe the statement I called S and its two conjunction terms. Arithmetic, being logical, is available to us in the IL. So we can readily form two sentences; one, call it D_1, stating that the first instants of the two durations coincide; the other, call it D_2, stating that the last instant of the one precedes that of the other. Now I transcribe the three statements by (I_1)'$lf(b, a) \cdot D_1$', (I_2)'$lf(b, a) \cdot D_2$', (I_3)'$lf(b, a) \cdot D_1 \cdot D_2$', respectively. '$D_1 \cdot D_2$' is not a contradiction; hence I_3 isn't. Thus the problem is solved. Or, if you please, the puzzle is dissolved. Three brief comments should settle the matter. One. A superficial similarity with Russell's analysis of definite descriptions suggests itself. Upon this analysis, the two sentences 'The present king of France is bald' and 'The present king of France is not bald' are no longer contradictions. Or, rather, their transcriptions are not. Second. As I interpreted 'lf', '$lf(c, d)$ can be truly asserted of any two individuals of a specious present, irrespective of how in this specious present they temporally lie to each other. That does not mean that we need two primitive notions of leftness; a crude one, which is the one I used; and a refined one, which involves synchrony. The point is, rather, that the refined one can, and for some purposes must, be defined in terms of the crude one

[5] See *Philosophy of Science*.

in conjunction with the two primitive temporal relations. Third. 'At first' and 'then', the two expressions I used earlier when, speaking commonsensically, I introduced the example, are correlative. They "presuppose" each other. 'D$_1$' and 'D$_2$' do not state correlatives in this sense. Noticing this, some one may wonder whether I$_1$ and I$_2$ can really serve as transcriptions of the two parts of S. Such a one worries about ordinary language. I leave him to his worries and conclude with a more general reflection.

Duration is a temporal notion. Continuity as such is not. Continuity is no doubt one of the essential ingredients of duration. Not being temporal, however, it cannot be the whole. The other essential ingredient of duration is the second kind of change. In the IL, this ingredient is accurately and adequately represented by the undefined name for overlapping. In this sense, the construction of time, a small part of which I have here considered, does full justice to duration. In another sense it does not and cannot. I need not and shall not argue whether or not "duration" is introspectively simple. Whether or not it is, it is sometimes wholly presented to us. It is in fact so presented whenever we find, in a specious present, the third kind of change, e.g., a spot (continuously) changing color. Yet, the IL refers to duration by means of a defined functor and not, as would seem more satisfactory, by an undefined descriptive term. Nor, for that matter, can the spot which changes color be named in the IL. That shows how things hang together. The dissatisfaction itself cannot be removed in any non-substantialist context. More radically even, as I have shown elsewhere,[6] we stand here at the natural limits of the analytical enterprise.

[6] See the last section of SRT.

Physics and Ontology*

THERE is *philosophy proper*, also called first philosophy or metaphysics, and there are the several *philosophies of* something or other. A "philosophy of," if it is to remain just that, must not cut itself off from philosophy proper. Deliberate confrontations from time to time should help to avoid such fatal severance. The heart of philosophy proper is ontology. For a while this insight was lost. Now it is being recovered. Thus it may help to confront some recent ontological thought with the recent philosophy of physics. This is what I propose to do. But I cannot of course on this occasion offer more than the barest sketch or outline, just as I shall have to leave unsupported much of even the little I can say.[1]

As to *method*, philosophy during the first half of the century has taken the linguistic turn. Words are used either philosophically or commonsensically. Philosophical uses are literally unintelligible. The task is to explicate them by talking commonsensically about them. This is the fundamental idea of the turn. By now it has fully emerged. How, then, does it affect the emerging concern with ontology as the main *content*?

Ontology asks what exists. This use of 'exist' is philosophical. An ontologist who has executed the linguistic turn will therefore not propose still another division of all entities into existents and nonexist-

* Philosophy of Science, *28, 1961, 1–14. Reprinted by permission. This paper was read, with some omissions, as part of a symposium at the 1960 International Congress for Logic, Methodology and Philosophy of Science held at Stanford University.*

[1] For supporting arguments, see *Philosophy of Science* and *Meaning and Existence.* Among older essays, see the two pieces on the philosophy of physics in H. Feigl and M. Brodbeck (eds.), *Readings in the Philosophy of Science* (Appleton-Century-Crofts, 1953). Among recent essays, see "Ineffability, Ontology, and Method," *The Philosophical Review,* 69, 1960, 18–40, and pp. 45–63 of this book, and "Dell'Atto," *Rivista di Filosofia,* 51, 1960, 3–51 and pp. 3–44 of this book.

ents. Rather, he will attempt to discern and state commonsensically the several and often conflicting intellectual motives which control the philosophical use of 'exist'. I just spoke of motives; I could instead have spoken of criteria. Both words, though, motive and criterion, may seem to impute critical awareness where its absence often has been crucial. So I shall avoid both, speaking of *patterns* instead. Of such patterns there are quite a few. Some I shall ignore or merely mention; to some others I shall attend. First, though, for the connection with physics.

(When used commonsensically, 'exist' can always be replaced by 'there is (are)'. In this essay I shall therefore not use it at all except in order to mention the philosophical uses. Other philosophical uses I must mention I shall mark by double quotes when they first appear and whenever it seems necessary to avoid confusion. 'Entity' has also been used philosophically. I use it here merely as an abbreviation, to avoid such commonsensical but tedious phrases as 'what an expression expresses or refers to'.)

Are forces and particles "real" or are they merely (methodological) "fictions"? At the time of Mach the particles were atoms. Nowadays they are the many entities of subatomic physics; and one may wish to include the psis. Within the philosophy of physics this change from, say, Mach to the present gave rise to a new group of special problems. One cannot tackle them successfully unless he understands what has not changed at all. 'Real' and 'fiction' in this question are used philosophically and exactly as a moment ago I used 'existent' and 'nonexistent'. That shows the connection between ontology and the philosophy of physics. The question I borrowed from the tradition thus opens the ontological *Problematik*[2] of physics. Forces and particles have also been called "theoretical" entities. This adjective, too, is compromised by a philosophical past. So I shall avoid it, speaking instead of the *problematic entities* of physics.

The problematic entities are very many. The patterns controlling the philosophical use of 'exist' are quite a few. Thus it may well be that the latter lead to a classification of the former, depending on which pattern or group of patterns is needed to clarify the status of the entity. Very roughly, there are two such classes. That is why I gave two illustrations, forces and particles. I shall first attend to the class represented by forces; then, after a digression about phenomenalism and realism, to that represented by particles.

---

[2] *Die Problematik, la problematica, la problématique* are handy nouns in German, Italian, and French. I often wish we had their equivalent in English.

What exists exists "independently." This is the *independence pattern*. The use of 'independent' is philosophical. According to one explication, only facts can be independent; according to another, only things may be. The alternative marks the deepest dividing line in the ontological tradition. That is why I mention it. But it has not affected the recent philosophy of physics. With but few exceptions, such as Whitehead's eventism, its practitioners are all implicit thing ontologists. That is why I shall say no more about this pattern.

What exists is what is "in" space and time. This is the formula of the *concreteness pattern*. As the crucial word is used, physical objects are in physical space and time; sensa, in phenomenal space and time. The pattern does therefore not commit one to either materialism or phenomenalism. On the other hand, properties and relations exemplified by either physical objects or sensa are not literally in space and time; either physical, in the case of the former; or phenomenal, in the case of the latter. That spots the place of the concreteness pattern in the nominalism complex.[3] This complex we can again ignore. One subpattern or component of the pattern, though, has been very important recently. Physical objects move in orbits. As some put it, that is indeed part of the notion of a physical object. Call this the *orbit subpattern*. Literally, the modern particles have no orbits. Everyone is familiar with the disturbance this feature has created.

We cannot know anything to exist unless we are "acquainted" either with it or with a part of it or, wholly or in part, with a thing of its sort. This is the formula of the *acquaintance pattern*. Its flavor is epistemological. In one sense, ontology and epistemology can indeed not be disentangled; in another, dialectically, they can. This I here take for granted.[4] The phrase to be explicated is, of course, 'being acquainted'. We are acquainted with what we *perceive*, or, synonymously, with perceptual things, i.e., with perceptual objects, such as stones and chairs, and with some of the characters they exemplify, such as colors, shapes, and distance. That is one explication. Upon another explication, we are acquainted only with what we are *directly aware* of; direct awareness being of phenomenal entities, i.e., such things as sensa and the characters they exemplify on the one hand and, on the other, mental acts such as perceiving, remembering, thinking, and, of course, direct awareness itself. The dialectics of this alternative, perception versus direct aware-

[3] Concerning the place of the independence pattern in the nominalism complex, see Edwin B. Allaire, "Existence, Independence, and Universals," *The Philosophical Review*, 69, 1960, 485–96.

[4] For argument, see my special review of Strawson's "Individuals," *The Journal of Philosophy*, 57, 1960, 601–22, and pp. 171–92 of this book.

ness, has dominated much of the tradition. Made fully explicit, it can be confined to philosophy proper. Implicitly, from Mach to Einstein, it has profoundly affected the *Problematik* of the particle. Retain, then, for future reference, that in this context I called stones and chairs perceptual rather than physical objects.

Some entities are "simples"; all others "consist" of simples; the former exist; the latter don't. This is the *simplicity pattern*. What is a simple? What does it mean for a thing to consist of others? The formula, we see, contains two philosophical uses. Each has produced a huge body of dialectics. I call them two bodies rather than one because up to a point one can examine each separately. To understand that, consider that one may disagree as to whether the "simples" are phenomenal, or perceptual, or even more fundamentally, whether they are facts or things, and yet agree on what it means for one entity to "consist" of others. In our subject the dialectics of consisting looms large, that of simplicity doesn't. So I shall ignore the latter, except for a digression that will permit me to complete the ontological schema as well as to relieve the dryness of the catalogue by at least a fragment of argument.

(One may accept the fundamental idea of the linguistic turn concerning the proper method without accepting another, concerning the proper technique. I accept both. The proper technique, expedient for all purposes, indispensable for some, is to talk commonsensically about a schema called the ideal language (IL). The IL I propose is built around a syntactical dichotomy called logical-descriptive. In the IL there are logical features, signs, and truths. The shapes expressing the type distinctions are among the logical features; the connectives and the quantifiers, among the logical signs. The explication of "analytic" rests on the logical truths.)

The philosophical uses of 'simple' are all misguided; attempts at explicating them show that none has a retrievable and important common-sense core. This is what the holists believe. If they are right, then I should not have listed the simplicity pattern. Since holism is now again fashionable, I shall in four steps sketch a partial defense of that pattern, exhibiting the role it plays in a crucial dichotomy which even some modern holists wish to preserve. 1. Philosophers have long tried to distinguish the world's "form" from its "content." This is the crucial dichotomy. It must of course be explicated. The world's form is expressed by what is logical (in the IL); its content, by what is descriptive. This is the one explication which has not yet broken down. 2. The world's content exists, its form doesn't. This is one of the classical gambits. I reject it, insisting that the world's form has some ontological status, though of course one radically different from that of its content. The latter exists, the former subsists. That is one way to express this gambit by a formula. The difference between the two gambits is fundamental. Yet it makes no difference for what I am about. 3. Consider the customary connectives on the one hand, the sixteen truth functions of two sentential variables on the other. There is no way of dividing these sixteen into two classes such that it would make sense to say that while the members of the one are simple, those of the other consist of them. At least, I know of no such sense of 'simple' and 'consist'. This shows in the case of the connectives what is meant by saying, truly I believe, that there are no logical simples. But let me add two comments. 3a. It does not follow that the connectives, those which we customarily use as well as those we could use, are in any sense metalinguistic. If they were, the logical entities they express would be either nowhere or, at best, in the mind. 3b. There is the obvious objection that the truth functions can all be "defined" in terms of either the stroke or the arrow function. I shall attend to it presently, after having said what needs to be said here about "definition." 4. Putting 2 and 3 together makes the lesson obvious. The logical entities do not exist. That is the gist of 2. There are no logical simples. That is the gist of 3. The idea of "simplicity" is indeed a crucial ingredient of that of "existence." That is the lesson. It concludes the digression.[5]

An entity "consists" of others if and only if the expression (of IL) referring to it can be defined in terms of expressions referring to those others. Structurally as well as historically, this is the dominant explication. To understand why and how it serves one must understand the nature of definitions. Call the two sides of a definition its left and its right, with the definiendum appearing on the left. Call the entity to which the definiendum refers the defined entity; those of which it consists, the defining entities. This will save breath and do no harm. Notice next that one always defines a character, never an object.[6] Let the left be 'x is a bay'; the right, 'x is a horse and x is tawny'. What we have defined is not an object but a character exemplified by all and

---

[5] Wittgenstein, in the *Tractatus* and earlier, was greatly impressed by this piece of dialectics. Unfortunately, he also insisted that form was literally nothing and strained toward the view rejected in 3a. These two errors were among those that propelled him toward the views he propounded in the *Investigations*. See also two essays by Edwin B. Allaire in *Analysis*: "*Tractatus* 6.3751," 19, 1959, 100–105, and "Types and Formation Rules: A Note on *Tractatus* 3.334," 21, 1960, 14–16.

[6] Philosophers will also notice that in order to avoid the dialectics of particularity and individuality, I have avoided both 'particular' and 'individual', used the rather ambiguous and noncommittal 'object' instead.

only those objects which are horses as well as tawny. Now for the main point. The left side is no more nor less than an abbreviation for the right. Thus, the notion of definition is essentially metalinguistic. The insight is fundamental. One would think that it is also obvious. Yet when one reads what is being written one wonders. It has at any rate three facets. First. Defined terms are eliminable. Second. The left and the right have by virtue of a notational convention the same referent. Third. One must not be misled by the circumstance that after a definition has been introduced, one may use the sentence which for the moment I call 'left if and only if right' *as if* it were a logical truth and not merely the reflection of a notational convention. The distinction is of the essence. For a notational convention does not express anything. A logical truth expresses part of the world's form. This is my cue for picking up a loose thread.

Remember the objection 3b above and consider the sentence 'not-p if and only if neither p nor p'. It expresses a logical truth. Thus it is not merely the reflection of a notational convention. Technically, in mathematical logic, it may be treated *as if* it were a definition. In the philosophy of logic and mathematics the distinction looms large. But we need not and must not pursue it on this occasion. The philosophy of physics is concerned with what exists rather than with what merely subsists.

In Newtonian mechanics force may be defined in terms of mass and acceleration. 'Mass' and 'force' may in turn be defined and therefore eliminated from the original definition. Continuing this descent, one may arrive at a right side mentioning only perceptual things (objects and characters). In the light of these facts, do forces exist? Some took the negative; some, the affirmative. We do not join the controversy, merely try to unravel the dialectic. It depends on four patterns, simplicity, acquaintance, concreteness, and a fourth which I shall presently introduce.

Those swayed by the simplicity pattern will of course take the negative. The role of the acquaintance pattern is not so unambiguous. Interpret it so that we are acquainted with what we perceive.[7] Everyone agrees that we perceive the defining entities. Do we perceive forces, densities, friction coefficients, and so on? The answer is No. If one stops there, the pattern provides an argument for the negative. But there is a counterargument which amounts to an amendment of the pattern. Borrowing the explication of 'consist' from the simplicity pattern, this counterargument reminds us that the left and the right sides have literally the same referent. Then it points out that we admittedly

[7] Just as the dialectics of simplicity and consisting can be separated, so for the point at hand it does not matter where we actually peg the level of acquaintance.

perceive all the defining entities. It concludes that, even though we do not perceive the defined entity, we are in the relevant sense acquainted with it. (Whether or not one moves on to broaden the use of 'perceive' so that we do perceive forces is merely a matter of words. The broad use, to be sure, would be rather technical. But that does not make it philosophical.) To understand how the concreteness pattern comes in, remember first the definition of 'bay'. The entities exemplifying the defined character, bay, and those exemplifying the two defining characters, horse and tawny, are of the same kind, objects in space and time. This is a source of resistance against the simplicity pattern, particularly if one forgets, as one well might under the influence of nominalism which has been rampant for so long, that what this pattern denies is not that there are bays but, rather, that the character they exemplify exists. (Whether or not the two defining characters of the illustration are simple obviously does not affect the point.) In the case of our problematic entities, the converse of these ideas becomes operative. These entities are either rather complex relational characters, exemplified not by a single object but jointly by several. Or, even more suspect to the implicit nominalist, they are characters of characters. Thus the concreteness pattern becomes plausible as an argument for the negative.

A *defined* entity exists if and only if it is significant; an entity being significant if and only if the expression *referring* to it occurs in statements of lawfulness which we have reason to believe are true. This is the *significance pattern*. By it, forces exist. That is again obvious. Something else, that should be obvious, nowadays isn't to some. Notice that I underlined 'defined' and 'referring'. A defined entity exists, and so on. Not just: an entity exists, and so on. If there is a definition, we know what the expression refers to. If there isn't, we do not know what we are talking about. Significance presupposes reference. The holists deny that. That is why I do not know what they take us to be talking about either in physics or elsewhere. That is my cue for the next point.

Let 'x is soluble (in water)' stand for the left; 'If x is put into water, then x dissolves', for the right. Upon this definition of the disposition term, Carnap's famous match which has never been put into water is soluble. In English, shifting to the subjunctive mode, 'if it were . . . then it would . . .', takes care of the awkwardness. Make the left '$f_3(x)$'; the right '$f_1(x) \supset f_2(x)$'. Now the shift requires the introduction of a new primitive[8] sign, say 'C', making the right '$f_1(x)Cf_2(x)$'. One sees

---

[8] If 'C' itself is not primitive, its definiens will contain a primitive constituent which is a quasirelation. Then the arguments apply to this constituent. The same goes for 'N' below.

now that the awkwardness is closely related to another. If one makes the closure of the conditional on the right, '$(x)[f_1(x) \supset f_2(x)]$', the paradigm of a law statement, then the difference between "laws" and "accidental generalities" is lost. Remember Chisholm's park bench in Boston Commons on which only Irishmen ever sat even though, had I sat on it, I would not be or have become an Irishman. These are the facts. What is the problem?

The awkwardness arises only if one insists on transcription into IL. Such transcription is the proper technique of ontological inquiry. That suggests that the problem is ontological. There are three alternative ways of handling it. Before turning to them, let me in the law case show a further connection. Let 'N' be the primitive name of a descriptive (i.e., nonlogical) relation of the second type such that $N(f_1, f_2)$ if and only if f_1 and f_2 are causally connected. This makes '$N(f_1, f_2) \equiv (x)[f_1(x) \supset f_2(x)]$' a synthetic truth or falsehood, depending on whether the generality is a law or accidental. N is in substance an Aristotelian nature. If the objects in question exemplify only two characters, then it literally is one. That supports the ontological diagnosis.

The *first alternative* is to introduce 'C' as a primitive sign. Syntactically, 'C' is a quasirelation, i.e., a sign combining either sentences or sentences and terms into sentences. So is 'M', the primitive sign for the logical nexus of meaning, in one of the several meanings of 'meaning', which connects the mental characters I call propositions with the states of affairs, expressed by sentences, which they mean. Three comments will illuminate the situation that produces. 1. The entity C is either logical or descriptive. If it is claimed to be descriptive, many will demur on the ground that they are not acquainted with it. 2. C must in fact be logical on structural grounds which lie much deeper than the acquaintance pattern. To see that, consider a (binary) descriptive relation, r. It is exemplified if and only if some sentence '$r(a, b)$' is true, which presupposes that the two objects called 'a' and 'b' exist. The one and only thing one could plausibly mean by a descriptive quasirelation C being exemplified is, analogously, that some sentence '$p_1 C p_2$' is true; 'p_1' and 'p_2' being two sentences referring to states of affairs. And it is part of the idea of a "descriptive" universal that it must make sense to say of it that it is "exemplified." Now assume 'If a were f_1, then a would be f_2' to be true in a case where a is in fact neither. Transcribed, the sentence is of the form '$p_1 C p_2$'. Hence, if 'C' is to express the causal nexus, this latter sentence would be true even though its two sentential constituents are both false. The quasirelation would thus be "exemplified" by two nonobtaining states of affairs. This clashes with the very idea of a descriptive entity, or, what amounts to the same, with the idea of an existent. To see that it does not so clash with the idea of a subsistent, one merely has to consider '$p_1 \lor p_2$'. It makes no sense to speak of a logical entity, such as the quasirelation of conjunction, as being exemplified. Hence, there is no absurdity whatsoever in counting '$p_1 \lor p_2$' as true in case either 'p_1' or 'p_2' is false.[9] 3. In case IL contains quasirelational primitives other than connectives and 'M', the two interdependent dichotomies "logical-descriptive" and "analytic-synthetic" cannot be adequately explicated. At least, no such explication has as yet been proposed. Nor can I conceive even the vaguest idea of one.

The *second alternative* is to accept "implicit definitions."[10] The simplest paradigm is '$f_1(x) \supset [f_2(x) \equiv f_3(x)]$', the bilateral reduction sentence, B, by means of which Carnap has proposed to "introduce" the predicate 'f_3'. In this context 'introduce' is anything but clear. Three comments will remove the blur. 1. What is being introduced is not just 'f_3' but also B. 2. B is not a logical truth (analytic). Thus it could not possibly in the language reflect a definition or notational stipulation about it. 3. Whether or not B is analytic, introducing it does not make 'f_3' eliminable. I agree with those who conclude that upon this alternative one would therefore not know what one is talking about when using 'f_3'. Reference is being sacrificed to significance in the manner of the holists. One reason the alternative seems nevertheless attractive to some is that it reflects the way we try out a new concept. But then, to use Reichenbach's pretty phrase, the context of discovery is one thing, the context of justification is another. To mistake the former for the latter is one of the hallmarks of holism. That confirms the diagnosis.

The *third alternative* is to accept the awkwardness that the disposition terms cannot *in closed form* and with anything approaching idiomatic accuracy be transcribed into IL. Such acceptance is made easy by considering what it amounts to in the law case. Upon this alternative, a law statement cannot *as such* in IL be distinguished from an accidental generality. Rather, the difference lies in the context, that is,

---

[9] As for '$\lor$', so for 'M'. Let 'p_1' be the propositional character which means p_1. M is a logical entity. Hence, there is no absurdity in "$p_1' M p_1$'" being true even though 'p_1' be false. If one is a thing ontologist (i.e., no "fact" exists, irrespective of whether it be "true" or "false"), that solves the problem of false beliefs. This too shows, as does the argument in the text, that there is a stylistic discrepancy, to say the least, between the very idea of a thing ontology and that of primitive quasirelations.

[10] Frege as early as 1903 rejected the idea of implicit definitions as inherently and irremediably confused. *The Philosophical Review* (69, 1960, 3–17) recently has earned our gratitude by printing an English translation of this impressive piece.

first, in the success as a premiss of the statement we call a law in those nontrivial cases where the match has been put into water, and, second, in its deductive connections with other such statements. A little reflection will show that this explication of the difference is but an up-to-date formulation of Hume's basic insight concerning causes, natures, and dispositions.

That much for the kind of problematic entity represented by forces; I turn to that represented by particles. The particle exists. This is one alternative. It doesn't exist, is merely a "construction" or "fiction." This the other. Commonsensically, we think of the particle as a kind of physical object. At least, we think or thought so of the particles of classical physics. That merely brushes aside what does not matter right now. It also helps to explain why and how the realism-phenomenalism issue, which belongs to philosophy proper, has so profoundly affected the status of the particle. Physical objects[11] exist. That is the realist thesis. They don't exist. That is the phenomenalist contention. Thus one may easily be led to argue that only a realist can consistently assert what a consistent phenomenalist must deny, namely, that the particle exists. To appreciate the impact of the argument, remember Einstein. He made no secret of his intense dislike for "positivism." The positivism he knew was among other things a kind of phenomenalism. Reading him, one discovers soon that the real object of his dislike was just that phenomenalism. On the other hand, he was profoundly committed to the particle, even the classical particle.[12] So he may plausibly have been swayed by the argument. Again, reading him shows that he was. So we better face the philosophical dialectic.

I begin by introducing two commonsensical distinctions and a new pattern. What I perceive when I see a chair or a stone I call a perceptual object, not a physical object. My seeing the perceptual chair has causes. Science tells me what they are. One of them—there is no need to elaborate the familiar—I call the physical chair. Colors, sounds, and smells are all perceptual things. But they have not for several hundred years been thought of as physical things. That makes the point rather forcefully. So I shall not belabor it. *Perceptual* things versus *physical* things: that is the first distinction. The second is between perceptual and phenomenal things. Sensa, toothaches, awarenesses, and so on, are phenomenal objects; the characters they exemplify, phenomenal char-

---

[11] More precisely, physical things, i.e., either objects or characters (i.e., either properties or relations). The point must by now be obvious. So I follow here and elsewhere stylistic convenience.

[12] The story of the shadow this commitment cast on his later life is well known. See also my review of the Einstein volume in The Library of Living Philosophers (*The Philosophical Review*, 60, 1951, 268–74).

acters. That is how, commonsensically, I use 'phenomenal'. Others use 'mental' instead. The perceptual chair I see obviously is not a phenomenal thing.

Perceptual things exist. This is the new pattern. It states fairly what the realist wants to maintain. So I call it the *realism pattern*. Say instead "There are perceptual things" and you have uttered a truism. The realist wants to say more. That shows that his use of 'exist' is philosophical. (That is why I speak of a pattern.) Presently I shall so explicate it that the pattern becomes true and commonsensical, though no longer truistic. But let us first look at the phenomenalist.

The phenomenalist starts from the acquaintance pattern, explicates it so that to be acquainted with something is to be directly aware of it. Since the only things we are directly aware of are phenomenal things, he concludes that perceptual things do not exist. That is so absurd (however you may explicate 'exist') that we cannot but immediately ask two questions. What is the minimum the phenomenalist must claim to deserve a hearing? What is the intellectual motive for his desperate gambit?

Starting from a class of definientia consisting only of sensa and some of their characters, which are all phenomenal things, one can define serviceable expressions for all perceptual things. This is the minimal claim. It has been and still is controversial. How tenable it is depends on how one interprets 'serviceable'. With a reasonable interpretation it is tenable as well as strategically important. This, though, is only half of the story. The other half is that to grant the claim is the quickest way to dispose of phenomenalism. Remember what has been said about definitions. The left and the right have the same referent. Thus, a consistent phenomenalist must hold that a perceptual object is, literally, a congeries, however complex, of phenomenal things. That is his fatal weakness.

The classical dialectic of perception revolves around two pivots. I perceive the tower to be round, the stick to be bent. Through further perceptions I come to know that the one is square, the other straight. There is perceptual error. This is one pivot. Veridical perceptions are not intrinsically distinct from others. The criteria are all contextual. This is the other pivot. The one and only way to master the dialectic is to grant *in this context* the phenomenalist's claim. That accounts for his intellectual motive. It is also his formidable strength.

Weakness and strength together have produced an agonizing stalemate. The way out leads through phenomenology. There are two kinds of phenomenal things; one I call *primary*; the other, in a narrower sense of the term, *mental*. Sensa and their characters are among primary things. Mental things are either awarenesses, which are objects, or their characters. I am not directly aware of the perceptual object. That is obvious. Nor am I in perceiving something directly aware of that mythical phenomenal object called a "percept." That, too, is obvious, although it has been temporarily obscured by what the classical realists in exasperation called the way of ideas. What happens when I am seeing the chair is, rather, that I am directly aware of an act, i.e., of an awareness and the two simple characters it exemplifies. One of the two is *perceiving*. (Others of this kind are remembering, thinking, doubting, and so on.) The best English name for the second character the awareness exemplifies is '*the proposition (that) this is a chair*'. So I call it a propositional character. Both these characters are nonrelational.[13] That gives the phenomenalist his due. The realist may take comfort from four other features. 1. Like pitches, hues, and all other simple phenomenal characters, the quality called perceiving is unmistakable and completely determinate. 2. The propositional character is simple. 3. The referential aspect of perception resides in the meaning nexus. This nexus is a logical quasirelation (M). It connects a phenomenal entity (viz., the propositional character) with a perceptual one (viz., the fact which the propositional character means). The sentence expressing it, e.g., 'The proposition this is a chair means this a chair', is analytic. 4. Primary facts, e.g., a (phenomenal) spot's being green, are sensed, not perceived. The awareness in the case exemplifies sensing and the appropriate proposition. In such cases, both terms of the meaning nexus are phenomenal objects, one primary, one mental.

Now remember the formula of the realism pattern: Perceptual things exist. I explicate this philosophical use of 'exist' so that it asserts those four features and nothing else. That makes the formula commonsensical, true, and anything but truistic. If some feel that it also makes me a realist, I shall not argue with them about the label, if only because I feel that none of the classical labels is worth arguing about.

What is the import of all this for the status of the particle? The classical particle is a kind of physical object. So I reword the question. What is the import of this phenomenologically chastened realism for

---

[13] This part of my analysis has a certain similarity with the Aristotelian-Thomistic solution. The second feature preserves what is sound in the Kantian notion of the transcendental unity of apperception. The third feature is the heart of the matter. The fourth provides, as it were, a phenomenal model of perception. That makes it structurally, if perhaps not genetically, the deepest root of the idea of an external world. The deepest root of the classical phenomenalists' failure is that they either ignored or misconstrued the mental things or even denied that they exist.

the status of physical objects? The gist of the answer is that it frees the philosophy of physics from the wrong kind of metaphysical pressure. If that is true, it is also important. So I must unpack it.

The distinction between perceptual and physical objects is beginning to pay off. So I shall venture another. According to the phenomenalist, a perceptual thing is literally a congeries of phenomenal ones. That is often expressed, very aptly I think, by saying that upon this view all nonphenomenal things are *constructions*. A construction, in this sense, replaces an entity which does not exist by one which does (or by a congeries of such). That sounds and is paradoxical, since one can of course not *re*place what is not there. The paradox sets off the distinction I am about to make. Without paradox science replaces perceptual things, which do exist, by certain others, namely, physical things, which latter in the very nature of the case we cannot know to exist in exactly the same sense of 'knowing' in which we do know that perceptual things exist. I express this as follows. Neither perceptual nor physical things are constructions. Rather, the latter are *reconstructions* of the former. The motive for reconstruction is of course scientific explanation; its only proper warranty, explanatory success. The new distinction is thus between construction and reconstruction. The former is ontologically problematic, the latter is not. That is its point. It takes the wrong kind of pressure off the philosophy of physics. Once this pressure is off, one can deal properly with those features of the particle which are peculiar to it and do need dialectical clarification. To this, my last task, I now turn. First, though, for two comments.

Several hundred years ago the perceptual object was so reconstructed that among other things it lost its colors. It is well to realize that the resulting physical object is as unintuitive as a classical atom or a modern light quant. The difference, if any, is at most a matter of degree. This is the first comment. Some may feel that what I say is obsolete since nowadays we actually "see" individual particles. The answer is that what we see (perceive) is not the particle but, say, a flicker on a screen. Or we hear a counter tick. Those who are not sensitive to the difference that makes simply lack the kind of sensitivity that makes philosophers. So I shall not argue with them, merely assure them that I am as convinced as they are that there are particles. That is the second comment.

Once more, does the particle exist? Once more, I do not take sides, merely exhibit the dialectic. In the case of the classical particle, the affirmative argument rests on two patterns. One we already know, the other I shall presently introduce.

The classical particle is in time and space and has orbits. Except for its size, it is in these fundamental respects like a macro-object of

classical physics (briefly: like a macro-object). Hence, by the concreteness pattern and its crucial orbit subpattern, the classical particle
exists.

The basic entities of the comprehensive process schema exist. This is
the *process pattern*. I could have called it the "deterministic" or the
"mechanistic" pattern. But the multiple ambiguity, including philosophical uses, of these two words is notorious. So I avoid them. A
schema (in physics) is comprehensive if and only if it explains all
(physical) facts. The claim of comprehensiveness is of course always a
matter of principle only, an expectation, or, if you do not object to the
phrase, a frame of reference. The flavor of 'schema' conveys some of
this idea. The notion of *process* is an abstraction from Newtonian point
mechanics. From a complete state description in conjunction with the
process law (which is part of the schema) such descriptions of all earlier
and later states can be deduced. *Basic*, finally, are those entities which
in an axiomatization of the schema correspond to its undefined nonlogical terms.[14]

Consider now the physics of, say, 1900. For macro-objects the limitation in some cases to statistical prediction was accepted. Atomistics,
however, served as a comprehensive process schema. The affirmative
side, those arguing for the existence of the classical particle, could therefore appeal to the process schema. The record shows that either implicitly or explicitly they did. But, of course, not all went smoothly for
long. It never does. So far, at least, every schema has had its crisis. The
one I allude to is the crisis of thermodynamics. It marked, as we now
understand, the transition to modern physics. Let us first look at the
negative side in the dialectic of the classical particle.

The entities of the model do not exist. This is the formula of the
model pattern. It underlies much that has been said on the negative
side. To understand it, one must understand this use of 'model'. To
understand this use, one must attend to a characteristic feature of all
particles, classical as well as modern. In describing the feature I shall
without further explanation speak of two languages and of translations
from one into the other. No harm will be done and much breath will
be saved.

---

[14] The strength of the process pattern shows itself in the classical dialectic of
the mind-body nexus. I have never really understood the alleged distinction
between epiphenomenalism and parallelism. All I can make out is this. The
bodily series, as it is called in these discussions, is part of a comprehensive process. The mental series neither is itself such a process nor can it plausibly be
thought of as part of one. The epiphenomenalist, *under the impact of the process
pattern*, expresses this difference by calling mind "merely" an epiphenomenon.
The parallelist shrinks from such verbal impiety.

The particles (micro-objects) must of course be "tied" to the (physical) macro-objects. (The latter are in turn "tied" to the perceptual objects. This, after what has been said, we may take for granted.) The macrolanguage mentions only macro-objects; the microlanguage, only micro-objects. The characteristic feature is that while every sentence of the macrolanguage is in principle translatable into the microlanguage, translations in the opposite direction are not available for all sentences but only for some. This state of affairs is very neatly described by saying that one may first develop the microlanguage as an uninterpreted calculus, then establish the required tie by "coordinating" some of its expressions to expressions of the macrolanguage. Hence the phrase: coordinating definitions.[15] Another phrase often used is: partial interpretation (of a calculus or model). That explains the relevant use of 'model'. The idea is this. As the vicissitudes of explanation require, one language which as such we do not understand, namely, that of the model, may be either attached to or detached from another permanent one, which we do understand, namely, that of the macro-objects. It is not hard to see how this idea may lead one to deny that the entities of the model exist. Hence the impact of the pattern. Yet, in classical physics it is easily challenged.

Natural and convenient as it is, the model way is not the only one of describing the situation. A classical particle is merely a macro-object reduced in size or scale. Such scale reduction is a purely arithmetical notion. Thus it is available to us as a part of the world's subsistent form. Hence particles (i.e., the predicate 'particle'; remember the bay horse!) can be defined as a kind of physical object.[16] Once the notion has thus become available, one can in the familiar fashion reconstruct the macro-object as a swarm or flock of micro-objects. In classical physics this alternative balances the arguments based on the model pattern. The modern particle, however, is not just a macro-object reduced in size. That of course affects the balance.

[15] As far as I know, the phrase is Reichenbach's. It will do no harm as long as one realizes that these "coordinations" are not really definitions. For a very thorough analysis of the several ways 'model' has been used by scientists and philosophers of science, see M. Brodbeck, "Models, Meaning, and Theories," in L. Gross (ed.), *Symposium on Sociological Theory* (Row, Peterson and Company, 1959), 373–406.

[16] For a more detailed statement of this point, see "The Logic of Psychological Concepts," *Philosophy of Science*, 18, 1951, 93–110. The reconstruction may in this case not unreasonably be called an *existential hypothesis*. I mention the phrase because it is being used by old-style realists, such as Feigl. The way they use it, it is ontologically problematic; the way I just used it, it is not. The difference is roughly that between construction and reconstruction.

Among the novel features of the modern particle two stand out. For one, it has in principle no orbit. That greatly weakens, if it does not altogether destroy, the usefulness of the concreteness pattern for those who want to argue that the particle exists. For another, the limitation to statistical prediction has, as it were, penetrated into the world of the particle. In classical physics the limitation applied only to some macro-situations. In modern physics all predictions about position and speed of the individual particle are in principle statistical. That deprives the arguments which draw upon the process pattern of their ground. But there is a twist here. The way the statistical predictions are achieved is most naturally and conveniently described in the model way. By means of very intricate translation rules a further calculus or model is attached to the properly modified atomic model. The advantage of this description is that it resolves all so-called paradoxes. The twist is that the second model, which is of course quantum mechanics, is again a process schema for which comprehensiveness may reasonably be claimed. Thus, by the process pattern, its basic entities would be what really exists. On the other hand, these entities have no longer even the remotest similarity with perceptual objects. That was and still is the source of much intellectual discomfort.[17] It almost seems that it takes a philosopher to appreciate that the difference in intuitiveness, or lack of such, between these entities and the colorless macro-objects of Descartes and Newton is at most a difference in degree.

I am ready to conclude. Do the problematic entities of physics exist? Starting from this classical question, I refused to take sides, exhibited instead eight major patterns that control its dialectic. Two of these, independence and realism, belong to philosophy proper. Yet the latter is needed to relieve the philosophy of physics of a burden only philosophy proper can bear. So is the distinction between perceptual and physical objects, together with the related one between construction and reconstruction. That leaves six patterns: concreteness (including orbits), acquaintance, simplicity, significance, process, and model. I have tried to sketch how each of these six may be used and I believe has been used, either explicitly or implicitly, in the controversy. A sketch cannot of course carry conviction in detail. I shall be very content if I have contributed to convincing you of something else, which is not at all a matter of detail, namely, that a philosopher of physics, unless he wants to become just another *Grundlagenforscher*, must not cut himself off from philosophy proper.

---

[17] For ample detail, see "The Logic of Quanta," which is reprinted in the Feigl-Brodbeck anthology. Also, in *The Philosophical Review*, 69, 1960, 267–270, the review of the recent symposium volume, *Observation and Interpretation*.

Ontological Alternatives*

IN A recent essay[1] Dr. Egidi, stating what she takes to be Frege's ontology, starts from and uses throughout as a foil what in another essay[2] I have said about Frege. She holds that Frege is an idealist, takes me to hold that he is a nominalist. As I use 'nominalism', Frege is not a nominalist. Nor did I ever say that he was one. I merely tried to show that there is in the very structure of his ontology a tendency toward nominalism. That makes the title of my essay, "Frege's Hidden Nominalism," suggestive rather than accurate. In spite of what Dr. Egidi says, I still believe that the nominalistic tendency is unmistakably there. Nor has she convinced me that Frege is an idealist. She has, however, shown very convincingly what I, for one, had not seen as clearly as she does, namely, that there is also an unmistakable structural tendency toward idealism in Frege's ontology. Thus, if I were asked to choose for her essay a title as suggestive and as exaggerated as mine, I would call it "Frege's Hidden Idealism."

Those who are merely clever sometimes discover tendencies which are not there. Those who discern hidden tendencies which are there think structurally and, sometimes, profoundly. In my judgment Dr. Egidi's essay is of a profundity that deserves high praise. Yet I also judge much of what she says to be radically mistaken. Because of these mistakes she makes an idealist out of Frege. Her mistakes reflect the idealistic ambience that has nourished her. So she should not be blamed

* This is the English original of "Alternative Ontologiche: Risposta alla Dottoressa Egidi," which appeared in Giornale Critico della Filosofia Italiana, 17, 1963. Printed by permission.

[1] "La Consistenza Filosofica della Logica di Frege," Giornale Critico della Filosofia Italiana, 16, 1962, 194–208. See also her "Matematica, logica e filosofia nell' opera di Gottlob Frege," Physis, 4, 1962, 5–32. The essays will be cited as CFLF and MLFF, respectively.

[2] "Frege's Hidden Nominalism," Philosophical Review, 67, 1958, 437–59. See also "Propositional Functions," Analysis, 17, 1956, 43–48.

for them too severely. Those who know how difficult metaphysics is also know that, since its core is dialectical, there is nothing paradoxical about judging an essay in metaphysics to be both profound and profoundly mistaken.

Dr. Egidi, I just said, makes an idealist out of Frege. This is not quite accurate and the inaccuracy is of a sort to which one as committed as she is to accurate intellectual biography might well object. Explicitly she merely claims that Frege's renovation of logic and, inseparably from it, his analysis of the simple clause '*a* is *F*' is implicitly idealistic, i.e., that it fits with or perhaps even suggests an idealistic ontology, just as in her opinion Aristotle's logic and philosophical grammar fit only with the realistic ontology he actually propounds. If you wish, replace "fits and perhaps even suggests" by "inspires and perhaps even is inspired by." The idea is clear. I express it by calling a claim of this sort structural. Structurally, Dr. Egidi claims, the philosophical grammar of the *Begriffsschrift* is idealistic.

My own concern is exclusively structural. That determines what I shall say as well as the order in which I shall say it. In Section One I shall state and unravel the relevant part of the fundamental ontological dialectic. Section Two is about Frege. In Section Three some of Dr. Egidi's arguments will be examined. In Section One, which must be most succinct, the main issues will be stressed at the expense of all the details which may be found elsewhere.[3] Since in Section Two it will be taken for granted that Frege's ontology is realistic, I refer to a recent essay by Reinhardt Grossmann[4] in which this appraisal, which as it happens is also the traditional one, has been freshly examined and impressively documented, structurally as well as biographically.

I

Mind is One; the world is Many. This is but an aphorism. Aphorisms must be unpacked. Yet they remain suggestive even after they have been unpacked. Also, they allow us to express our sense of debt to and continuity with the tradition. That is why I shall try to expose the deepest roots of the idealism-realism issue by unpacking this particular aphorism. Nor, since they are so deep, are they the roots of just this one issue. But I shall focus on it.

To exist or to be an *entity* is one and the same. Your or my now or at some other time perceiving or remembering or imagining that Peter is blond is called an *act*. Peter's being blond is the single *intention* of

[3] See in particular the first four essays of this book.

[4] "Frege's Ontology," *Philosophical Review*, 70, 1961, 23–40; see also his "Conceptualism," *Review of Metaphysics*, 14, 1960, 243–54.

these several acts. Acts are *mental* entities. Peter's being blond is a *nonmental* entity. The intentions of some acts are mental; those of some others, nonmental. Restating these bits of common sense shows how, commonsensically, 'entity', 'act', 'intention', 'mental' and 'nonmental' will be used. Idealism holds that all entities are mental; materialism, that they are all nonmental. Only realism$_2$ sides with common sense, asserts that (1) some entities are mental, some nonmental. Materialism we may safely dismiss as absurd. (1) by itself is an empty husk. Realists$_2$[5] also must assert and justify that (2) minds can know what is nonmental. To justify (2) is to present and to defend against all dialectical attacks an ontological assay of acts and their intentions that fulfills two conditions. (a) When I believe what is false, the act is there, its intention is not. The assay must account for such acts. (b) The assay must provide a "connection" between an act and its intention which is so "close" that it justifies (2), irrespective of whether the intention is (α) mental or (β) nonmental. (α) leads to the dialectic of the Cartesian *Cogito;* (β), to that of (2). An example will help. According to the Aristotelian-Thomistic account of perception, when I perceive a tree, two substances, mine and the tree's, exemplify one universal. Clearly, this "connection" is sufficiently "close." The dialectical difficulties of (a) and (b) are notorious. So I need not and shall not here consider them except as they impinge upon that particular piece of the dialectic I propose to unravel.

(What has been said in the last paragraph suffices to unpack the aphorism that *epistemology is merely the ontology of the knowing situation.* This use of 'knowing' is of course generic, comprehending the several *species* of perceiving, remembering, believing, imagining, doubting, entertaining, and so on. Henceforth 'species' will be used only for these kinds of "knowing.")

Yesterday I perceived that Peter is blond. The act that would have occurred if instead of perceiving this fact I had remembered it is different from the one that actually occurred. This no philosopher has ever questioned. That shows that they all take two things for granted, namely, first, that an act and its species are both mental entities, and, second, that the latter is a constituent of the former. If instead of perceiving that Peter is blond I had perceived that Mary is tall, is the act that would have occurred different from the one that actually occurred? Their intentions are different, but they are both nonmental.

---

[5] The meaning of 'realism' in 'realism-nominalism' is radically different from that in 'realism-idealism'. The first dichotomy, being one of general ontology, lies deeper than the second. The choice of subscripts reflects this difference.

Prima facie that provides an ontological alternative. One may hold that the "two" acts are one and not two. Or one may hold that each act has a constituent such that in two acts this constituent is the same if and only if they have the same intention. Call a constituent of this sort a *thought*. As one ordinarily speaks, 'thought' is used in two ways. Once the word stands for the act itself; once for a constituent of it which varies with its intention. That makes our use of 'thought' in this essay technical, although only in the very limited sense that we shall employ the word in only one of the two ways in which we employ it when speaking as we ordinarily do. (Some philosophers use 'thought', technically, as I use 'intention'. The dangers and inconveniences of this use are obvious.) Thoughts, as we use the word, are constituents of acts. Hence, *if* there are thoughts, they are mental entities. If there are none, then what I am about to assert of them holds of acts, i.e., of those mental entities which, speaking as we ordinarily do, we sometimes also call thoughts. That is why I need not as yet commit myself as to whether or not there are thoughts.

An ontology is an inventory of what exists (is there). In his own peculiar way and for his own peculiar purposes, an ontologist, therefore, describes the world. His description is inadequate unless it accounts by what is for what is (phenomenologically) presented to us. I shall next call attention to two striking features of what is so presented. *No* ontology, therefore, is adequate unless it accounts for both of them. That is why I shall not make any specific ontological commitment until these two features have been stated and the dialectics which because of them *every* ontology must face has been exhibited.

Call a thought unitary if and only if it has no constituent which is itself a thought. All thoughts are unitary. This is one of the two striking features. Call it the *unity of thought*. Replace 'unity' by 'One', 'thought' by 'mind' and you will see that the first half of the aphorism is already unpacked.

Some hold that awareness is propositional, i.e., that there are no thoughts whose intentions are not represented by sentences. If so, then all thoughts whose intentions are represented by simple clauses are unitary. Take the thought whose intention is represented by 'Peter is blond'. The only thoughts that could be constituents of it are those of Peter, of is, and of blond. If awareness is propositional then there are no such thoughts and the unity thesis asserts something new or further only for those thoughts whose intentions are represented by compound sentences. As it happens, though, the arguments for such thoughts being unitary are the same as those for all thoughts being unitary. Thus, once more, we need not commit ourselves.

If the unity of thought is a striking (phenomenological) feature, what need is there for arguments to support it, what point in arguing against it? The question is reasonable indeed. The reasonable answer is that the arguments in support merely clear up the misunderstandings which have been caused by the (phenomenologically) inaccurate way in which many philosophers and psychologists have described what is called introspection or introspective analysis. Introspection presumably "decomposes" thoughts into their constituents. What actually occurs when one introspects a thought is a series of further thoughts that fulfills certain conditions. Two such conditions are, first, that the intention of each member of the series is a constituent of the intention of the thought that is being "decomposed," and, second, that the intentions of all members of the series are all the constituents of the intention of that thought. A thought's being unitary (a) and its intention having no constituents (b) are two propositions and not one. The invalid inference from (a) to (b) is one of the pivots of the traditional dialectic. Of that more presently. The invalid inference from the negation of (b) to the negation of (a) is the main source of the misunderstandings that may weaken one's grasp of the unity of thought. The premiss as well as the alleged conclusion of an invalid inference may be either true or false. (a) is true. How about (b)? One's answer depends on his grasp of the second feature.

Unless some intentions were mental, we could not know that there are minds, just as we could not know that there are nonmental entities unless some intentions were nonmental. The difference between the mental and the nonmental is itself (phenomenologically) presented to us. Call the part of the world which is nonmental the truncated world. The idealists claim that the truncated world does not exist. The second feature strikes us most forcefully in nonmental intentions. As to whether it is also a feature of minds we need not as yet commit ourselves. I shall therefore call attention to it by attending to some nonmental entities *as they are (phenomenologically) presented to us.* And I shall save words by omitting the italicized phrase. That the omission does not prejudge anything will soon be clear beyond doubt.

Take a spot which is red and round. The spot is an entity; its shape (round) and its color (red) are two others. The latter (red, round) are *constituents* of, or as I shall also say, they are "in" the former (the spot). An entity which has constituents is *complex* or a complex. If you challenge any of this, I answer that the example shows how in ontology I use 'constituent' and 'complex' and that therefore there is nothing to be challenged.

Take two spots; one red and round, the other green and square. Red and round are "tied" together. So are green and square. Red and square are not. Nor are green and round. That is why there are two spots and not four and why these two are what they are. That shows two things. *First.* There is a sort of entities which are constituents of others and yet so "independent" that a complex is more than, as one says, the sum or class of them. Entities of this sort I here call *things.* This is of course a very special use of the word. *Second.* The something more, the "tie" which makes a complex out of the class, must have an ontological ground. Everything except sameness and diversity must have an ontological ground. One who does not understand that does not understand the task and nature of ontology. The entity or entities which are the ground of the "tie" I call *subsistents.*

In the *truncated* world *as it is (phenomenologically) presented to us* there are many things. This is the second striking feature. If it were not for the italicized word and the italicized phrase, we would already have unpacked the second half of the aphorism: The world is Many. It will be better if before finishing this job I interrupt for four comments which, although they are badly in need of expansion, may yet help to avoid puzzlement.

1. Not all subsistents are "ties," but they are all "dependent" in the sense in which things are "independent." Since the distinction corresponds to the traditional one between *categorematic* and *syncategorematic,* I shall also use these two words even though the traditional distinction is among words rather than, like mine, among the entities which I hold these words represent. That is not to say that there are two (or more) modes of exist*ing.* 'Exist' is univocal indeed. Otherwise I, for one, do not know what it means to exist. But there are several kinds of exist*ents* and the differences among the highest kinds or *modes* are very great indeed. Categorematic and syncategorematic are two modes.

2. A thing that has no constituent which is a thing (except, as the mathematicians speak, trivially itself) is called *simple* or a simple. What has been said so far does not at all depend on whether or not there are simples. Among subsistents the distinction simple-complex does not even make sense. Nor do syncategorematic entities need further ones to connect them with the categorematic entities they connect. (Thus Bradley's paradox is avoided.)

3. Complexes are constituents of other complexes. They are also "independent" in the sense in which I just used this ambiguous word. As I proposed to use 'thing', that makes complexes things, which is rather awkward, since the most interesting complexes are of the kind one would rather call facts, in ontology as well as when speaking as we

ordinarily do. The cause of the awkwardness is that any classification of complexes, e.g., in "facts" and "complex things," requires some of those specific ontological commitments which I as yet wish to avoid. In an ontology that admits simples, for instance, one could reserve 'thing' for simples and divide all "independent" entities into two kinds, things and complexes.

4. Minds are in the world, of course. Are they, too, Many? Less aphoristically, are acts complex? I have not as yet committed myself. But we understand already why, *if* acts are complex, this feature imposes itself less forcefully in their case. Thoughts are unitary, i.e., they have no constituents which are thoughts. That is not the same as being things and being simple. Yet the ideas are close. Nor is there any doubt that even if its thought is merely one among the constituents of an act, it imposes itself so forcefully that the others are easily overlooked.

The task of ontology is to account for what is (phenomenologically) presented to us. If one holds that awareness is propositional, he must also hold that all (nonmental) intentions are complexes. Everyone agrees that some are. Every ontologist must account for this manifold (complexity). The realist$_2$ accounts for it by a corresponding manifold in the truncated world of which, unlike the idealist, he claims that it exists. At least, that is for him structurally the obvious way to account for the second striking feature. Nor do I know of any articulate realistic$_2$ ontologist who has found another way. That fully unpacks the second half of the aphorism. The world is Many.

The basic dialectic that controls the realism-idealism issue has *three centers*. The interactions among these centers determine the ontological alternatives which are or seem available to us.

Most ontologies, whether realistic$_2$ or idealistic, recognize that there are things, be they mental or nonmental or either. Very few recognize the ontological status of the subsistents, i.e., they do not recognize that the syncategorematic *terms* represent *entities*. The only two recent exceptions from this almost universal neglect are Frege and the early Husserl, i.e., the author of the *Logische Untersuchungen*. That is indeed one very major reason for my admiration of these two thinkers. Characteristically they are both realists$_2$. Ontologies which do not recognize the syncategorematic entities I call *reistic*. For an ontology to be realistic$_2$ is one thing; to be reistic is quite another thing. A reistic ontology, we know, cannot be adequate. It cannot even account for the truncated world. This impossibility is the *first center*. The unity of thought must be adequately accounted for. That task is the *second center*. To spot the third, remember the old idea of adequation, *ade-*

quatio rei et intellectus. If mind (thought) is One and the (truncated) world is Many, how can a unitary thought be adequate to a complex intention? This difficulty, or apparent difficulty, of reconciling the One and the Many in the knowledge situation is the *third center*.

A realistic₂ ontology cannot be adequate unless it fulfills three conditions. It must not be reistic. It must account for the unity of thought. It must resolve the difficulty of adequation. Or, to hark back to what has been said earlier, the realist₂ must show that in his world the "connection" between a unitary thought and the complex it intends is so "close" that he can defend against all dialectical attacks the proposition which he must hold lest his realism₂ remain an empty husk, namely, that minds may know what is nonmental. That unpacks and thereby gets rid of that old phrase, *adequatio rei et intellectus.* (Let me point out, in parenthesis, since at this point I neither need nor wish to make any specific ontological commitment, that as far as the third center is concerned it makes no dialectical difference whether the complex intention is mental or nonmental. That is why I am convinced that the crucial task is an adequate ontological assay of the act and that the realism-idealism issue *as such* is rather shallow, or, at least, that it does not lie as deep as it was thought to lie during the last three hundred years or so, ever since the structural drift toward idealism which has still to be stopped got its start for reasons that will be touched briefly at the very end of this essay.)

Let us look at the alternatives open to one who does not know how to meet all three conditions. An ontology which is reistic as, alas, almost all are, cannot even adequately account for the truncated world. This inadequacy and its source need not be clearly seen in order to be more or less strongly felt as a difficulty. Its source, we know, is the second feature, which, as we also know, imposes itself more forcefully in the truncated world. That shows how one may be tempted to choose the idealistic alternative.

If one shrinks away from the absurdity of idealism he still has two alternatives left. He may relieve the pressure from the third center by opting for materialism. If one also shrinks away from the absurdity of materialism he has only one alternative left. He may relieve the pressure from the second center by doing violence to the feature that is its source, making thought complex. That also removes the pressure from the third center (adequation). Thus, if he remains insensitive to the subtler pressure from the first center (inadequacy of all reistic ontologies), he may be content. This is the choice or, at least, it is the tendency as well as the basic weakness of the British succession from Locke to Russell. In Locke and Berkeley it remains a tendency; they at least still recognize the act. Hume makes the choice. For him, all mental entities are mosaics of sense data. Literally, the phenomenalism which so frequently also appears in this succession is of course a kind of idealism. Structurally, though, as well as in flavor, it is more often than not materialistic. Russell oscillated between these two equally unattractive alternatives, phenomenalism and materialism, all through his career.[6]

I am ready to state my own ontological commitments and to show that they meet the three conditions every adequate realistic$_2$ ontology must meet. But it will be better if first I say what in ontology I mean (and what I believe most philosophers have meant) by 'universal' and 'individual', and, also, how I use the two labels 'realism$_1$' and 'nominalism'.

Take two spots of exactly the same color, say, red. An ontologist may account for their both being red by a single entity which is "in" both of them. Such an entity is a *universal*. Ontologists who hold that there are universals may differ in what they hold about them.

Assume that two spots agree exactly not only in color but in all (nonrelational) properties. (I ignore in this essay relational universals as well as those of higher types. Relations, however, are not "in" any of the several entities they relate.) Every ontology must solve the problem of individuation, i.e., in the example, it must account for there being two spots and not just one. One way of solving the problem is by two entities, one "in" each spot. Such an entity is an *individual*. All ontologists who accept individuals make them *things*, not subsistents. There is also always more or less clearly the idea that an individual is a *simple*. I say more or less clearly because the conflict between this idea and some others which philosophers also have had about individuals is notorious.

(The expressions referring to) individuals cannot be predicated of anything. All ontologies recognize this obvious difference between individuals and universals. Some ontologists introduce another. Universals,

---

[6] The concern here is only with intellectual *reasons*, not with personal or cultural *motives*. *Of course* there are such motives. They may and often do affect the choice. For *many* they are indeed its only determiners. The absurd doctrine that these motives are the only determiners, or the only important or perhaps even the only valid ones for *all* is not, alas, limited to Italy, but I notice of late a certain recrudescence of that doctrine in the neo-Croceans of both extremes. If these gentlemen were right, then there wouldn't be any history of philosophy for them to write about. Nor, if it were not for the *few* who are sensitive to dialectical pressures, would there be alternatives for the many to choose from according to those motives. One need not reject what makes sense in either Marx or Croce to avoid such intemperate extremes.

they hold, differ qualitatively; individuals are merely numerically different. In the Anglo-Saxon tradition such individuals are called *bare particulars*. Ontologists who accept bare particulars implicitly recognize that sameness and diversity are primary, i.e., that they and they alone need no ontological ground. An ontologist who explicitly recognizes that faces squarely the striking feature Aristotle first faced when he introduced his notion of matter. The difficulties of that notion are notorious. Yet, every adequate ontology must come to terms with the feature.

Bare particulars are one extreme, individual substances are the other. In most classical ontologies, particularly those of the Aristotelian-Thomistic variety, individuals are substances. Substances and universals are both things, i.e., they are both "independent" (as I used this ambiguous word), but there is nevertheless an ontological difference between them which (in another sense of the word) makes the former "more independent" than the latter. Clearly that depresses the ontological status of universals as compared with individuals.

Few ontologists have completely ignored the problem of accounting for "sameness in diversity" in such cases as that of the two spots of exactly the same color. Quite a few, though, took the problem rather lightly. Perhaps they were too concerned with epistemology, not enough concerned with ontology. Some of these tell psychological stories which may or may not be more or less true but are completely irrelevant to the ontological problem. To call only such patently inadequate assays nominalistic seems to me a waste of a good word. I rather speak in such cases of dead-end nominalism.

I call an ontology *realistic₁* if and only if its individuals and its universals are both things and there are only two fundamental ontological differences between them; one, the obvious one; the other, that individuals are only numerically different (bare).[7] To call all other ontologies *nominalistic* may seem and, as things now stand, probably is idiosyncratic. But it is anything but idiosyncratic to insist, as I do, that any ontology which depresses the ontological status of universals as compared with individuals is *nominalistic in tendency*. Every one familiar with the *structural* history of the dialectic will appreciate that. In ontologies which make universals syncategorematic entities the nominalistic tendency is as pronounced as it can be, stops just one step short of the dead end.

---

[7] There is the *prima facie* possibility of realistic₁ ontologies in which the only difference is the obvious one. But they encounter structural difficulties that lead quickly to catastrophe.

In my world there are individuals and universals (characters). All individuals are simple and bare. A character is either simple or complex. In all other respects, except for the obvious difference, individuals and characters are alike. That makes me a realist$_1$. In my world there are also subsistents. Not being reistic, my ontology fulfills the second of the three conditions every adequate realistic$_2$ ontology must fulfill. Its fundamental tie is *exemplification*. In 'Peter is blond' it is represented by 'is'. Peter's being blond is a complex of the kind called a *fact*. (The other kind are the complex characters. Their ontological status, though, is merely derivative. Thus we can safely ignore them in this essay.) "In" the fact represented by 'Peter is blond and Mary is tall' there are two others, Peter's being blond and Mary's being tall, as well as the subsistent, represented by 'and', which ties them together. And so on. The idea is clear, I trust. My world is not "atomistic"; it is not just a class or collection of disjoined entities. Rather, it is *completely structured*.

(A *Begriffsschrift* or ideal schema (language) reveals the explicit or implicit ontology of its author. Although I shall presently introduce a few abbreviations, I shall not in this essay use a schema of my own. But it will help to bring out an important point if we consider what in such a schema the transcription of 'This spot is red and round' would be. If 'a', 'red', and 'round' are made to represent the individual and the two characters "in" the spot, respectively, then the transcription reads 'a is red and a is round'. Thus it looks very much like the sentence which it transcribes even though 'a' does not represent the spot but, rather, the individual "in" it. The spot itself, in this world, is the fact represented by the sentence! That is the point which the schema helps to bring out.)

In my world acts are very similar to spots. Take a case of my perceiving the fact P, namely, that Peter is blond. In my world there are thoughts, e.g., the-thought-that-Peter-is-blond ($\ulcorner P \urcorner$). An act is an individual exemplifying two simple characters; one is a species (perceiving, believing, remembering, and so on); the other is the thought "in" the act. The act in question, for instance, is the fact which (in my schema) is represented by 'b is perceiving and b is $\ulcorner P \urcorner$', with b representing the individual "in" it.[8] Such (mental) individuals I call aware-

---

[8] 'b is perceiving' is not very idiomatic. We would rather say 'b is a perceiving' and 'b is a thought-that-Peter-is-blond', just as we say 'Peter is a man' rather than 'Peter is man' even though we also say 'Peter is blond'. If perceiving, the-thought-that-P, man, and blond are four characters, as in my world they are, then such idiomatic strain or awkwardness is irrelevant. Nor could a schema be what it is supposed to be if it conformed in *all* contexts to the idioms of this or that language.

nesses. $\ulcorner P \urcorner$ is simple. *All thoughts are simple characters.* Thus I account for the unity of thought, meet the first condition every adequate realistic ontology must meet. Notice, too, that since thoughts are universals, you and I may literally have the same thought although a thought is a mental entity and although of the two individuals which exemplify it when you and I both have it one is in my mind and one is in yours.[9]

In my world there is a subsistent, M, such that $\ulcorner P \urcorner MP$ is a formal fact. 'M' transcribes the word 'means' as we sometimes use it in such sentences as 'the-thought-that-Peter-is-blond means (intends, is about) Peter is blond'. A fact is formal or a fact of (in) the world's form if and only if the sentence representing it is analytic.[10] Through the thoughts "in" them, acts are by the subsistent I call M "connected" with their intentions. That immediately raises three questions.

First. Is the "connection" sufficiently "close" to fulfill the third of the three conditions? One only has to consider such complex facts as P-and-Q and P-or-Q in order to realize that some subsistents establish connections which are very loose indeed. (If they were closer, fewer ontologies would be reistic.) Thus the question is very reasonable. All I can say here is that the required closeness is accounted for by $\ulcorner P \urcorner MP$ being a fact in the world's form.

Second. The-thought-that-Caesar-was-murdered and the-thought-that-Calpurnia's-husband-was-murdered are two, not one. Yet they *seem* to mean (M) the "same" fact. Can two thoughts mean a single fact? The affirmative answer bogs down in difficulties which are insuperable. This is the logical problem of intentionality; or, rather, it is the logical aspect of the problem of intentionality.[11] Since it can be kept out, I shall keep it out of this essay, merely drop a hint that will come

---

[9] Frege tried very hard to account for this piece of "realistic" common sense. That is indeed a major intellectual motive for his inventing those nonmental entities he calls senses (*Sinn*) and which therefore, revealingly even though most misleadingly, he also calls thoughts.

[10] This is merely a convenient hint. Lest it be misleading, I add that the basic idea (the world's form) is ontological, not logical (analyticity). A world's form is what it is because its subsistents are what they are. Our notion of analyticity is grounded in the form of the only world we know.

[11] It is a measure of Frege's greatness that he was (as far as I know) not only the first who clearly saw the logical problem of intentionality but that he also realized its ontological import. That provided *another* major intellectual motive for his eventually hypostatizing senses (thoughts) as nonmental entities. That he missed the solution, in spite of this hypostatization and even though he recognized that some subsistents exist, is a measure of his failure. His fear was that he would have to give up all definitions. How typically a mathematician's fear! See also *Meaning and Existence*, p. 217, and the crucial passage from "Begriff

in handy soon. The key to the solution is the recognition that the subsistents exist. For, if they exist, then two facts (complexes) are literally the same, i.e., one and not two if and only if (1) the simples in them are the "same" and (2) these simples are "tied" to each other in the same way. Upon this strict use of 'same', P and Q may therefore be two facts and not literally one even if P-if-and-only-if-Q is a fact in the world's form (i.e., if 'P if and only if Q' is analytic).

Third. What if P does not exist? More precisely, how can $\ulcorner P \urcorner$ MP be a fact if there is no fact for $\ulcorner P \urcorner$ to intend?[12] Once more, the answer depends on M being a subsistent. For P-or-Q to be a fact it suffices that either P exists or Q exists. This could not be so if or were not a subsistent but a relational universal, such as, say, being to the left of, which is a thing. This book being to the left of something else, for instance, is a fact only if that something else exists. Not so, we just saw, for or. As for or, so for M. (In my world a fact that isn't there yet exists, though only in the *mode of possibility*, which is of course the lowest ontological status of all. I call such "nonexistent" facts p-facts.[12] Nor is that an *ad hoc* construction. But I cannot here pursue this matter.)

Succinct as it is, almost desperately so, this sketch of an ontology will do as a foil for what must be said about Frege before I can intelligently attend to what Dr. Egidi says about him, except that the sketch could not even serve this purpose without some indications as to the ontological assays of judgment and of truth which it implies.

A judgment is an act. It will keep out issues that can be kept out of this essay without prejudging anything that will have to be said if we take it for granted that the species "in" an act of judgment is believing. That makes for a threefold distinction:

$$(\alpha) \qquad P \qquad\qquad \ulcorner P \urcorner \qquad\qquad\qquad G(P).$$

P is the fact intended. $\ulcorner P \urcorner$ is the thought "in" the judgment. $G(P)$ is the judgment itself. P is never a constituent of $G(P)$. If P is nonmental, which is the only case we need consider, that is obvious. $\ulcorner P \urcorner$ is merely one constituent of $G(P)$. The other two are the species believing and the awareness which "individuates" the act, e.g., my judgment now that P, yours tomorrow, mine yesterday. 'Truth', or, rather, 'true' has

---

und Gegenstand" which is there quoted (p. 46 of the Black-Geach translation). Structurally the deepest root of this failure is that in his world there are no facts (complexes). See below.

[12] P obviously exists or doesn't exist depending on whether the sentence 'P' is true or false. It is by now equally obvious, I trust, why at this point I avoid 'true' and 'false'. The root of all matters philosophical, including logic, is ontology.

(at least) four uses; one is primary; the second derives from the first; the third from the second; the fourth from the third.

In the *primary* use, 'true' and 'false' are predicated of thoughts, which are characters. A character is true if and only if there is an entity such that the character means (M) it and it is a fact. A character is false if and only if there is an entity such that the character means it and its negation[13] is a fact. This assay has two consequences. First. *True and false, as represented by the primary use of 'true' and 'false', are subsistents.* More specifically, they are subsistents of the kind some call defined logical characters.[14] Other entities of this kind are the integers, integer itself, transitivity, reflexivity, and so on. *Subsistents are neither mental nor nonmental.* Second. (1) $^\lceil P^\rceil$ being true and (2) P itself are two facts, not one. That is again obvious, if only because (1) does while (2) does not contain the constituent $^\lceil P^\rceil$. Nor is it a source of difficulties that the sentence '$^\lceil P^\rceil$ is true if and only if P' is analytic. Just remember the hint of which it was said a moment ago that it would come in handy soon.

In their *secondary* use, 'true' and 'false' are predicated of judgments. A judgment is true (false) if and only if the thought "in" it is true (false).

An assertion is a kind of linguistic gesture. Typically, it involves the utterance of a sentence. Typically, it communicates a judgment of the one who makes the assertion. In their *tertiary* use, 'true' and 'false' are predicated of assertions. An assertion is true (false) if and only if the judgment it communicates is true (false).

The sentence involved in an assertion represents the fact the judgment communicated intends. What a sentence of a natural language represents depends on the context in which it is uttered. This is not so for the schemata called ideal languages. The fact represented by a sentence of an ideal language (*Begriffsschrift*) is completely determined by the sentence itself.[15] In their *fourth* use, 'true' and 'false' are predicated

[13] Negation being a subsistent, 'P' and 'not-P' both represent entities, one a fact, one a p-fact.

[14] 'Defined' suggests complexity. If one holds, as I do, that among subsistents the dichotomy simple-complex makes no sense, then the word is misleading. So, since characters are things, is 'character'.

[15] To realize the dependence of natural languages on context, consider (1) 'It is cold today' and (2) 'I am cold'. What (1) represents depends on when and where it is asserted; what (2) represents, on when and by whom it is asserted. The independence, in this sense, of schemata called ideal languages is one of the radical differences between them and natural languages. Because of this difference, those schemata could not even in principle be used for communication. Also, this difference unpacks part of the metaphor that an ideal language is, or purports to be, a picture of the world.

of the sentences of ideal languages. Such a sentence is true (false) if and only if what it represents is a fact (*p*-fact).

II

Some of the terms Frege chose are very awkward. Probably he sought for words to serve him as weapons in his life-long struggle against psychologism. For instance, he calls "thoughts" entities which he himself strenuously insists are nonmental and which one would therefore much rather call the (potential) intentions of thoughts (or of judgments, or of acts in general). Under the circumstances I shall continue to use my own words with the meanings I have given to them, make a special point of avoiding his use of 'thought'. It will be convenient, though, occasionally to replace 'mental-nonmental' by 'subjective-objective', which is the dichotomy he happened to prefer, probably because he felt that it stressed his opposition to psychologism.

Begriffsschrift appeared shortly before 1880, *Function und Begriff*, *Ueber Sinn und Bedeutung*, and *Ueber Begriff und Gegenstand* shortly after 1890. The three later essays present an explicit and rather detailed ontology of the objective (truncated) world. About minds as such they tell us nothing. They merely specify the objective entities which are the (potential) intentions of subjective acts. Nor does the earlier essay contain an ontology of mind. Yet it makes in §2 an important contribution to the ontology of judgment. To this contribution, as far as I know, none of Frege's later writings adds anything. Some even blur it. Perhaps that is why that early contribution has been somewhat neglected. It is a great merit of Dr. Egidi to have called attention to it. I shall next describe this partial ontology of judgment, then the eventual ontology of the objective world.

The heart of §2 is a distinction among three entities, represented by

$$(\beta) \qquad\qquad P, \qquad -P, \qquad \vdash P,$$

respectively. If you compare (β) with (α) above, you will be able to guess what I take to be the natural reading of the paragraph. $\vdash P$ is the judgment, the entity I call $G(P)$; $-P$ is the entity I call $\ulcorner P \urcorner$, i.e., the thought "in" the judgment; P is its intention, or, as Frege here calls it, its "content." A string of six comments will support this reading and prepare the ground for what follows.

1. Frege here says nothing about whether P is simple or complex. Nor does anything he says depend on that. This is not to deny, though, that in his eventual ontology (of the objective world) all (potential)

intentions are simple. 2. $-P$ is called a "complex of ideas" (F2).[16] That shows three things. (a) $-P$ is a mental entity. (b) Frege had not yet hypostatized thoughts into objective entities to serve as the intentions of judgments. (c) Verbally at least, he was still not completely free from the tradition that makes thoughts complex. 3. $-P$ is not the judgment itself but, rather, that constituent of it which also occurs in an act of merely entertaining P without either believing or disbelieving it. That shows that $-P$ is $\ulcorner P \urcorner$. 4. Of the horizontal stroke in $-P$ it is said that it "combines the symbols following into a whole" (F2). Literally that does not make sense. For one, the symbols of a well-formed sentence are a whole. Thus the stroke would be redundant. For another, this whole is a nonmental entity. The only way of making sense out of the passage is to read it, with Dr. Egidi, as an assertion of the unity of thought. So read, it far outweighs the evidence to the contrary from 2(c). Or so at least it seems to me. One must not forget after all how very difficult it was in 1879 to speak about these things accurately. Nor is it very easy today. 5. Even though Frege insists that $-P$ is not the whole of $\vdash P$, he does not tell us what else there is "in" $\vdash P$. *At this place he leaves a blank. Eventually the blank will become a blur.* 6. P and $-P$ are two entities, not one. Nor is there anything to indicate that P is "in"—P. That shows that *the contribution is realistic₂*, or, at least, that it is compatible with realism₂.

In the eventual ontology (of the objective world) each entity is of one of two kinds. It is either a *Gegenstand* or a *Function*. The former are "independent" in exactly the same sense in which (in my world) things are. That makes them *things*. Frege's notion of function is mathematical. A function projects or maps one thing (or an ordered pair of things, etc.) on another thing. That makes a function "dependent" on the things mapped and mapped upon in exactly the same sense in which (in my world) the subsistents called ties are "dependent" on the things (and facts) they tie into complexes. Nor does a function need a further tie to tie it to what it maps and maps upon. That makes functions *syncategorematic entities*.

Things are of three kinds. The only members of the *first kind* are the two truth values, the thing True (T) and the thing False (F). The things of the *second kind* are all "senses," e.g., the sense-*that*-Peter-is-blond, the sense-*of*-Caesar, the sense-*of*-Calpurnia's-husband. Judgment is propositional, of course. Hence, only the senses whose names contain 'that' are the (potential) intentions of judgments. But Frege is

---

[16] "F2" refers to page 2 of the Black-Geach translation. But I have the German text of *Begriffsschrift* before me. 'Complex of ideas' stands for '*Ideenverbindung*'.

not (as far as I know) committed to the view (which happens to be mine) that all awareness is propositional. Thus the senses whose names contain 'of' could be and probably are in his world the (potential) intentions of other acts, e.g., of perception. *All possible senses exist.*[17] The things of the *third kind* are either ordinary "things" such as Peter or Mary or a colored spot; or they are integers, classes, and so on. For our purposes it will be safe to ignore all but the "ordinary" members of this kind. (The quotation marks around 'thing' are a reminder that in my world a colored spot is a fact, just as numbers are subsistents of the kind some call defined logical characters.)

Functions are of two kinds. One is exemplified by blond, tall, and so on.[18] Frege calls them concepts (*Begriffe*), but we can do without this word. The other kind is exemplified by the connectives, i.e., by the entities represented by 'and', 'or', 'if-then', and so on. The connectives map (ordered pairs of) truth values on truth values. The other kind of function maps ordinary things (or ordered pairs of such, etc.) on truth values. Blond, for instance, maps the thing Peter on either the thing T or the thing F depending on whether Peter is or is not blond.

Blond and tall being universals, this is the proper place for saying what little needs to be said about Frege's "hidden nominalism." Since his universals have ontological status in the objective world, he is not a dead-end nominalist. On the other hand, since his universals are functions and functions are "merely" subsistents (syncategorematic entities), his nominalistic tendency is as pronounced as it could be, stops just one step short of the dead end. A comment may add perspective. The ontological status of the connectives is very "weak," so weak indeed that the reists either overlooked it or quite explicitly insisted that they had none. Frege recognized that they have some. That is one of his glories. On the other hand, he depressed the ontological status of universals by lumping them with the connectives. That is one of his fatal errors.

Are Frege's things all simple or are some of them complex? We are not told; as far as I know, he ignores this fundamental dichotomy. Structurally, that is perhaps the most striking feature of his ontology. As far as I know, his is indeed the only articulate ontology of this kind.

[17] I.e., if the dots in 'sense-that- . . . ' are replaced by a well-formed sentence, the resulting expression is the name of a thing that exists. Similarly for 'sense-of- . . . '. 'Sense' stands of course for Frege's *'Sinn'*.

[18] Or, more accurately and in the spirit of the system, being-blond, being-tall. But I permit myself this simplification, just as I ignore, safely for the purposes of this essay, the problem of the appropriate ranges (domain and counterdomain) of functions, which is of such crucial importance in the foundations of arithmetic.

The only way, therefore, of arriving at an answer is to infer it from the structure of what we are told. Presently I shall propose an answer. *Frege's things are all simple.* First, though, I shall explain why the dichotomy is so fundamental that one cannot thoroughly discuss his ontology without answering the question.

Remember what was said earlier. The world is not just a class or collection of disjoined entities; it is completely structured. I say and mean the world as a whole. But we may once more focus on the objective world. To account for the world's structure is an obvious task or problem every adequate ontology must solve. Recognizing a task and tackling it in a certain way or style is one thing. The adequacy of a solution proposed is another thing. Consider a world (ontology) all whose things are simples and all whose complexes are facts. That merely brushes aside details. In such a world one may try to solve the task by making things (simples) constituents of facts (complexes) which are in turn constituents of other (more complex) facts. This is *a* style. As it happens, it is *the* style of virtually all articulate ontologies. The key to it is the dichotomy simple-complex. That shows why the dichotomy is so fundamental. This is one thing. That a reistic ontologist cannot in this style arrive at an adequate solution is another thing.

Let us check how the prevailing style works in my world. Assume for the sake of the argument that Peter and blond are simples. Consider Peter's being blond. Four entities are involved: (1) the simple thing (individual) Peter, (2) the simple thing (character) blond, (3) the subsistent called exemplification, (4) the fact of Peter's being blond. (4) is the complex which exists because (3) "connects" (1) and (2); thus making (1), (2), and (3) constituents of (4). The world of my ontology is completely structured.

There are two reasons for holding that Frege's things are all simple. One of them I am not yet ready to state. The other is as follows. Frege recognized the need for subsistents. That makes it more than plausible that he also recognized that there cannot be complexes unless there are some subsistent ties which make complexes out of simples. Yet none of his subsistents is a tie; they are all functions; and a function, rather than making a complex out of, say, two things, maps one of them upon the other.

I take it, then, that Frege's things are all simple. It does not follow that his (objective) world is completely unstructured. His functions do establish "connections." Not to recognize that is to miss the very point of their having ontological status. On the other hand, since functions do not make complexes, these "connections" are not, as I use the word, facts. *In Frege's world there are no facts.* It may help, though, if occasionally we speak and think of his "connections" as "facts." (This is a recognition of, as well as an attempt to overcome, the difficulty of speaking without distortion about a style radically different from one's own.)

In Frege's world Peter's being blond involves at least four entities; (1) the thing Peter; (2) the thing T; or, if Peter is not blond, the thing F, but the difference makes no difference for what we are about; (3) the function blond; (4) the thing sense-that-Peter-is-blond. (3) maps (1) on (2). That is the "fact" in the case, which itself is not an entity. (1) and (2) are nevertheless objectively "connected" by (3). There is, however, no objective "connection" whatsoever between (4) on the one hand and (1), (2), (3), on the other. That shows that *Frege's world is not completely structured.*

One may try to remedy the defect by bringing in two more things, namely, (5) the sense-of-Peter and (6) the sense-of-(being)-blond. (6) is the sense of a function. Are there in Frege's world such senses? Whatever expedients either he himself or his disciples may have resorted to, structurally, I believe, the answer is No. But we need not insist, may even for the sake of the argument assume that there are such senses. If so, then (4) will be "connected" with (1), (2), (3) if and only if the following two conditions (a) and (b) are fulfilled. (a) (5) and (6) are constituents of (4). (b) (5) and (6) are "connected" with (1) and (3), respectively. (a) makes (4) a complex. Hence, if all things are simple, the attempt at remedying the defect fails on this ground alone. But let us waive that argument, look at the first half of (b), i.e., at the two things Peter and sense-of-Peter. There is no objective "connection" whatsoever between them. To appreciate the gravity of the point, introduce two more things, Mary and the sense-of-Mary. There is no "connection" between any two of these four things. What, then, one must ask, is the objective "fact" that makes the sense-of-Peter the sense of Peter rather than that of Mary and conversely? I conclude that the things Frege calls *senses are totally disjoined from all other entities of his objective world.* Nor is that surprising. Senses, after all, are merely the (objective) hypostatizations of (subjective) thoughts.[19]

Assume next, for the sake of the argument, that there is an objective "connection" between (4) on the one hand and at least one of the entities (1), (2), (3) on the other. The only likely candidate is (2), the thing T. Assume, then, contrary to fact, that there is an objective

---

[19] The two major dialectical motives for this hypostatization are Frege's antipsychologism and his awareness of the logical problem of intentionality. See fns. 9 and 11.

"connection" between (4) and (2), i.e., between the sense-that-Peter-is-blond and T. If this were so, since (1), (2), (3) are "connected," (4) would over (2) also be connected with (1) and (3) and this world would in its own peculiar way be completely structured. To appreciate how peculiar that way would be, consider that, if Mary is tall, the "connection" among the three entities Peter, blond, and the sense-that-Peter-is-blond would be exactly the same as that between the three entities Peter, blond, and the sense-that-Mary-is-tall. One could argue that such a "connection" is worse than none. That shows the absurdity of hypostatizing the two subsistents true and false into the two things T and F.

Virtually all studies of Frege start from and are dominated by his *semantics*. I deliberately stated his ontology without any reference to his semantics. This is not to deny the crucial importance of the linguistic turn or even of ideal languages. Their importance, though, is methodological. Once one has either by this or by any other method enucleated an ontology, either his own or another's, he will be well advised to check his result by trying to state it without even mentioning words. Otherwise he will be in danger of mistaking for ontology what is merely semantics. In Frege's case, he may mistake for objective a "connection" which is merely semantical and therefore in the relevant sense subjective even though words as such and the ways we use them are of course "objective" facts of the world "as a whole." Or is it not obvious that an objective "connection" between objective things does not depend on whether or how we or any one else talks about them? What if there is no one at all to talk about them or, for that matter, about anything else? Isn't that just another bit of realistic₂ common sense?

In Frege's semantics 'Peter' and 'Peter is blond' are expressions of the kind he calls saturated. Every saturated expression has a double semantical tie, one to the thing called its sense (*Sinn*), one to the thing called its reference (*Bedeutung*). The sense and the reference of 'Peter' are the sense-of-Peter and Peter; those of 'Peter is blond' the sense-that-Peter-is-blond and the thing T, respectively. In this way the two things Peter and sense-of-Peter are linked semantically. So are the two things T and the sense-that-Peter-is-blond. Thus, if a semantical link were what of course it is not, namely, an objective "connection," Frege's objective world would be completely structured.

Words are objective (nonmental); judgments are subjective (mental). Yet the former are used to express the latter. There is a cue here. Following it, we shall discover that there is in Frege's world as a whole a mental "connection" between such nonmental things as, say, T and the sense-that-P even though in his objective world these two things remain totally disjoined.

Sinn und Bedeutung contains two crucial passages[20] (F65, F78) to the effect that *a judgment is the "advance" from a sense-that to "its" truth value.* I do not quote the passages only because I continue to use my own words. 'Advance' and 'its', though, are Frege's. They leave no doubt that the advance is held to provide a mental link between such nonmental things as, say, T and the sense-that-P. Thus, the "connection" established is at best subjective. Unfortunately, though, the very idea of this advance is irremediably confused. Frege himself was not wholly at ease. Otherwise he would not have warned (F65) against mistaking the italicized formula for a definition. The formula is nevertheless the heart of his irremediably confused eventual ontology of judgment. *The blank of the early contribution has become a blur.* I shall remove the blur by stating the only clear idea of an "advance" in this context.

Suppose that three acts occur successively in my mind. The species of the first is entertaining (without either believing or disbelieving); the species of the second is perceiving; that of the third, believing. The intention of all three is the same, P. The thought "in" all three is the same, $\ulcorner P \urcorner$. That is merely a schema of course, but it will serve. One starts by entertaining P; one ends by judging that P (believing that P). Or is there any other way of "advancing" toward a judgment? In the schema, the "advance" is from an entertaining through a perceiving to a believing; the thoughts and the intentions of the three acts happen to be the same. I say happen partly because not all "advances" are that simple; partly because I want to repeat that even if there were such objective things as the sense-that-P and T and even if these two things were the intentions of the first and the third act, respectively, the "connection" which the "advance" establishes between these two objective things would still be subjective. Nor, alas, is that all. T is a thing. Thus it could not in Frege's world be the intention of a judgment. That alone shows that the confusion is irremediable. Notice, too, that unless a judgment has actually occurred, there is no actual but at most a possible "connection."

Since some of its things are totally disjoined from all others, Frege's truncated world is not completely structured. If, however, one follows him in adding to the (nonmental) "connections" available in this world some

---

[20] Characteristically, they are also crucial for the problem, from which the whole essay is developed, of how, if 'a' and 'b' are both "names," '$a = a$' and '$a = b$' can differ in "cognitive value." See also below.

others which are mental and therefore not available at all unless there are minds, then, after a fashion at least, his truncated world becomes completely structured. (I say after a fashion because of the blur.) This is the diagnosis at which we have arrived. It suffices to identify the idealistic tendency in Frege's ontology. But it will be better if we postpone this job, turn first to some comments that will support and round out what has been said so far.

The early contribution to the ontology of judgment, although sound, was yet fragmentary. Eventually the blank became a blur. Can one so fill this blank that Frege's world as a whole becomes completely structured? Since he tells us but very little about minds as such, the question is rather moot. Yet the answer may, and I believe does, yield some dialectical insight. My answer has two parts. 1. As we just saw, one would have to make truth values intentions and admit merely possible "connections." Both emendations are antistructural. (This is but another way of saying that the confusion requiring them is irremediable.) 2. Remember the problem of false belief. Since the intentions of *some* acts do not exist, the "connection" between *any* act and its intention cannot be a relation. In my world the difficulty is solved by making it a subsistent (M). Frege has no difficulty. All possible senses exist. Thus one could fill the blank by making minds things which are "connected" with their intentions by relations. Or, to say the same thing in Frege's style, one could add to his world things which are minds and an appropriate class of binary functions. The modified Frege-world which is the result of this addition and of the counterstructural emendation is indeed completely structured. Yet it has three peculiar features. (a) Certain "connections" among objective things remain as subjective as before. (b) If I judge that P then, irrespectively of whether my belief is true or false, the believing-function maps my mind and the thing T on T. That makes it embarrassingly clear that the judgment as such is completely disjoined from the sense, even though one may have "advanced" to the former from entertaining the latter. 3. If acts are relational, then the mental entity the early Frege called $-P$ has no place in the system. Thus a further emendation is required. We must abandon a most valuable part of the early contribution.[21]

---

[21] All this is further evidence that senses are but hypostatized thoughts. But there is here a striking dialectical connection with representative realism in the style of, say, Locke, which has been pointed out to me by E. B. Allaire. In those ontologies a mind is "connected" to that wholly mythical entity called a percept by a relation which corresponds structurally to one of the binary functions I added to Frege's world. The only difference is that while all Fregean intentions are nonmental, percepts are meant to be mental entities. The more striking it is

In Frege's semantics all sentences and all definite descriptions are *names*. 'Peter is blond', for instance, is a name of T or F, depending on whether Peter is or is not blond. 'Calpurnia's husband' is another name of Caesar.[22] This is the second structural reason for holding that in Frege's ontology all things are simple. Since it is semantical and since, for a reason that has since been explained, I did not want to introduce Frege's semantics before having stated his ontology, I did not state this second reason when stating the first. Now I am ready.

Speaking as we ordinarily do, we use 'name' very broadly. In this century the philosophers who were most influenced by Frege used the word very technically. Their use, which is very narrow, carries more or less clearly three connotations. (1) A name represents a simple thing. (2) A name tells nothing about the entity it represents.[23] (3) In a well-constructed *Begriffsschrift* (ideal language) a name does not occur unless the entity it purports to represent exists. Had Frege himself always and clearly used 'name' with all these connotations, I would in view of (2) have made my point. I do not make so extreme a claim concerning Frege's use of the word. I merely claim that all these connotations are more or less clearly implicit in the way he uses it. Just remember how it puzzled him that '$a = b$', where 'a' and 'b' are names, can convey any information.[24] Nor is it just chance that in the post-Fregean debate these connotations became ever more clear and explicit.

In my world, you will remember, P and $\ulcorner P \urcorner$ being true are two facts, not one. In Frege's world there are no facts. Literally, therefore, he cannot either agree or disagree. But he comes as close to disagreeing as he can by asserting (F64) that the sense-that-P and the sense-that-P-is-true are one thing, not two. We ought to be able to understand how he came to assert that. Let us see.

In his world there is only one kind of "fact." Something maps some-

---

that in spite of this difference the two worlds suffer from the same structural weakness. Just as the representative realist cannot bridge the gap between the subjective percept and the objective entity of which it is the percept, so the "connection" between a sense and what it is the sense of remains even in the modified Fregean world subjective.

[22] According to Frege, a description that fails names the arithmetical thing Zero. In *Meaning and Necessity* Carnap, prone as always to mistake a mathematical construction for a philosophical idea, recently revived this infelicitous "stipulation."

[23] Except, by its shape, about the ontological kind (individual or character) to which it belongs. This, though, is another detail we may safely ignore.

[24] See fn. 20.

thing on something else. Blond mapping Peter on T is such a "fact." Call it α. 'P' does not really state α; it is merely a name of T. Let us express this by saying that 'P' corresponds to α. The sentence corresponding to $\ulcorner P \urcorner$ being true is '$P = T$', with '$=$' representing an identity function,[25] i.e., a binary function projecting two things on T if and only if the "two" are one. The identity function projecting P and T on T is a "fact." Call it β. Are α and β two or one? I am prepared to argue that by the logic of "facts" they are two. If you disagree I shall take your disagreement to show how very difficult it is to think and talk about a world without facts (not: "facts"!), particularly when one is committed to a schema whose sentences do not even state "facts" but are merely names of T or F. Fortunately we need not argue. For I also believe that Frege agreed with you, held α and β to be one. Thus, whether or not you agree with me that they are two, we can agree that he wanted to assert their being one. Moreover, it is obvious that he could not possibly assert that by asserting that 'P' and '$P = T$' both name T. For, that would imply that the two "facts" by virtue of which Peter is blond and Mary is tall also are one. So he asserts instead that the sense-that-P and the sense-that-P-is-true are one. That leads to two further observations.

First. If 'P' is false, then it is a name of F while '$P = F$' names T. Hence 'P' and '$P = F$' do not have the same sense. That shows that the symmetrical treatment of T and F is mere sham. Nor is that surprising, since T (but not F) does the job which in my world is done by exemplification and exemplification produces entities which are not merely in the mode of possibility.

Second. Consider the infinite series

$$(P = T), \qquad (P = T) = T, \qquad [(P = T) = T] = T, \ldots,$$

all of whose members are well-formed, compare it with the familiar classical regress

I know P,   I know that I know P,
I know that I know that I know $P, \ldots$;

notice that in my schema the mark for the subsistent true cannot be iterated without adding corners

$\ulcorner P$ is$\urcorner$ true, $\ulcorner\ulcorner P \urcorner$ is true$\urcorner$ is true, $\ulcorner\ulcorner\ulcorner P \urcorner$ is true$\urcorner$ is true$\urcorner$ is true, $\ldots$;

---

[25] In *Begriffsschrift* identity holds between names, which makes even identity subjective. Eventually Frege introduces an objective identity function. Grossmann argues convincingly that this change occurred at the approximate time of the three great essays.

and you will see that T also does the job of that mental character which I call the species "in" an act of judgment. Or are we to infer that only a true judgment is ontologically a judgment, only a true belief a belief?

These observations show the absurdity of hypostatizing true and false into two objective things. The next paragraph is not strictly necessary in the context of this essay. Yet it is short and it at least states the answers to some questions that must have arisen in the mind of the reader. So I shall indulge in the digression.

In a schema that reflects a world like mine no compound expression is a name. A name is a primitive symbol that represents a simple thing. No simple thing has more than one name. Sameness and diversity themselves are not represented but merely "show themselves" by the sameness and diversity of (types of) expressions. (That shows, once more, that ideal languages are not really languages. Also, it unpacks part of the metaphor that they are pictures of their worlds.) Two things are identical and not one, or, as one says, the same, if and only if whatever can be said about the one also can *salva veritate* be said about the other (Leibnizian identity of indiscernibles). Identity is represented in the schema (Leibniz-Russell definition of identity). It is, however, a categorial feature of the *truncated* world that no two simples are identical. Two awarenesses, it seems, can be two and yet identical (discernibility of identicals). All this unpacks part of the aphorism that sameness and identity are primary. Notice, finally, that in Frege's case I spoke of an identity function, not of a sameness function. A sameness function would be a monadic function mapping every thing on itself.

Subjective idealists hold that only minds exist. Upon the common-sensical use of 'mental' and 'nonmental', which I shall not abandon, some things are mental, some are nonmental. That makes subjective idealism absurd. Objective idealists hold that all nonmental things are, in a very special sense of the word, "mental." The only way to find out what this very special sense is, is to state commonsensically those features or alleged features of the nonmental which are held to make it "mental." Thus one can discover the dialectical core of objective idealism. Its proponents may or may not add that the nonmental (the truncated world) is literally a Mind of which our own minds are "moments." That is merely speculation. So I merely ignore it. But I reject any ontology, with or without speculative accretions, whose dialectical core is absurd. *The dialectical core of objective idealism is the proposition that minds contribute (create) the structure of the nonmental.* That is absurd.

Frege's truncated world is not "mental." Nor does he claim that it is.

That makes him a realist₂. He is indeed one of the very few realists₂ whose truncated world is at least partly structured. That makes his realism sturdier than most others. For the inadequacy of reism creates a very strong pull toward idealism. That we saw when we discussed the interaction between the three centers of the basic dialectic. On the other hand, according to the diagnosis at which we arrived some time ago, *part* of the structure of his truncated world is contributed by mind. That makes his ontology idealistic in tendency.

Frege also hypostatized mental things (thoughts) into nonmental ones (senses). Does that make his ontology materialistic in tendency? A materialist either denies that there are mental things, which is absurd, or, which is equally absurd, he "identifies" them with "ordinary" nonmental things. Frege's T and F and his senses are, alas, most "extraordinary" nonmental things. That is why they do not make him a materialist. Rather, they testify to the tenacity with which he clung to his realism₂ under dialectical pressures to which no one before him had been as sensitive as he was.

III

Dr. Egidi is exquisitely sensitive to the pressures from the three centers of the basic dialectic. Her strongest and clearest commitment is to the unity of thought. In her own way she insists on the inadequacy of reism. She is aware of the problem of adequation. This is her profundity. She sees no realistic₂ way of resolving the basic dialectic. That is why, under the pressure of her strongest commitment, she opts for objective idealism. But she not only makes a choice, she also makes a claim. Structurally, she claims, Frege is an objective idealist. Not surprisingly, the argument or reasons by which she supports her claim depend on those by which she supports her choice. That is why before examining the former I shall examine the latter. The conclusion at which I shall arrive is that none of her arguments, either for the choice or for the claim, is a good argument.[26]

Dr. Egidi believes, with one qualification, that one must choose between Aristotelianism and objective idealism. The qualification concerns those who see through the inadequacy of Aristotelianism, yet persist in rejecting objective idealism. These, she believes, are forced to withdraw into the desert of dead-end nominalism. Since she also

---

[26] Notice once more the heavy emphasis on the dialectic. I need not and do not claim that her ontology is "false" or that her reading of Frege is "mistaken." I merely claim that the reasons or arguments she gives for them are not good reasons. This is just one of the many lessons I have learned from G. E. Moore.

seems to believe that I am among the dwellers in this desert, I shall try to convince her that I am not by showing first of all what is or ought to be obvious, namely, that dead-end nominalism is not a way out of the impasse of reism.

Realists$_1$ hold that "in" Peter's being blond there are two things, Peter and blond. Reistic realism$_1$ fails because it cannot "connect" the two. Dead-end nominalists find "in" this fact only one thing, namely, Peter. Hence, if they could otherwise solve the problem of universals, i.e., if they could assign an ontological ground to Peter's and Mary's both being blond, they would not at this point have to face the problem no reist can solve. Yet they would be up against it at the very next step. What "connects" the several facts of their world? Since they are all reists, any two facts (or should I say things?) remain disjoined. That shows that the only way out of the impasse of reism is not dead-end nominalism but, rather, the recognition of the ontological status of a class of subsistents sufficient not only to make realism$_1$ viable but also to account for a world that is completely structured.

Aristotle's individuals are substances; his characters, attributes.[27] The former "create" or "produce" the latter, the latter "inhere" in the former. The traditional words ('create', 'produce', 'inhere') suggest a characteristic feature. Attributes "depend" on substances in a sense in which the latter do not "depend" on the former. That spots a nominalistic tendency. On the other hand, Aristotle's substances and attributes are both things. Any one who does not use the word as narrowly as I sometimes do will therefore call him a "realist$_1$." Nor is it fair to call him a reist. "Inherence" or, conversely, "creation" is a sort of tie. The trouble is that closer analysis reveals it to be irremediably anthropomorphic. This is the fatal flaw not just of Aristotelianism but of all substantialist ontologies.[28]

Dr. Egidi identifies Aristotelianism (substantialism) not only with realism$_1$ but also with reism. More fatally still, since Aristotle is of course a realist$_2$ and since she sees in him the only alternative to either objective idealism or the nominalist desert, she identifies realism$_1$ and realism$_2$. Thus she fails to distinguish between any two of four things as different from each other as Aristotelianism (substantialism), realism$_1$, realism$_2$, and reism. This is her *first major mistake*. It vitiates all her arguments.

---

[27] For our purposes it is safe to ignore the distinction between attributes and accidents.

[28] This shows how the issue of bare particulars versus substances ties into the basic dialectic.

Aristotle, like Frege, was not only an ontologist but also a logician. That makes it convenient to introduce next some distinctions Dr. Egidi misses in the area of logic, even though this second failure affects the arguments for her claim more than those for her choice. First, though, I must delineate a subarea of this area on which we completely agree.

Logic without ontology is merely a calculus. A calculus acquires philosophical import only if its author claims that it is an ideal language (*Begriffsschrift*), i.e., that it perspicuously reflects an adequate ontology. I shall mark this distinction by consistently so using the two words that 'calculus' stands for what is merely a calculus, 'logic' for a calculus to which that claim has been attached. Ordinary grammar or language, although we cannot but start from it, is not a reliable guide to logic. Our (Indogermanic) languages are all of the subject-predicate form. Aristotle's logic more or less perspicuously reflects his ontology. His calculus is an *exaggerated subject-predicate calculus*, i.e., it hugs the subject-predicate form of ordinary grammar so closely that it reflects (rather perspicuously) certain specific inadequacies of his ontology. The subject of 'Peter loves Mary' is 'Peter'; that of 'Mary is loved by Peter' is Mary. In an exaggerated subject-predicate calculus that is an important difference. Yet there is an important sense of 'same' in which both sentences represent the same fact.[29] 'Loves Mary' in 'Peter loves Mary' is construed as is 'is red' in 'This is red'. That reflects an inadequate ontological assay of relations. The transcription of 'All dogs are mammals' into the calculus preserves the subject-predicate form. That reflects an inadequate ontological assay of generality. And so on. (Ordinary language is not an exaggerated subject-predicate calculus simply because it is not a calculus. That is why on the one hand it is flexible enough to represent everything while, on the other, there is much which it does not represent perspicuously.)

It is a great merit of Dr. Egidi to have seen all this very clearly, more clearly indeed than many in whose ambience these insights are more widely spread than in hers. As far as I know, she is also right in insisting that Frege was the first who saw all this; and I share her admiration for his momentous achievement. There, though, our agreement ends.

A calculus may be a *moderate subject-predicate calculus*, i.e., it may be of the subject-predicate form without hugging this form so closely that any ontology it perspicuously reflects must suffer from those specific

[29] 'Peter loves Mary if and only if Mary is loved by Peter' is analytic. But we need not at this point commit ourselves as to whether the-thought-that-Peter-loves-Mary and the-thought-that-Mary-is-loved-by-Peter are two things or one.

inadequacies with respect to relations, generality, and so on, which mar Aristotle's. I am not sure that Dr. Egidi disagrees. But I am very sure, alas, that she believes any such calculus to be inadequate in an even more radical sense. According to her, any ontology perspicuously reflected by a moderate subject-predicate calculus must be reistic. This is her *second major mistake*. Four comments will show how bad a mistake it is and at the same time prepare the ground for the third major criticism.

1. *Principia Mathematica* (PM) is a moderate subject-predicate calculus. Yet it can be used and in fact has been used for the correction of those specific inadequacies of the Aristotelian ontology. 2. Notice the condition of perspicuous reflection. To unpack this label is a very major job. Also, the matter is very technical. If one understands it completely, then he sees that a calculus which perspicuously reflects a (non-reistic!) world whose fundamental tie is exemplification must be a moderate subject-predicate calculus and conversely. This is not to say that all philosophers who propounded a PM-type logic realized that the syncategormatic entities exist. But, then, neither did they fully understand those very technical matters. (3. Presently we shall see that in all calculational respects Frege's logic is a moderate subject-predicate calculus. Its perspicuity is a different matter. That we have seen already.) 4. I believe, first, that the logic of the truncated world is of the PM-type. I believe, second, that the logic of our world as a whole, that is, including minds, is not of this type. Or, to say the same thing in a way that suits our purpose, while such a calculus can be used to represent perspicuously all nonmental intentions, it contains no means for so representing either the subsistent I call M or the simple characters I call thoughts ($\ulcorner P \urcorner$) or the facts called acts and, in particular, judgments ($G(P)$). (This fits nicely with the materialistic (behavioristic) tendencies of most "PM-philosophers.")

Peter's being blond (P) is *one* fact. Your or his or my judging that Peter is blond ($G(P)$) is an*other* fact.[30] Dr. Egidi would not put it this way, yet she would agree. She also holds that a calculus may perspicuously represent one of the two facts, namely, P, without so representing

[30] If the first fact is represented by 'P', then the second is in my world represented by 'a is believing and a is $\ulcorner P \urcorner$', where $\ulcorner P \urcorner$ is a simple character and a the individual "in" the act. Thus, the first fact is not upon this assay a constituent of the second, the "connection" between the two being accounted for by the analyticity of '$\ulcorner P \urcorner M P$'. Of the third, formal fact represented by the latter sentence both P and $\ulcorner P \urcorner$ are constituents.

the other, namely, $G(P)$. With this I agree. This is indeed the very point of what I just said. A PM-type calculus can be used to represent perspicuously every nonmental intention but contains no means for so representing $G(P)$. There, though, our agreement ends.

Dr. Egidi holds that no calculus can perspicuously represent the act of judging. Any logic for which this claim is made (as I make it for mine) she calls "formalistic." The idea is that no formalistic logic can perspicuously represent an adequate ontology. This is her *third major mistake*. Some of my reasons for judging it to be a mistake may be merely implicit in Sections One and Two. Most of these reasons, though, are quite explicit in what has been said so far. Repetition is tedious on any occasion. Complete explicitness is not practical on this occasion. So I shall next show that the intellectual motive behind the mistake is structural idealism.

Dr. Egidi's ontological assay of judgment is idealistic. According to such an assay, the mind first "posits" what, after having posited it, it judges. To posit something, in this sense of the word, is to create or produce it; or, at least, to "contribute" to the "product" something without which it would not be what it is. That makes the idealistic assay of judgment the structural heart of idealism. Thus, if she will permit me to say so, Dr. Egidi shows even in some of her mistakes the flair of those who can think structurally. Rightly or wrongly, she goes to the heart of the matter.

To connect this diagnosis with what she actually says, turn to CLFC 203–205. Rather than quote, I shall express her ideas in my own words. Without the unitary act, she holds, there would not be that manifold which is such a striking feature of its (nonmental) intention. Logic (language) can only represent the manifold which is, wholly or in part, the product. It cannot represent the producing. Or, to say the same thing differently, language (logic) can only represent what we know. It cannot represent the "ideal conditions" which make it "possible" for us to know what we know.[31] That shows beyond doubt that the intellectual motive behind Dr. Egidi's third major mistake is the structural core of idealism.

That much for her choice. I now turn to her claim.

Her claim stands or falls with her contention that Frege's ontology of judgment is structurally idealistic, i.e., that implicitly at least it agrees with hers. The main evidence she has so far produced for this

---

[31] I am of course aware of the Kantian flavor of this 'possible'. Dr. Egidi would not, I think, repudiate the structural connection thus hinted at.

contention is what is said about judgment in the *Begriffsschrift*, particularly in §2. Let me once more draw a clear line between agreement and disagreement. She gives Frege credit for distinguishing between $\vdash P$ and $-P$, i.e., between a judgment and what I call the thought "in" it. If you recall what has been said about that early contribution in Section Two, then you will see that I agreed. She takes what Frege says in §2 to be an assertion of the unity of thought. I agreed that he may plausibly be credited with this fundamental insight. There, though, our agreement ends. For I also believe to have shown three things which are incompatible with her contention. First. The natural reading of §2 is realistic$_2$. Second. This early contribution to the ontology of judgment is fragmentary; it leaves a blank. Third. Eventually the blank becomes a blur. Frege's idea of judgment as an "advance" from a sense to a truth value is irremediably blurred.

Dr. Egidi takes advantage of the blur by filling the blank with her own idealistic ontology of judgment. In this she shows once more her keen sense of structure. For the blur is indeed the seat of the idealistic tendency of the system. If you want to verify this diagnosis, turn to MLFF 19, where she says perhaps most bluntly what more subtly she intimates again and again, namely, that a Fregean "advance" is really a Fichtean "posit."[32] It does not follow, alas, that her claim is sound. Frege's T and F and his senses are most "extraordinary" things indeed. So are his functions, even though to a mathematician bent above all on refuting psychologism that may not have been as obvious as it really is. Yet all these entities are clearly nonmental. For one, Frege himself, as far as I know, has never claimed them to be either mental or "mental." For another, irrespective of what he himself may or may not have said or believed, they all are structurally nonmental. That is indeed the argument of Section Two. So I shall without repeating myself conclude this examination by attending to two of Dr. Egidi's arguments for her claim, both of which I find rather disappointing.

Are functions and ordinary things, say, blond and Peter, "determinate" entities "independent" of the acts which posit them? The two words between double quotes are hers, not mine. Yet there is no doubt what the question means. Are these entities objective or nonmental in my (and, if I am right, Frege's) sense? Dr. Egidi consistently denies that they are. Functions in particular she calls "ideal" entities in the

---

[32] Idealistic ideas are not easily explicated by means of a calculus; not, alas, because Dr. Egidi is right but, rather, because they are so vague and elusive. If I were to try, though, I would say that according to Dr. Egidi the mind in its advance "posits" the identity $(\vdash P) = T$. I merely add that while '$\vdash (P = \mathrm{T})$' is at least well-formed, '$(\vdash P) = T$' is ill-formed in the Fregean calculus!

sense that they make "experience" possible. She also calls them "objective." But then it transpires (CLLF 207) that all she means by that is that the experience they make "possible" is independent of its linguistic representation in exactly the same sense in which a certain fact that was mentioned earlier is independent of its being represented by either 'Peter loves Mary' or 'Mary is loved by Peter'. This I find disappointing.

Frege, like his successor Russell and like Russell's successors, writes '$f(x)$', '$r(x, y)$', and so on. The only difference is in the semantics. For Russell, the substitution instances of '$f(x)$' represent facts or possible facts; for Frege, they are names of either T or F. And so on. That makes it obvious that *in all calculational respects* Frege's logic is a moderate subject-predicate calculus. But it will help if before turning to the second argument I state the two qualifications which are covered by the italicized phrase. (a) On the one hand, the assertion sign ('$\vdash$') and the horizontal stroke ('$-$') do not fit into a moderate subject-predicate calculus. On the other hand, Frege himself makes no real calculational use of them. That is why the later logicians were puzzled by them and eventually dropped them, which in turn fits well with what Dr. Egidi and I agree upon, namely, that Frege in §2 introduced the two signs in order to make by means of them a point in the ontology of judgment. (b) 'T' and 'F' do not fit into a moderate subject-predicate calculus. More precisely, if they are taken to represent things, then '$P = T$' and '$P = F$' are in such a calculus ill-formed. But then, as far as I know, neither Frege nor, with the possible exception of Alonzo Church, any of his followers have paid any attention to these two expressions. Rather, it was I, who, for a purpose of my own, insisted that they are, or, at least, that they ought to be considered as well-formed. My purpose, or, rather, the use to which I put them in Section Two, was to expose by means of them some of the perplexities of Frege's ontology as well as the lack of perspicuity with which it is reflected by his calculus.

Dr. Egidi makes much of the fact that in dealing with the sentential calculus the Frege of the *Begriffsschrift* uses sentential variables, writing 'p' instead of, say '$f(x)$'. This she takes to be *his* assertion of the unity of thought, upon which she foists *her* ontology of judgment. The truth of the matter is that no mathematician of even the most moderate skill who had either conceived or been told the idea of the sentential calculus would in constructing it use any but sentential variables. Sentential logic is the most fundamental part of logic. To have recognized that is without doubt one of Frege's major achievements. But it is disappointing to see Dr. Egidi build so much of her argument on the trivial fact that he writes the sentential calculus in sentential notation. Besides, if it were the job of the single variable to express the unity of thought, may I ask how she would explain what she also asserts, namely, that the same job is also done by the horizontal stroke?

The indictment I have drawn up against Dr. Egidi is severe. Yet I do not want to end on a note of disappointment. So I shall change sides, from the prosecution to the defense, as it were, and conclude with some remarks which will add perspective in a way that amounts to a plea of attenuating circumstances.

The basic dialectic of the realism-idealism issue lurks in the things themselves. The trend toward idealism began only about three hundred years ago, that is, roughly, at the time of the Cartesian revolution. Why did this trend start at just that time? The gist of what I believe to be the right answer can be stated very briefly.[33] The Aristotelian-Thomistic account of perception, which was dominant until then, is realistic₂ in structure. A single substantial form informs the mind of the perceiver and the thing perceived. This account was supported by and is compatible with the idea that a mind can only know what is "in" it. The revolution overthrew the old account of perception. The idea continued to be taken for granted. That suffices to account for the rise of the trend.

The lure of idealism continues undiminished. The structure of Deweyan instrumentalism is idealistic.[34] The same is true of the present misery, at Oxford and elsewhere, which goes by the name of ordinary-language philosophy. If the temptation of a philosophy so absurd continues so strong for so long, it stands to reason that, for all its absurdity and even though at a prohibitive price, it accounts more adequately than its competitors for at least one striking feature of the world. The thing to do, therefore, is to identify this feature and try to do justice to it in a realistic₂ ontology. Then and only then will the temptation cease.

The role of minds in the world is unique. This is the feature. The idealists' way of safeguarding it is to insist, with or without some attenuation, that minds "create" their intentions, which is absurd. My way of safeguarding it is different.

Consider (1) 'P and Q', (2) 'not-(not-P or not-Q)', (3) 'P and Q if and only if not-(not-P or not-Q)'. Call the facts represented by (1) and (2) F_1 and F_2, respectively. Are F_1 and F_2 two or one (the same)? There is an important meaning of 'same' upon which they are the same. This

---

[33] For a more detailed statement see essay XII of this book.

[34] See May Brodbeck, "La filosofia di John Dewey," *Rivista di Filosofia*, 50, 1959, 391–422.

meaning I explicate by the analyticity of (3). Since the subsistents exist, there is also a stricter meaning of 'same', such that two facts are the same if and only if the same simples are in the same way connected by the same subsistents. With this meaning of 'same', F_1 and F_2 are two and not one. The subsistents and the truths which depend only on them are "the world's form." The ontological ground of F_1 and F_2 being two and not one thus lies not in the world's things but wholly in its form. Yet there are in my world two things, namely, the-thought-that-P-and-Q and the-thought-that-not-(not-P-or-not-Q) which are two and not one for the sole reason that if the world's form is taken into account the facts they represent are two and not one. There is thus a kind of things, namely, thoughts, which are unique in that they and they alone among the world's things reflect its form.[35] This, I submit, is an adequate realistic₂ account of the feature.

I shall of course not convince Dr. Egidi. To expect that would be merely presumptuous. But I do nourish a more modest hope. I may convince her that there are realists₂ who in *their* way try to resolve the dialectical tensions to which she so keenly responds. If this hope is justified, then I am confident she will eventually find *her* way of rejecting idealism.

[35] This is also the deepest structural reason for so explicating 'analytic' that $\ulcorner P \urcorner MP$ becomes analytic or, synonymously, that it becomes a truth in the world's form. There are also quite a few logical (calculational) reasons for this step. Philosophically, though, such reasons do not carry conviction unless they support and are supported by a structural reason that lies rather deep.

Inclusion, Exemplification, and Inherence in G. E. Moore*

GREEN and good are both simple properties. In this they are
alike. Green is a natural property; good, a nonnatural one. In
this they differ. That is the key formula of Moore's *Principia
Ethica*. Take two green spots. Some philosophers hold that their both
being green is accounted for by a single entity, green, which, in a sense
to be specified, is a constituent of both spots. Such entities are called
universals. The "properties" of the formula are universals. About that
there is no doubt. A property that can be referred to by a compound
expression such as 'green and square' is not "simple." One which in
direct reference can only be named is simple. Much unpacking as that
needs, it will do. And, again, there is no doubt, this is what Moore had
in mind. What though did he mean when he called some properties
natural; some others, nonnatural? There has been much doubt and a
great deal of discussion. No satisfactory answer has come forth.
Moore's dichotomy almost seemed a riddle. I shall here propose a solution of the riddle. For this choice of topic I have two reasons, one personal, one structural.

I am your guest. A guest ought to put his best foot forward. One of
the best things, if not the best, a philosopher can credibly say for himself is that he has found some younger men, willing to call themselves
his students, who have grown up to make some substantial contributions. The basic idea for the solution of Moore's riddle is not mine.
Rather, it is a substantial contribution of one of my most gifted stu-

* The is the first of two essays which appeared under the title "Meaning and
Ontology" in Inquiry, 5, 1962, 116–42. Reprinted by permission. The essay by
Herbert Hochberg has in the meantime appeared under the title "Moore's Ontology
and Non-natural Properties" in The Review of Metaphysics, 15, 1962, 365–95.

dents, Herbert Hochberg, who has elaborated it in a paper as yet unpublished. This is the personal reason.

In what a great philosopher says there is a pattern. It all flows from one source, a few fundamental ontological ideas. In the light of this source and only in this light, it can all be understood. In this sense, ethics properly understood is but a corollary of metaphysics; and the heart of metaphysics is ontology. I want to drive home this point by showing that Moore's puzzling dichotomy can be understood only in the light of his ontology. That is the structural reason for my choice of topic.

To speak of Moore's ontology in the singular is misleading. There are at least two, probably more. An early version, explicitly stated in some papers published around the turn of the century, even though never mentioned in *Principia Ethica,* yet controls this book. That, specifically, is Hochberg's precious discovery. One later version is recorded in *Some Main Problems of Philosophy,* a course of lectures delivered in the 'twenties, published only in the 'fifties. This later and that earlier version throw much light upon each other. Speaking about them, I shall simply call them Moore's first and second ontology.

Moore always knew where he wanted to arrive. But, alas, he never found out how to get there. There are minds as well as bodies. Also, a mind may know a body, for instance, by perceiving it. If that is called realism, Moore wanted to arrive at realism. There are not only valuings but also values. Goodness, for instance, is in some things valued, not just in the minds valuing them. If that is called objectivism, Moore wanted to arrive at objectivism.

What does it mean for anything to be in a thing? One cannot answer the question without first answering another: What is a thing? The kind of answer required is, of course, an ontological assay. Before turning to Moore's early answer, some general remarks are in order.

Take two spots; one, green and square; the other, red and round. The green goes with the square, not with the red; the red with the round, not with the square. Hence, there must be something that makes these items go or hang together as in fact they do. In assaying that something there are two possibilities. Either the tie required is in the mind of the beholder. That is the road to idealism. Think of Kant's transcendental unity of apperception. Or the ties are in the things themselves. In this case an infinite regress threatens. What ties the tie to what it ties? The question reveals the threat. The only way out is to give ontological status to entities I call *fundamental ties* or nexus. A fundamental tie needs no further tie to tie it to what it ties.

Take now two green spots. There is identity as well as diversity to be accounted for. The two spots are identical in being both green. The universal accounts for the identity. They are different in being two, not one. The ontological assay must account for that difference. In traditional words, all philosophers embracing universals are faced with the problem of *individuation*. Basically, there are two ways of solving it. I shall call them *A* and *B*.

A. There is a kind of simples called individuals. In the example there are two, each spot being a complex containing one individual and the color. An individual once presented could not, if presented again, be recognized as such. That is why individuals are also called bare, or bare particulars. Their sole function, as it were, is to individuate. Accordingly, the spatial and temporal relations, assayed as relational universals, obtain among individuals and among them only. Space and time thus are assayed as being in essence relational. The nexus between individuals and universals is called *exemplification*. Individuals and universals belong to different types. That means, first, that of two entities of the same type, say, two individuals, none can exemplify the other. It means, second, that exemplification is intransitive; i.e. if α exemplifies β and β exemplifies γ then α cannot exemplify γ. The complex, finally, the individual exemplifying the universal, is of a third type. *B*. All simples are universals. The basic tie is *inclusion*.[1] A simple may be included in a complex. "Two" complexes are one if and only if they include the same simples. Individuation is achieved by a special class of nonrelational spatial and temporal universals. Call them here, there, now, then, and so on. One of the two spots, for instance, is a complex including green and there, the other, one including green and here. Space and time, one sees, are assayed as being in essence nonrelational.[2] Simples and complexes are of the same type. More poignantly, there are no types. Accordingly, if α includes β and β includes γ then α includes γ. This gambit cannot but remind one of Scotus', with the special class of space-time properties corresponding to his *haecceitates*.

Think of *cognoscere* and *recognoscere*, *erkennen* and *wiedererkennen*. "What cannot be recognized cannot be known. Bare particulars cannot be known. Hence, there are no such entities." That is the structural

---

[1] This is rough. The complex ought to be built up from what it includes by some tie or ties of "affiliation." For my limited purposes, though, the roughness helps a good deal without spoiling anything. Inclusion is, literally, one of Husserl's basic ties. The two with which Goodman begins are "affiliations."

[2] Notice that I use 'relational' and 'nonrelational' instead of the conventional 'relative' and 'absolute'. There are good reasons for that.

root of the resistance against A-ontologies. At least, it is a very important root. "Space and time qualities are not presented to us. Hence, there are no such entities." That is the structural root of the resistance against B-ontologies. At least, it is a very important root. A- and B-ontologies must both face the problem of relations. That is, they must in their respective assays indicate the constituent or constituents which account for, say, this spot being to the left of that. A consistent A-ontologist accounts for it by a relational universal, exemplified by a pair of individuals. Exemplification, being either unary, or binary, or ternary, and so on, thus becomes subdivided. But the A-ontologist needs, up to this point, no other fundamental tie.

There is throughout the tradition a tendency to favor individuals over universals, to deny the latter the same ontological status as the former. One of its roots is the pattern according to which what exists is "in" space and time or localized, in the sense in which the universals of either A or B are not and the individuals of A are localized. In this sense, in B nothing is in space and time. Rather, certain complexes are individuated by the combination of spatial and temporal universals they include. There is also a tendency to discriminate among universals, in favor of nonrelational ones (properties, qualities), against relations. Its root, somewhat inconsistently, is the same pattern as before. The relation, spanning this spot and that spot, is not localized. I say somewhat inconsistently because, strictly speaking, no universal is localized in the sense in which the individuals of A are. The inaccuracy testifies to the strength of the tendency.

Put yourself now in the place of a B-ontologist clever enough to know that relations must be given some ontological status. This spot is to the left of that; this other to the left of that other; and so on. Clearly, he must assay relations as universals. Equally clearly, he must tie the relational universal, say, being to the left of, to the two complexes of properties which in his assay are the two spots. But then, even more clearly if anything, the relation, spanning both spots, is not included in either, in the sense in which "its" properties are included in each. As far as I can see, there is only one way out. Our B-ontologist must introduce a second fundamental tie which in all respects is like relational exemplification, except that the exemplifying entities are not the bare particulars of A but, rather, the complexes of B. Call this tie relational B-exemplification. Thus where the A-ontologist makes shift with one nexus, the B-ontologist needs two; inclusion in the spots, if I may so put it, as well as B-exemplification by the spots.

What exists is independent. Less radically, the more independent an entity is, the higher or fuller its ontological status. Throughout the tradition, this pattern has been as influential as any.[3] By it, our *B*-ontologist's assay of relations, while giving them some ontological status, still discriminates against them in favor of properties. For the relation to be exemplified, the two complexes of properties must be there. A property, say, green, does not so "depend" on another, say, square, in order to be individuated, which in *B* corresponds to its being exemplified in *A*. The analogy, such as it is, is, rather, to how the "ordinary" properties in a complex, the colors, shapes, and so on, depend for their "individuation" on those spatial and temporal properties which are as characteristic of *B*-ontologies as they are, alas, problematic. But, then, these peculiar properties are themselves nonrelational. This shows how relations "depend" on properties in a way in which properties do not depend on each other, or, if you please, depend only on each other.

Except for one feature, to be taken up presently, the *B*-ontology with relations I just described is G. E. Moore's first ontology. Its simples are all universals. Universals are of two kinds. Those of the first kind are included in complexes; those of the second, *B*-exemplified by complexes. The dichotomy coincides with another. All universals of the first kind are nonrelational; all of the second, relational. For one of the first kind to be a relation is, as we saw, counterstructural. What spans both spots cannot be included in either. But there is no structural reason whatsoever why there should not also be properties (nonrelationally) *B*-exemplified by complexes. Good as assayed in *Principia Ethica* is such a property. Or, to say the same thing differently, to be a nonnatural property is to be a nonrelational universal of the second kind (in a *B*-type ontology). That is Hochberg's thesis, his solution of the riddle. In his forthcoming study he will no doubt most ably defend it, as it must be defended, namely, by showing that it permits one consistently to make sense out of what Moore has said about nonnatural properties, in *Principia Ethica* and elsewhere. I shall in the rest of this paper stay with some points of general ontology.

If the issue is whether something is either "in" the beholder or "in" the thing beheld, universals of the second kind surely are "in" the thing. Moore's assay of goodness thus achieves his objectivist aim. It discriminates nevertheless among natural and nonnatural properties in favor of the former. (That is one plausible reason for calling the latter nonnatural.) In the case of relations I just showed that by means of the independence pattern. One sees easily that what in this respect

[3] See E. B. Allaire, "Existence, Independence, and Universals," *Philosophical Review*, 69, 1960, 485–96.

holds for relations also holds for nonnatural properties. The two are in the same boat, as it were. Considering the strong tendency to deny all ontological status to relations, that may be significant in itself. Some reflections show that it is.

In A-ontologies individuals and universals are two different ontological kinds, just as among universals properties and relations are two subkinds. But these kinds and subkinds all enjoy the same status. A-ontologists, that is, are free from the "nominalistic" tendency to discriminate against universals in favor of individuals and, among universals, against relations in favor of properties. Now there is *one* obvious sense in which to the universals of A-ontologies correspond, in B-ontologies, those and only those of the second kind. One may express this by saying that in *this* sense only the universals of the second kind are true universals. A true universal, then, is either a "nonnatural" property or it is "merely" a relation. The "nominalistic" tendency behind all that is unmistakable. In *another* sense which is equally obvious, properties of the first kind are universals. Considering that, ask yourself what the outcome will be if, in a philosopher who started as Moore did, the "nominalistic" tendency eventually prevails. Again, the answer is obvious, or all but obvious. The only universals, in *any* sense, that will be left in his eventual ontology will be either "nonnatural" properties or relations. We shall see that this is what happened in Moore's case. First, though, we must attend to that feature of his early ontology which so far has been ignored.

Believing, remembering, perceiving, and so on, are species of awareness. Epistemology or theory of knowledge is nothing but the ontological assay of the awareness situation. Realists have a tendency, easy to understand, of assaying the several species of awareness as relations, such that, when a mind is aware of something, say by perceiving it, perceiving is relationally exemplified by this mind and whatever it perceives. For a relation to be exemplified, the entities exemplifying it must be there (exist). For this spot to be left of something, for instance, the something must be there. Consider now a false belief. In this case what I believe is not there (does not exist). Nor is what I perceive, in the case of perceptual error. Yet there is, in either case, an awareness situation! Any relational assay of such situations must face the dialectical problem that presents. It may help you to recognize it if I remind you that Frege tried to solve it by giving ontological status outside of minds to what he called *Sinn*. Details apart, some British philosophers spoke instead of *propositions*. There are good reasons, one of which I shall eventually mention, for the belief that Moore's first ontology was above all designed to solve this problem. Later on, turning to ethics, he found in this ontology the ready means for achieving his objectivist aims. That shows how the several answers of a great philosopher all hang together, flow as they all do from the same source, a few fundamental ontological ideas.

In Moore's first ontology, natural properties fall into three subkinds. Two we have encountered. The third is the missing feature. Only one of the three is unproblematic. A natural property either is (1) what a moment ago I called an ordinary property, a color, a shape, a pitch, a loudness, and so on. Or it is (2) one of those "coordinate qualities," as one might call them, a here or a there, a now or a then. Between A- and B-ontologists at least, (1) is unproblematic. To A-ontologists, and not only to them, (2) is problematic. In the third category there resides in lonely splendor (3) the single entity which the young Moore calls *existence*. That (3) is problematic needs no argument. The job is, rather, to show accurately what the problem is. First, though, let us check how with (3) one can solve the problem of false belief, erroneous perception, and so on.

Return to the green spot. In the case of veridical perception, I perceive it and it is there. Or, rather, it is there, it exists, and I perceive it. In the case of perceptual error, though I perceive it, it is not there. Upon the relational assay, there must be, in either case, a complex to be perceived. Now the existing spot, in the case of, say, veridical perception, is assayed as a complex including some members of (1) and (2) and, in addition, the lonely member of (3), existence. In the other case, say, of perceptual error, the complex has the same members, except existence. That gives the idea. No doubt the problem is solved. Indeed one can hardly escape the impression of a construction *ad hoc*, the reason, or, at least, a very major reason for (3) being the felt urgency of the problem of false beliefs. The price paid for the solution is the new entity. Let us now look at it more closely.

Does existence exist? That is the question. Less dramatically, are we dialectically forced to acknowledge some such entity? Is it redundant? Does acknowledging it inevitably lead to dialectical disaster? Ontological kinds do or may differ in ontological status. There is thus a range of possible affirmative answers. Existence may be assayed as a property among properties, it may be assigned a higher status, it may be relegated to a lower one. The one point I wish to make here is that Moore's answer in his first ontology is at the upper extreme of the range. Formally or officially, if I may so express myself, he makes existence a universal among universals, a natural property among natural properties, a simple among simples. Structurally, it is a very peculiar universal, just as Frege's True and False, though officially things among things, are two very peculiar things. The comparison with Frege, though, is too rough to be very illuminating. The one which serves best is with Thomas. Take a tree. As Thomas assays it, it has a nature and it has being. But its being is anything but one among the attributes in or of its nature. To use the traditional words, it is, rather, the divine fulguration creating the tree, endowing a mere nature with—Being. Moore's existence (3), though formally a property among properties, is thus structurally much more than just that, enjoys an ontological status much higher than that of a "mere" property. That Moore's first ontology is part Scotist in structure we saw before. Now we see that it is also part Thomist. Each feature corresponds to one of the two problematic subkinds of natural properties; existence (3) to Thomas' being, the coordinate qualities (2) to Scotus' *haecceitates*.

Some Main Problems is among all Moore's writings the one I love best and admire most. Yet it is, in the manner which is so characteristic of him, as inconclusive as any. In the concluding chapters, the second ontology is discussed, very accurately and in great detail. The discussion, call it the second, centers on the issue of universals. The middle chapters contain a discussion, call it the first, equally accurate and detailed, of the problem of false beliefs. I shall next give the gist of the second ontology, or, to say the same thing differently, of the second discussion.

Take once more two spots, one here, one there; both green; both round. Disregard all other "ordinary" properties they may or may not have. In Moore's first assay, of the *B*-type, each spot contains, in addition to the tie of inclusion, three universals; one, say, the one to the left, here, green, round; the one to the right, there, green, round. Green is one entity, contained in both spots. So is round. That is indeed what is meant by saying that upon this assay they are universals. In both spots, taken together, there are thus four universals: green, round, here, there. (With respect to the last two that is inaccurate. They ought to be replaced by classes of "coordinate qualities." But the inaccuracy merely avoids details which do not matter for what I am about.) These four are also simples. In the second ontology these four entities are replaced by six: this-here, this-green, this-round; that-there, that-green, that-round. This-green and that-green are two entities, not one. So are this-round and that-round. Also, notwithstanding the necessity of referring to each of them in English by connecting two English words through a hyphen, they are all simples. There being (in this case) six such simples is what is meant by calling each of them a *perfect particular*. So far, the second assay of, say, the left spot has thus yielded three perfect particulars, this-here, this-green, this-round.

It also yields a fourth entity which is not a tie. This fourth entity is an *individual substance*.

The individuals of an *A*-ontology cannot be recognized. They are bare. An individual substance is not bare. It is a nature and it has a nature. 'Nature', you will gather, has been used ambiguously. So perhaps I had better say, an individual substance is a *dynamic* nature and has a *definitional* nature. The former creates, or produces, and supports the latter. The ineradicable anthropomorphic flavor of these three notions, creation, production, support, is only too obvious. But it is not and could not be my purpose here either to criticize or to explicate completely these classical notions. I merely try to state intelligibly what I need. Four remarks should be helpful. 1. A Leibnizian monad is an individuated dynamic nature. 2. A definitional nature is the class of attributes the substance has "by its nature." These attributes are enumerated in what the tradition calls a real definition. That is why I chose the phrase, definitional nature. 3. I neglect here the classical distinction between attributes and accidents. 4. I am of course committing myself on Moore. But I neither need nor wish to commit myself here as to whether either the attributes or the accidents of any other philosopher are either universals or perfect particulars.

What is the nexus between an (individual) substance and one of its attributes? The affiliation between two items in a *B*-complex is symmetrical. To whatever extent the idea applies, they support each other mutually and equally. The substance supports the attribute, but not conversely. The nexus we are looking for thus is not inclusion. Exemplification, either *A* or *B*, is completely free of what is conveyed by the ideas of either creation or production. The nexus we are looking for thus is not exemplification. It follows that this nexus, the fundamental tie between substance and attribute, is *sui generis*. The tradition speaks of *inherence*. The attribute inheres in the substance. I shall use the traditional word.

The spot is a complex containing four entities which are not fundamental ties, one individual substance, three perfect particulars. The tie which makes them a complex is inherence. Each of the three perfect particulars inheres in the individual substance. This is not yet all of Moore's second ontology, but as far as the single spot is concerned, it is its gist. Three comments will illuminate its structure.

First. Remember the realism Moore always wanted to arrive at. To be consonant with this aim, an assay of the perceptual situation must do equal justice to two features. (1) In a very "close" sense of presentation, the properties of the body perceived are presented to the perceiving mind. (2) These properties are nevertheless "in" the body. 'Nevertheless' spots the tension between (1) and (2). The closer the presentation, the stronger is the pull on the properties away from the body, toward the mind, or, in the limit, into the mind. The more firmly the properties are anchored in the body, the more strongly they are pulled in the opposite direction. If, as in B-ontologies, the body is merely a complex of properties, there is danger that the pull toward the mind will prevail. Making the properties inhere in an individual substance lends them support against this danger. This, I submit, is the intellectual motive, or, at least, it is a very major intellectual motive for the appearance of individual substances in the second ontology. That also shows the exact sense in which in the second ontology individual substances do the job existence does in the first, which shows in turn that existence (3) is indeed a most peculiar universal. Presently we shall see that this universal, just because it was officially assayed as a nonrelational and natural universal, was in the second no longer available for that job.

Second. However problematic the idea of a perfect particular may be, such hyphenated expressions as 'this-green', 'that-round', represent it very aptly, neither adding nor subtracting anything to or from the problem. That is not so in the case of such expressions as 'this-here', 'that-there'. They seem and in fact are redundant. Their verbal redundancy, it may seem, gratuitously adds to the problem. In fact, it is merely the symptom of a structural redundancy. In the first ontology such coordinate properties as here and there are needed to do the individuating job. In the second, where this-green and that-green are two entities, no special further entities are needed to do this job. That makes such perfect particulars as this-here, that-there structurally redundant. Since the second ontology, in this respect like the first, contains spatial and temporal relations, that raises a question. Why do these peculiar perfect particulars occur at all? Or, what amounts to the same, why did not Moore in the second ontology abandon the earlier nonrelational assay of space and time in favor of a relational one? The answer I propose is structurally enlightening. For one, the ontological status of relations in either ontology is not as good as that of natural properties in the first or that of perfect particulars in the second. For another, the better the ontological status a philosopher who wants to arrive at realism can assign to space and time, the closer he will plausibly think he has come to his goal. Take these two ideas together and you will see what I believe is the intellectual motive for the occurrence of those redundant perfect particulars in the second ontology. Another cause, if not motive, is that they are the successors, or, rather, the survivors of the spatial and temporal properties (2). I add, in fairness to Moore, that these peculiar entities are nowhere mentioned in *Some Main Problems*. But a nonrelational assay of space and time is most vigorously propounded throughout the book. And this assay cannot without those entities be reconciled with the second ontology.

Third. What exists is localized, is in space and time. We know the pattern and its power. In the second assay the constituents of the spot are one individual substance, three perfect particulars, and the nexus of inherence. Individual substances and perfect particulars are localized. The pattern has prevailed. Universals, not being localized, ought not to exist. That is the "nominalistic" urge. A philosopher feeling the urge, as Moore did, may yet know, as Moore also did, that one cannot get along without universals. The one thing he can do to satisfy the urge is to depress their ontological status. How that is done in the first ontology we have seen. As a result, all its true universals are either "nonnatural" properties or "merely" relations. In an ontology of the *B*-type, such as the first, this result is easily achieved. The goal of the second ontology is the same. All its universals ought to be either relations or, presumably, the nonnatural properties of *Principia Ethica*.[4] This time I call it a goal rather than a result, because in an ontology of perfect particulars it cannot be reached unless a certain difficulty has been overcome.

This-green and that-green are two entities, not one. That is half the gambit of perfect particulars. They are both simples. That is the other half. There is something in or about them which makes them two greens.[5] There is no such something in the case of, say, *a* green and *a* round. This something must be ontologically grounded, accounted for. That is the difficulty. For, since all greens are simples, the something cannot be a constituent of any of them. That is indeed what is meant, or a part of what is meant, by calling them simples. The only way out is a relation of similarity exemplified by any pair of greens, any pair of rounds, reds, and so on. The idea is not new of course. New, or at least rare, is the candor with which Moore acknowledges that this relation must be given some ontological status. Thus the difficulty is overcome, the goal reached. Except presumably for nonnatural properties, the

[4] I say presumably because these properties are not mentioned anywhere in *Some Main Problems*. But, then, neither is any problem of either ethics or aesthetics.

[5] Neglecting shades, as I have throughout, or, what amounts to the same, using the adjective for just one shade, this use of the plural and the indefinite article is of course, as one now says, the grammar of perfect particulars. I have avoided it in all other contexts.

universals of the second ontology are all relations exemplified by perfect particulars; "ordinary" relations such as being to the left of, and, in addition, *similarity*.

Pick *a* green; no matter which. The *complex* property of being either identical with it or similar to it is coextensive with the *A*-ontologist's simple universal green. In this sense, as Moore knows and explains very well, there are universals in the second ontology. Why, then, we must ask, are his "nominalistic" sensibilities not offended by the occurrence of these complex universals. Notice that I speak of occurrence rather than of existence. The wording hints at the pattern in which I believe the answer lies. Only what is simple exists. This pattern, too, has been very powerful throughout the tradition. Taking it into account, we can now complete the inventory of the second ontology. Disregarding non-natural properties, there are three kinds of simples, namely, in descending order of ontological status, individual substances, perfect particulars, relational universals. The fundamental ties among them are inherence and exemplification. Universals are exemplified by perfect particulars which in turn inhere in individual substances. It will be remembered that I took this ontology, which I call Moore's second, from what I have called the second discussion in *Some Main Problems*.

The first discussion centers around the problem of how to account for false beliefs within a relational assay of awareness. Moore with great accuracy and considerable detail explains first the problem, then the only solution he can think of.

There are things, e.g., Peter, facts, e.g., Peter's being blond, and propositions, e.g., the proposition that Peter is blond. If Peter is in fact blond, both the fact and the proposition exist; if he isn't, only the proposition does. What is believed is always a proposition. A belief is true or false depending on whether or not the fact that corresponds to the proposition believed exists. Propositions are very similar to those complexes of the first ontology which do not contain existence. I say very similar rather than the same because there is also a difference. Existence is, throughout the book, not only called a property but also treated as such. Or, at least, an attempt is made to treat it as such. But the similarity by far outweighs the difference. Let me describe this state of affairs by saying that the first ontology, of about 1900, is implicit in the first discussion, of the 'twenties. At the end of this discussion Moore tells us that since he cannot bring himself to countenance such entities as propositions, he must reject the solution, even though he knows of no other. In *Some Main Problems*, or, what amounts to the same, in the second ontology, the problem of false beliefs thus remains unresolved. Surely this is a striking instance of that inconclusiveness which is as characteristic of the man as are his candor, his accuracy, and his profundity.

Let me now make a schema. Throughout his career Moore thinks of awareness as relational. Throughout his career he has therefore a characteristic problem concerning false beliefs, perceptual error, and so on. In his first ontology the problem is soluble. In the second it is not. In the book in which he expounds the latter, Moore not only candidly tells us so but also expounds at great length, if only in order to reject it, a solution in which the first ontology is implicit. Remember now that I promised to give a reason for the conjecture that even though the first ontology subsequently provided him with the ready means for achieving his objectivist goal in ethics, that early ontology was above all designed to solve the problem of false beliefs. Look at the schema and you will see the reason. If you don't see it or if you do not think it is good enough, consider that not much really depends on whether a conjecture of this historical or, rather, biographical kind is held to be properly substantiated. My main purpose in advancing it was indeed structural. It helped me to show how in the thought of a great philosopher everything hangs together, everything depends on his answers to a few fundamental questions. Let me conclude with another lesson of this kind.

Throughout this paper I have not tipped my hand. At least, I have tried not to tip it. If I succeeded, you may wonder what my own views are. If you do, I am pleased to oblige. I am an A-ontologist; I am a realist; I am not an objectivist. I believe that we are dialectically forced to give existence some ontological status but that this status is neither that of a property among properties nor higher. All this, though, is beside the point. The point, or the lesson, is that I could say quite a bit about the problems without offering any solutions, and, if I succeeded, without even tipping my hand. That shows how very, very much of philosophy is dialectics and nothing but dialectics.

Strawson's Ontology*

ABOOK may be important because what it says is excellent. Or, provided it be competent, it may be important without being excellent because what it says is original. In these two ways a book may be intrinsically important. Some books become historically important because of their impact on the course of events. The two kinds of importance need not go together. Of Gellner's *Words and Things*, which is right now making such a stir, one may reasonably judge or hope, as I do, that it will turn out to be historically important without, as I don't, judging it to be intrinsically so. Strawson's latest book[1] I believe to be historically important in the same context as Gellner's. But I also judge it to be competent and original. That makes it an unusual book. Unusual books deserve notices of unusual length, so-called special reviews. They also deserve intellectual courtesy. I shall pay my respects by attending first and at great length to what Strawson says and its dialectical context, and only at the end very briefly to the contemporary situation.

Criticism searching enough to be worthwhile often requires some exposition of the critic's views. The latter, in turn, requires space beyond the limits of a standard review, the proper protagonist of which is always the author, never the reviewer. In a standard review, therefore, criticism often and quite properly takes second place. A special review may preserve this proportion. Or it may try to achieve worthwhile criticism by using some of the additional space available for a more balanced exposition of both the author's and the critic's views. A special reviewer thus has a choice. This piece is a story without a single protagonist. So I shall first give three reasons why I believe that under the circumstances that is the proper choice.

* The Journal of Philosophy, *57, 1960, 601-22. Reprinted by permission.*

[1] P. F. Strawson, *Individuals: An Essay in Descriptive Metaphysics* (London: Methuen, 1959).

171

Strawson has written a treatise on ontology. About that no doubt is possible. Nor do I doubt, from what he says in this treatise, that, as to *content*, he considers ontology to be the heart of the philosophical enterprise. I agree. The agreement is fundamental. At present, among linguistic philosophers, it is also rare. But the ontologies we propound differ so radically that our disagreement in this respect is almost equally fundamental. Confrontation thus looks promising. It is also economical. I called the book original. Originality presupposes a thorough, though not necessarily a scholarly, grasp of the dialectical tradition. For it consists in a novel arrangement of the traditional dialectical patterns. Only that excellence which is most rare achieves more, adding a pattern or two to the treasure. Strawson is a clever rearranger. To bring out his cleverness, one must bring in the tradition. One very economical way of bringing it in is to confront his ontology with one almost diametrically opposed. This is the first reason.

As to *method*, Strawson is a linguistic philosopher in the good sense. That is, he does not philosophize, if that be the word, about language but, rather, by means of language, about the world. At least, that is what he tries to do. I, too, am a linguistic philosopher in this sense. At least, that is what I try to be. But again, there is disagreement as fundamental as this agreement. Strawson is an ordinary-language philosopher; I philosophize by means of an ideal language. Happily, we are both moderates or even rightwingers. For Strawson, I take it, would reject the claim, reputedly made by one of the leading Oxford extremists during a recent visit to this country, that what he does and all he cares to do are "prolegomena to a future science of language"; just as I shrink away from those "formalists" who consider mathematical logic the heart of philosophy. Once more, therefore, confrontation seems promising. This is the second reason.

The book is crammed full of arguments. That is one of its more unusual virtues. The arguments are always careful; often ingenious of their kind; sometimes profound, in spite of their kind. I am tipping my hand, deliberately of course. Since he is by temperament a metaphysician, Strawson strains toward the schematic, away from the wrong kind of detail. Since he has imagination, he constructs "possible worlds." Current fashion at Oxford frowns on all this. He, while writing, quite naturally tends to think too much of his associates. Since he hails from Oxford, that puts the rest of us at a disadvantage. For instance, he is often defensively prolix when, outside of Oxford, no defense is needed. Nor would I, from where I stand, choose to use the additional space available for either exposition or criticism of even those *detailed arguments from use* which, from where he stands, are essential; simply because, quite rightly I think, outside of Oxford such arguments do not carry conviction. But I shall of course try to do justice to their gist. This is the third reason.

One more word about strategy. Since Strawson reshuffles the onto-logical deck rather thoroughly, I shall, before describing his game, say a few things about how it has been played traditionally; just as I shall separate the exposition of his system (I hope he will not take offense at the word) from that of the arguments by which he supports it. First of all, though, I shall lay the ground for worthwhile criticism by attend-ing to two matters, first the *epistemological predicament*, then the *lin-guistic turn*, which affect all possible games.

Ontology tells us what there is (what exists), irrespective of whether or not we know it. Taken the wrong way, the clause starting with 'irrespective' seems too exclusive. Taking it the right way, one sees that it really isn't. Consider the absolute idealists, who are the most likely ones to be excluded. What they tell us is, roughly, that know-ings are the only things there are. So stated, even their ontology falls as a limiting case under the formula. The difficulty lies elsewhere. One can only tell what he knows. Speaking traditionally, it seems impos-sible to disentangle Being and Knowing as radically as the formula requires. This is the epistemological predicament. Head on, the obstacle, or limitation, is indeed insurmountable. Some even object, quite rightly, to the very words, 'obstacle' or 'limitation', as pampering aspirations that make no sense. Fortunately, the "obstacle" can be outflanked. There are not, to be sure, two things, ontology and episte-mology, as there are, say, Greek and pre-Columbian history. But there are dialectical contexts which it makes perfect sense to call either onto-logical or epistemological, as the case may be. I am not quite sure whether Strawson would agree. But I am very sure he agrees that if there be such flanking manoeuvres, more light will be shed on their nature by proceeding to cases rather than talking about it in general. The case or point I select is crucial for what is at issue between author and critic. Naturally, therefore, the point lies deep. Like all such points, if one knows how, one can reach it quickly by starting from a common fact.

Let us agree to use 'entity' neutrally, i.e., without ontological com-mitment, for anything an expression may refer to. (Sentences are counted as a kind of expression.) Many philosophers, including author and critic, use 'particular' and 'universal' to refer to two categories (i.e., ontologically interesting kinds) of entities. That does not mean they all agree on which entities fall into which category. In Strawson's world, for instance, physical objects (bodies) are particulars; in mine, they aren't. At the moment, the difference makes no difference, partly because the perceptual (or, if you wish, physical) properties of bodies, say colors, are universals in his world as well as in mine. So I shall talk about bodies. Irrelevancies apart, when a universal, having been presented to us once, is presented to us again, we *recognize* it, directly, as one says, or immediately, or as such, without having to resort to a "criterion." Particulars we do not recognize as such. Roughly again and much complexity apart, chairs, for instance, we recognize only mediately, making use of two (kinds of) criteria. We may recognize (as such) a combination of properties the chair exemplifies. This illustrates the first criterion. It often fails. (I cannot, in isolation, tell my dining room chairs from each other.) "Physical objects move in spatiotemporal orbits." Let this formula stand for a large and complex but also familiar group of facts (laws). In applying the second criterion we draw (consciously or unconsciously) upon our knowledge of this group. In sum, while we do recognize universals as such, we do not so recognize particulars. This is the very common fact I mentioned. Differently exploited, it yields two different, though of course not unrelated, pieces of dialectics, one epistemological, one ontological. The epistemological predicament being what it is, that is not surprising.

M. I know what is (has been) presented to me. *D*. I know only what, if it has been presented to me, I can recognize when it is presented to me again. Some philosophers explicate 'know' so that *M* is true; some others, so that *D* is. The alternative is the starting point of the epistemological dialectic. (The appropriate sense of 'being presented' is not here under consideration.) The gambit is so fundamental that, historically, it marks the deepest dividing line in the epistemological tradition. Not by chance, therefore, this line, too, divides author and critic. Strawson opts for *D*; I, for *M*. The gambit also is so fundamental structurally that one cannot argue directly for his choice, although he can of course point out consequences and offer elucidations, both historical and philological. In a sense, this essay is nothing but a study of the consequences of Strawson's choice. Philologically, think of '*cognoscere*' and '*recognoscere*' and recall that 'to know' is a very accurate translation of the former. I also recall Schlick's formula, *Kennen ist wiedererkennen*, which played such a large role not only in *Allgemeine Erkenntnislehre* but also in his lectures until, during the last years, Wittgenstein's influence submerged everything else. Historically, remember the powerful tradition according to which the only things the mind (intellect) can grasp (know) are universals, i.e., entities which in fact are directly recognizable. Remember the related dualism of sense and intellect and the rather pretty metaphor of the two eyes that goes with it: the mind's eye which "sees" the "concept" and the eye of the senses which, "seeing" only the "particular," is really blind. Strawson is in excellent company. Few philosophers, if any, as much as saw the monistic alternative M, let alone its significance. (The letters M and D are of course taken from 'monistic' and 'dualistic'.)

Yesterday I sat at this desk. Today, recognizing it when entering the room, I might have said "This is the same desk." The analysis of identity, or, as I would rather say, of *sameness*, is the ontological piece of dialectics involved. I distinguish three uses of 'same'; call them logical, epistemological, and ontological. 'Red or blue' and 'not-(not-red and not-blue)' are analytically equivalent. Their referent(s) are not two but one (the same). This illustrates the logical use. For my point it does not matter; I mention it merely to avoid misunderstandings. Whether or not "two" things *are* really one (the same) is one thing. Whether or not we *know* it is another thing. In the first context (they *are*), 'same' is used ontologically; in the second (we *know*), epistemologically. To emphasize this distinction, as I do and Strawson doesn't, is to perform one of those flanking manoeuvres the epistemological predicament forces upon us. Again, the gambit is too fundamental for direct argument in its favor. But again, one can, and I shall, elucidate and point at consequences.

Ontologically, nondiversity and diversity (sameness and difference) are primary. Let me unpack this formula. Consider a phenomenal field consisting of two simultaneous tones differing in pitch. When I "have" such a field, as I sometimes do when introspecting though of course not when perceiving something, I am directly aware of two particulars (as I use 'particular'). I do not, for instance, know that they are two and not one merely by virtue of my also being directly aware (in exactly the same sense of 'aware', since I embrace M) of the different pitches they exemplify. Rather, they must be two for there to be anything in which they differ. On the other hand, their diversity is not presented to me as such, in addition, as it were, to themselves, as are their pitches. The ontological use of 'same' corresponds to direct recognition; the epistemological, as in 'This is the same desk', to recognition by criteria. Where there is a criterion, there is, or can be, a question. About what is primary, there is not.

Strawson wants us to know (be acquainted with) bodies. His intellectual motive, not surprisingly, is realistic. Being a D-theorist, though, he must hold that the unrecognizable is also the unknowable. (He says so himself, p. 210 fn. He even rubs it in by a historical allusion, speaking of an unknowable substratum; rather ironically, I think, since the notion of a substratum is typical of D-theories.) But bodies are in fact not recognizable as such. So he plays down, epistemologically, the distinction between the two kinds of recognition, and, ontologically, puts the full burden of the ontological use on the 'same' in 'This is the same desk'. As a consequence his argument for realism fails. We observe something for a while; then we don't; then, observing it again, we say "This is the same." It follows that "it" existed while we did not observe it; hence it existed independently of our observing it. Bodies, therefore, are not just constructions out of what we observe. This is the gist of the argument. It would be better than it is if the use of 'same' on which it rests were ontological. As long as this use itself rests, as it does, on a criterion, the constructionist (phenomenalist) can account for it as convincingly as anyone else. At this point the very idea of a criterion smacks of constructionism! All this is only too familiar. So I turn to four brief comments, to conclude this crucial topic.

First. Like Strawson, I believe that an adequate "realistic" argument can and must be made. This is not the place for it.[2] I merely wanted to show that, as a consequence of his opting for *D*, his major argument will not do. *Second*. It is a consequence of my option *M* that the ontological 'same' is merely a "lazy word" and cannot without either futility or at a prohibitive price be introduced into the ideal language. I wish to leave no doubt that I accept this consequence. For argument in its favor this is, again, not the place. *Third*. Since my particulars (e.g., sensa) are all momentary things, the question of recognition does not arise. If it did, they could not be recognized as such. They are, as one says, bare particulars. Since we can in fact not even recognize bodies as such, my choice of particulars is perhaps not as wild as some think. Even so, I am convinced that only one who recognizes the significance of *M* can make this choice without getting into trouble. The opposite, as it were, of bare particulars are substances. So it makes sense that, as we shall see, Strawson also accepts the root idea of all substantialism—with a modification, as we shall also see; the very modification in which his originality consists. *Fourth*. I read not long ago what Thomas Reid has to say about (personal) identity in the third chapter of the third of his *Essays on the Intellectual Powers of Man*. Identity, he argues, presupposes temporal continuity. Brooding over his argument, I felt that, as one says at Oxford, something had gone radically wrong. What went wrong, I submit, is that Reid recommends a criterion for the ontological use of 'same'.

That much for what is best said in connection with the epistemolog-

---

[2] See "Dell'Atto," *Rivista di Filosofia*, 51, 1960, 3–51, and pp. 3–44 of this book.

ical predicament. Now for what must be said in connection with the linguistic turn.

All linguistic philosophers talk about the world by means of talking about a suitable language. This is the linguistic turn, the fundamental gambit as to method, on which ordinary and ideal language philosophers (OLP, ILP) agree. Equally fundamentally, they disagree on what is in this sense a "language" and what makes it "suitable." Clearly, one may execute the turn. The question is why one should. Why is it not merely a tedious roundabout? I shall mention three reasons. Strawson might not approve of the way I shall state them but, being moderate and fair-minded, he probably would approve of their spirit. Extremists, of either camp, wouldn't.

First. Words are used either ordinarily (commonsensically) or philosophically. On this distinction, above all, the method rests. The prelinguistic philosophers did not make it. Yet they used words philosophically. *Prima facie* such uses are unintelligible. They require commonsensical explication. The method insists that we provide it. (The qualification, *prima facie* is the mark of moderation. The extremists of both camps hold that what the classical philosophers were above all anxious to express is irremediable nonsense.) *Second.* Much of the paradox, absurdity, and opacity of prelinguistic philosophy stems from failure to distinguish between speaking and speaking about speaking. Such failure, or confusion, is harder to avoid than one may think. The method is the safest way of avoiding it. *Third.* Some things any conceivable language merely shows. Not that these things are literally "ineffable"; rather, the proper (and safe) way of speaking about them is to speak about (the syntax and interpretation of a) language. Consider exemplification. It shows itself by juxtaposition of subject and predicate, which latter two stand for, or represent, the entities to which they refer. Except at the price of either futility or threatening paradox, exemplification cannot be so represented.

OLPs talk about the language we speak (OL); hence the tag applied to them. More precisely, they study *communication;* exploring how we manage to learn OL and, having learned it, to communicate with each other by means of it. That is of course a psychological study. As the extremists pursue it, it is nothing else. Think of the "prolegomena to a future science of language." The fact remains that, including even OLPs outside of their studies, we all communicate about the world, i.e., that part of it which is not language. In some entirely noncommittal and nonspecific sense of 'picture', OL must therefore be a picture of the world and thus, in a minimal sense, a "suitable" language. The ILP, or at least this ILP, acknowledges that. In a general way, he acknowledges it by taking common sense for granted, in this following G. E. Moore. More technically, he acknowledges it by explicating all philosophical uses commonsensically. He insists, however, that just because its primary purpose is communication, OL is most unsuitable as a tool for his purpose, i.e., as a "language" by means of which (not: in which!) to philosophize. This point, decisive as it is, or perhaps because it is so decisive, cannot be argued in general. Once more, one must proceed to cases. Presently I shall.

The very phrase, ideal language (IL), is a misnomer. The IL is merely the skeletal schema of a language. Much more importantly, even if it were not just that, it could not be used for communication. Nor is it a schema of what some call the inner monologue. Rather, it is a *picture* of the world, in a specific and specifiable sense of 'picture'. In making this sort of picture of it, we are stepping outside of the world. That, of course, is merely a metaphor. Literally, the marks the ILP makes on paper are as much a part of the world as is OL. Logically, though, to vary the metaphor, these marks are nowhere. One may indeed wonder why such a picture or schema has ever been called a "language." (I by now often wish it hadn't.) One large part of the explanation, with which I shall not tarry, is historical. The other is structural. Remember the three reasons, all of which have something to do with real languages, which I gave for the linguistic turn. Talking about his marks on paper, the ILP is in an excellent position to observe the three injunctions which correspond to the three reasons. I should like to add that, to the extent an OLP ignores or rejects these three reasons, he is left without any good reason for the linguistic turn. Thus he is in danger of talking merely about language. The extremists among the OLPs have succumbed to the danger. The extremists on the other side talk merely about calculi. At times I do not know which bores me more.

I shall now indicate in what sense IL is a picture by presenting the case I shall also use to show that while an IL is, OL is not a suitable tool. The case involves another disagreement between author and critic, so fundamental that it, too, must be brought out into the open. It is also very familiar. But I prefer first to present it on its merit and only then apply the familiar tag.

In a phenomenal field consisting of a colored spot and nothing else I am presented with two entities, the spot and its color; and three logical features, particularity, universality, and exemplification, shown by the spot, the color, and the fact of the former's exemplifying the latter, respectively. My IL represents the two entities by two syntactically primitive marks, of the kind called undefined descriptive; the three logical features, by the shapes of these marks and their juxtaposition. Since neither chairs nor sensa are directly recognizable, it makes no difference for what I am now discussing that I "attach" some of my primitives to sensa rather than to chairs. On the other hand, I do not wish to prejudge what is indeed a third fundamental disagreement between author and critic, namely, whether or not when having such a field I am presented with two entities or with only one. But again, this further disagreement does not affect what is now under discussion. The example indicates why and how I use 'picture'. It also shows that the IL essentially contains labels. The labels are of course the two marks. Since their shapes show the ontological categories of the entities they represent, they are not "pure labels." Yet they are labels in that (1) they tell (or show) absolutely nothing else about the entities; and (2) their place in the IL is *fully justified* and their meaning, in one of the several meanings of 'meaning', *completely specified* by their having been "attached" to what they are to represent, even though in case the entity represented is a particular (sensum or chair), they could not be correctly "reattached" on the basis of *direct* recognition. It follows that on this ground alone IL could not be used for communication. Or, to say the same thing differently, for the purposes of communication the meaning of these crucial marks would not be completely specified.

OL contains what grammarians call proper names such as 'John' and 'Venice'. But we can communicate by means of 'John' only because both speaker and hearer would recognize John—*indirectly*. I express this by saying that OL does not essentially contain labels. Surely, the familiar tag, *logically proper names*, is by now on every likely reader's lips. I dislike the phrase very much. Strawson uses it, though, and it has been used widely. So I shall for the moment use it, too. Now for three comments.

First. The IL contains essentially logically proper names; OL doesn't. On this author and critic agree; then they immediately part ways. Strawson, dominated by his concern with communication, rejects the idea of an IL on this ground alone. I, prompted by my desire for a suitable picture, reject on this ground alone OL as a suitable tool. IL is suitable (in this respect) because I know of no better (and safer) way to speak of some crucial ontological matters than to point out that certain entities could not in any conceivable "picture" be directly represented except by logically proper names. (An indirect way of referring, as I just used 'direct', would be by definite description.)

Second. Depending on what is the case, every well-formed sentence of the IL is either true or false. 'John smiles' is a well-formed sentence of OL. Depending on whether or not John smiles while it is asserted, it is sometimes true, sometimes false. That does not disturb the OLP. For sentences as such, he tells us, the question of truth or falsehood does not even arise. It arises only when a sentence is uttered in accordance with the rules for its use in order to make an assertion. Again, this shows as clearly as anything in what sense the IL is and OL is not a picture of the world.

Third. Everyone familiar with Strawson's "On Referring"[3] knows that it contains a lucid and forceful presentation of the two groups of ideas, on logically proper names and on truth, which I just attributed to the OLP. The same ideas dominate *Individuals*. About the first group we are told a good deal; the second is more or less taken for granted. One could even say that the book is merely an elaboration of the essay. To me, that is high praise. Good philosophers, I am convinced, do not pursue too many ideas. Rather, they are pursued by a few, which they ponder ever more deeply and know how to elaborate ever more richly.

When we speak commonsensically, we say that there are bodies, thoughts, facts, numbers, and so on. Or we say, synonymously, that these entities exist. As the ontological game has been played, some philosophers have denied that the instances of some of these kinds "exist." To rid such talk of the flavor of absurdity that clings to it, one must first of all realize that in it 'exist' is used philosophically. As a second step, one must state commonsensically what the philosophical use stands for. The tradition has been dominated by three major ideas: *I*. What "exists" exists *independently*. *S*. What "exists" is *simple;* whatever else there is (exists, not: "exists"!) *consists* of simples. *C*. All "existents" are in space and time, in the sense in which bodies are; or, at least, they can be located there, *more or less directly*. These are the three ideas; the three letters being taken from 'independent', 'simple', and 'concrete'. I marked the philosophical use of 'exist' by double quotes. I shall continue the praxis whenever it seems necessary, also for other ontological key terms. The words italicized in *I*, *S*, *C* are themselves used philosophically in these propositions. Thus, however briefly, I must comment.

Concerning C. Even though I italicized 'more or less directly', this use is not necessarily philosophical. But one must be prepared to specify what the phrase is made to stand for.

Concerning S. (*a*) An entity is "simple" if and only if it cannot in any conceivable language be directly referred to except by labels. (*b*) An

---

[3] *Mind*, 59, 1950, 320–44.

entity "consists" of certain others if and only if the expression directly referring to it (in IL) is definable in terms of the expressions which so refer to those others. Jointly, (a) and (b) indicate the drift of the ILP's explications. (b) implies the claim that whatever is not itself a simple consists of such. (Once a use has been explicated, I drop the quotes.) "Reductionism" is the tag for this claim. All OLPs are antireductionists. That shows a connection. Their rejections of logically proper names and of reductionism reinforce each other. The tag itself, reduction, is from a long history burdened with derogatory connotations. So I shall henceforth avoid it, speaking of definitionalism and antidefinitionalism instead.

Concerning I. Taking 'independent' causally, one inevitably ends up an extreme ontological monist. The idea which guides philosophers who shun this gambit is best understood when one considers that we are never presented either with a particular that is not qualitied or with a universal that is not exemplified. But a particular's exemplifying a universal is a fact, not a thing. Thus one may say, not unnaturally, that while facts, or at least some facts, are independent, no thing is. That gives the idea of the explication. The use of 'fact' and 'thing' in it is commonsensical. At most, it lies at the border between the two uses. If I were challenged nonetheless, I would so explicate it that a "fact" is referred to by a (true or false) sentence; a "thing," by a nonsentential (descriptive) expression (of IL). The crucial point is that with this most natural explication *I* and *S* clash. Even the "simplest" fact, referred to by a subject-predicate sentence, has two constituents, referred to by subject and predicate, which are things. Thus, in an obvious sense, no fact can be as "simple" as a thing may be. Those in whom *I* wins out become *fact ontologists* ("only (simple) facts exist"); those with whom *S* prevails, *thing ontologists* ("only (simple) things exist"). Their disagreement marks the deepest dividing line in the ontological tradition. *Substance ontologists* try to have the best of both worlds. To see that, consider that as 'substance' is used philosophically, a "substance" is a thing which, by virtue of being this thing, exemplifies certain characters. But a thing's exemplifying a character is a fact! That spots the tension.

Having made so many preparations, I can now at least before turning to detailed description characterize Strawson's ontology in one fell stroke. Basically, it is a remarkably explicit fact ontology. (Like every consistent ILP, I am a thing ontologist.) Less basically, to be sure, it has many substantialist (Aristotelian) features. Why not? Having paid the price one may as well enjoy his purchase. The central and original idea is that there is a kind of fact, so far unnoticed, which is even simpler than those facts with two constituents which we have so far thought were the simplest. And of these very special facts everything else, whether thing or fact, "consists"; as I would put it, though, as we shall see, not Strawson. In one of the rare purple passages (p. 212) set off against his enjoyably low-keyed prose, he even calls those newly discovered "simples" the true atomic facts. The way I am telling the story, the reader may be ready with a shrewd guess as to the nature of that novel simplicity, that new expedient to relieve the tension between I and S. I am not yet ready for the denouement. After this glimpse at the heart of the system, I turn next to some comments that should help to penetrate its surface.

The characteristic ontological use of 'exist', we saw, is narrower than the ordinary. The same goes for 'individual', which ontologists tend to use synonymously with 'particular'. Strawson so uses 'individual' and 'exists' that whatever may be referred to by the subject word or phrase of a true sentence (of OL) is an individual and exists. That makes everything an individual; facts, bodies, thoughts, colors, numbers, and so on. His use of these two key terms is thus as broad as it is unproblematic, except that it makes the book's title rather inexpressive. "Facts and Particulars" would be more appropriate. But I understand the lure of elegant one-word titles; so I shall not grumble. 'Particular' he also uses much more broadly than is usual, though more narrowly than 'individual'. This use is controlled by C, which in turn controls his argument. So I shall explain it later, when presenting the gist of his argument.

If 'a' is definable in terms of 'b', 'c', 'd', then a "consists" of b, c, d; and the latter three are "simpler" than a. That is the definitionalist ILP's high road to the explication of S. Among OLPs, the extremists, having renounced and denounced the goal, need no road that leads to it; the moderates must look for an alternative. Strawson's alternative is *conceptual analysis*, or, as he says, analysis of the structure of our conceptual scheme. His key words, corresponding to 'simple' and 'consist', are 'basic' and 'folding'. The less basic "unfolds" into what is more so; the latter, in turn, "folds up" into the former. After a fashion, there is thus an ontological hierarchy, even though all its members "exist" and are "individuals." I am reminded of certain commonwealths in which all citizens are equal, except that some of them are more so.

Since definitionalism and antidefinitionalism are now again battle cries, they affect the style of many current debates. The issues debated are of course not all fundamental. Among the few which are, one is at the root of what was originally at stake, before the rubrics themselves again became battle cries. In favor of this one issue I brush aside all others. Conceptual analysis yields what OLPs call "conceptual truths"; or, synonymously, "linguistic truths," "logical truths," "analytic truths." The ILP's explication of 'analytic' is narrower. Both sides agree that 'Either it is raining or it isn't' is analytic. On 'No body is at the same time in two places' they disagree. For the OLP it is analytic; for the ILP it isn't. For the ILP definitions are a proper tool of onto-logical analysis because they are (in his sense) analytic; so-called "con-ceptual truths," because they are (in his sense) synthetic, are not. The issue at the root is thus the nature of "logical truth." Once more author and critic are in fundamental disagreement. Where it most crucially matters, Strawson's analysis is, as I shall point out, definitional. Or, at least, whatever difference there is makes no real difference. (That is one reason why I admire him.) But he himself does not see that. So he remains the victim of *two illusions*. It is a familiar formula that in philosophical analysis the appeal to "logical truth" is conclusive. As the ILP explicates 'logical truth', the formula is true enough as far as it goes. As OLPs explicate 'logical truth', the formula spawns the illu-sion that when they appeal to what they call conceptual truth their analysis, or argument, is as conclusive as it would be if they had appealed to what the ILP calls logical truth. This illusion, call it the first, Strawson shares with all OLPs. The formula I just called true enough so far as it goes is the last truth. We can go that far and no further. This illusion, call it the second, is much subtler than the first. Strawson shares it with all those, including many ILPs, who hold, or could consistently hold, that logic is the world's "form," in an inher-ently confused sense of 'form' which leaves logic without ontological grounding. I registered my dissent when I insisted that such logical features as particularity, universality, and exemplification are pre-sented to us.

It will pay if I support the generalities of the last paragraph, about conceptual analysis and the two illusions, with an illustration simpler than anything I could cull from the book. Consider 'longer-than', 'equal-in-length', and 'length', as applied to straight sticks. Since the two hyphenated expressions give away the "conceptual structure" involved, replace them for the moment by two opaque marks, 'R_1' and 'R_2'. There is a small group of true generalities, call it G, some men-tioning only R_1, some only R_2, some both. E.g., R_2 is transitive and symmetrical; R_1, transitive and asymmetrical; and so on. The story is very familiar. Add an equally familiar definition, D, for 'length'; more precisely, for 'having-a-certain-length'; still more precisely, a schema of definitions, one for each length. Why bother with the familiar? Consider finally two propositions: (1) Lengths are linearly ordered. (2) Length is a property (of sticks). This is the illustration. *The ILP speaks about it as follows.* Both (1) and (2) can be nontrivially deduced from *D* and *G*; all members of *G* are synthetic; so, therefore, are (1) and (2). 'Deduced' is used in the strict sense which goes with the strict sense of 'analytic'. 'Nontrivially' has to be added because every tautology can be trivially deduced from any premiss. *Strawson would have to say* that, first, (1) and (2) are conceptual truths about length; and, second, since the concept length can be unfolded into the two concepts R_1 and R_2, the latter are more basic than the former. For criticism I separate (1) and (2). *Concerning* (1): Moving downward, to what is more basic, the OLP must consistently hold that the members of *G* are in turn conceptual truths about the concepts R_1 and R_2. Overtly or covertly guided by the psychologistic identification of the "contradictory" with the "unimaginable," OLPs notoriously hold this view. Moving upward, they would have to maintain that all generalities are conceptual truths. For there is upon their account no criterion to separate "conceptual (analytic)" from "empirical (synthetic)" generalities. That makes statements of individual fact the only "empirical" ones, which to me is absurd. Strawson does not openly embrace this absurdity. But we shall see that he comes remarkably close to it in sentiment. *Concerning* (2): Being a property (or even: a property of sticks) is a conceptual property of the concept length. That is but another way of stating (2). For it is part of the notion of conceptual truth that a concept's having a "conceptual property" is itself such a truth. This kind of talk needs explication. I take it to mean that from a word's being of a certain kind, e.g., an adjective, the rules by which it combines with others into well-formed sentences can be deduced. This is patently false. The mistake is most easily spotted if we turn for a moment to calculi. The so-called formation rules of a calculus have two parts. In the first part one distinguishes several kinds (shapes, types) of signs, e.g., x-shapes and f-shapes; in the second, one specifies the combinations making well-formed sentences, e.g., '$f(x)$' but not either '$f(f)$' or '$x(x)$'. Both parts must be stated; the second cannot be deduced from the first. (Wittgenstein made the same mistake when he argued, in *Tractatus* 3.333, that the type *rule* is contained in the type *distinction*.) Clearly, this mistake relates to the second illusion, just as what was said concerning (1) relates to the first.

There are entities which are "facts" and yet so "simple" that they have only one "constituent." Since so far no one has understood their nature I shall call them the hidden simples. Into these entities everything else unfolds. *This is Strawson's central and original idea.* If it stands up under close scrutiny, then it is indeed the denouement, not only of my story but of the age-old tension between fact and thing ontologies. The idea does not stand up. This is the center of my criticism. If that criticism stands up, then Strawson has failed. I shall argue my case in three steps.

First. What are these hidden simples? Is their single constituent a universal, or like a universal, in which case the nominalists would object? Is it a particular, or like a particular, in which case the realists would demur? From these questions, one should think, all criticisms must start. Yet there is one even more radical. The purpose of philosophical analysis is not to confuse or perplex us but, rather, to enlighten us in a commonsensical way. The idea of a single-constituent fact fills me with irresoluble perplexity. I hear the words. But nothing comes through. The commonsensical distinction between thing and fact, or, if you would rather have it this way, between term and sentence, cannot be talked away. For me, this alone is decisive. But it is not all I have to say. In the next step I shall identify the hidden simples, arguing that in fact they have two constituents. That is why I call Strawson a fact ontologist. In the last step I shall argue that if one grants what Strawson claims to be their nature, they cannot, as he also claims, be folded up into bodies.

Second. When I behold a white expanse of a certain kind, the simplest among all the facts presented to me is, according to Strawson, correctly expressed not by 'This is snow' but, rather, by 'Snow'. So used, 'snow' is said to refer to a *feature*. A feature is the single constituent of a hidden simple. It is, we see, a universal, or like a universal. Remember now the disagreement I was careful not to prejudge when I insisted earlier that, being presented with a red spot and nothing else, I am presented not with just one thing but with two, a particular ('this') and a universal ('red'). Now I must judge. How should I proceed? Philosophy is a dialectical structure erected on a phenomenological base. Questions located where the structure rests on the base have a delicacy all their own. I, of course, have convinced myself that I am actually presented with two things. Yet I am loath to rest the case on this conviction; for I am also convinced that a very major part of it is dialectical. So I ask dialectically how, if I were not also presented with particulars, I could ever know it if a second spot, of exactly the same shade, made its appearance beside the first. I add in dialectical support that after the appearance of the second spot the first is exactly what it was before. If an objector reminds me that I could say, very simply, that while at first I had one red, red_1, later I had two, red_1 and red_2, I reply, equally simply, that for all that matters (since the realism-nominalism issue is not directly involved), the indices have the logical force of particulars. (Indexed universals are at least very close to the "perfect particulars" of the tradition. Strawson, p. 169 fn., is of course aware of the connection.) Remember also what has been said about nondiversity and diversity being primary. But the dialectic is complex indeed. So I let it go at that, adding instead a word about Strawson's intellectual motives. The 'This' he suppresses in 'This is snow' refers to what is as momentary as and no more recognizable as such than is my sensum. That is why he suppresses it. This shows the close structural connection between his two most fundamental gambits, his choice of a dualistic epistemology (D over M) and his identification of ontological and epistemological sameness, on the one hand, and the central idea of his ontology on the other.

  Third. Can bodies be *unfolded* into features, i.e., as we just saw, into unindexed universals, by means of the (presumably conceptual) truths about the spatial and temporal relations obtaining among features? Strawson's answer is Yes. I submit that he is mistaken. The problem is complex; but it has been explored; so I shall limit myself to three comments. First, though, I should like to point out that for all I can tell, Strawson in the few passages he devotes to this crucial and complex problem proceeds as if the 'unfolded' I italicized could be replaced by 'defined'. That is what I had in mind when claiming earlier that where it most crucially matters his analysis is definitional rather than conceptual. (*a*) Consider a field consisting of three spots, green to the left of red to the left of green. 'Green to the left of green', 'green to the left of red', 'red to the left of green' will all be true. This shows that the "structure" of the "spatial" relations among features is very different indeed from that of the relations ordinarily called spatial. I found no evidence that Strawson even noticed that. (*b*) A particular exemplifies more than one universal. Traditionally speaking, the latter *coin*here in what is, upon D, an unknown substratum. Strawson, in order to succeed, must make his features *co*here, the way they actually do, without making them *in*here in anything. I call this the bundling problem. In an essay called "Russell on Particulars"[4] I have shown that upon Strawson's terms it is insoluble. (*c*) Strawson rejects absolute space and time. Thus he cannot introduce a certain class of universals whose introduction amounts to accepting absolute space and time. This is what I mean by his terms. If one waives them, the bundling problem, though still very difficult, can be solved. Nelson Goodman has shown that in

---

  [4] *The Philosophical Review*, 56, 1947, 59–72 (reprinted in *The Metaphysics of Logical Positivism*).

The Structure of Appearance. Like Strawson, I reject absolute space and time. Nor is that the only reason why I reject Goodman's ingenious construction. But I greatly admire the accuracy with which he has thought about some matters so subtle and so fundamental that in thinking about them accuracy and profundity are one thing and not two. In the matter just discussed Strawson was not as accurate as he might have been had he not been hampered by those two irremediably inaccurate notions, conceptual analysis in general and his hidden simples in particular.

The ontological building stones of Strawson's world are the hidden simples. As he speaks, they are most "basic." Putting 'exist' to its traditional philosophical use, one might call them the only "existents." On that base his ontological hierarchy rests. Next to its base we find his "particulars." Among the latter, some are more "basic" than others. To understand their subhierarchy, one must grasp the idea controlling his use of 'particular'. To understand this use, one must in turn understand the gist of the arguments supporting the system. That determines my strategy.

As far as communication is concerned, there are no logically proper names. This we saw earlier. Let us now explore a bit further. Tom, while talking with Dick, who does not know Harry, points at a tall, blond man just walking past and says 'This is Harry'. Assume that on this occasion (context) the definite description 'the tall blond man walking past' is unambiguous. If so, Tom would not have needed to point. Moreover, whether or not Tom pointed, Dick's using on another occasion, say, the next day, 'Harry' correctly and as far as communication goes successfully, *presupposes* his being able to recognize Harry, which in turn *presupposes* that on the first occasion, when he learned how to use 'Harry', he was presented with the fact (or facts) which made the definite description true and unambiguous. Communication would be impossible were it not for a class of entities which speaker and hearer can thus "identify" and "reidentify." (These are two of Strawson's key words; I avoided them, deliberately of course, because of what I had to say about sameness.) This class is that of bodies, i.e., commonsensical physical objects such as chairs but not, say, electrons. That makes bodies the "basic particulars." This is the idea. Now for a string of comments, expository and critical.

First. Remember the ontological predicament. An ontological hierarchy is an order of Being, not of Knowing. The principle of Strawson's hierarchy is not even Knowing. His is an order established by Communicating. His hierarchy is thus ontological only after a fashion. To speak as I did earlier, he once more fails to execute the proper flanking manoeuvre. Even worse, he falls behind what so often has been achieved before, since he does not even operate on the level of Knowing but, at an irrelevant further remove, on that of Communicating. It is clear, I trust, how this failure derives from his fundamental gambits.

Second. As Strawson uses 'particular', a sensum, a chair, an electron, my beloved's last smile when I last saw her, the battle of Waterloo, the impending spring flood of the Iowa River are all particulars. What makes this hodgepodge into an ontological category? The answer lies in two ideas. Communicating about any of these entities, we "identify" them through definite descriptions. I myself just so referred to three of the six I mentioned. If a definite description fails to single out the entity for the hearer, we try again by offering further descriptions for what some words or phrases in the first refer to. Pursuing this descent as long as is necessary (for successful communication) we arrive if necessary at bodies, at which level we *necessarily* succeed. This is *the first idea*. It makes bodies basic among particulars. (Since they unfold directly into the hidden simples, they are, next to them, the most basic.) Bodies are directly in space and time. The entities of the hodgepodge category are all indirectly located in space and time through the location of the body or bodies mentioned in the definite descriptions to which theoretically we may have to descend in order to achieve "identifying reference." The longer the descent, the less direct the location, and therefore, as one might expect, the less basic the particular. Now remember *C*: what "exists"is what is directly or indirectly located in space and time. *The second idea* obviously is *C*. Nor is *C* just a matter of communication. It explicates a genuine ontological idea, even though one of which I don't happen to think much; it is too "materialistic"and "Aristotelian" for my taste. If this diagnosis is correct, then, however covertly, Strawson's particulars (and the hidden simples) should be the only "existents" of his world. He himself doesn't say that. Nor could he, given his all-encompassing use of 'exist'. And, of course, he is much too clever overtly to embrace nominalism. Have we then perhaps come upon one of the motives for that all-encompassing use? Be that as it may, we shall soon come upon two outcroppings of this Aristotelian bedrock.

Third. Bodies do, of course, provide a "coordinate system" for unambiguous reference. This is so because of a class of generalities, call it again *G*, of which 'No body is at the same time at two places' is as good a representative as any. *G* was mentioned once before, as the body of fact (law) yielding the residual criterion for the indirect recognition of bodies. Now consider three things. Consider first the idea mentioned a while ago that an analysis is complete and conclusive in a special way if it has penetrated to the level of the "logical." Consider, second, that as he consistently must, Strawson considers the members of G to be all "conceptual truths" about bodies. Consider, third, that for the OLP the adjectives 'conceptual', 'linguistic', 'logical', and *necessary* all combine with the noun 'truth' into synonymous phrases. With these three things kept in mind two more become clear. First, Strawson bolsters the ontological status of bodies by pointing out that in virtue of the supposedly conceptual truths G they *necessarily* produce the coordinate system required for communication. Second, by thus bolstering the ontological status of bodies he bolsters his "realistic" sentiment. I have no quarrel with the sentiment; I am merely analyzing the structure of a very complex argument. For the ILP, of course, the members of G are synthetic. The contrary belief is but an instance of the first illusion (i.e., that, say, the axioms of geometry are conceptual truths). Presently we shall come upon two instances of the second illusion.

Fourth. Universals exist for Strawson; of course they do; everything does. Where, though, do they have a place in his hierarchy? My answer is that there is no good place for them. I acknowledged that a while ago when, following Strawson, I called the hidden simples the only building stones of his world, thus excluding what consistently I (and he) ought to have included, namely, the spatial and temporal relations (universals) which the hidden simples exemplify. Even this omission could be counted an outcropping of that Aristotelian bedrock. Two others are more conspicuous. Particulars, we are told, are "complete" in a sense in which universals are not. For this alleged ontological asymmetry there are two elaborate arguments. Replace 'complete' by 'independent', remember I ("What "exists" exists independently") and you will in these two arguments recognize the two outcroppings. Both arguments, (a) and (b), are in a special sense "linguistic." A little reflection will show that they are both instances of the second illusion (the subtle one, concerning the world's "form").

(a) Unlike the words and phrases referring to universals, those referring to particulars express "complete thoughts." The reasons Strawson gives for this claim are, as he knows and tells, more or less Oxfordish variations of Frege's ill-begotten idea of propositional functions. A "name" of an "object"—I use the two words as Frege does—can stand by itself; an adjective, e.g., 'green', is merely a part of a propositional function, e.g., ' . . . is green'. This is the idea. It clarifies nothing; confuses everything; merely expresses, rather than supports, a preconceived ontological asymmetry. What can be done with it can be done as well or better without it. One who does not see that will argue as Strawson here does and as Wittgenstein did, also under the influence of Frege, in *Tractatus* 3.333, which I mentioned earlier for this very reason. That also shows where the illusion comes in.

(*b*) As 'empirical' has been used for quite some time, everybody is an empiricist, just as everybody is against sin. So I don't use the word anymore. Strawson, who uses it rarely, once uses it emphatically (p. 238), speaking of the natural determination "to wed the notion of existence to empirical fact—the ultimate stuff with which we have to deal—and hence to those items, viz., particulars, the designations of which necessarily presuppose empirical facts." What is this ultimate stuff? What are these empirical facts? (By the way, does anyone still wonder why I called Strawson a remarkably articulate fact ontologist?) An "empirical fact," the context shows, is an individual fact involving a body, e.g., the fact expressed by 'This is a tall blond man'. This is the passage I had in mind when I claimed that even though he does not say so outright, Strawson is in sentiment remarkably close to the absurd position that true statements of individual fact about bodies in space and time are the only nonconceptual truths. As far as the argument at hand is concerned, recall the story of Tom, Dick, and Harry, in the paragraph in which 'presuppose' is twice italicized. The correct use of proper names ('Harry') or definite descriptions ('the tall blond man') referring to particulars *presupposes* the knowledge of "empirical facts." Call the last sentence (1). Particulars (bodies) *presuppose* empirical facts. Call this sentence (2). Passing from (1) to (2) is to pass from communication theory to ontology. Strawson, for whom this transition is only too easy, argues from (2) that bodies are ontologically "complete" in a sense in which their properties (i.e., ordinary universals, not just features) are not. I need not at this point explain why from where I stand the argument fails. I add, though, that 'presuppose' is here used exactly as in "On Referring," where we are told not only that (the correct use of) 'The king of France is bald' presupposes that there is a king of France, but also that to be thus presupposed is to be "in a special sense, implied." Implication is a syntactical notion. This is the cue as to where the second illusion comes in. (2) is not just a conceptual truth. It is supposedly a conceptual truth of that special kind, "logical" or "linguistic" in a special sense, which I illustrated by 'Length is a property'. Once more, the illusion helps to exalt the ontological status of bodies.

It is time that I confess an omission. Bodies are not really the only basic particulars of the system. That has something to do with Strawson's analyses of the mind-body nexus and of our knowledge of other minds. Here and there an insight shines brightly, now and then a comment intrigues in what he says, and he says a good deal, about these two important problems. By and large, though, I find this part of the book much less interesting and not at all original. Some of it I find quaint. Thus, since I had to select, I made a choice. But I shall now, with apologies, characterize this part as briefly as in a standard review. The extremists among the OLPs either overtly or covertly embrace metaphysical behaviorism (materialism). Strawson is much too sensible for that. His goal is, rather, an overt reasoned rejection of this absurd doctrine. His starting point is the supposedly conceptual truth 'I do not have your experiences'. Ordinary language analysis, as first practiced by the later Wittgenstein and following him at Oxford, provides the way by which he arrives from this starting point at that goal. The price he pays is the doctrine that "persons" are particulars which are both basic and logically primitive. One can of course not be sure what 'logically primitive' means in the mouth of an antidefinitionalist. It seems to mean that a person cannot be defined in terms of his body and his "experiences." This doctrine I find quaint. When introducing the alleged conceptual truth, 'I do not have your experiences', Strawson very cautiously refers to Schlick's last essay "Meaning and Verification."[5] He need not have been so cautious. Nor is it accidental that, as Allaire quite recently pointed out in "Tractatus 6.3751,"[6] Schlick in another late essay anticipates some of the later Wittgenstein's ideas about the nature and function of linguistic analysis.

Now to conclude with a few reflections of a very different kind. Strawson is charmingly eager to convince his readers that what he does is metaphysics, the same thing, in spite of all the differences, which the classical philosophers did. The eagerness is most naturally explained by his long association with the Oxford movement, since at Oxford for quite some time now and until most, most recently, to say the least, the very word, metaphysics, was taboo. This reader is convinced. Nor am I just charmed. I am almost touched, remembering how sternly admonished I was by some high dignitaries of another movement shortly after I had first used that bad word, metaphysics, in the title of an essay. Eventually I was even excommunicated. Strawson's fate, I believe, will be less harsh (if that be the word). There have been quite a few signs lately that the Oxford movement is about to collapse. Or perhaps it is just petering out. There is that book I mentioned at the beginning. More pertinently, there have been a few remarkable pieces

---

[5] *The Philosophical Review*, 45, 1936, 339–69.
[6] *Analysis*, 19, 1959, 100–105.

in recent British journals. These I don't mention, partly because I do not wish to put the finger on anyone. In this country, there is the recoil from those frankly professed "prolegomena to a future science of language." There is, most ominously of all, The Big Yawn, often no longer covered by a polite or diplomatic hand. The signs add up. Strawson's book is more than just a sign. It shows a way out to those who, partly because of the way he says what he says, are more likely to listen to him than to anyone else. From where I stand, I had to make it clear that I judge him to have failed. But then, in philosophy, who hasn't failed or doesn't fail eventually? It is enough, more than enough, to have done as well as Strawson did. *In magnis voluisse sat est.*

The Ontology
of Edmund Husserl*

THERE is reading and reading. We insist that our students read some of the classics. Most of them do not know what they have read. They just read *in* them. Recently I spent several months reading Husserl.[1] Naturally, I had read in him before, though not very much and not during the last fifteen years or so, while I worked out my own views. Now, having really read him, I am profoundly impressed by the greatness of his achievement. I also see how much of what slowly and painfully I have discovered for myself I could have learned from him. I thus paid the usual price of ignorance. Ignorance, or even its confession, is hardly an excuse for an essay. Again as usual, though, there is a twist. Had I in good time learned from Husserl all there was to be learned, I probably would not have avoided what, from where I now stand, I take to be his fatal mistakes. In a sense, though not exclusively to be sure and not I hope in a niggardly fashion, those mistakes are the subject of these *méditations husserliennes*.

In first philosophy, 'realism' has two major uses. Call realism as opposed to nominalism, realism₁; as opposed to idealism, realism₂. If challenged to squeeze as much as possible about Husserl into three short sentences I would say this: Taught by Brentano, he started from and always held fast unto the act; at first, he was a realist₂; eventually he became an idealist. These three things I had long known, of course, from having read in him or, even, about him. They were in fact what

---

* Methodos, *12, 1960, 359–92. Reprinted by permission.*

[1] This essay is based on a complete reading of *Logische Untersuchungen, Ideen* (Erstes Buch), *Méditations Cartesiennes, Erfahrung und Urteil.* I have also read much of the material now being published as *Husserliana* by the Husserl Archive, particularly the later books of *Ideen.* But I shall not, except at a few salient points, either quote or cite.

now led me to read him. To explain the attraction, I must talk about myself. My first teachers were the logical positivists who, whether or not they know it, are all either materialists or phenomenalists. Phenomenalism is a kind of idealism. When, dissatisfied, I tried to think for myself, I discovered the act. (In this, as it happened, I took the cues from Moore and Brentano rather than from Husserl.) Guided by the discovery, I now find myself structurally a realist$_2$. I say structurally, because the classical realists would probably not welcome me into their company. But this I believe is so merely because, while they philosophized before, I philosophize after the linguistic turn. In other words, the anticipated rejection reacts to my method of philosophizing rather than the structure of my philosophy.

Husserl built everything on the act. So do I. In this there is no difference. He moved from realism$_2$ to idealism. I traveled in the opposite direction. The difference is massive and striking. Yet the differences between our analyses of the act seem, and in many though not in all respects in fact are, minor. What, then, are the major structural differences to account for the opposite movements, towards and away from idealism? The question drove me to the books. The answer I found there is that Husserl made two major mistakes. For one, he is a nominalist. For another, his analysis of relations is inadequate. From these two mistakes, either by themselves or in conjunction with a few subsidiary patterns, all others follow. Both already occur in the *Untersuchungen*. In fact, they dominate them. This is the case I shall argue. If I am right, then the later idealism is already implicit in this explicitly realistic work. (I am a realist$_1$, and, taught as I was by Russell, started with an adequate analysis of relations.)

Calling Husserl a nominalist jars. So I hasten to add that there are several kinds of nominalism. All but one are rather shallow dead ends, mere variants of that "psychologism" Husserl himself tracked down so relentlessly. His is the one serious kind. I hope to give good reasons for calling it conceptualism rather than nominalism. But there are also several kinds of conceptualism. Again, all but one are shallow dead ends, more or less "psychologistic." And again, Husserl's is the one serious kind, which is really a variant of Platonism. Of all this presently. Now I merely want to make sure that the reader will keep his peace until I have had my say.

Even mere exposition often gains from what a critical discussion cannot do without, namely, a foil. What has been said makes it plausible that my own ontology is a suitable foil for Husserl's. Nor does the interest of the purely structural points which are my main concern and which this foil sets off depend on original and foil being held in equal esteem. Thus I feel free to proceed as I shall. And I shall, for brevity's sake, speak of Husserl's and my ontology as the *system* and the *foil*,[2] respectively.

Nothing is ineffable. Some things, though, are peculiar in that before they have been said it seems very difficult to say them while afterwards they seem very simple. These things are then called ultimate or profound. Naturally, they have a lure all their own. The danger is that one mistakes for profound what is merely trivial. In philosophy both lure and danger are greatest in what (I believe) Wolff first called *ontologia generalis sive formalis*. Its air is thin and heady indeed. No matter what mistakes Husserl may have made in it, he was one of its few recent masters. I am becoming ever more sensitive to its lure. So I shall court danger by starting with some reflections on general ontology. Next I shall very briefly outline my own; then with much more detail Husserl's. Next I shall exhibit the two fundamental mistakes. Then I shall be ready to attend to some of their consequences. At that point the further order of exposition will be obvious.

I

Ontology asks what there is. The answer expected is or yields a classification. The use of 'is' in the question is philosophical. A phrase and a word will help us to avoid it. Whatever is assigned a place in the classification is given some *ontological status*. To have some ontological status is to be an *entity*. Call the most comprehensive or highest classes (ontological) *modes*; those immediately below them, (ontological) *kinds*. How many modes does an ontologist recognize? How many kinds in each mode? How many entities in each kind? The questions direct us toward salient differences among ontologies. Traditionally, 'real', 'ideal', 'existent', 'subsistent' indicate (membership in) modes. Since the traditional uses are all philosophical, the safest thing is to set them off, say, by double quotes. But since I shall never employ either these or any other words from the traditional vocabulary without eventually explicating how philosophers have used them, and, for a few of them, how I use them myself, we shall be safe without typographical pedantry. 'Exist' will be used mostly for a mode, but occasionally also as a convenient substitute for the clumsy 'having some ontological status'. The latter use will always be marked by double quotes.

Ontologists disagree on which entities, if any, should be classified

---

[2] For exposition, see *Meaning and Existence* and two later essays: "Dell'Atto," *Rivista di Filosofia*, 51, 1960, 3–51, and pp. 3–44 of this book; "Ineffability, Ontology, and Method," *Philosophical Review*, 69, 1960, 18–40, and pp. 45–63 of this book.

as individuals and characters respectively. Some propose such things as apples and their (perceptual) colors. Others propose instead sensa and their (phenomenal) colors. With a certain precaution, individuality and universality are nevertheless good examples of ontological kinds. The precaution has something to do with things to come. Some philosophers are so impressed with the dialectic of the One and the Many that, building their whole ontology around it, they assign whatever they call individuals and characters not only to different kinds but to different modes. Others are content to make individuality and universality two kinds of one mode. The latter I call *realists*$_1$*;* the former, *nominalists*. There are of course also those who deny all ontological status to colors. They too are called nominalists. But they are merely stuck in a shallow blind alley.

Some ontologists wish to speak so that there is only one entity; others, so that there are several. The former are called *monists;* the latter, *pluralists*. Monism I shall not consider. The pluralists all have a problem in common. To spot it, I introduce an example from which we shall get a lot of use.

I hear a dichord; c and e of the middle octave; the former soft, the latter loud. Since we have no ready words for loudnesses, let me use '*sft*' and '*ld*' for these two particular ones. That makes '(c, sft); (e, ld)' an adequate notation for the dichord. Hearing it, I do not hear (c, ld); (e, sft), which is another dichord. Hearing them both, in succession, I know them from each other. That is so because in the one c is tied to *sft* while in the other it is tied to *ld*. Correspondingly for e. In the notation the parentheses represent the ties which make the difference.

Assume that c, e, *sft*, *ld* are all counted as entities. The tones themselves, (c, sft), and so on, may or may not be so classified. If one counts them as entities, one will naturally call them *complex entities*. Otherwise one will speak of *a complex of entities*, thus by implication denying ontological status to complexes. In this respect pluralists have a choice. In another they don't. No pluralist can get along without at least one of the two, complex entities and complexes of entities. What "makes" either is of course the tie. The tie itself must therefore be grounded ontologically. From here a single step will quickly take us to the problem all pluralists must face.

Notice first how the example was put. One hears a dichord. One hears another. One knows them from each other. The example was put epistemologically, as one says. As so often, this is a most natural way to introduce an ontological issue. It is also a proper way, since whatever we perceive and whatever we know, as well as our perceiving or knowing it, must be grounded ontologically. On this all philosophers who know their business agree. Their disagreements lie elsewhere. An idealist, for instance, may ground either in Selves or in their characters what a realist$_2$ grounds in entities which are neither.

The only way to ground the tie is to make either it or an "ingredient" of it an entity. Choosing the latter alternative, one arrives after some steps at the former. So we may as well start with the former. Calling the tie 't', we may then consistently write (c, t, sft), (e, t, ld), and so on, for the four tones. The parentheses spot the problem. How are the three entities c, t, sft tied together? We cannot dodge the question. Yet we seem to be started on an infinite regress. There are but two ways of avoiding it. One may at this juncture opt for monism. This is what Bradley did. Or one admits at least one entity which ties others into complexes (or complex entities) without need of a further entity to tie it to what it ties. Any such entity I shall call a *fundamental tie*, or a *nexus*. We may say, then, that a pluralist must give ontological status to at least one fundamental tie. Ever since Bradley this should have been a truism of general ontology.

Every workable ontology contains in fact a plurality of nexus, which plurality divides into kinds. As to the number of such kinds ontologies significantly differ. Consider as an abstract possibility one with two modes. It must contain at least one kind (if only with a single member) to connect (tie) entities from different modes. Otherwise the world falls apart. (Platonic participation is such a tie.) Also, it will plausibly contain two more kinds, one "within" each mode. Presently we shall see that the system realizes this possibility. It looks as if by pursuing such patterns we may gain some rather radical structural insights. Unhappily, we are also approaching the point where the price of complete generality is either tedium or emptiness or both. One more comment, though, is perhaps worthwhile. No matter how many fundamental ties or kinds of such there are, each is itself an entity and the ontological classification is all-inclusive. Where then, in it, fall the fundamental ties? There are two styles, as it were. One may gather into one mode all the fundamental ties and *whatever goes with them* but nothing else. Or one may make this class but a kind within a mode. The latter, we shall see, is the system's style; the former, the foil's.

To unpack next the italicized phrase. The ontological categories are themselves entities; otherwise the classification wouldn't be all-inclusive. Consider now an ontology containing two kinds and an (asymmetrical) tie connecting two entities, one from each of these two kinds, and no others. The two kinds will then "go with" this tie. That unpacks the phrase. For an example, think of (the realist's) individuals and (nonrelational) characters as the two kinds. That makes (nonrelational) exemplification the tie; individuality and (nonrelational) universality, the two entities that "go with" it.

One more comment about fundamental ties as such. Remember that I wrote $c, t, sft; e, t, ld$; and so on. (The parentheses are now suppressed; the semicolons will do.) Had I sought generality for its own sake, I could have written $c, t_1, sft; e, t_2, ld$; and so on. As far as I know no one has ever explored this possibility. That is, the "sameness" of a nexus in its several "instances" has never been probed dialectically. Or, as some now may want to put it, the grammar of 'same', 'instance', and 'nexus' is such that the phrase 'instance of a nexus' makes no sense. I nevertheless just introduced the dialectic of the One and the Many into that of the nexus. True, I introduced it only in order to dismiss it. Yet there is some small point in confronting the two. Some ontologies, we know, are built around the One and the Many. If such an ontology has been built by a master, then we shall expect to find all nexus, no matter what they connect, in the mode of the One. This is the point. The master I have in mind is Husserl.

Speaking as we ordinarily do, whenever two or more "things" are somehow "connected," we say that they are related. I spoke instead of a fundamental tie or nexus. Only a philosopher with an axe to grind would do that. Let me unsheathe the axe. In the foil, something being green involves two entities which are not nexus, call them for the moment ordinary entities, held together by the nexus of (nonrelational) exemplification. Similarly, something being to the left of something else involves three ordinary entities, one of them an ordinary *relation*, held together by the nexus of (relational) exemplification. To propose this account is to claim that there is at least one striking difference between an ordinary relation and a nexus. One who uses the same word for both is in danger not only of prejudging that claim but also of making mistakes in his analysis of (ordinary) relations. Husserl did use the same word, calling inner and outer relations what I call a nexus and a relation, respectively.[3]

Take a tone which is c and sft. In the foil it assays as follows. In addition to c and sft, which are counted as (simple) characters, there is a third entity, which is counted as an individual. These three are held together by two (kinds of) nexus. Conjunction ties c and sft into the (compound) character c-*and*-sft; the latter and the particular are tied

___

[3] In the foil and elsewhere a distinction is made between descriptive (e.g., being to the left of) and logical (e.g., being the converse of) relations. The point above does not depend on the example being descriptive. Brentano's analysis of relations is as inadequate as Husserl's; for details see R. Grossmann, "Acts and Relations in Brentano," *Analysis*, 21, 1960, 1–5.

into one fact by exemplification. Alternatively, exemplification ties each of the two (simple) characters to the individual, thus yielding two facts, which conjunction in turn ties into one. The difference between the alternatives makes no ontological difference. (More precisely, it makes no difference provided all facts are considered compounds and no compound an entity.) In the system, the tone's ontological assay is quite different. Of this presently. Now I merely want to call attention to the *connectives*, conjunction, disjunction, and so on, since they are a kind of nexus. Both system and foil account for them. Nor will it be necessary for us to examine either account. That is why I mention the connectives now, lest not mentioning them at all in a discussion of fundamental ties cause either puzzlement or confusion.[4]

II

There are really two systems; the first, that of the *Untersuchungen*, realistic₂ at least in intent; the second, of the *Ideen* and thereafter, explicitly idealistic. I turn now to what I take to be the first system of a *truncated world*, i.e., a world otherwise like ours but without minds. Again, it will help to begin with the truncated foil.

An entity either *exists or subsists*. Existence and subsistence are the two modes of the foil. Existents are either *individuals* or *characters* (relational or nonrelational). The nexus between the two kinds is exemplification (unary, binary, and so on.) Except for the connectives, *exemplification is the only nexus*. The only subsistent entities are the fundamental ties and, roughly, what "goes with them." I say roughly because while some entities, such as individuality and universality, obviously go with them, this is not so obvious for quantity (all, some) and arithmetic. That dialectic, though, is not the concern of this study.

What "exists" is simple. In this formula 'exist' and 'simple' are both used philosophically. Unexplicated, the formula thus literally makes no sense. After the two uses have been explicated, it will be either true or false, depending on the two explications. That shows in which sense I do not take a stand on the classical issues. Rather, I insist that in order to understand some of the classical ontologies, one must realize that their authors, speaking philosophically, used their words so as to make the formula true. A formula that provides this sort of key I call a *pattern*.[5] This particular ontological pattern is the simplicity pattern.

---

[4] On the connectives, see "Ineffability, Ontology, and Method."

[5] Recently I exhibited the eight (!) patterns on which the realism-phenomenalism controversy, as it reflects itself in the philosophy of physics, depends. See "Physics and Ontology," *Philosophy of Science*, 28, 1961, 1–14, and pp. 108–23 of this book.

For existents, though not for subsistents, an explication (we need not tarry with it) for this use of 'simple' is provided in the foil; 'exist' is so explicated that only simples "exist." (In its commonsensical use 'exist' is here always replaced by 'there is'.) In this sense, the foil may be said to accept the *simplicity pattern.* Some *things,* i.e., all individuals and some characters, are simples; even the "simplest" *fact,* an individual exemplifying a (simple) character, is not. Hence, no fact "exists."

The existents of the foil are all phenomenal entities, either sensa or characters they exemplify. Which pattern controls this choice? How can a realistic$_2$ ontology be built on it? The questions are urgent. Yet, expository strategy requires that the answers be postponed. The deliberate abstractness of the exposition serves among others the purposes of this strategy. But strategy must not be carried to extremes. The hint just dropped permits a comment now in order.

Earlier, simultaneous, to-the-left-of, extended, and so on, are either temporal or spatial characters, the first three relational, the fourth nonrelational. The only entities exemplifying them are sensa. This is expressed by saying that the individuals of the foil are *in* (phenomenal) *space* and *time.* Characters, including of course the spatial and temporal ones, are not in this sense in either space or time. Hence, only individuals are. Perceptual objects (apples and chairs) are not phenomenal ones. But again, perceptual objects are in perceptual space and time; their characters are not. That shows how I use 'phenomenal' and 'perceptual'. It also shows that the matters touched upon lie deeper than the phenomenalism-realism$_2$ issue. Perceptual objects, however, are *continuants* (in time); sensa are momentary. Hence, *no existent is a continuant.*

If a character which was presented to me yesterday is presented to me again today, I recognize it, directly or as such. Sensa, being momentary entities, are in fact never presented twice. Yet, if one were presented to me twice, I would not the second time recognize it as such. (This holds also for perceptual objects and their characters; which shows that this matter, too, lies deeper than the phenomenalism-realism$_2$ issue.) Entities not recognizable in this sense I call *bare.* (The traditional phrase, which I shall avoid, is *bare particulars.*) One who grants ontological status to bare individuals must consistently also grant it to exemplification. Remember the dichord. If, being presented with it, I were not also presented with exemplification, how would I know which characters go together, i.e., are exemplified by the same bare individual? And one can of course not be presented with anything having no ontological status. Behind the refusal to grant such status to anything bare is a pattern. *We know only what, if it be presented to us again, we recognize.* Call it the *recognition pattern.* As stated, it is epistemological rather than ontological. To grasp its ontological impact, build a verbal bridge, replacing 'know' by 'know to exist'. Since it makes no sense to talk of what "cannot be known," the bridge is plausible.

That will do for the foil; now for the system.

An entity is either *real* or *ideal;* if the latter, it is called an *essence;* if the former, I shall call it an *item.*[6] Reality and the realm of essences are the two modes of the system. Behind the dichotomy are two major intellectual motives, each corresponding to a pattern. *What "exists" is localized in space and time.* This is one of the two. Call it the *localization pattern.* 'Localized in' is stronger than 'in'. A continuant, for instance, though in space and time, is not localized in time. Husserl's own phrase, *hic et nunc,* surely is as strong as one can make it. As it stands, the pattern leads to catastrophe, either materialism or Humeism, depending on whether time and space are taken perceptually or phenomenally. Husserl avoided both traps. Yet he was swayed by the pattern. So he modified it: What is real (though, since there are also essences, not every "existent") is localized in space and time. That shows the power the pattern had over him. Notice an immediate consequence. *No item is a continuant.*

What is an item? There is a red round spot on my blotter. What I see when now looking at it involves three items. Call them red_1, $round_1$, $spot_1$. Tomorrow, when I shall look at the spot again, there will be three further items, red_2, $round_2$, $spot_2$; and so on. In this respect, simply because they are *hic et nunc,* items are like sensa. Also, items, like sensa, are things. Yet an item is *not* a phenomenal thing. They are all (rudimentary) perceptual ones. To make that as clear as possible I use an ink spot rather than a tone. But a tone, as I hear it, also involves three items, say, c_1, sft_1, $tone_1$.

The system does distinguish between simples and compounds. In the example, $spot_1$ and $spot_2$ are compounds; the other four items are simples, or so I assume for the sake of the argument. But the system rejects the simplicity pattern. That is why we have here six items and not just four. Accordingly, the thing-fact distinction is less crucial than in other ontologies. A compound is also called a *whole.* A whole is what-

---

[6] Because of the clash with 'idealism', 'ideal' will henceforth be avoided. Husserl typically uses several words for one idea. I always use only one and stay as close as possible to English usage, either literally translating (e.g., 'essence' for *'Wesen'*) or approximating (e.g., 'item' for *'Moment'*) the most suitable one among the several.

ever has *parts*. *Red₁* and *round₁* are severally parts of *spot₁*; *red₂* and *round₂*, of *spot₂*; c_1 and *sft₁*, of *tone₁*.

Being-a-part-of is the only fundamental nexus between items. I shall occasionally mark it by '**C**', e.g., *red₁* **C** *spot₁*. What does '**C**' stand for? We are at the limits of communication. That makes it easier to say what it doesn't stand for. Certainly not for the homonymous set-theoretical relation. Nor simply for the geometrical one, as is shown by *sft₁* **C** *tone₁*. On the other hand, take the two halves into which a diagonal divides the area of a square. More precisely, take a triple of corresponding items. The two triangular ones are said to be parts of the square. The notion thus comprehends the geometrical one. It is in fact very broad. Distinctions can and must therefore be made. Of these later, in Section Three.

All fundamental ties—except for **C** and of course the connectives we do not yet know what they are—as well as what "goes with them" are essences. Despite the differences among the ties themselves, in this respect there is no difference between foil and system. Essence, however, contains two further kinds. This difference in style was mentioned in Section One. One additional kind are the *universals*. Red or redness though not of course *red₁*, *red₂*; *c* and *sft* though not of course c_1, and so on, are universals. So are triangle or triangularity, pitch, tone, and countless others. The second additional kind are the *essential facts*, i.e., all and only those facts whose constituents are all essences. Since the simplicity pattern is rejected, we are not surprised to encounter this kind. Nor shall I make much of it, any more than of the thing-fact dichotomy. Notice, though, that while universals, like items, are things, *red₁* **C** *spot₁*, being expressed by a sentence, is what everyone would call a fact although, two items being among its constituents, it is not an essential fact. Since all real entities are items, which are things, facts like this one are ontologically homeless. Such impoverishment of reality as compared with the realm of essence is striking. It will be well to keep it in mind.

Pitch **C** *tone* is an essential fact; so is *red is a color*. The first shows that **C** is also a nexus among essences. In the second sentence, 'is' stands for *predication*, the second nexus, one among essences and essences only. The linguistic connotation of the word, predication, makes it awkward. Yet, 'exemplification' is pre-empted, and I know of no better word. It is at any rate Husserl's own; just as he himself insists that the copula in the commonsensical 'This is red' does not stand for predication.[7] The latter sentence will be discussed in Section Six.

---

[7] *Logische Untersuchungen* (Niemayer, 1922) II, 1, p. 125 (hereafter *LU*).

Redness is One; "its" items are Many. The system's universals are not, but correspond to, the foil's (nonrelational) characters. The system's items are not, but correspond to, the foil's individuals. Items are, rather, what the British tradition calls perfect particulars. One salient difference is that, unlike the foil's individuals and characters, items and universals belong to different modes, the latter being classed with what in the foil "merely" subsists. To say the same thing differently, for once taking advantage of the flavor of philosophical uses, if in the foil I were to use 'real', I would insist that individuals and characters are both real. These are good reasons for calling Husserl a nominalist.

Items are not bare. If they were, why call them as they are called, red_1, sft_1, and so on?[8] The recognition pattern thus had its part in shaping the system, even though items, being *hic et nunc*, are in fact never presented twice. Items not being bare, is there anything in or about them to gather them, as somehow they must be gathered, under "their" universals? Those answering Yes will soon bog down in the dialectic of the Third Man. The answer at least implicit in the system is that, say, all "red" items are tied to their universal, red, by the third and last nexus of the system. I call this nexus *participation*, mark it occasionally by ' $<$ '. $Red_1 < red$ is a fact. Retain that it, too, is without ontological status. Only essential facts "exist." Notice also what from the viewpoint of general ontology is perhaps the major structural difference between foil and system. While the former (aside from the connectives) has only one, the latter has *three fundamental ties*.

Since participation, being an essence, has ontological status, it may, just as the foil's exemplification, be presented to us. In terms of structural economy, items might therefore as well be bare, just as the foil's individuals are. Yet they are not. Such redundance is a flaw, indicating a tension in the structure. Its plausible cause is aversion to bareness. A plausible effect, we shall see, is that in the second system the items of the first have become hypostatized sense qualities. The choice of the Platonic term, participation, is deliberate, of course. Even so, I shall not defend it historically. 'Conceptualism', which I also used, covers a lot of confusion. To place the One as "concepts" in the mind is a shallow dead end. The expository device of the truncated world makes that even more obvious. Husserl was not shallow. The only serious alternative to either realism$_1$ or dead-end nominalism is to grant ontological status to both the One and the Many while at the same time setting them ontologically as far apart as possible. Husserl did just that.

---

[8] For the dialectic of bareness in connection with independence and existence, see E. B. Allaire, "Existence, Independence, and Universals," *Philosophical Review*, 69, 1960, 485–96.

That is why I called him a conceptualist, in the only worthwhile sense of the term I can think of.[9]

The localization pattern was introduced as one of two major motives for the dichotomy of the realms. *The essential (universal) is the intelligible and the necessary.* This is the second major motive. Call it the *intelligibility pattern.* The implied synonymy of 'essential' and 'universal' in this and other contexts is more than authorized by the texts. Historically, it is easy to understand why the pattern swayed one on whose philosophical horizon Kant loomed as large as on Husserl's. It is not at all easy to say commonsensically what the formula might mean. Universals are recognizable (knowable); the distance between certain philosophical uses of 'knowable' and 'intelligible' is not large; there is thus some overlap with the recognition pattern. This, though, is merely a nuance. "All essential facts (truths) and only essential facts are both intelligible and necessary." That is how in the system the formula is understood. That leads to the core. *Red is a color. The triangle is a plane figure. Red and green exclude each other* (in the familiar sense). These are three essential truths. A large part of the tradition staked out a claim of peculiar status for them by calling them and their like *a priori.* Again, this philosophical use of 'a priori' is not easily explicated. But its connection with some uses of 'intelligible' and 'necessary' is at least very familiar. I cannot here possibly go beyond this hint. But I can and shall next show, first, how the pattern may make one insensitive to another flaw in the system; and, second, how the system's notion of necessity cannot even within it do the job it is supposed to do. This is not just a flaw; it is a mistake.

First. Green is a color; red is a color; and so on. The colors are Many; color is One. Nor of course are the colors parts of color. A master does not make this kind of mistake. Like participation, predication is therefore threatened by the dialectic of the Third Man. The only way to avoid the threat is, again, to give predication ontological status. The system does just that. Thus predication may be presented to me. The trouble is that if it must be presented for me to know that, say, green is a color, just as in the foil I must be presented with exemplification in order to know that a certain individual exemplifies a certain character, then it is no longer easy to see why this fact, green's being a color, is "intelligible" in some special sense of the word. Perhaps we shall be told that it is intelligible because it is also "necessary." Maybe so. For me, nothing comes through. I merely see another flaw.

Second. Red and green exclude each other. Call this essential truth

---

[9] For further comments on conceptualism, see R. Grossmann, "Conceptualism," *Review of Metaphysics*, 13, 1960, 243–54.

S. We need not completely assay it if the reader is willing to take on trust that all its constituents are essences. Let now red_i and $green_j$ be two items and consider S': red_i and $green_j$ exclude each other. Unless S' is also necessary, the "necessity" of S does not do its job. So far, exclusiveness having been introduced as an essence, it is not even clear what the sentence expressing S' means. The system, as it must, takes it to mean $(red_i < red)$ and $(green_j < green)$ and S.[10] The last of the three conjunction terms is necessary; the other two, since they contain items, are not. Hence, S' is not necessary. This is the mistake. We had better explore its cause immediately. That requires mention of (mental) acts, which in the truncated world surely are out of place. But I shall once more compromise with the strategy lest the combination of abstractness and disjointedness become unbearable. The new notions of the next paragraph will be taken up in Section Four.

We have two eyes, one the mind's, one the senses', the latter being blind without the former, the former staring into the void without the latter. The metaphor is as old as it is beautiful; so beautiful that one is tempted to call it a pattern. Of course it is not unrelated to the recognition pattern. In the system it lives in the distinction between two kinds of acts. (Some) items are the intentions of (acts of) *sensory intuition;* (some) essences (things and facts) those of (acts of) *eidetic intuition.* Assume now that an act intuiting red_1 is immediately followed by one intuiting *red*. If so, the former is a part of the latter. If that part-nexus itself immediately becomes the intention of a third act, the highest degree of evidence is bestowed upon $red_1 < red$. Phenomenologists may find this account a bit rough. For our purposes the roughness does not hurt. (My callousness indicates rejection of certain familiar excesses of phenomenological microscopy.) What does matter is that "evidence" is held to pertain to an act or acts and not to the intention $red_1 < red$, which is, we notice, the first constituent of S'. The high degree of evidence thus bestowed on but not pertaining to the first two constituents of S' is, I submit, the reason why it was not seen that necessity cannot consistently within the system be attributed to them and, therefore, not to S' itself. More crudely, what pertains to the intention (the "object") has been put into the act (the "subject"). That is the essence of psychologism. Husserl, of course, was its most implacable enemy. Yet, at this subtle point he became its victim. That is why the mistake is bad indeed, not just a subtlety missed.

III

To be louder, larger, later, are all *relations*. In the foil some relations are entities (simple characters), some are compounds. The latter are

[10] *LU*, II, 1, p. 256.

accounted for in terms of the former. The details don't matter. In the system, no entity is a relation. How then does it account for any? The answer requires another glance at the part-nexus.

Pitch and loudness are parts of tone. Neither part can be without the whole and, therefore, without the other. Two such entities are said to *found each other*. Consider next our dichord. There can be a tone without a dichord, but there cannot be a dichord without two tones. That is expressed by saying that while the tones jointly *found* the dichord, tone(s) and dichord do not found each other. All this goes for items as well as essences.

Our dichord is a third. Add another, the fifth on the same base. How is the difference between the two accounted for? In the foil the answer is obvious. To make it short, assume that *hg'* and *hg''* are simple relational characters, the first exemplified by any (ordered) pair of (tone) individuals which make a third; the second, by any pair making a fifth. In the system, the two intervals, call them *thrd* and *fth*, are wholes, even though not "independent" ones, since pitches and loudnesses found each other. That, though, does not matter here. Consider now (1) $(c_1 \text{ C } thrd_1)$ *and* $(e_1 \text{ C } thrd_1)$, (2) $(c_1 \text{ C } fth_1)$ *and* $(g_1 \text{ C } fth_1)$, (3) $(x \text{ C } z)$ *and* $(y \text{ C } z)$. (3) shows that as far as their part-whole structure is concerned, (1) and (2) are indistinguishable, which shows in turn that the difference between the two intervals cannot be accounted for in terms of this structure alone. Nor does the system attempt to do that. It accounts for it in terms of this structure and of something else.

I spoke about items. I could instead have spoken in terms of the three universals, *c, e, g*. So far, that would have made no difference. The something else, however, lies in the realm of essence. What it is will be better understood if we first understand what it is not. If there were two relational universals corresponding to the foil's *hg'* and *hg''*, then the two intervals could be distinguished from each other, e.g., c_1 and e_1 making a third, could be construed as $(c_1 < c)$ *and* $(e_1 < e)$ *and* $(hg'(c, e))$.[11] Within the system at least, that would be an adequate solution. From the outside, all one could say against it is that it betrays once more a tendency to impoverish reality in favor of essence. This, however, is not what is done. In the system nothing is a relation.

What then is that something else? We are told, first, that *c, e, g* all have their own "natures." If that is taken to mean that they are recognizable then it can be understood. We are told, second, that these

---

[11] The parentheses in the third conjunction term are borrowed from the logical notation to stand for predication.

(nonrelational) natures "found" the (relational) intervals; e.g., c and e jointly found the third. This, too, I understand if I may take it as before. But then, we saw that by itself their part-whole structure does not suffice to distinguish the intervals. Hence it must mean something more. What is this something more? The only answer I can think of leads to catastrophe. Consider in addition to c and e the pairs d, f; e, g; and so on. They are all thirds. Hence, they must all have something in common with each other but not with, say, the pairs "of" the fifth. This something, we saw, is not a relational essence predicable of these and only these pairs. The only other alternative is that there is a something that is shared by the "natures" of the two members of each pair of, say, the third but not, of course, by any other pair. The interval thus is the One; the pairs, the Many. Hence, as twice before, the Third Man threatens. Seen from the foil, the only difference is indeed that this time we deal not with exemplification between individuals and characters but, rather, between characters of the first and the second type. The first two times the threat could be avoided, even though at the price of a flaw. This time it is fatal.

A plausible reason why all this was not seen is not hard to come by. C and e making a third is counted as an essential truth and therefore as intelligible. The threat remained hidden behind the blur produced by the notion of intelligibility. Recall an Aristotelian pattern preserved in ordinary speech, for the most part quite harmlessly, like an insect in amber. "It is in the nature of this thing to have that property; hence its actually having the property is intelligible." That makes the occurrence of 'nature' at this point a give-away cue. The point is that the notion of an intelligible nature blurs the distinction between things and facts. The two things in the case are the two (nonrelational) universals; the (relational) fact, their making a third. Whether or not this diagnosis is correct, the system fails to account for relations. Such failure of so great a master seems almost incredible. So I cite the text.[12] Yet, Husserl is not the only one to have failed at this point. I am becoming ever more convinced that Russell was the first who really understood relations. That is one measure of his greatness.

Much of space and time is relational. Hence this large part of them cannot be accounted for either. Nor is that all. Assume for the sake of the argument that the system's account of all other relations is adequate. It would still be inadequate for all spatial and temporal ones, unless moments and places are counted as items so that "their" uni-

[12] *LU*, II, 1, p. 283.

versals may have (or be) natures. The first system is thus committed
to making the "objective" space and time of nonmental reality absolute.[13] The only alternative is to make both space and time wholly
mental or "subjective." This is of course what happens in the second
system, where everything real is mental. Space, since I must limit
myself, I shall ignore. To time, since it is crucial in the transition from
the first system to the second, I shall return.

IV

The time has come to introduce *mind*. In the first system, that requires of course new entities, items as well as essences, but no new
"ordinary" kinds[14] in either realm nor, at least explicitly, a new nexus.
The same goes for the foil, except that there a new nexus is needed.
The foil thus really has two nexus: exemplification, which is pervasive;
and one other, as yet unnamed, which is the hallmark of mind. The
vehicle of awareness in both system and foil are (mental) *acts*. 'Awareness' is used generically. The several species of this genus are perceiving, remembering, imagining, thinking, doubting, and so on. In the
foil, though not in the system, sensing is also an act.

The foil's act is a fact, an individual's exemplifying two simple characters. These three "new" entities are called mental. All mental entities are of course phenomenal ones. As the words are here used, the
converse does not hold. Sensa and their characters, though of course
phenomenal, are not mental. In the last Section that will become important. Mental individuals, like all others, are momentary and bare.
As such, a mental individual is therefore not an awareness. (It has no
"nature.") Loosely speaking, though only loosely speaking, the two
characters it exemplifies make it an awareness, just as certain other
characters make the individuals exemplifying them tones. One of the
two mental characters I call a *species*; the other, a *meaning*. The several species are perceiving, remembering, imagining, and so on.

A meaning *means* its *intention*. When I doubt that it will rain tomorrow, doubting is the species of the act; its raining tomorrow, the

---

[13] This fits well with the affinity to Leibniz which later on Husserl himself
stressed. Concerning the important sense in which Leibnizian space and time are
absolute, see the Leibniz essay in *Meaning and Existence*.

[14] Since the first system is here identified with the *Untersuchungen*, it should
perhaps be mentioned that this is not quite accurate for the transitional sixth
Inquiry where, to say the least, the concern with Self comes to the fore. Since
Selves (and Time) are the only continuants, one will want to call them a "new"
kind.

intention. 'Means', I shall sometimes mark it by 'M', stands for the foil's second nexus. When in a second act I am aware of one of my acts, the intention of the second act is phenomenal. The intention of an act of perceiving, say, that Peter is blond, is a perceptual fact, Peter's being blond. Some may wonder why I consistently avoid the more common 'physical' and 'material', using 'perceptual' instead. The reason is, simply enough, that it helps to keep out from where it does not belong the further question about how we come to replace what we perceive, say, a chair, by the denizens of science, say, a cloud of electrons. *A meaning and its intention are always two, never one.* That is, of course, the great lesson of Brentano.

The foil's intentions are all facts. Facts are expressed by sentences. That is why elsewhere I call meanings propositions. In the system intentions are either things or facts. Later on I would therefore have to speak of propositional and nonpropositional propositions, which is very awkward. So I replace here 'proposition' by 'meaning', which as it happens is also the best translation of Husserl's own word, *Bedeutung*.

M is a nexus, connecting the act, which is phenomenal and even mental, with its intention, which often is neither. That is one of the pillars of the foil's structural realism$_2$. It also raises an immediate question. One term of the nexus is a meaning which, being simple, exists and is exemplified whenever the act occurs. But how about the second term, the intention, in case of, say, a false belief? A detailed answer may be found elsewhere. However, since the point is structurally crucial, I shall comment briefly. First. The difficulty is, of course, that the intention of a false belief, say, the fact of the moon's being made of green cheese does not exist (is not the case). Commonsensically we speak without hesitation about facts not existing. Those trying to get us into trouble are starting on the dialectic of the philosophical uses. Second. The foil is a thing ontology. Thus in it no fact "exists." Third. Let $\ulcorner S \urcorner$ be a meaning; S, the fact which is its intention. In the foil '$\ulcorner S \urcorner M S$' is analytic. Everyone accepts 'S or not-S' as analytic, even though one of the two constituent facts is not the case.

That will do for the foil; now for the system.

About one half of the *Untersuchungen* is an analysis of the act, interwoven with a penetrating examination of the tradition as well as a good deal of psychological material. The whole is of a subtlety and richness which make it an imperishable masterpiece. This I now appreciate. Yet we need not be overawed. In many respects the system's and the foil's analyses agree. The differences are of three kinds. Some do not matter for what really matters. Some, without being important in themselves, merely reflect important differences between the two ontologies. Three, we shall see, are crucial.

The system's acts are real things. An act is thus a "new" item. Every act has two parts. Being themselves items, the two parts are not, but correspond to, the foil's species and meaning. This, though, is just one of those differences which flow from the difference in the ground plan without making much difference for our purpose. No harm will therefore come to us if we call these two part items of an act item its *species* and its *meaning*. Neither a species nor a meaning is ever simple; they are themselves wholes; of this presently. *A meaning and its intention are always two, never one.* In the language of the system, even (what I call) a phenomenal intention is never literally a part of its act. This is again the great lesson of Brentano. Husserl acknowledges it with the generosity of one who can well afford to be generous.

How are a meaning and its intention connected? In the system they remain unconnected. That is the *first crucial difference.* If it seems surprising, consider that in ontology fundamental ties and relations (in combination with fundamental ties) are the only means of "connecting" anything with anything else. Participation and predication are obviously unsuited for the purpose; and we have seen that an act's intention is never a part of it. Yet there are no other nexus in the system. Nor are there "ordinary" relations. But one need not rely on inference. We are told most explicitly that while meanings are nonrelational they do yet by their "nature" point beyond themselves at their intentions. They are, as it were, intrinsically relational. This is absurd. So I cite again the text.[15] Failure to understand relations as well as lack of clarity[16] concerning the distinction between fundamental ties and relations are two plausible reasons why the absurdity was not felt. Whether or not the diagnosis is correct, there is in the system no ontological bridge between the perceptual world and that of the mind. Calling them two worlds rather than one is therefore not just a metaphor. Small wonder, then, that in the second system the perceptual world no longer "exists." That is why the difference is crucial.

The system's meanings are all wholes. How then are their constitu-

---

[15] *LU,* II, 1, p. 368, 435. The "intentional relation," we are told, must be "purely descriptively understood as the intrinsic nature" of the (nonrelational) act. Remember the two pitches which, though nonrelational, by their intrinsic natures found the interval. The case in hand is only more extreme.

[16] That is most strikingly revealed by *LU,* II, 1, p. 280, where in a polemic against Twardowski Bradley's problem, whose solution as we know depends on recognizing the need for fundamental ties, is used as an argument against granting ontological status to relations.

ents held together? In the foil, all meanings are simples. Hence the question does not arise. This is the *second crucial difference*. In the system, the only consistent answer is that a meaning's ultimate constituents are its simple parts. Presently we shall see that this answer is not available, which makes the difference crucial. To understand that in detail, one must first understand the third difference.

In the foil sensing is an act. In the system it is not. This is the *third crucial difference*. What, then, is the system's account of *sensation*? Even though the word sensation (*Empfindung*) is Husserl's, I use it reluctantly since, as G. E. Moore pointed out in the *Refutation*, it blurs the distinction between sensing and the sensed. To this extent, Moore, too, knew the great lesson. It has been conjectured that it came to him from Brentano, either directly or through Stout. Perhaps that is why, at least after a fashion, British philosophy could afford to ignore Husserl. Yet it is a pity.[17] In the foil, of course, 'sensation' is expendable. There are sensa and their characters; there is the species called sensing; and there are the suitable meanings.

The system's sensations are not bare. In this one respect they are like items. A case could perhaps be made that officially they are items. Really they are not; or so at least I am prepared to argue. They are too amorphous for that, as it were; they are all ὕλη and, except for not being bare, completely devoid of μορφή. The Greek words are again Husserl's own, taken from the *Ideen*.[18] The idea is already in the *Untersuchungen*. Two modifications I shall permit myself in arguing the point will help to bring it out without distorting it and, at the same time, simplify the exposition. In the second system there are Selves. I shall introduce them into the first. That is one modification. Sensing not being intentional, if there are Selves, what else could sensations be but (momentary) properties of (continuant) Selves? I shall assume that they are just that. This is the second modification. Both merely anticipate the second system. Husserl also speaks of sensory qualities. But one must not be misled by either 'property' or 'quality.' Since these entities are (and remain) real, they are of course not universals. Still another warning about words may help. When you sense red, you have, Husserl says, a *Rotempfindung*. In German a single word is conveniently available. In English we must choose between 'sensation

---

[17] Husserl's students haven't helped, alas; least of all the existentialists who acknowledge a debt to phenomenology. Nor I suppose has Ryle's completely negative, though in certain respects very acute review of the Farber commentary in *Philosophy*, 21, 1946.

[18] *Ideen zu einer reinen Phaenomenologie und Phaenomenologischen Philosophie*, Erstes Buch (Niemayer, 1928), p. 172 ff. (hereafter *Id*).

of red' and 'red sensation'. The first phrase suggests intentionality; the second that the entity it stands for is complex. Both suggestions mislead. The second phrase seems to me the lesser evil, if only because in writing it can be mitigated by a hyphen. So I shall speak of red-sensations, green-sensations, and so on.

Represent a Self by a solid sphere; its now having a red-sensation, by the sphere's surface now being red all over. Think of the red surface as a coat that can be put on and lifted off the solid. Imagine that there are many such coats, to be put on and lifted off, one for each sensory quality. When the Self has several sensations simultaneously, the solid wears more than one coat. When, for instance, two color spots are perceived, since extensions are sensed, there are (at least) four coats. These coats surround the solid in a certain order, say, in the direction from the center, first the two color-coats, then the two extension-coats. In this respect the representation is richer than what it represents. There is no order or any other sort of structure among simultaneous sensations. Notice, too, that the two color-coats, each covering the sphere all over, are in this sense compatible. Since color-coats are not color-items, there is no contradiction; yet there is food for thought. All this shows what I meant by calling sensations too amorphous to be items. What in particular could possibly by meant by saying that any two of them, say, two all-over extension-coats support a part-whole nexus? I, for one, find the whole doctrine absurd, if only because I am not acquainted with those amorphous entities. That is why I resorted to a representation. Yet this is unquestionably Husserl's doctrine, in both systems. Nor is it just his. It is indeed a large part of the meaning of the metaphor that the eye of the senses is blind. One consequence of this strange doctrine is easily explained. Yet, structurally crucial as it is, it deserves a Section of its own.

V

Return for the last time to the dichord as I now hear it; writing it $[(c_1, sft_1), (e_1, ld_1)]$. Call the wholes corresponding to the two parentheses $tone_1$, $tone_2$, respectively, and that corresponding to the bracket, which is the dichord itself, ch_1. Consider next the alternative dichord $[(c_1, ld_1), (e_1, sft_1)]$. Call its three nonsimple items $tone_3$, $tone_4$, ch_2. Ch_1 and ch_2 and their subwholes differ; the simples founding them are the same, c_1, e_1, ld_1, sft_1. Their part-whole structures as such are also indistinguishable. The only difference is that while in ch_1, for instance, c_1 and sft are parts of a subwhole, in ch_2 they are not; and so on. Simples not being bare, this difference suffices, *objectively* or on the side of the intentions, to distinguish between the two dichords. The example is so

chosen that the system's inadequate account of relations does no harm.
For the argument at hand one may even assume that this latter account is adequate throughout. That merely strengthens the argument and illuminates the strategy.

Subjectively or on the side of the acts, the two meanings having the two chords as their respective intentions must differ; otherwise we wouldn't know the two chords from each other. Yet they are both *colligated* from the same material, a c-sensation, an e-sensation, a sft-sensation, and a ld-sensation. Everything will therefore be well if and only if the "nexus" I just called colligation establishes among these four sensations the same structure as the part nexus establishes among the simple items of the chords.

Sensations, we saw, are too amorphous to support the part nexus. What, then, could colligation be? In the first system there is no answer. The only way out is to make it issue from the Self. In the representation, imagine a hand reaching out from the center of the sphere and, in order to produce the meaning which goes with ch_1, first colligating the sensations corresponding to c_1 and sft_1, then the two corresponding to e_1 and ld_1, then the two products with each other. Correspondingly for ch_2. How does the hand or Self know in which of the two alternative ways to proceed when one of the two dichords is perceived? The answer is that it doesn't. That spells disaster. As once before, what is "objective" has been put into the "subject." The first time it was a subtle point about necessity. This time the account of perception has collapsed. This time therefore the charge of psychologism is not strong enough. We are half way on the road to idealism.

The hand performs an *act*. The word is old; the meaning is new. In performing those "acts" of colligation, the hand is "active" in the categorial sense in which an Aristotelian or scholastic Self is active. Colligation is neither passive nor an item. An act in the original sense of the first system is both. In this system there is of course no Self and no hand. Nor did I claim that it is explicitly idealistic. I merely undertook to show that the later idealism is implicit in its structure.

'Colligate' has been suggested to me by the French *colliger*, which is one of the key words of the *Méditations*. In this very late book there is very much about wholes. But these wholes are all products of colligation and all the colligating is done by a very "active" Self. It is indeed, as the author insists, virtually a Leibnizian Self.

The "active" Selves of the tradition are all continuants and they are not bare but have "natures." That holds also for the Self of the second system. Of this later. One structural reason, though, for the Self which has been anticipatorily introduced not being bare is implicit in what has been said already. To make it explicit, it will be best to start from the foil.

The foil's mental individuals (loosely: awarenesses) are both momentary and bare. Again, when sensing something, say, a single qualitied sensum, I am not thereby aware of my sensing it. As Husserl says, poetically rather than accurately,[19] I live not in the act but in its intention, the qualitied sensum. Yet, an act of sensing is there and its being there accounts for there being consciousness (awareness) of the qualitied sensum. What then, one may reasonably ask, accounts in the system for a property of the Self, whether sensory quality or act item, being conscious? The only answer I can think of is: It is conscious because it is a property of the Self. But to say that and to say that the "nature" of Self is consciousness is ontologically one thing and not two. One is reminded of Descartes' Self whose nature is indeed consciousness (thought) and which therefore, since it is a continuant, always thinks.[20]

VI

Looking at the ink spot on the blotter, one may say 'This spot is red'. How does the first system ontologically assay what the sentence expresses? The answer can be read off from its transcription into the notation we incidentally developed. The only possible transcription is '$(red_1$ C $spot_1)$ and $(red_1 < red)$ and $(spot_1 < spot)$'. Nor is it implausible; in the system, therefore, it will do. But assume now that on the same occasion '*This is red*' has been uttered. This even simpler sentence cannot within the system consistently be transcribed. To be precise, the difficulty is not to transcribe '*This is red*' but, rather, '*This is red_1*'. For, once a transcription of the latter sentence is available, one of the former can immediately be obtained, in the spirit of the system, by conjoining it with '$red_1 < red$'. In the *Untersuchungen* the difficulty is clearly stated but not resolved. Its resolution in the second system is not only explicitly idealistic but very close to the core of the idealism if not, perhaps, its very core. That is the claim of this Section. Before arguing it, it may be well to locate the claim in the tradition. That will show that it is neither as bold nor as extravagant as it may seem.

Items have here been marked by attaching subscripts to the names of universals, red_1, red_2 and so on. Husserl speaks instead of *this red*

---

[19] Thereby hang some differences between system and foil which are anything but negligible, even though here they can safely be neglected, in the account of perception. For the latter, see "Dell'Atto."

[20] Eventually the Self, whether or not it actually thinks (is aware of something), becomes indeed "the pure *cogito*." See, e.g., *Husserliana*, IV, pp. 102–105 (Nijhoff, 1952), which is the second book of *Ideen*.

or *that red* or a red-item. (*Rotmoment* is conveniently one word.) The verbal distance between the phrase and the sentence, 'this red' and 'this is red', is small. The difference between what they purport to express is large; that is why I resorted to numerals. Yet, both expressions are blurred. Items are not bare. That accounts for the adjectival component of either expression. The second component, be it numeral or demonstrative, is the cause of the blur. Directly or as such, items cannot be recognized. (Nor, as we know, can sensa or chairs.) In other words, there is nothing in the item itself to make it either *this* or *that*, or the *first* or the *second*. The second component of either expression therefore marks merely the times one has encountered a red-item, which is something "subjective" and not "objective." Objectively, therefore, the second component is redundant.[21] Negatively, it merely reminds us that in the context 'red' does not stand for a universal. Positively, it tells us that 'red' is used as one "name" to name indifferently more than one thing. I do not know what it means for a name to name more than one thing; hence the quotation marks around the word. The *common-name* doctrine is nonetheless one of the classical gambits of nominalism. Husserl, making $red_1 < red$ available elsewhere in the system, escapes one of the difficulties most variants of the gambit are up against. He does not escape another. If 'this' and 'red_1' both stand for the item—one as a proper, the other as a common name, as one says—then the copula in *'This is red'* cannot but stand for identity. But this is not what the sentence purports to express. Hence, the sentence cannot be transcribed. That is the difficulty, shared with all other variants of the common-name doctrine, which the first system does not escape. Let us next inquire into the form it takes there, or, if you please, how it came to be noticed.

First. Meanings, being items, are not bare. If they were, how could they participate in recognizable universals? Nor are we surprised. We know by now that nothing is bare. *Second.* A propositional meaning is a whole. Its parts are the meanings of the words that occur in the sentence expressing it.[22] And, of course, every act has a meaning. *Third.* The propositional meaning of 'This is red_1' has as its parts the meanings of 'This', 'is', and 'red_1'; just as three acts with these three partial meanings are among those founding the one with the propositional

---

[21] For a closely related argument, see R. G. Turnbull, "Ockham's Nominalistic Logic: Some Twentieth Century Reflections," to appear in *The New Scholasticism.*

[22] Words in this sense are those of "pure grammar," which in a natural language may have to be expressed by phrases. With the notion of a pure grammar Husserl clearly anticipates certain aspects of what is now called an ideal language.

meaning. *Fourth.* Consider now these three acts. Treat 'red₁' frankly as a common name and you will convince yourself once more that the partial act intending the item has a meaning which is not bare. Whatever the difficulties connected with 'is' may be, the nexus it stands for is recognizable. Again, therefore, the act intending it has a meaning which is not bare. Not so for the act relating to 'This'! To put it as before, numeral or demonstrative pertain to the act, not to its intention. That does not mean that all acts intending a This and nothing else do not have something in common. Only, this Something pertains to them, not to their intentions. The meaning of these acts would therefore be bare. I say would because, in the first system and not only there, such an act is an absurdity. That is how the difficulty arises there and is noticed.[23]

The resolution is one of the themes pervading *Erfahrung und Urteil.* Thus there is no need to quote or cite much. This text, one of the latest, is of course most explicitly idealistic. It also carries phenomenological microscopy to extremes. I am aware of a red-item in an act of sensory intuition. The microscopist notices that sometimes in becoming aware of the item, in focusing on it, as it were, all one is fleetingly aware of is a wholly indeterminate Something, a This, a τόδε τι.[24] He concludes that even the simplest act of sensory intuition is already founded (a whole). As the characteristic founding part he proposes an "act" by which the Self hypostatizes (objectivates, externalizes, posits) one of its sensory qualities, i.e., the sort of thing I call phenomenal, into a Something or This, of the sort I call perceptual, without as yet further determining it as, say, a red-item. To use once more the metaphor, at the risk of straining it, this time the hand reaching from the center of the sphere does not just colligate what it finds on the surface. In this particular instance it does in fact not colligate anything. Rather, it grasps what it finds there and, piercing the surface, holds it out into space, thus making it into a simulacrum of something neither mental nor even phenomenal. This is the founding "act"! I need not, I trust, once more justify the quotation marks. It is not an act in the original sense but, rather, the activity of a Self creating the world. *Vergegenstaendlichung ist immer eine active Leistung des Ich.*[25] We are in plain idealism.

Preferring an anticlimax to loose ends, I raise two questions. Has the

[23] *LU,* II, 1, p. 83 and II, 2, pp. 18–22. The first passage, from the first Inquiry, where the difficulty is noticed, is cited in the second, from the transitional sixth Inquiry, where the idealistic "solution" is all but explicit.

[24] *Id,* p. 28, cited in *Erfahrung und Urteil* (Academia-Prag, 1939), p. 160.

[25] *Erfahrung und Urteil,* p. 64.

difficulty, as it originally presented itself, really been resolved? The answer is, perhaps, that in the second system the craftsmanship is not as exquisite as in the first. Does the realm of essence, too, eventually lose its ontological status? The answer is Yes. Consider an act of eidetic intuition intending the universal red. It is founded by the one of sensory intuition just considered. And from nothing nothing comes. Simulacrum spawns simulacrum, as it were.

VII

The strategy must by now be obvious. Step by step the system has been unfolded against the foil. At each step a tension point came into view, each a corrosion of nonphenomenal existence. Their effect is cumulative. Moreover, they make a *crescendo*. The first was a subtle point about necessity. With the last we landed, *fortissimo*, in plain idealism. Yet idealism is hard to swallow. Swallowing it took Husserl some time, probably also some struggle. *Which pattern or patterns controlled this last decisive step?* Before the job is done, the question must be answered. Three further ones were left pending. The foil's building stones (simples) are all phenomenal entities. *How can such an ontology be realistic₂ in structure?* A Self was introduced as an expository device into the first system. *How and why is it actually introduced into the second?* Finally, *how is time eventually accounted for?* The answers to all four questions depend, though of course not exclusively, on a single pattern. That is why they are gathered together in this single Section. After they shall have been answered, one last task will remain. In the introduction Husserl's movement from realism to idealism was attributed, though again of course not exclusively, to two major "mistakes," his nominalism and his failure to understand relations. Formally, this diagnosis is the major claim of the study. The justification, such as it is, of that claim is its body. The last task and proper conclusion will be to spell it out.

Everything we know is analyzable in terms of what we are *acquainted* with (otherwise we would not know what we are talking about). The parenthetical clause shows not only that as it stands the formula is epistemological but also its ontological impact. As we ordinarily use 'acquainted', we have acquaintance with phenomenal as well as with perceptual objects. Yet there is a difference. Phenomenal objects are the only ones with which we are *directly acquainted*. That is one traditional way of expressing the difference. If our formula is taken to speak of direct acquaintance only, it becomes the formula of the *Cartesian turn*, which was the true Copernican revolution in philosophy.

What sort of thing is the "analysis" the formula mentions? We need not tarry to answer beyond pointing out a connection all uses of 'analysis' and 'simple' preserve. One thing having been "analyzed" in terms of some others, the latter are said to be "simpler" than the former. That suggests combining the Cartesian turn with the simplicity pattern. The result is a further pattern. *All "existents" are phenomenal* (simples). Call it the *acquaintance pattern.* Many philosophers adopted it because they were convinced that large blocks of the traditional dialectic cannot be mastered without "in the last analysis"[26] resorting to phenomenal entities. The trouble is that they seem thereby committed to phenomenalism which, being a kind of idealism, is hard to swallow.

Commonsensically, there are (exist) minds as well as bodies. One who has executed the linguistic turn always speaks commonsensically. Literally, therefore, the foil could not possibly accept any pattern. Yet it accepts the Cartesian turn. After a fashion it therefore also accepts the acquaintance pattern; insisting that all statements mentioning anything nonphenomenal can be replaced, *adequately for all purposes of philosophical analysis,* by statements mentioning only phenomenal simples. Method and tradition being what they are, that makes all ontological building stones phenomenal. The italicized clause must of course be dialectically defended. If the defense fails, so does the foil. This is not the place to defend it once more. Nor can I here fully expound how such an ontology manages to be realistic₂ in structure. But I must briefly state six points on which the case rests.

1. To say that statements about chairs can for certain purposes be replaced by statements about sensa, is not to say that chairs are or consist of sensa. This point was seen clearly by the so-called linguistic phenomenalists who flourished earlier in the century. 2. Since commonsensically there are phenomenal as well as perceptual things, one who appreciates the fundamental distinction between ordinary and philosophical uses could not possibly take the acquaintance pattern to mean that there are only phenomenal things. To the extent that they more or less implicitly appreciated the distinction, the linguistic phenomenalists more or less clearly saw this second point, too. Both points are *negative.* Thus they do not by themselves suffice to refute the charge of a "phenomenalistic structure." In the case of the linguistic phenomenalists the charge is indeed irrefutable. The remaining four points are all *positive.*

3. The simples of the foil, though all phenomenal, are yet of two radically different kinds. Sensa and their characters are the only non-

---

[26] The phrase is barbarous. Yet here for once it serves well.

intentional entities.[27] Every mental individual exemplifies a meaning which by M is tied to the fact it intends. 4. Sensing something and being aware of sensing it, one is directly acquainted with both sides of a meaning nexus. Direct awareness contains, as it were, a model of perception. 5. While of course not directly acquainted with what we perceive, we are so acquainted with the species perceiving. 6. Since mental individuals and the two characters each of them exemplifies are simple, even if one were to use 'exist' philosophically as in the acquaintance pattern, one would have to hold that bodies and minds enjoy the same ontological status! Such counterfacturals are I think very useful in demonstrating that an ontology in the new style, in this case the foil, has the same structure as some classical ontology, in this case some realistic$_2$ ones.

Like all modern masters, Husserl always held fast to the Cartesian turn. The distinction between the two uses he did not make, naturally not, since it was still far in the future.[28] That alone suffices to set up, by the acquaintance pattern, a drift toward idealism. There is quite a skein, though. The localization pattern and, in conjunction with the notion of eidetic intuition, the intelligibility pattern are as decisively involved. To disentangle the skein one must first consider another question.

What makes phenomenal entities so desirable as a last resort? Two features stand out. (a) They are what they appear to be. That is *certain*. To *doubt* it doesn't even make sense. (b) If presented at all, they are *wholly presented*. That is part of their being *hic et nunc* (the localization pattern!). Universals or, for that matter, characters not being in space and time, (b) causes a difficulty. There are three ways of handling it. One may introduce a special device. Husserl's special device, not unrelated to the intelligibility pattern, is eidetic intuition. Or one may get lost in some kind of dead-end nominalism. Or one may sever the idea of being wholly presented from that of *hic et nunc*, insisting that when, say, sensing a green sensum, one is wholly presented with the color character it exemplifies. This is done in the foil.[29] Nor do I see what else a consistent realist$_1$ could do.

[27] This neglects "affective" individuals and characters. See the later remark about their neglect in the account of the system.

[28] This is not to say that Husserl's sensitivity and skill in making linguistic distinctions are not among the most extraordinary on record. The *Untersuchungen* abound with examples. The chapter on the thirteen (!) uses of '*Vorstellung* (idea)' is as richly satisfying as a Bach concerto.

[29] See the essay on Elementarism in *Meaning and Existence*.

When I perceive a chair, there is not necessarily a chair; I may be the victim of error or even illusion. (To those who now object to this use of 'perceive' I point out that, first, there are no intrinsic criteria of veridical perception, and, second, the act involved is in both system and foil a perceiving.) A phenomenal *hic et nunc*, on the other hand, *necessarily is* "as it presents itself." The phrase in quotation marks drops out only too easily. The verbal distance between 'necessarily is' and 'necessarily exists' is short. The verbal bridges among 'necessary', 'indubitable', and 'certain' ((a) above), treacherous as they are, have been much trodden. Appreciating all this, one will not find it strange that in the *Ideen* Husserl proclaims what he now takes to be the one proper and essential sense or meaning of 'exist'.[30] In this sense, act items and their constituents exist; chairs do not. That shows how, *negatively*, (a) and (b), with the patterns involved, account for the last step in the transition to idealism.

Positively, Selves and Time are the "new" existents of the second system. Nor do they just exist, they are "absolute" existents. Yet a Self, being a continuant, is not *hic et nunc*; nor of course, whatever else it may be, is Time. How, then, is their exalted ontological status secured? Eidetic intuition does the job. Acts and sensory qualities, unlike Selves and Time, are momentary. They are also experiences (*Erlebnisse*). The universal, experience, is supposedly available to eidetic intuition. Eidetic intuition, we remember, presents, with the highest degree of evidence, not only some universals but also some essential truths. The following are held to be three essential truths so presented. (1) Experience presupposes an experiencer. (2) Every experience has duration. (3) Duration presupposes time. The idiom of presupposing in (1) and (3) can be replaced by that of founding. The experiencer in (1) is a Self. (3) is unpacked to mean that a duration, even if short enough to be contained in a *nunc*, cannot be "conceived" except as a "segment" of "Time." (*Nunc* is indeed not a mathematical point but more nearly a specious present.) This is how the ontological status of Selves and Time is secured.

The last paragraph states the gist of the *Ideen*. The elaboration there is very rich, of course, and it is indefatigably continued in all later writings. Disciples and commentators have dwelt on these ideas at the expense, alas, of that masterpiece, the *Untersuchungen*. Once more, there is therefore no need for documentation. For our purpose the gist will do. Nor do I wish to be tedious or appear disrespectful to

[30] The several strands are all clearly visible in *Id*, p. 86, where this wide-arched argument begins. Its triumphant conclusion, as far as that book is concerned, is on p. 296.

Husserl by presenting criticisms which are familiar, belong to a different tradition, and, worst of all, fall outside the rather severely limited dialectic of this study. Four comments, though, all within the limits, will serve the purpose.

First. In the second system acts and their constituents, including sensory qualities, are indubitably properties of Selves.[31] What then, one may reasonably ask, is the nexus between a Self and one of its properties. Both are real. Predication connects only essences. Hence the nexus cannot be predication. Is it exemplification? Textually, perhaps because of the lesser craftsmanship of the later years, the question is moot. Structurally, exemplification is the most reasonable answer. That illuminates the importance of the nexus which in the foil singly holds the truncated world together but has no recognized place in either system. *Second.* In the first system red_1 and $spot_1$ belong to reality. The fact red_1 **C** $spot_1$, because of its essential constituent (**C**), does not. Nor does it fit any other ontological slot. That is why I once called it ontologically homeless. Essential facts (truths) do have a safe slot in the realm of essence. The contrast spots a tension. Its resolution in the second system is radical though no longer surprising. Selves and their properties are the only "existents." They are also real. To be real and to be an "existent" has become one and the same. A Self exemplifying (?) one of its properties is a real fact. Nor are there any others.

Third. An experience as lived is, as one says, a Now. Now is an essence![32] Thus it is all μορφή. The contrast with the τόδε τι, which is all ὕλη, is striking. *Hic* and *nunc* have parted ways, as it were. I am equally struck by the fact that if the formula is to be taken literally, then in the second system Time is not only, like everything else, "subjective" but also absolute. *Fourth.* Self and Time are "absolute" existents. Let me show how such things may come to be said by playing for a moment with 'constituting' and 'founding'. The Self, which is a continuant, by colligating and hypostatizing its momentary sensory qualities constitutes (founds) all other momentary existents, i.e., its own acts and their parts, as well as all simulacra of (nonphenomenal) existence. Time and the Self found (constitute) each other. They are the only existents which mutually constitute themselves. That makes them not just existents but the active and necessary ground of all existence (reality). Time lies even deeper than the Self.[33] One may get a glimpse of what that could mean by reflecting that the Self cannot

[31] E.g., *Id*, p. 175.
[32] *Id*, p. 164.
[33] *Husserliana*, IV, p. 103

colligate what does not lie in the same specious present. Unhappily, the same reflection makes one wonder whether anything has been said at all. But one must not be too analytical when standing at the threshold of mystery. For the rest, one is reminded of a Hegelian dictum: *Das Sein des Geistes ist die Zeit.*[34] Literally that is absurd. As an aphorism it is arresting. Time is indeed the substance of the world. Or, rather, that is the aphorism I prefer. However inadequately expressed, the insight is as deep as any. Quite a few have been haunted by it. To be haunted by it is one thing; to articulate it dialectically is quite another thing. Anyone who can articulate it as richly as Husserl did I salute as a master. But, alas, he did not know how to disentangle Time and Self. That made idealism the price he had to pay for thinking so deeply about time. The price is prohibitive.

Two brief comments which fit here as well as elsewhere may forestall puzzlement. The psychologists whom Husserl read and criticized distinguished sensory and affective elements. Not surprisingly, therefore, there are probably also affective qualities in the system(s). If so, they surely remain in the background. Moreover, since they are as amorphous as their twins, the sensory qualities, they make no difference for what has been discussed. So I ignored them. As I speak, one may wonder whether the second system is solipsistic. In fact it is not. If anything, it is Leibnizian. The further step or steps by which that is achieved I do not find very interesting.[35] Nor do they affect what is here discussed. So, again, I ignored them.

The structures of both systems now lie before us. So does the foil's. The differences responsible for the opposite movements, toward and away from idealism, have been pointed out. Even so, I should like to state or restate two of them. The first will not take us long. The sec-

---

[34] There is more than one Hegelian echo in the later texts. Merleau-Ponty caught this one very well: *Si nous devons résoudre le problème . . . de la subjectivité finie . . . ce sera en réfléchissant sur le temps et en montrant comment . . . cette subjectivité est le temps lui-meme, comment on peut dire avec Hegel que le temps est l'existence de l'espirit ou parler avec Husserl d'une autoconstitution du temps.* (*Phénoménologie de la perception* [Gallimard, 1945], p. 278). I take the reference from Francesco Valentini's remarkably readable *La filosofia francese contemporanea* (Feltrinelli, 1958), p. 69.

[35] The later Husserl attempted an *Aufbau*, as the logical positivists called it. The point is that in his *Aufbau* "The Other," the "Thou" is reached before the perceptual object. The latter cannot be reached without the former. Whether or not that is merely an idiosyncratic mistake, as I believe it is, it helps one to understand how within one short generation an analytical philosopher of the first rank became one of the patron saints of the existentialist *Lebensphilosophen.*

ond, which deserves closer attention, also provides the promised conclusion by bringing out how fundamental the two major "mistakes" are.

In the second system, sensory qualities are properties of Selves. In the foil, a qualitied sensum or two sensa exemplifying a relation are the simplest phenomenal facts not involving mental entities. As was pointed out earlier, such facts serve as a phenomenal model of perceptual facts. One reason they can so serve is that they are not characters (properties) of the mental individual that is also there when they are sensed. The characters this individual exemplifies are, rather, the species sensing and the meaning which intends what is sensed. This is the first difference. Restating it concisely will show how crucial it is. In the second system everything is constituted from properties of "minds." How then could there be anything but minds and their properties? In the foil not even sensa or their characters are properties of "mind." The reason why 'phenomenal' and 'mental' have been distinguished must by now be obvious. The idea behind the distinction also guided G. E. Moore. Unfortunately, he bogged down in trying to make sensa parts of perceptual objects. All this also shows how important structurally it is that in the foil sensing is an act and that all awareness is propositional. The difference between a fact and a character is a bit too gross to be overlooked.

Everyone speaks of perceptual *judgments*. The idea controlling the use of this word is that in a judgment one asserts more than what is, in a suitable sense, presented to him. Call this more the excess of judgment over presentation. Where there is such an excess, the mind is, in an obvious sense, active. In the foil this activity is harmless; even in the first system it is not. That is the second difference. Let us see.

Assume that when judging the tower to be round, I am presented with some phenomenal facts. Schematically, that is in the foil a suitable sense of 'presentation'. I say "schematically" and I said "assume" because literally I hold all this to be false or, at least, grossly inaccurate, if only because while towers are perceived, (nonmental) phenomenal facts can only be sensed and a deliberate shift from perceiving to sensing is not easy to achieve. Even so, the schema does very well for the two points that matter. First, the excess consists of further phenomenal facts. *Excess and presentation are thus of the same kind*. That makes the activity of the mind harmless since it does not, in a sense, add anything. It merely anticipates more of the same. Second, phenomenal facts, as presented, are *fully structured*. Sensa, (nonrelational) characters, and relations are all presented as such; so is the nexus of exemplification they support. In this respect, there is no scope for activity. The reason for there being none is that the foil is realistic₁ and adopts Russell's view on relations.

Both systems find an excess wherever the foil does. The suitable sense of 'presentation' is different. That is why even the first system finds an excess where the foil doesn't. To be presented is to be given in sensory intuition. The only things thus given are perceptual items. So dim is the eye of the senses. Hence even the nexus in a fact as simple as *red₁ **C** spot₁* is an excess over what is presented.[36] That makes even the assertion of this simple fact a perceptual judgment, notwithstanding that the fact, or at least all the items in it, is *hic et nunc*. Furthermore, *excess and presentation are not of the same kind*. The excess, which is a universal, is seen only by the mind's eye. The metaphor of the two eyes spots a tendency: *What is seen only by the mind is contributed by the mind*. The tendency is away from Platonism, which is hard to swallow. In the first system Husserl resisted it. That is why his conceptualism is not shallow. But then, the tension was there; or so at least one may judge from the outcome. Given its reins, this tendency makes the structure (essence, form) of (in) even the simplest perceptual fact a contribution of the mind. That shows that this time the mind's activity is anything but harmless. There would be no scope for such activity if the perceptual items, which are all that is ever presented, were not so *unstructured*, i.e., if they were not all, except for not being bare, mere τόδε τι. Again, presentation could not be so unstructured if the system were not nominalistic. All this, we now fully understand, hangs by Husserl's assay of a fact as simple as *red₁ **C** spot₁*. When relations enter, the need for a contribution of the mind becomes even more urgent. That we have seen.

[36] *LU*, II, 2, p. 152.

The Glory and the Misery of Ludwig Wittgenstein*

THE *Tractatus logico-philosophicus* appeared in 1921; the *Philosophical Investigations*, posthumously, in 1953. Wittgenstein will live through these two books. The contrast between them is striking. In the author's view, and not in his alone, the second repudiates the first. As his epigones see it, his glory is the second. The first they consider, however tenderly and reverently, a relative failure. As I see it, Wittgenstein's glory is the *Tractatus;* his misery, the *Investigations*. The disagreement could not be more complete. Yet I agree with the epigones that the connection between the two books is very close indeed. I see in the second the reaction, dictated by the council of despair, to the relative failure of the first.

The *Tractatus*, then, if I am right, is a glorious failure. It is also, I am deeply convinced, an achievement of the first rank. Nor is that paradoxical. None of our predecessors achieved more. No one among us and our successors will do better. The fundamental metaphysical problems are too difficult for this to be otherwise. Fortunately, their number is small. Even the secondary ones, though quite a few, are not too many. Good philosophers therefore do not pursue many questions. Rather, they are pursued by a few which they articulate ever more richly and explore ever more deeply, down toward the fundamental ones. The few great among the good can rethink a fundamental problem on their own. Such a problem always consists of a group of dialectically connected questions. To rethink it is either to discover a new dialectical connection within the group or, at the very highest, to affect these connections even more radically by discovering a new

* This essay appeared in Italian translation in Rivista di Filosofia, *52,1961*, *387–406*. Printed by permission.

question to be added to the group. The new question permits and requires new answers. The glorious failures are those who knew how to ask the new question but did not find the new answer.

Wittgenstein all through his philosophical life was obsessed by two fundamental problems. What is the nature of logical truth? Call this the first. What is the nature of mind? Call this the second. Both have shaped both books. The first dominates the *Tractatus;* the second, the *Investigations.* On the first, he asked the decisive new question, led a part of the way toward the new answer. On the second, he merely misled, lending specious plausibility to a stale old answer.

(1) There are no philosophical propositions. Those passing for such are neither true nor false but, literally, nonsense. (2) The illusion that keeps us from seeing through this sort of nonsense is linguistic. (3) To destroy the illusion, or, in a phrase that has become famous, to show the fly the way out of the bottle, is to direct attention to the ineffable, which language shows but cannot say. That is Wittgenstein's conception of the philosophical enterprise. (1) states his nihilism; (2) is the root of the linguistic turn; (3), that of the therapeutic approach. I reject (1) and (3). There are philosophical propositions. Nor is there anything ineffable. Wittgenstein's insistence on the linguistic turn, more radical and more profound than Russell's, is the other half of his glory. But he executed it wrongly, herostratically. That makes (2) his other glorious failure, which, since our questions as well as our answers depend on our conception of the philosophical enterprise, made the other two, the glorious as well as the miserable one, inevitable. So I shall next execute the right linguistic turn.

(1) Words are used either *commonsensically* or *philosophically.* A proposition in which at least one word is used philosophically is a philosophical proposition. As such, philosophical uses are unintelligible. But they can and must be made intelligible by explicating them, i.e., by talking commonsensically about them. Thus explicated, a philosophical proposition says something about the world, which, as the case may be, is either true or false. (2) Every systematically constructed language *shows* some things which cannot without futility be *expressed* in it. These things, though, far from being ineffable, can and for certain purposes must, be expressed by talking about the language and what it talks about. Jointly, (1) and (2) are the gist of the right linguistic turn. Technically, they are equally fundamental. Nontechnically, (1) is the heart of the matter. So I leave (2) until later, comment next on (1).

"Bodies don't exist, only minds do" is a classical philosophical proposition. "Minds don't exist, only bodies do" is another. "Characters don't exist, only individuals do" is a third. If the words are all taken commonsensically, such propositions are not at all nonsensical. Rather, they are patently and blatantly false; so patently and blatantly indeed that only a madman could assert any of them. Yet each has been asserted by some philosophers. According to Wittgenstein, these men either futilely tried to express the ineffable, or, confusingly and themselves confused, presented as an assertion about the world what is at best one about the way we use language. I believe that these men often succeeded very well in directing attention to certain pervasive, or, as one says, categorial features of the world. Only, I also insist that these features can and must be talked about commonsensically.

Classical ontology is dominated by the several ontological uses of 'exist' and 'existence'. Since the core of all fundamental problems is ontological, I shall next indicate the explications of two such uses.

(a) *If something is presented to me, so is its existence.* The formula explicates the use. To have "existence" in this sense and to have "ontological status" is one thing and not two. The idea is commonsensical. Yet some comments will be helpful. *One.* Something may exist without being presented. If converted, the formula is no longer commonsensical. *Two.* Perception is one kind of presentation. Direct awareness is another. Do both kinds make the formula the truism it must be if it is to serve its purpose? By this question hangs a huge body of dialectic. For my purpose tonight the answer does not matter. *Third.* In such sentences as 'There is a coffee house around the corner' existence is represented by the phrase 'there is'. Existence(a) or ontological status can always be so expressed. But we also say, commonsensically, that there is a prime number between 4 and 6. Are we then prepared to grant some ontological status to such "entities" as numbers? Wittgenstein, we shall see, is not. I am. The way I just used 'entity' is ontologically neutral. It will be convenient to have this neutral word available.

(b) *What exists is simple.* The formula explicates another philosophical use of 'exist', provided only we understand this very special, though commonsensical use of 'simple'. An entity is thus simple if the only way of directly referring to it, in any language, is by naming it. A *name*, in this very special sense, is also called a label. That conveys the idea that a name can only be attached to what is or has been presented. There is also the idea that a label as such does not tell us anything about what it labels except, of course, that it exists(a). This, though, we shall see, is not quite correct in the case of linguistic labels or names. In a systematically constructed language a name is, of course, a primitive descriptive sign. Notice that an equivalent formula has become available: An entity exists(b) if and only if, provided it is presented, it can be named. Notice, too, that an entity which could not be named, or, more precisely, as we shall presently see, an entity which could not be named without futility, may yet be presented and even be represented in the language by something which is not a name. Such an entity would exist(a) without existing(b).

The sentential tautologies so-called are familiar instances of logical truth. What is the structure of such truths? We are ready for Wittgenstein's first fundamental problem. Rethinking it, he discovered the new question which is his glory. How does any sentence, whether or not it expresses a logical truth, manage to express what it does? In appearance the new question is unduly linguistic, in an obvious bad sense of 'linguistic'. In substance, it points to the ontological core of the problem. Even better than that, the right answer provides an invaluable lesson, teaching us how to do ontology after the linguistic turn. That is why the glory of the one who first asked the question is great, even though his answer went wrong. Here is what we are told. Take the (written) sentence itself as a fact. This (linguistic) fact shares with the fact it expresses a "logical form." That is how the former manages to express the latter. 'Logical form' is used philosophically and, unhappily, remains unexplicated. So we are not surprised when we are also told that "logical form" is ineffable, merely shows itself. There is an easy transition, noticed, or, more likely, unnoticed, from being ineffable to being nothing, or, what amounts to the same, not having any ontological status, not existing(a). This sort of transition I call a verbal bridge. The original question Wittgenstein answered as follows. A truth is logical if and only if the sentence expressing it is true by virtue of its "logical form" alone. But, then, we are also told that a sentence expressing a tautology (logical truth) really says nothing and is therefore not really a sentence. This supports my belief that, unwittingly, Wittgenstein walked that bridge. Whether or not he did, his answer does not recognize the ontological status of what, speaking philosophically, he calls "logical form." That is the fatal flaw. The right answer, conversely, crucially recognizes the ontological status (existence (a)) of what I call the world's *form*. And, of course, it provides an explication for this use of 'form'. Notice, for later reference, that I suppress the adjective, 'logical', speak of the world's form instead.

These are the bare bones of my thesis. Putting some flesh on them, I shall first state the right answer. But, of course, if that needs to be said at all, without Wittgenstein's glorious failure, there would be no right answer today.

Suppose that, being presented with a green spot, I say, truly, 'This is green'. Limiting ourselves to true sentences merely avoids problems which, though most weighty in themselves, can at this point be avoided. What an (indicative) sentence expresses is a fact. The fact in the example is the spot's being green. Call it F; the sentence, S. S and F, each in its way, is as simple as a fact or a sentence can be, though of course neither is simple(b). Now if S is true, there must be something that makes it true. Or, as one says, the truth of S must be grounded ontologically. On this first move idealists and realists agree. The only difference between them is that for the realist the ground is independent of the mind to which F is presented, while for the idealist F depends on, or even more strongly, is the activity of this mind. But, then, do not in the idealist's world minds and their activities have ontological status?

S thus is true because it expresses F and F exists(a). If, therefore, we want to know how S manages to express F, we must first find out what there is to be expressed. In other words, we must begin with an onto-logical assay of F.

I hold that there are individuals and characters, all of the former and some of the latter being simple(b). Calling them both *things*, I also hold that, when presented with F, I am presented with two things, an individual named 'This' and a simple character named 'green'. Hence, my assay of F yields *at least* two simples. That raises two questions. (1) Is this assay complete? More strongly, could it possibly be complete or must it yield something else? (2) Is it correct as far as it goes? (2) may be controversial; (1), to my mind, is not. As it happens, my main point hangs on (1).

Simples enter into complexes. F, for instance, on any assay I can think of, is a complex. Take now two spots, one green and square, the other blue and round. If my assay is correct as far as it goes, there are thus six things "tied" into two complexes. You see already the deeper point. There must be "something" which ties anyone's simples (or, for that matter, things, if there should be no simples) into complexes. Also, this "something" must be presented. For, if it were not, how could I know that in the example, say, green goes with square but not with either blue or round. It follows that there must be ties, having onto-logical status, which tie the simples into complexes. What then, one may ask, ties the ties to the simples? There are only two possibilities. One is, paradoxically, an infinite regress, which is the way Bradley took to monism. The other is my solution. There are *fundamental ties*, I also call them *nexus*, which tie without themselves being tied to what they tie.

The nexus which ties an individual and a character into a fact I call *exemplification*. It follows that the ontological assay of F yields at least three constituents, two simples and exemplification. Notice, too, that a fundamental tie is not a relation. In the complex 'This is louder than that', for instance, there are three simples, this, that, and the relational character louder-than, held together by (relational) exemplification.

Further analysis, which I cannot tonight reproduce, shows that the complete assay of F yields two further nonthings, individuality and universality. When I am presented with an individual, I am also presented with its individuality. For, if I were not, how would I know that it is one? As for individuals, so for characters. As I use 'form', these three nonthings, exemplification, individuality, universality, are constituents of the world's form. As I use 'subsist', their peculiar ontological status is *subsistence*.

Does Wittgenstein agree with what has been said so far? There are very, very many passages in the *Tractatus* which seem to make it crystal clear that he, too, so assays F that 'This' and 'green' in S name two simples in F. I say seems because there are also many passages, such as 3.1432, which have been much written about recently, that cannot be reconciled with those very, very many others. On the nominalism-realism issue—for that is, of course, what the matter amounts to—the *Tractatus* is confused. Historically, I believe, that has something to do with the great impact Frege's views had on its author. Concerning exemplification, turn to 2.03: *Im Sachverhalt haengen die Gegenstaende ineinander wie die Glieder einer Kette.* That is exactly what they don't do.[1] If they did, there would be no need for a nexus. The image, admirably clear, leaves no doubt that Wittgenstein is radically wrong, making exemplification a part of that "logical form" which is "nothing."

How does S manage to express F? In a systematically constructed language S becomes 'Ga', i.e., in essence, the juxtaposition of two marks of different shape (capital and lower case). 'a' names or labels the individual; its shape represents, without naming it, the individuality of the thing named. As for 'a', so for 'G'. Names are thus not pure labels. Their shapes, which are geometrical characters, represent, without naming them, ontological categories. Exemplification, finally, is represented, though, again, not named, by the relational geometrical character of juxtaposition. S is a geometrical fact. Between certain

---

[1] Or, if you care to put it this way, things are *independent*. The philosophical uses of 'independent' are crucial. The formula "Only what is independent exists" controls indeed several philosophical uses of 'exist'. E. B. Allaire (*Philosophical Review*, 69, 1960, 485–96) has very ingeniously distinguished four relevant commonsensical uses of 'independent'. If I am not mistaken, I just identified a fifth.

geometrical features of S on the one hand and the constituents of F there is a one-one coordination of the kind called isomorphism. To understand a language is to know the rules of this isomorphism. Or to say the same thing differently, S manages to express F by virtue of this isomorphism. This is my answer. Let us confront it with Wittgenstein's.

S manages to express F by virtue of a shared "logical form," which is ineffable. That is his answer. The isomorphism mentioned in mine is anything but ineffable. I just stated it by speaking commonsensically *about* F and S. Now this isomorphism is also the only explication I can think of for Wittgenstein's philosophical use of 'logical form'. The explication makes his answer intelligible. Rather strikingly, it also makes it false. Nor is that difficult to show. Assume for the sake of the argument that the two marks in S are individuals. Then the geometrical fact S has five constituents which are things, namely, the two marks the two geometrical characters which are the shapes, the relational geometrical character of juxtaposition; and, in addition, individuality twice, universality thrice, exemplification thrice. That makes 13. F, we remember, has all together 5 constituents. And there is of course no one-to-one coordination between 5 and 13. Such are the bitter fruits of using words philosophically, without explication.

The ontological distance between, say, an individual and individuality is tremendous. Wittgenstein safeguards it without effort. For him, the individual exists; individuality, being part of "logical form," is nothing. For me the two are alike in both having ontological status (just as they are both presented). The difference so far is merely that in the language I constructed the individual is named while its individuality is otherwise represented, namely, by the shape of its name. That is not yet enough to secure that tremendous distance. I secure it by showing that the subsistents could *not without futility* be named. Take individuality. Let us try to name it. If it is a thing, then it is of course a (simple) character. Name this alleged character by 'I'. That makes 'Ia' the crucial sentence. The point is that it says what it says, namely, that a is an individual, only because the shapes of a and I and their juxtaposition represent, without naming them, individuality, universality, and exemplification, respectively. That shows what I mean when I say that the introduction of 'I' is futile.

If one wishes, one may put the last point as follows. a's being an individual is *shown* in the language by the shape of its name; but one cannot without futility *say* in this language that it is one. Remember now the second part of the right linguistic turn: Every systematically constructed language shows some things which cannot without futility be expressed in it. When first stating this part, I postponed comment. Now, without further comment, we understand. We have recovered all that is recoverable from Wittgenstein's famous ineffability thesis. The rest is nonsense, not because it is metaphysics, but because it is bad metaphysics.

There is of course much more to the world's form than is represented in S, just as there are many more facts than can be expressed by sentences as simple as S. We have had no more than a glimpse. And, of course, we cannot pursue. So I must venture to state the idea. Philosophy is a dialectical structure that rests on a phenomenological base. What is presented to us is a matter of phenomenology. If certain entities were not presented to us, we could not know what commonsensically we do know, e.g., that this is red, that green, this to the left of that, and so on. That is the dialectical twist. What must be presented to us must also be represented in our language, otherwise it could not express what it does. That is how language may be brought in. Then we are ready for the linguistic turn. 'Ontological status' has been used philosophically. I explicate this use by the formula: What must be represented has ontological status. That, though, is only the beginning. The furniture of the world is not all of one kind. The different kinds, even the glimpse we had taught us that, are represented very differently, i.e., in the written case, by very different geometrical features of the language. Or, rather, that is how I explicate the traditional ontological vocabulary. Enough has been said to support a claim made earlier. The right answer to Wittgenstein's new question is the key to the new ontology.

We are ready for the original question. What is logical truth? It is nothing. Nor is the sentence expressing it really a sentence. That, succinctly, is Wittgenstein's answer. I answer that it is a fact of (in) the world's form and that the sentence expressing it is a sentence like any other, except, of course, that its truth depends only on those of its geometrical features which represent constituents of the world's form. Lest the difference between the two answers seem slight, let me point out two consequences which loom large.

1. The connection between the philosophical uses of 'logical' and of 'necessary' is very close. "A logical truth is a necessary truth, and conversely." We all know this classical proposition. Partly because of it, I avoid 'logical' wherever I can, speak instead of formal truth (instead of: logical truth) and of the world's form (instead of: logical form). And I explicate the philosophical use of 'necessary' in that classical proposition so that a truth is necessary if and only if it is formal. That turns the proposition into a tautology. Wittgenstein disagrees. According to

him, the formal truths of our world are also the formal truths of all possible worlds. Replace 'formal truth' by 'logical form' and you will see the verbal bridge. "Logical form" is nought; and nought, as it were, is the same in all possible worlds. But, then, what shall we make of that phrase, 'all possible worlds'? Clearly, it is used philosophically. So it must be explicated. I can think of two explications. One turns the proposition into a tautology: Every world which has the same form as ours has the same form as ours. With the other explication, the proposition says that any world *must* have the same form as ours. I simply do not understand this *must*. If the logical is to be identified with the necessary, in some unexplicated and inexplicable sense of 'necessary', then, if you permit me an aphorism, there is nothing logical about logic. Technically, upon the explication which does not trivialize it, Wittgenstein's thesis, that the logic of our world is that of all possible ones, is simply false. I must not be technical tonight. But I can identify for you another bridge he walked on this as well as on many other occasions, all through his work. It leads from 'possible' to 'conceivable'. That is his psychologism. For it puts into the act what, if it is what it is supposed to be, must be a feature of the act's intention. Historically, Wittgenstein inherited this fateful mistake from Kant.

2. There is a class of truths, Kant calls them synthetic a priori, which are clearly not formal. "Nothing is (at the same time all over) both red and green" is a familiar example. Many philosophers tried to secure for these truths a special status, in the same boat with formal truths. In Wittgenstein, throughout his philosophical life, the urge was very strong. (In this, too, he shows the influence of Kant.) In the *Tractatus* he satisfies it by the claim that the sentences expressing those truths are, like tautologies, true by virtue of their "logical form" alone. That clashes with the very numerous passages according to which only tautologies can be true by their "logical form" alone. There is in the *Tractatus* one lonely passage (6.3751) which shows unmistakably that Wittgenstein himself was not wholly at ease. In the short paper of 1929, the only other publication during his lifetime, he returned to the attack; but again, alas, to no avail. This dissatisfaction may well have been one of the major intellectual motives for his eventual repudiation of the *Tractatus*.[2]

This chair's being brown is a physical fact. That water if heated boils is another. Your perceiving that the chair is brown is a mental

[2] E. B. Allaire has argued this point very convincingly in the first of two short but very weighty papers he has already published on Wittgenstein (*Analysis*, 19, 1959, 100–105 and 21, 1960, 14–16). Frequent discussion with him during the last years has been invaluable to me.

fact. So is my wondering whether this speech is too long, his remembering something, and so on. That there are both physical and mental
facts, or, for short, both minds and bodies, is common sense. Perceiving something, remembering something, thinking of something, are
mental facts of the kind called *acts*. There are also others, but we can
safely ignore them. The fundamental task is the ontological assay of
the act. In this task Wittgenstein failed. His way out was to reject it.
There is nothing to be assayed; there are no minds. The failure is foreshadowed in the *Tractatus*. The *Investigations* are virtually materialistic. Materialism is absurd. That makes the failure so miserable. We
shall understand it better if I first tackle the task.

What one perceives when perceiving something, what one knows
when knowing something, and so on, is the act's *intention*. To perceive
something, to know this thing, to remember it, are different acts with
the same intention. What they differ in I call the act's *species*. Acts
thus may differ in species and intention. Acts are mental, of course;
intentions, either physical or mental. What we perceive is physical;
that is part of what perceiving means. No thing is both physical and
mental. In perceiving, therefore, the act and its intention have no thing
in common. (I say no thing, rather than nothing because the world's
form is pervasive and neither physical nor mental.) This, by the way, is
true for all acts. But we can tonight stay with perception, where the
distinctness of act and intention is, if anything, even more obvious.

The perceptual complex has three constituents, (1) the act, (2) the
intention, (3) the body, i.e., the relevant physical facts about the perceiver's body. 'Complex' I use advisedly, to remind you that if there
is to be a complex, its constituents must be tied together. Now for
three constituents to make a complex there must be at least two and
there may be three ties. (2) and (3) are both physical. (2) causes (3).
This is the tie the scientists investigate. The tie between (1) and (3)
is that between a mind and its body. This tie I take to be parallelistic.
The third tie, call it the *intentional tie*, connects (1) and (2), the act
and its intention. Its nature is the heart of the problem.

Do not confuse the intentional tie with the mind-body tie. When I
perceive a landscape I perceive a landscape, not the relevant facts it
causes in my body. Since the landscape is causally tied to the body
and the body in turn parallelistically to the mind, there would still be
a complex even if there were no intentional tie. To say the same thing
differently, one may try to replace the direct intentional tie by a chain
with two links, one causal, one parallelistic. For two weighty reasons
that will not do. (a) I perceive the square tower to be round. More
dramatically, I have a hallucination. In the first case, the physical fact

invoked differs from the intention. In the second, there is none. (b) Some sentences are compounded of others. A language is called truth-functional or extensional if and only if the truth value of a compound depends only on the truth values of its components. Consider now the compound 'Smith believes that Caesar was murdered'. Assume it to be true. Replacing the true component 'Caesar was murdered' by the equally true 'The husband of Calpurnia was murdered' one obtains 'Smith believes that Calpurnia's husband was murdered'. Unless Smith knows that Caesar was Calpurnia's husband the new compound will be false. As for believing, so for all species. Statements expressing the intentional tie are not extensional. The causal tie, on the other hand, as well as the parallelistic one can be expressed in an extensional language. So, therefore, can the two-link chain. It follows that the intentional tie is a direct tie between the act and its intention. What, then, is its nature? Before I answer, one more idea must be introduced. But notice first that the author of the *Tractatus* was profoundly committed to the thesis that everything can be expressed in an extensional language.

None of the three constituents of the perceptual complex is a simple. Thus they, too, must be ontologically assayed. Crucial, of course, is the assay of the act. The tradition is dominated by one idea. Its formula is: A mind can only know what is *in* it. Everything depends on what the 'in' stands for. The tradition thinks of the mind as an individual of a very special kind, called a substance, and of its properties and only its properties being in it. What the mind knows is in it as its color or its shape are in the flower. That makes what I call the species a case of exemplification, or of whatever comes closest to it in these ontologies. The trouble is that in all of them, except perhaps the Aristotelian-Thomistic one, the intentional tie cannot be accounted for. In the perceptual case, for instance, the intention is itself a substance with properties. *And how can a substance be a property of another substance?* Dialectically, this is the deepest root, much deeper than the relatively shallow skeptical one, of the development from Descartes to idealism. Be that as it may, I am now ready for the answer.

An act is an individual exemplifying two simple characters. This individual is not at all a substance—there are none in my ontology—but momentary and bare, a bare particular so-called. One of the two properties is the species. The other I shall here call a *thought*. The intentional tie is between the thought and the intention. When we say, for instance, that the thought that Peter is tall *means* that Peter is tall, 'means' represents this tie. I say represents rather than names and also speak of the *meaning tie* because it is a nexus and, as such, belongs to the world's form. So, by the way, do the causal and the parallelistic tie. Only, they also belong to the form of a world otherwise like ours but without mind. In this sense, intentionality is the essence of mind.

How does this assay account for those cases, false belief, imagination, and so on, in which the fact S intended by the thought $\ulcorner S \urcorner$ does not exist(a)? Or, synonymously, if 'S' is false, how can '$\ulcorner S \urcorner$ means S' be true? If the meaning nexus were a relation, it couldn't. Since it is a part of the world's form, there is no difficulty. To get a glimpse of the idea, consider 'S or not-S', where the nexus is "or." Either S or not-S does not exist(a).[3] Yet, 'S or not-S' expresses a truth in the world's form. So does '$\ulcorner S \urcorner$ means S'.

Turn now to *Tractatus* 5.542. 'A believes that p', 'A thinks that p', and so on, all mean no more nor less than 'The sentence 'p' means p'. That is the gist of this passage. The sentence, here as always, is for Wittgenstein a physical fact. Substituting the sentence for the thought, he thus substitutes a physical fact for one that is mental. That is the decisive step toward materialism. Abstract thought is indeed, as one says, largely verbal. Properly understood, though, that means merely that such thought consists largely of awarenesses of words and sentences! Wittgenstein's 'says', if it means anything at all, stands for my 'means'. If so, then, even with the substitution of the sentence for the thought, ' 'p' says p' is no longer extensional. Nor is that all. The sentence 'p' "says" p only by virtue of a shared "logical form," which is ineffable. Hence, ' 'p' says p' is not really a sentence. The only thing that makes sense to me in all this is that the intentional nexus is indeed part of the world's form. For Wittgenstein, being part of "logical form," it is nothing. Once more, therefore, the act and its intention have fallen apart. The two ways out are idealism and materialism. Husserl took the first; Wittgenstein, the second.

This is the place to call attention to an ambiguity in the use of 'express'. A sentence as such does not "express" anything. We express a thought by means of it. This can be done because of the isomorphism between certain geometrical features of the sentence and what it "expresses." The ambiguity, if unnoticed, leads to disaster in the philosophy of mind. Outside of it, no harm is done. That is why I let it pass until now.

Materialists replace philosophy by science. Or they mistake the latter for the former. The later Wittgenstein is no exception. Not surprisingly in one as preoccupied with language as he was throughout his career, the key science is the psychology and sociology of language, or,

---

[3] More precisely, one of the two exists merely in the mode of possibility. This point, though of the greatest importance in some other contexts, may be safely ignored in this essay.

if you please, of communication. Not that the *Investigations* is a conventional scientific book. It is merely a medley of comments. Some are very keen; some others, more or less obvious; the rest, standard armchair psychology in the standard behavioristic style. Underneath, and not just underneath, there is always the effort to convince us—or should I perhaps say to convince himself?—that philosophy is all a mistake. The author was nevertheless a profound philosopher. So one comes every now and then upon a profound philosophical insight. The buzzing of the fly intrigues.

Assume that one tries to teach his language to one with whom he cannot talk at all. To teach the color words, he may use color charts, will do a good deal of pointing, and so on. As for the color words, so, with two differences, for the words referring to mental things. For one, the physical aspects of behavior will be much more prominent among the cues given by the teacher and taken by the pupil. (I put it this way because pointing is also behavior.) For another, the pupil could not learn unless he knew, from his own mind and body, which states of the two typically go with each other. The important truism that basically language must be learned and taught this way is characteristic of methodological behaviorism. Metaphysical behaviorism is materialism. The former makes sense, the latter doesn't. The transition from the one to the other is fallacious. The Wittgenstein of the *Investigations* makes it. Or he nearly makes it. Here and there a tortured qualification betrays the uneasy conscience and the inner struggle.

How does the teacher know that the lesson has been learned? When the pupil comes to use the words correctly, thus showing by his behavior that he knows what they mean. That is the root of the formula before which the epigones prostrate themselves: (1) meaning is use. 'Meaning' itself, of course, has many uses. Its use in the *Tractatus* may be epitomized by two formulae: (2) meaning is reference, and, (3) the meaning of a sentence is the method of its verification. Each of the two transitions, from (2) and (3) to (1), relates to a philosophical problem. Had Wittgenstein been able to solve these problems, or, what amounts virtually to the same, had he been able to make the required dialectical distinctions, he would not have made the transitions.

Take an individual and its name. By (2) the former is the meaning of the latter. Imagine that you are with only two persons in a room; one is your friend; the other you have never seen before. In this "context" your friend says, with or without pointing, "This is Peter." Because of the context you understand what he says. The next time you meet Peter you will recognize him. But you will recognize him only by the combination of characters he exemplifies. We do not recognize individuals as such, whether you use 'individual' as I just did or so narrowly that only sensa and their like are individuals. Thereby hangs an important philosophical point. Much less importantly, it follows that, first, communication depends on context, and, second, since a design of marks or noises not relying on context would have to contain names of individuals, we could not by means of it communicate. (That is the heart of the overblown quarrel about "ideal languages.") The epigones, convinced that there are no names are in danger of convincing themselves that there are no things to be named. There is only language. Hence, in spite of the materialistic substitution of words for thoughts, the idealistic structure so clearly discernible in so much of what they say.

One knows what a sentence means if and only if one knows what to look for in order to decide whether it is true or false. If one can look, he must inspect what he finds. Then he can actually decide. Negatively, a sentence is meaningless, not really a sentence, unless it can in this sense be "reduced" to what can be inspected. Much detail apart, this is the gist of (3). 'Inspect', which I use advisedly, has two connotations. By one of these hangs a fundamental philosophical problem. 'Inspection' may connote public inspection, i.e., not only by myself but also by others. With this connotation, since obviously we cannot inspect each other's minds, (3) obviously entails philosophical behaviorism. Statements about minds, to be meaningful, must be construed as statements about bodies. With the other connotation, one can inspect only what can be checked and rechecked. But one can only check and recheck what persists more or less unchanged. In this sense, mental individuals cannot literally be inspected, not because they are private, but because they are momentary. Yet there is a substitute. The mind within one specious present often shifts back and forth between an awareness and the awareness of this awareness. Assume three such shifts to have occurred. Then there are six awarenesses, two groups of three, the members of each group of the same kind. This is the substitute. Dialectically pursued, it leads to the fundamental problem of time and identity. For all other problems, the substitute will do. Wittgenstein, I believe, did not start out a materialist. But it seems that in the fashion of the phenomenalists he always thought of mental facts as sense data, or something like sense data, always completely missed the act. Sense data are awarenesses, of course. But the awareness of an awareness is always an act. Hence, if there were no acts, there would not even be the substitute for the inspection of mental things. This, I suggest, is the structural root of that underground affinity between phenomenalism and materialism which causes some to seesaw between the two. One cannot but think of Russell.

Remember, finally, that festering dissatisfaction about the synthetic a priori. The formula that meaning is use offers a specious way out. One who knows the rules for the use of language knows that 'this is both red and green' violates these rules. Or, as it is now put, nothing being both red and green is part of the meaning of the words 'red' and 'green'. Still differently, 'nothing is both red and green' is true not because the world is what it is but because we use language as we do. I merely ask two questions. Is every true (general) sentence true by virtue of the meanings of the words that occur in it? If not, where and how do you draw the line? The second question has no answer. One may try to answer the first by admitting, or even insisting, that the meaning of a word changes as we discover what is true and false about what it represents. There is of course *a* meaning of 'meaning' for which this is true. If, however, this were *the* meaning of 'meaning' in which we must first know what a sentence means before we can even ask whether it is true or false, then we could never know whether any single proposition containing a word is true without first knowing the totality of propositions which contain the word and are true. The holistic and idealistic structure of the doctrine is unmistakable. The ultimate subject of all predications is the Absolute. John Dewey, another structural idealist, propounds substantially the same doctrine of meaning. His Absolute is the sociopsychological process of inquiry. The epigones' Absolute is language.

Wittgenstein is a philosopher of the first rank. So we must study his work for its own sake. But we also may and should relate it to that of his peers, particularly if they are his contemporaries. So far, this century has seen four philosophers of the first rank. The other three are Husserl, G. E. Moore, and Russell. Moore, for whom I have a very special affection, was an *éminence grise*. Either one says very much about his contribution or one better says nothing. Tonight I shall say nothing. Russell's lasting achievements are easily identified. Tremendous as they are, they lie all in the area of logic, in the narrower sense of 'logic'. If asked to list four, I would mention his analysis of relations, the theory of types, his analysis of definite descriptions, and the logization of arithmetic. If asked to select among these four the one of greatest philosophical import, I would without hesitation point at the first. No one before Russell really understood relations. Wittgenstein has learned much from Russell and Moore. The most interesting confrontation is nonetheless with Husserl.

The world of my ontology, or, for short, my world is structured. The entities structuring it all have ontological status. Otherwise there would be no structure. No structure and no world is perhaps not quite the same. But the difference, if any, is not great. Among the entities which provide the structure there is one major division. Some are relations. Some belong to the world's form. Relations are things, share the ontological status of nonrelational characters. That is Russell's epochal insight. The Husserl of the *Untersuchungen*, who was still a realist of sorts, did see that the world's form has ontological status. Unfortunately, he located it, together with all characters, in a realm of Platonic essences. That is one seed of his later tragedy.

Most of my world is physical. Some of it is mental. Through the intentional tie, minds may know the world. In this sense, minds may also know themselves. In another sense, they don't. The awareness of an awareness is always a second awareness, never a part of the first. From this one point, which he took from Husserl, Sartre spun his philosophical fable.

The minds or my world do not create its structure. Nor do they impose it on what is without structure presented to them. Rather, it is presented to them. Our minds are of course active and even creative in many commonsensical ways. Or, alas, some minds are at some times. But, just as there are in my world no substances, there is nothing in it which, in this philosophical sense, is either creative or even active. Nor is that a coincidence.

The minds or Selves of the great tradition are not bare individuals. They are individual substances. If an image will help, think of such a Self as the inner of a sphere; of its properties, which you remember are the only things it can know, as coatings of the surface. The inner either actively creates these everchanging coats; or, at least, it actively imposes a structure upon what is, without one, impressed on the surface from without. Just think of Kant's synthetic unity of apperception! One who sets his feet into this path and walks it steadily will arrive at idealism.

Husserl's incomparable glory is the ontological assay of the act in the *Untersuchungen*. Yet, he understood neither relations, nor the need for fundamental ties, nor the difference between them. That is the other seed of the tragedy. Had he understood these things, he would not have said that the constituent of the act which I call the thought is "intrinsically relational." Nothing is intrinsically relational. The very phrase is a contradiction in terms. In particular, act and intention remain unconnected. Eventually, therefore, one or the other will be lost. That makes even the *Untersuchungen* a glorious failure. Eventually, deeply rooted in the Leibniz-Kant tradition as he was, the master dialectician of the *Untersuchungen* became the idealist of the *Ideen.*

Wittgenstein came as close to the correct ontological assay of the extensional part of the world's form as Husserl came to that of the act. Yet he shrank away from giving ontological status to what he was the first to see so clearly. Nor did he countenance active minds which might have provided that status. The possibility of minds which can know the world without being active in that certain philosophical sense he did not see. Thus mind was lost, the world left without form. Such a world is not much of a world. Thus, eventually, the world was lost. The epigones talk about language.

Stenius on the Tractatus[*]

A BIOGRAPHER'S subject almost always becomes his hero. Only
the exceptional biographer knows how to avoid this trap. As
with biographers, so with commentators. Only the exceptional
commentator will not twist and bend his chosen text to make it say
what he himself believes. At least, he will try to make it consistent.
Stenius' book[1] on Wittgenstein's *Tractatus* is exceptional in this admirable sense. Nor is it just a commentary but, rather, less as well as
much more. It is less because it is selective. The principle of selection
is again admirable. Stenius selected those passages concerning a few
fundamental and controversial issues out of which he believed he
could make sense. Trying to find this sense, he thought for himself. The
task he set himself, the sense he sought and found, are thus philosophical, not merely exegetic or biographical. That makes the book
much more than just a commentary. It is itself a philosophical treatise,
and a very considerable one indeed.

Stenius knows and shows that there are two groups of crucial passages in the *Tractatus* which cannot be reconciled with each other.
Then he opts for one. Thus he "corrects" Wittgenstein. (The word is
his, not mine.) The idea of, or behind, the correction is the central idea
of the book, its major contribution. I judge it to be original and ingenious as well as radically mistaken, in a way that is extraordinarily illuminating. To justify these judgments is the task I set myself in this study.
To solve it properly Stenius' ideas must of course be presented, which
cannot be done without also presenting Wittgenstein's. Nor can a
judgment be justified without some exposition of the ideas on which it
rests. That makes three sets of ideas. To present them completely
takes three books, Stenius', the *Tractatus*, and the one I haven't writ-

[*] Theoria, *29, 1963*, 176–204. *Reprinted by permission.*
[1] Erik Stenius, *Wittgenstein's Tractatus. A Critical Exposition of Its Main
Lines of Thought* (Blackwell, Oxford, 1960).

242

ten. The only way out is selection. The first selection determines the other two. Pride of place belongs to Stenius, of course. I select his central idea, the "correction."

Since I must justify my judgments, considerable space will have to be allowed to my views. Yet I shall be most succinct in stating them. Hans Hahn, who was a great teacher as well as a great mathematician, once said to a seminar of which I was a member: "Just knowing how a proof goes, you know nothing. When you know why it goes this way rather than that or that other way, then you begin to know something." I must state what I believe to be the right answers to some philosophical questions. But I shall achieve that extra succinctness by not arguing that just these and not those or those other answers are right. Those who care for the argument I refer to six recent essays[2] as well as to five others, by Allaire[3] and Grossmann,[4] discussion with whom has become so indispensable to me that sometimes I cannot tell who first said what.

How does a sentence manage to say what it says? The question dominates the *Tractatus*. Stenius rejects its answer. So let us take our bearings from the question. As Stenius and I use 'sentence', a sentence is a physical fact. Physical facts do not *say* anything. As it stands, the question is blurred. Replace 'says' by 'expresses' and the blur remains. Physical facts don't *express* anything. It is we who express our thoughts. More precisely, one expresses a thought by uttering a sentence which represents the thought's intention, i.e., the fact which the thought is about. That splits the question into three. (1) How does a sentence manage to represent a fact? (2) What is the connection[5] between a thought and its intention? (3) What, if any, is the

---

[2] "Ineffability, Ontology, and Method," *Philosophical Review*, 69, 1960, 18–40, and pp. 45–63 of this book; "The Ontology of Edmund Husserl," *Methodos*, 12, 1960, 359–92, and pp. 193–224 of this book; "Acts," *Indian Journal of Philosophy*, 2, 1960, 1–30, 96–117, and pp. 3–44 of this book; "Generality and Existence," *Theoria*, 28, 1962, 1–26, and pp. 64–84 of this book; "Meaning and Ontology," *Inquiry*, 5, 116–42, and pp. 85–97, 158–70 of this book; "La Gloria e la Miseria di Ludwig Wittgenstein," *Rivista di Filosofia*, 52, 1961, 387–406, and pp. 225–41 of this book. The present study elaborates a few of the many points rather briefly touched upon in the Italian piece on Wittgenstein.

[3] "Tractatus 6.3751," *Analysis*, 19, 1959, 100–105; "Existence, Independence, and Universals," *Philosophical Review*, 69, 1960, 485–96; "Tractatus 3.333," *Analysis*, 21, 1961, 14–16.

[4] "Conceptualism," *Review of Metaphysics*, 13, 1960, 243–54; "Frege's Ontology," *Philosophical Review*, 70, 1961, 23–40.

[5] 'Relation' and 'nexus' I use technically, 'connection' nontechnically and so broadly that a relation as well as a nexus is a connection.

connection between a sentence and the thought intending the fact it represents? (1) is still blurred. Physical facts do not *represent* anything. It is we who may or may not be able to make them represent (stand for) something. (1) can pass only as an abbreviation for (1'): What is there about a sentence that enables us to make it represent a fact? I shall save words by using (1) as an abbreviation for (1'). The question that dominates the *Tractatus* relates most closely to (1). So I shall start and for a long time stay with (1).

The heart of philosophy is ontology. Epistemology is but the ontology of the knowing[6] situation. The linguistic turn merely provides the method. Preoccupation with language as such is fatal to philosophy. (1) merely seems unduly preoccupied with language. If one wants to find out how a sentence manages to represent, he must first find out what there is to be represented. So he must begin with ontology. (Methodologically, we shall see, the order may be reversed.)

I present next my own answer to (1).

To *exist*, to be an existent, to be an entity, to have ontological status is one and the same. To say that something of a certain kind exists is the same as to say that there is something of this kind. This is the commonsensical use of 'exist'. I shall avoid all others.

Let S_1 be a pair of spots; one, red and round; the other, green and square. Green, red, round, square are four entities; S_1 itself is a fifth. Some existents are constituents of others. The two colors and the two shapes are constituents of S_1. To ask for all the constituents of an entity is to ask for its ontological assay. Two entities are different, i.e., two and not one, if and only if the assay of at least one yields at least one constituent which is not a constituent of the other.

Are the two shapes and the two colors all the constituents of S_1? Let S_2 be another pair of spots; one, red and square; one, green and round. Red in S_1 and S_2 is one entity, not two. So are green, round, square. Hence, if the assay of S_1, and therefore also that of S_2, yielded only these four entities, S_1 and S_2 would be one and not two. Yet they are different. In S_1 round is "tied" to red, while in S_2 it is tied to green; and so on. That shows the way out of the difficulty. One will so assay S_1 and S_2 that each yields in addition to the four entities called *things* (red, green, round, square) two occurrences of a fifth entity, called a *fundamental tie* (*nexus*), which in S_1 ties red to round, green to square, while in S_2 it ties red to square, green to round. That resolves the difficulty, provided an assay does not list a nexus just once but lists each of its occurrences (in this case, two), together with the entities it ties.

---

[6] This use of 'knowing' is generic, comprehends the species of perceiving, believing, remembering, doubting, and so on.

(Even if both spots were red, red would be listed only once.) In this sense a thing is and a fundamental tie is not an *independent₁* entity. That is one ontological difference between things and fundamental ties.

A *complex* is an entity among whose constituents are at least two things. A thing which is not a complex is a *simple*. Simples, to form a complex, must be connected by fundamental ties. (A class of simples is not a complex.) A fundamental tie needs no further tie to tie it to what it ties. (Otherwise we would be faced with an infinite regress *à la* Bradley.) In this sense things are and fundamental ties are not *independent₂*. That is another ontological difference between things and fundamental ties.

The things we have so far encountered are commonsensical. Common sense calls them (nonrelational) properties (characters). Now let S_3 be one spot, S_4 two spots, such that the three spots agree in all nonrelational properties. S_3 and S_4 are different, of course. Yet, if commonsensical properties were the only simples, they would yield the same assay. There are two ways out of the difficulty. One gives ontological status to bare individuals; the other, to such noncommonsensical properties as being at a certain place or a certain time. Faced with such an alternative, how does one decide? Urgent as the question is, we need not stay for an answer, since both alternatives recognize the ontological status of fundamental ties, which is the crucial issue between Wittgenstein and Stenius on the one hand and myself on the other, while, as it happens, aside from that issue and what it implies, Wittgenstein, Stenius, and I have all chosen the first alternative.

As I assay S_1, it yields six simples, four *characters* and two *individuals*, as well as four occurrences of an asymmetrical nexus I call *exemplification*. Nonrelational exemplification connects a character and one individual. Or, as one says, an individual may exemplify a character, a character may be exemplified by an individual. Relational exemplification connects two individuals and a relational character, which latter is not a nexus but a thing. Individuals never exemplify individuals. Characters never exemplify characters.[7]

If we may judge from what is presented to us, every individual exemplifies at least one character, every character is at least once exemplified. Call this the *Principle of Exemplification*. In this respect, individuals and characters are equally *dependent₃*. In two others, they differ. (A) Individuals exemplify characters, but not conversely. This is of course but another way of stating the asymmetry of exemplification. (B) The difference between two characters is of the kind called

[7] I limit myself to binary relations and the first two types. No harm will be done.

qualitative. Two individuals differ only in being different, i.e., in being two and not one. That is what is meant by calling them bare.

'Nominalism' and 'realism' have been used in many ways, some not very precise, some not very helpful, some neither. So I propose to use them in a new way, calling a realist₁[8] one who holds that (A) and (B) are the only differences between individuals and characters; or, if you wish, that they are the only differences fundamental enough to be called ontological. All others I call nominalists. That makes for several kinds of nominalism. One kind rejects the Principle of Exemplification, holds that characters but not individuals are independent₃. Its usual name is Platonism. Frege, we shall see, reverses Plato. According to him, only individuals, he calls them things, are independent₃; characters, he calls them a kind of function, are not just dependent₃ but dependent₁.

The ontological ground of the difference between two characters is the characters themselves. Or, with a twist, the differences called qualitative need no ontological ground. The difference between individuals and characters is not qualitative. Nor is being an individual or being a character itself a character (universal); otherwise we would be faced with an infinite regress. What, then, is the ontological ground of the difference? I ground it in two dependent₁ entities, call them *individuality* and *universality*.[9] Dependent₁ entities being so radically different from all others that it is convenient to have a name for them, I appropriated one from the tradition, call them *subsistents*. The tradition calls a *summum genus* of the ontological inventory a mode. That makes subsistence a mode of existence.

Individuality, universality, and exemplification are three subsistents. The connectives, negation, conjunction, disjunction, and so on, are others.[10] There are still others. But we need not pursue. I shall manage without detailed examination of any but those three, individuality, universality, and exemplification.

Red-or-green is a character. It is also a complex. The nexus that makes it one is disjunction.[10a] Characters are things. Some things are

---

[8] Realism₂ is opposed to idealism. See below.

[9] More precisely, nonrelational and relational universality are two entities. So are nonrelational and relational exemplification. When it makes no difference, I permit myself this inaccuracy.

[10] It is clear, I trust, that I use these words not for the marks sometimes so called but for the entities I claim they represent.

[10a] This seems to me now an awkward way of putting the matter. Let f_1 and f_2 be two simple characters. Let '$(f_1 \cdot f_2)$' represent the complex character exemplified if and only if there is a particular which exemplifies both f_1 and f_2. What makes the expression awkward is that '$(f_1 \cdot f_2)$' is merely an incomplete symbol intro-

thus complex(es). But not every complex is a thing. A complex is either a character or a *fact*. (All individuals are simples.) One individual exemplifying one simple nonrelational character is a fact. So are two individuals exemplifying one simple relational character. These two kinds of fact are called atomic. An atomic fact has no constituent which is itself a fact; hence the name. Notice, for later reference, that facts are independent₃.

How does a sentence manage to represent a fact? It will still be possible to join the issues if we limit the question to atomic facts. The "language" I shall examine, following Stenius who in turn follows Wittgenstein, is the familiar fragment of the lower functional calculus.

The fragment contains an indefinite number of marks of three different shapes, lower-case letters ('a', 'b', . . .), upper-case letters ('F', 'G', . . .), Greek letters ('ρ', 'σ', . . .). It will save words and do no harm if we assume that each mark is a (geometrical) individual exemplifying one of three simple (geometrical) characters (upper-case, lower-case, Greek). A mark thus is a fact. It occurs in the fragment only if there is a simple which it has been made to represent. The individual in it stands for the thing; the shape in it, for the thing's type; lower-case for individuality, upper-case and Greek for nonrelational and relational universality, respectively. Marks representing in this way are called *names*.[10b] Strings such as 'Fa' and '$b\rho c$' are made to represent atomic facts by making two kinds of juxtaposition such as 'F' followed by 'a' and 'b' followed by 'ρ' followed by 'c' represent the two kinds of exemplification.

In the fragment facts are thus represented by strings of marks, simples by the individuals in the marks, the subsistents by properties of and relations among these individuals. That illustrates a feature of all systematically constructed languages. Each ontological kind is represented in one and only one way; different kinds in different ways. That makes these languages useful tools for ontological analysis. On the other hand, not every constituent of the representing fact (mark or string) is made to represent something. The shape of a mark, for instance, is tied to the individual in it by exemplification. Yet (this occurrence of) exemplification is not made to represent anything.

---

duced by the definition that makes '$(f_1 \cdot f_2)(x)$' an abbreviation of '$f_1(x) \cdot f_2(x)$'. (More precisely, the "definition" is merely a definitional schema.) Whether or not $(f_1 \cdot f_2)$ exists actually or merely as a possibility depends of course only on whether there is an individual which exemplifies both simple characters. The definition, however, *if* introduced, is well-formed irrespective of whether or not there is such an individual. That reflects the ontological feature expressed by calling $(f_1 \cdot f_2)$ a p-character in case there is no such individual. [Added in 1963.]

[10b] See fn. 1a on page 49. [Added in 1963.]

The above description of the fragment is of the kind called seman-tical. A syntactical description, also called formation rules, attends only to the representing[11] facts. In our case it is very simple. First three kinds of marks[11] are singled out and distinguished by their shapes. Call this the *type distinction*. Then the two familiar kinds of strings are singled out as well-formed (sentences[11]). All other strings are ill formed. Call this the *type rule*. If the formation rules of a language were not what they are, it could not represent what it represents. *Our language is what it is because the world is what it is.*

Not every sentence represents a fact. That is of the essence of lan-guage. *'Fa'* represents a fact if and only if *a* and *F* are tied by exempli-fication. Otherwise there is no fact for it to represent. It does not fol-low that in this case it represents nothing. Since the formation rules are what they are because the world is what it is, the difference between *'Fa'*, which is well formed whether or not it represents a fact, on the one hand, and such ill-formed strings as *'FG'*, *'aa'*, *'aFb'*, and so on, on the other, must have an ontological ground. I identify this ground by saying that a sentence represents either a fact or a possible fact and making *possibility* in this sense a mode of existence.[12] Since this is a very special use of 'possible', I mark it by saying that a sentence repre-sents either a fact or a P-fact. If at this point some are shocked, what shocks them is merely the peculiar flavor of the traditional ontological language.

How do *'Fa'* and *'bρc'* manage to represent? To each constituent of the fact represented corresponds one constituent of the representing fact. The nexus connecting two simples, actually or P-wise, is repre-sented by a relational thing connecting the two individuals which represent the simples. Such a correspondence is called an *isomorphism*. The language represents by means of an isomorphism. To understand the language is to know this isomorphism, which is *partial* and *external*. It is partial because, as we saw, not every constituent of the represent-ing fact (sentence) represents something. It is external because the represented and the representing constituents need not and often are not of the same ontological kind. In the fragment all subsistents are represented by characters; characters are represented by individuals. Only individuals are represented by individuals.

Wittgenstein and Stenius make the same fundamental mistake. Neither recognizes that the subsistents exist. Wittgenstein,[13] because

---

[11] This is of course a proleptic use of 'representing', 'mark', and 'sentence'.
[12] As for facts, so for complex characters. 'Centaur' represents a possible character.
[13] "Wittgenstein" is throughout this study the author of the *Tractatus*.

of this fundamental mistake, provides no answer to the question how sentences manage to represent facts. Stenius answers it, in spite of the fundamental mistake. From where I stand his answer is wrong. But it is not wrong because of the fundamental mistake. Rather, it is wrong because of the nominalism it implies but which Stenius himself does not notice. If the task were merely diagnosis, I would now be ready to conclude. Since the task is also analysis and justification, I have barely begun. It will in fact be best if before turning to Wittgenstein and Stenius I make four further points.

First. Remember what was said earlier. The heart of the matter is ontology; the linguistic turn merely provides the method. That is why I began with ontology. But the traditional ontological talk is problematic, sometimes even shocking. The thing to do therefore is to make it commonsensical. That is done by reversing the order, beginning with language. We know, commonsensically, that this is red, that green, this to the left of that, and so on. Language represents what we know, otherwise it could not do the job it does. Hence it must represent what must be there if we are to know what in fact we do know, e.g., that S_1 differs from S_2, S_3 from S_4. The method first identifies the representing features of language. Then it explicates the ontological kinds as corresponding to the different ways in which different features represent. If these ways were arbitrary, the method would fail. Thus one must show that in a relevant sense they are not arbitrary. I shall show that, hastily, in one case. Assume that individuality can be represented by a capital letter, say, '*I*'. (If the method works, that amounts to assuming that individuality is a simple character.) Consider now '*Ia*'. This sentence manages to represent what it represents, namely, that *a* is an individual, only because we know already what the shapes of '*a*' and '*I*' and their juxtaposition have been made to represent. In this sense the sentence represents *only with futility*. Or, if you please, the language "shows" what cannot in it without futility be "said." That is the recoverable core of Wittgenstein's famous ineffability thesis. The argument also supports a point made earlier. Systematically constructed languages are useful because they represent the different ontological kinds in different ways. (Natural languages are universal, i.e., in them everything can be said; hence the troubles of philosophy before the linguistic turn.)

Second. The overwhelming majority of modern philosophers failed to recognize that the subsistents exist. Among recent ones the only exceptions I know of (and admire) are Frege and Husserl. In Frege's world, though, exemplification does not exist. Yet he managed to fill the gap. Since in this study exemplification is the crucial issue and since Frege's influence is clearly visible in the *Tractatus*, we had better understand how he managed. His things are independent₃. His notion of function is taken from mathematics. A function is a "mapping" of entities on entities.[14] That makes it dependent₁ on those entities. Hence it needs no tie to tie it to them. The connectives are one kind of function; characters are another. Characters thus have the same ontological status as the connectives, to which the overwhelming majority of modern philosophers gives no ontological status whatsoever while in my world they "merely" subsist. That makes Frege a nominalist. (It also shows that there is some point in my new way of using that old label.)

Among Frege's things there are two noncommonsensical kinds, propositions and the two things True and False. In my world, a sentence represents either (a) a fact or (b) a P-fact. In his world there are no facts. Rather, each sentence represents two things, one as its *Sinn*, one as its *Bedeutung*. In case (a) it represents a proposition and the thing True; in case (b) the same proposition and the thing False. Notice now, first, that the proposition is a thing in either case, e.g., in the paradigm, whether or not exemplification occurs between *a* and *F*.[15] Notice, second, that the occurrence and nonoccurrence of exemplification is "represented" by the two things True and False, respectively. That shows how Frege managed. The price he paid for not recognizing the ontological status of exemplification was the two noncommonsensical kinds of things.

Third. If one says that there are six possible ways of selecting two things out of four, ten to select three out of five, and so on, he uses 'possible' combinatorially. This use needs no explication. Two others do. Both are often marked by the adverb 'logically'. In other words, I claim that 'logically possible' has been used in two different ways, each of which needs explication. As for 'possible', so of course for 'impossible' and 'necessary'. For the time being I suppress the adverb, distinguish the two uses by subscripts.

'*Fa*' is well formed; '*FG*' is not. It is possible₁ for '*Fa*' to represent something; it is impossible₁ for '*FG*' to do so. That is the cue. It is possible₁ for a well-formed string to represent something, impossible₁ for one that is ill-formed. Notice also what I did not say, namely, that a well-formed string represents a possible entity. For, whether a sentence represents a fact or a P-fact is an entirely different matter. In

[14] See "Frege's Hidden Nominalism," *Philosophical Review*, 67, 1958, 437–59; reprinted in *Meaning and Existence*.

[15] A P-fact is there (exists in the mode of possibility) if and only if there is no fact for the sentence to represent. That alone shows that a P-fact is not a proposition.

other words, the ontological use of 'possible', which was explicated earlier and marked by 'P', is a third use.

Replace in a fact all the simples among its constituents so that, first, different ones are replaced by different ones, and, second, each is replaced by one of its own kind, individuals by individuals, and so on. Considering all "possible" replacements, there are two "possibilities." (The two uses of 'possible' in the preceding sentence are combinatorial!) The resulting "complexes" either are all facts or some are P-facts. If and only if they are all facts then all these facts, including the original one, are necessary$_2$, or, synonymously, they are facts of all possible$_2$ worlds. As for facts, so for P-facts. If for a P-fact all possible replacements yield P-facts, then all these P-facts, including the original one, are impossible$_2$, or, synonymously, they are P-facts in all possible$_2$ worlds.[16]

If you doubt whether the two uses are really different, consider a contradiction. Since it is well formed, it is possible$_1$ for it to represent something. Yet what it represents is impossible$_2$. If you are still doubtful, try to use the phrase 'possible world' in connection with possibility$_1$. In this context "all possible worlds" are those corresponding to all possible formation rules. Our world, or, rather, and this is where the difference shows, *all* possible$_2$ worlds are just *one* such "possible world." Or, if you want to say the same thing still differently, possibility$_1$ determines the class of all complexes and P-complexes; necessity$_2$ and impossibility$_2$ single out two subclasses of this class.

While combinatorial possibility enters explicitly into the notion of possibility$_2$, it does not so enter into that of possibility$_1$. Yet there is a connection. To know all "possible" well-formed strings is the same thing as to know for which strings it is possible$_1$ to represent something. In the fragment that amounts to knowing all "possible" strings of two or three names that are well formed. The two uses of 'possible' in this paragraph that are marked by quotation marks are combinatorial. That shows the connection.

Fourth. What is the ontological ground of an isomorphism? The answer requires some preparation. "Subsistent characters"[17] are a special kind of subsistent. If there are three chairs in this room, the character chair-in-this-room "exemplifies" the "subsistent property"

---

[16] More usually one would say that the representing sentences are necessarily$_2$ true (false) or that they are true (false) in all possible$_2$ worlds. But there is some point in avoiding 'true' and 'false' in this study. So I make a point of avoiding them.

[17] More usually they are called *logical characters*. But it will help the explication of how Wittgenstein uses 'logic' and 'logical' if I avoid using them myself.

of being a triple. In a monogamic society the characters husband and wife jointly "exemplify" the "subsistent relation" of equinumerosity. Subsistent characters are not characters; nor are they really exemplified by anything; hence the quotation marks; otherwise the expressions within them may mislead. Individuality and triplicity are both subsistents. Yet there is a difference. That an entity is an individual cannot as we saw (without futility) be said (in a systematically constructed language). That the chairs in this room are a triple can be said. If the statement saying it is appropriately abbreviated by means of definitions then the subsistent appears to be represented by a defined predicate. As for triplicity, so for all subsistent characters; hence the name which may mislead.

There is an isomorphism between A and B if and only if they jointly exemplify a subsistent relation of a certain kind. That answers the question which opens the last paragraph. Two comments will show its importance. First. Complete philosophical understanding of a statement is inseparable from the identification of its ontological ground. It follows that one cannot fully understand the nature of an isomorphism without realizing that the subsistents exist. Second. We say that we discover an isomorphism, that we establish one, and so on. Discovering and establishing involve mind. We speak of formation and interpretation[18] rules. Again, rules involve mind. That makes it important to grasp firmly that the isomorphism between a sentence and the fact (or P-fact) which by the virtue of this isomorphism it represents involves nothing mental but merely the sentence itself, the fact, and certain subsistents.[19]

I turn to Wittgenstein.

Stenius and I use 'sentence' for the physical fact; Wittgenstein doesn't. I shall continue to use the word as before, mark Wittgenstein's use by capitalizing its initial (*Sentence*). What matters is not of course how a word is used but, rather, the distinctions which a use helps or hinders.

What is a mind? What is a thought? What is the right assay of the knowing situation? The three questions are but three facets of one. Call it the *problem of mind*. Remember now three other questions. (1) How does a sentence manage to represent a fact? (2) What is the connection between a thought and its intention? (3) What, if any, is the connection between a sentence and the thought intending the fact which it

---

[18] To make the individual in a name stand for a certain simple is an instance of an interpretation rule.

[19] The fact represented may of course itself be mental. Reread what has been said at the beginning about (1) being merely an abbreviation of (1').

represents? One cannot solve the problem of mind without clearly distinguishing among (1), (2), (3), nor without realizing that the answer to (1) must not involve mind. My answer to (1), we saw, is of that kind. So, we shall see, is Stenius'. His and my use of 'sentence' helps the relevant distinctions. The *Tractatus* is hopelessly blurred on the problem of mind. Call that its *fundamental blur*. Of this more later.

A Sentence is, *roughly*, a sentence plus the relevant (formation and interpretation) rules. The question which dominates the *Tractatus* is not (1) but, rather, (1″): How does a Sentence manage to represent a fact? Now there is of course in this context a way of referring to rules which does not essentially involve mind and which is therefore as harmless as it is often convenient. If the rules ingredient of a Sentence were harmless in this sense, the difference between (1) and (1″) would be merely verbal. Unhappily this ingredient is anything but harmless. Thought is essentially involved. The fundamental blur thus spreads to Sentences. The ontological status of their rules ingredient remains hopelessly blurred. I shall mark that blur by once more capitalizing an initial, say that a Sentence is a sentence plus the relevant *Rules*. Nor is that the only reason I said "roughly." Some passages may plausibly be taken to imply that a Sentence is something wholly mental. More precisely, they may be taken to imply that the thought of a fact, i.e., a Sentence, and the thought of a sentence representing this fact are one thing and not two. The right answer to (3) is that these are two thoughts and that the connection between them is merely causal.

What is Wittgenstein's answer to (1″)? I limit the task as before. How does an atomic Sentence manage to represent an atomic fact? As before, we cannot answer without answering another question first. According to Wittgenstein, what is there to be represented? A sentence may of course represent a P-fact. But it will be safe to ignore this complication until we come to the only point where it matters.

There is no disagreement about those constituents of atomic facts which are things. The only issue are the three subsistents, individuality, universality, and exemplification. Wittgenstein denies that they exist. That is his *fundamental mistake*. One cannot understand it accurately without understanding why the way in which he disposes of the first two differs from that in which he disposes of the third. Individuality and universality he calls internal properties, argues with great care that as such they do not exist. Exemplification he overlooks. Or, at most, he brushes it aside, denies the need for it in one striking passage. The structural reason for this difference is that he attends, again with great care, to something else, he calls it an internal relation,

which is not exemplification but which conceivably even though not
plausibly may be mistaken for it. Notice that I speak of a structural
reason rather than a cause, just as I do not claim that Wittgenstein
mistook that internal relation for exemplification, or, even, that he
overlooked the need for the latter because of his preoccupation with
the former. For I am not in the least interested in biographical con-
jectures.

The striking passage[20] just mentioned is 2.03:

> Im Sachverhalt haengen die Gegenstaende ineinander, wie die
> Glieder einer Kette.

The image is admirably clear. The links of a chain hang in each other,
need no tie to hold them together. There is no need for exemplification.
It is nothing, less than nothing. To be nothing and to have no ontological status is the same. And there is of course no lesser ontological
status than none. Thus I spoke metaphorically. Internal characters
(properties and relations), we shall see, have no ontological status, are
nothing. Exemplification, however, has not even the "status" of an
internal relation. That unpacks the metaphor. To say the same thing
still differently, even if internal relations existed, it would not follow
that exemplification exists.

(a) Individuality and universality are internal characters. (b) Internal characters do not exist. (a) and (b) jointly imply that individuality
and universality have no ontological status. Wittgenstein obviously
holds (a). The strongest evidence for his also holding (b) is a fragment
from 4.123:

> Diese blaue Farbe und jene stehen in der internen Relation von
> heller und dunkler eo ipso.

Remember what was said earlier. Difference, whether qualitative
between two characters or, as one says, merely numerical between two
individuals, needs no ontological ground, i.e., no third entity in addition to the two things. But a relation between two things is a third
entity. Nor is it just a subsistent, it is a third thing. The strength of
the evidence lies partly in the fragment's being so patently wrong.
Partly it lies in the "eo ipso," which leaves no doubt that the two
colors are the only entities in the case, or, what amounts to the same,
that the alleged internal relation has no ontological status whatsoever.

[20] I approve and therefore follow Stenius' practice of quoting the German
original.

It is possible₁[21] for any individual to exemplify any character.[22] Wittgenstein expresses this by saying that an internal relation, call it R, obtains between each individual and each character. R is the connection of which I claimed that it might conceivably be mistaken for exemplification, or, less strongly, that preoccupation with it might cause one to overlook exemplification. The distinction depends on the distinction between possibility₁ and the mode of possibility (P). Take a and F. Exemplification either does or does not occur between them. If it does, they jointly form a fact; if it doesn't, a P-fact. But R obtains between them in either case. Hence R and exemplification are two, not one. That is one way of putting the matter; let me try another. If R and exemplification were one, 'Fa' would merely represent its own being well-formed, which is absurd. What it does represent (by means of juxtaposition!) is either a fact or a P-fact; which of the two we are of course unable to tell by looking merely at 'Fa'. If one is overimpressed by this inability, as I believe Wittgenstein was, and if one does not clearly distinguish between possibility₁ and the mode of possibility (P), the distinction between R and exemplification may become blurred.

The Sentence represents the fact by sharing its "logical form." That is Wittgenstein's answer to (1″). He also calls internal characters structural, or formal, or *logical*. What, then, is his notion of logic? A thread I left dangling will lead to the answer. Possibility₁ and possibility₂ are two, not one. Yet they have both been called "logical possibility." Is there a notion of logic that fits both (undistinguished) uses? Combinatorial possibility, we remember, is an ingredient of both. Mistaking this common ingredient for what it is not, a common core, one arrives at the following notion: "Logic encompasses all possibilities. The nonlogical is the impossible; the logical, the necessary. The necessary, not depending on any one possibility, is common to all possible worlds." This is also Wittgenstein's notion of logic. I shall first connect it with his notion of internal (logical) characters, then show why it is confused.

Let E_1 and E_2 be two sentences. E_2 follows deductively from E_1 if and only if 'If E_1 then E_2' is a tautology. According to Wittgenstein, a Sentence's being a tautology is an internal (logical) property of it; E_2's deductively following from E_1, an internal (logical) relation between the two Sentences. A tautology, we remember, represents a

[21] As explicated earlier, possibility₁ involves marks. But no harm will come from using the term also as above.

[22] The extension of the argument to relational characters, ordered pairs of individuals, and relational exemplification is obvious.

necessary₂ fact. That shows the connection of logical characters with possibility₂. The connection with possibility₁ we know already. 'Fa' is well-formed because the logical relation R obtains between a and F.

Wittgenstein's notion of logic makes both being well-formed (possibility₁) and being a tautology (necessity₂) a "matter of logic."[23] That is the root of the confusion. Its bitter fruit is either failure to distinguish between formation rules and tautologies, or, even worse, to mistake the former for a species of the latter. Wittgenstein himself virtually makes that mistake when he asserts in 3.332, 3.333 that the type rule (e.g., that 'ab' and 'FG' are ill-formed) follows deductively from the type distinction (e.g., between 'a' and 'F').[24] The mistake is (or may be) facilitated by the equally confused idea that if an internal relation obtains between two entities, then the sentence expressing this fact is a tautology. The internal relation in the case is of course R, which obtains between a and F but not between either a and b or F and G.

The only clear use of 'logic' and 'logical' is the narrow classical one that relates to deductive inference (necessity₂). The broader the use, the blunter the tool, the greater therefore the confusion. Wittgenstein's broad use opened the door to even broader ones. His epigones at Oxford rushed through the door. Stenius, even though in most other respects laudably unaffected by Oxford, is also given to a very broad use. This aspect of his book I admire least. That is why I did not select it for examination.

The Sentence and the fact share a *logical form* (logical structure, internal structure). That is how, according to Wittgenstein, the former manages to represent the latter. What, then, is the logical form of an atomic fact? It is a "something" that consists "somehow" of three internal characters, the relation R and the two properties corresponding to individuality and universality. R connects individuals and characters, not individuality and universality; and a structure is not just a class, its constituents must be connected; hence the quotation marks around 'somehow'. But let us waive this objection. Perhaps the blur it spots can be cleared up. Internal characters are nothing, have no ontological status whatsoever. What consists of nothing is itself nothing. Logical form is literally nothing; hence the quotation marks around

[23] The phrase is vague. But square pegs do not fit round holes. A vague phrase sometimes helps taking apart a confusion. This particular confusion has also been promoted by multiply ambiguous uses of 'formal' and 'linguistic'. These I examined elsewhere; so I ignore them here.

[24] See Allaire's paper on 3.333 cited in fn. 3. The mistake is further facilitated by Fege's notion of function. See also my "Propositional Functions," *Analysis*, 17, 1956, 43–48.

'something'. What two entities literally share is itself an entity, has ontological status. If what the Sentence and the fact share has none, then there is nothing they share. This objection is fatal. Wittgenstein's *explicit answer* to (1″) is no answer. If we merely wanted to judge, we could stop. Since we also want to understand as accurately as we may, we must continue.

After a fashion, we know what the logical form of the nonrelational atomic fact is. Let us see whether we can find it in the Sentence. The Sentence is the sentence plus the Rules. Let us first look at the sentence, say, '*Fa*'. The three shapes (lower-case, upper-case, Greek) are nowhere mentioned in the *Tractatus*; nor is juxtaposition.[25] A sentence is considered to be a fact; a mark (name), an individual.[26] The logical form of two individuals, or, even, of two individuals in juxtaposition is not that of the nonrelational atomic fact. Yet the latter is supposed to be in the Sentence. Since we haven't found it in the sentence, we must look for it in the Rules. These, I submit, "correspond" to the formation rules. I say "correspond" rather than "are" because, we remember, Rules either are mental, or, at least, essentially involve mind. Even so, we have come upon Wittgenstein's implicit answer to (1″). The sentences (or Sentences) of the fragment manage to represent because there is a one-one correspondence between the members of the class of all possible$_1$ atomic facts and P-facts on the one hand and all combinatorially possible well-formed strings (Strings) of the fragment on the other; with the formation rules determining what is combinatorially possible. What is thus really "shared," not to be sure by any pair of corresponding members but, at least, by the two classes themselves is this one-one correspondence. We know that a one-one correspondence is an elementary isomorphism whose ontological status is that of a subsistent relation, which is not "shared" but, rather, jointly exemplified by the two classes; hence the quotation marks around 'shared'.

Is Wittgenstein's implicit answer to (1″) really an answer? If sentences (or Sentences) were names (or Names), it would be one. Since they are not, as he himself so admirably insisted against Frege, and since he overlooked exemplification, he can not really tell how a string (or String) manages to represent what it represents. Hence not even his implicit answer is really an answer.

Wittgenstein denies that the subsistents exist. That is his fundamental mistake. Since the subsistents are nothing, logical form is nothing. The status of mind in the *Tractatus* is hopelessly blurred.

[25] See, however, what is said below about Stenius' "second group of passages."
[26] Or, if you insist on the type-token distinction, a character. The difference makes no difference for the argument.

That is its fundamental blur. One can even argue what presently I shall at least assert, that in the *Tractatus* world mind is nothing. On the side of the Sentence, we saw, the logical form, which is nothing, resides in the Rules which, being mental or at least essentially involving mind, are either themselves nothing, or, at best, something whose ontological status remains hopelessly blurred. That shows how the fundamental mistake and the fundamental blur curiously supplement each other, jointly produce the semblance of an answer where there is none.

Why did Wittgenstein overlook exemplification? Intellectual biography is one thing; connections among ideas are another. To explore the *structural* reasons which *may* plausibly have shaped a man's thought is merely one way of exploring connections among ideas. Sometimes it is the most convenient way. I suggest next two further structural reasons why Wittgenstein may have overlooked exemplification.

First. The commonsensical use of 'exist' is also the broadest. (1) To exist is to be an individual. (2) To exist is to be a simple. (3) To exist is to be in space and time. (4) To exist is to be a thing. (5) To exist is to be a fact. (6) To exist is to be an atomic fact. Each of these six sentences is the formula of a narrow use of the kind I call philosophical. (There are still others.) Once a philosopher has adopted such a use he never permits its formula to become false. That may lead him to reject the commonsensical use; or he may fail to distinguish the latter from his own. In either case he will be in trouble.[27] That is indeed one way of diagnosing *the* trouble of classical ontology.

Wittgenstein, with a difference, adopts (2) and (6). I say with a difference because in his world the ontological status of atomic facts (6) is "higher" than that of simples (2). The more "independent" an entity is, the "higher" is its ontological status. That is the idea behind the difference. Its influence throughout the history of philosophy is very great indeed. To understand the difference (and unpack the metaphors between the quotation marks), remember the Principle of Exemplification. Facts (5) are and things (4) are not independent$_3$. Simples (2) are the "simplest" things (4); atomic facts (6), the "simplest" facts (5). The "simpler" an entity is, the "higher" is its ontological status. That is another idea whose influence throughout the history of philosophy is very great. It accounts for the replacement of (5) and (4) by (6) and (2), respectively.

R's being an internal relation expresses the dependence$_3$ of individuals and characters on each other. That is why what follows merely

---

[27] If, for instance, wittingly or unwittingly he adopts (1), he may say that characters don't exist without noticing that what he says is patently wrong if 'exists' is taken in its one clear and commonsensical meaning.

adds a nuance. *Each* individual has *a* character (or some) on which it depends₃; each character, an individual (or some). Call this the general dependence of the two kinds on each other. It needs no further ontological ground; that is why R is superfluous and why its being nothing does not hurt. On the other hand, *this* individual depends₃ on *this* character and not on that or that other. This specific dependence does need an ontological ground. Otherwise, what would be the difference between the two pairs of spots with which I began? To put the ontological status of facts "higher" than that of things is to be overimpressed with the general dependence of the latter on each other. If one is so overimpressed then he may overlook the need for ontologically grounding their specific dependence. That is the nuance.

Second. In Frege's world, we saw, there are no facts. There are, instead, the two noncommonsensical kinds of things, propositions and the two things True and False. I say instead because, as we also saw, these two strange kinds enabled Frege to construct an ontology which has no gap at the place which in other ontologies is taken by exemplification. Call this the function of the two strange kinds. Wittgenstein rejected them both. In this I believe he was right. But, then, he cannot have fully understood their function. Otherwise he would not have overlooked exemplification. Call this the negative influence of Frege. Being negative, it does not show in the text. Another one does.

A function, being a mapping and as such dependent₁ on the entities mapped and mapped upon, needs no nexus to tie it to these entities. Wittgenstein, partly under Frege's influence, partly because of his preoccupation with combinatorial possibility, thinks of '*Fa*' as a "propositional function" of '*F*' and '*a*'. The sense that makes is obvious and irrelevant; the nonsense, subtle and disastrous. Replace either of the two names by another and you obtain another sentence. That is the sense. Keeping one name unchanged, you may, if you wish, replace the other in all possible₁ ways. That shows the connection with the preoccupation. The nonsense is that a character does not "map" an individual into a fact. Nor of course does an individual so map a character. Rather, an individual and a character, if connected by exemplification, jointly "make" a fact. That shows why one who in thinking about a world in which there are facts thinks about sentences as "propositional functions" may overlook exemplification.

I turn to Stenius.

Unlike Wittgenstein, Stenius, as one must, answers (1), not (1″). His assay of the atomic fact agrees with Wittgenstein's; yields one or, in the relational case, two individuals, one character and, literally, nothing else. For, like Wittgenstein, he does not recognize the ontological status of the three subsistents. Yet, he does not overlook exemplification.[28] That is why, unlike Wittgenstein, he is able to produce an answer. More precisely, what he says becomes an answer as soon as one recognizes that exemplification exists.

'Fa' is for Stenius a fact. Wittgenstein and I agree. 'F' and 'a' he takes to be individuals. Wittgenstein agrees, I don't. With the qualification that disagreement implies, all three agree that 'a' represents the individual in the fact as its *name*. Stenius' innovation concerns 'F'. This letter for him is not the name of the character in the fact. The linguistic representative of that (nonrelational) character is, rather, the (nonrelational) character standing-to-the-right-of-'F' (on paper). The letter itself is merely an ingredient of the representative, he calls it its characteristic, probably because one can by means of it establish the required one-one correspondence between representing and represented entities; where standing to the left of 'F', of 'G', of 'H', and so on, correspond to this, that, and that other character, and so on. Whether one calls these representatives of characters names is a matter of words. How one uses a word, provided only one knows how one uses it, does not matter. But it will facilitate the exposition if we avoid 'name', speak instead of *character-representatives*.

To each represented individual corresponds one representing individual, its name, and conversely. To each represented nonrelational character corresponds one character-representative, which is itself a nonrelational character, and conversely. The represented fact or P-fact consists of an individual exemplifying a character, actually or P-wise; the representing fact, the sentence, of the representing individual exemplifying the character-representative. That is an isomorphism. Stenius' answer to (1) is that the sentence represents the fact by virtue of this isomorphism. Notice that each entity corresponds to one of its own kind, individuals to individuals, nonrelational characters to nonrelational characters, (occurrences of) exemplification to (occurrences of) exemplification. In other words, the isomorphism is internal. Notice, too, that *as long as the marks are assayed as individuals* each constituent of the representing fact, *except the mark 'F' itself*, is made to represent something. With these two qualifications, which apparently he did not notice, the isomorphism of Stenius' answer is complete. Thus he thinks of it as both *internal and complete*.

Let us compare the three answers, assay them ontologically. According to Wittgenstein, the Sentence and the fact "share" something.

---

[28] Overlooking exemplification is one thing. Assigning it the "status" of an internal relation is another thing. That should by now be clear.

That is how the former manages to represent the latter. The something "shared" turns out to be nothing. That is why his explicit answer fails. So, we saw, does his implicit answer. According to Stenius the sentence represents the fact by virtue of an isomorphism. If exemplification is given ontological status, that isomorphism is really there. With this obvious qualification, Stenius' answer is really an answer. We know that an isomorphism is a subsistent relation which is not "shared" but, rather, jointly exemplified by the two members of each corresponding pair. This knowledge, though, requires the correct ontological assay of an isomorphism, which in turn requires the insight that the subsistents (not just the three to which I limited the issue) exist. Stenius, who does not have this insight, *seems* to hold that something is "shared." The two individuals, for instance, the represented and the representing one, share individuality. To see how wrong that is one merely has to remember that individuality, being dependent₁, never occurs as such in an ontological assay. Rather, an assay lists occurrences of individuality. In our case, individuality occurs twice, once in the represented, once in the representing fact. Hence, obviously, neither of the two occurrences is "shared" by the two facts. As for individuality, so for universality and exemplification. I said "seems" when attributing to Stenius the belief that something is "shared" because inevitably at this point he is not as clear as one could wish. Yet no harm is done. He makes his idea perfectly clear nevertheless. Since they "share" something and/or the isomorphism is internal and complete, the sentence and the fact are *similar*. That is the idea. The corresponding entities of an external and partial isomorphism are not similar in this sense. The isomorphism of my answer is external and partial.

If you try to apply Stenius' innovation to the relational atomic fact represented by '*aρb*', you will see that the representative of the relational character must itself be such a character. Hence it can only be standing-to-the-left-and-right-of-'*ρ*' (on paper), with the letter '*ρ*' as its characteristic. Reread now 3.1432:

Nicht: "Das komplexe Zeichen '*aRb*' sagt dass *a* in der Beziehung *R* zu *b* steht," sondern: Dass "*a*" in einer gewissen Beziehung zu "*b*" steht, sagt, dass *aRb*.

and you will, if I am not wholly mistaken, for the first time understand the passage. I have been puzzled by it for years. From time to time I brooded over it, to no avail. Others, equally puzzled, remained equally in the dark. Stenius has solved the puzzle. That makes our failure the measure of his ingenuity. But then, one may ask, how does his reading of 3.1432 fit the rest of the text. He himself provides the answer by calling attention to two groups of passages.

One fairly large group, taken in isolation, leaves no doubt that '*a*', '*F*', '*ρ*' are names in exactly the same sense, represent in exactly the same way. That contradicts 3.1432.[29] Since Stenius very carefully points that out himself, I need not quote from that first group.

I made much of 2.03, the metaphor of the links in the chain, claimed that it was the only passage that at least implicitly deals with exemplification, if only to brush it aside, dismiss it as superfluous. Given my lack of text-critical enthusiasm in general and the nature of this text in particular, I am not prepared to press the claim. Rather, I agree with Stenius that there is a small group of passages which, taken in isolation, permits, even though it does not require, an interpretation that contradicts my claim. 3.21 is a passage of this second group as characteristic as any:

Der Konfiguration der einfachen Zeichen im Satzzeichen entspricht die Konfiguration der Gegenstaende in der Sachlage.

I incline to the belief that any such passage is merely another tedious reference to that tedious and useless nonentity *R*. That is why I said "permits even though it does not require." Stenius reads "verhalten" to stand for exemplification, once of the character by the individual in the fact, once of the character-representative by the name in the sentence. He adds with his usual acuity and candor that with this reading the two groups contradict each other. Then he proposes to disregard the first, *that is his correction*, and bases his interpretation on 3.1432 and the second. But, then, why call interpretation what is really an original idea that may or may not have been suggested by a text which is notoriously contradictory as well as opaque?

Remember the method. Unless secured by the linguistic turn, ontological talk remains problematic. Two entities are of the same ontological kind if and only if in a systematically constructed language they are represented in the same way. Remember next what was said about nominalism and realism$_1$. (A) Individuals exemplify characters but not conversely. (B) The difference between characters is qualitative, that between individuals merely numerical. (A) and (B) are the only differences between characters and individuals. Anyone who either explicitly or implicitly adds another is a nominalist. According to

---

[29] More precisely, it contradicts the first half of 3.1432, up to "sondern." The contradiction does therefore not depend on accepting, as I do, Stenius' reading of the whole passage as the only intelligible one.

Stenius, individuals are represented by names; characters, by character-representatives. The difference in the way of represention could hardly be more striking. It makes Stenius a nominalist.[30] To me that alone suffices to reject his answer to (1). It is only fair to add that he himself has the good sense to reject nominalism. In fact, he rejects it rather emphatically. But, then, in philosophy it is not enough to reject or deny something. The task is to get rid of all its equivalents and traces in what one asserts. (I have had the good sense to reject phenomenalism long before I knew how to get rid of it completely.)

Recall the task. I promised to present Stenius' central idea and to justify the judgment that it is mistaken. The promise has been fulfilled. But I also undertook to justify the further judgment that Stenius' mistake is extraordinarily illuminating. To this remaining part of the task I now turn. It requires that we face the problem of mind, or, what amounts virtually to the same, the ontological assay of the act,[31] which in turn requires some preparations. Then I shall again confront the three bodies of ideas. This time, though, I shall reverse the order, attend first to Stenius' ideas, then to Wittgenstein's, only at the end say a few words about my own. For this is of course not the place to expound once more my own philosophy of mind.

You perceive that this tree is green. He knows that two and two are four. She remembers that her lover admires Rilke. I doubt that I shall ever see Vienna again. These are four acts. What one perceives, remembers, and so on, is the act's *intention*. Perceiving, remembering, and so on, are its *species*. My now perceiving something, my having perceived it yesterday, your perceiving it tomorrow are three acts, not one. Acts are *individuated*. Acts (minds) exist. What, then, is the ontological assay of an act, or, what amounts virtually to the same, of the knowing[32] situation? A philosopher's answer depends on his ontological ground plan or schema. The task requires that we attend to the classical (Aristotelian-Thomistic) schema even though, fortunately, we can ignore all its details. So I shall, in presenting it, rather recklessly schematize the schema. But notice first that no assay can be adequate unless it accounts for the three dimensions of each act, i.e., its intention, its species, and its being individuated.

Individuals exist independently; their attributes exist dependently; nothing else exists. That is the classical schema. Its individuals are

---

[30] I see another symptom of his (and Wittgenstein's) nominalistic tendencies in their assaying marks as things rather than facts.

[31] I.e., in terms of the trio of questions I set up, questions (2) and (3).

[32] Since in this phrase 'knowing' is used generically, the several species are species of "knowing." See fn. 6.

substances, not bare. (Substances are continuants, not, as the individuals of my world, momentary.) Their attributes are nonrelational characters (universals). Since substances are not bare and exist independently in a sense in which attributes do not, the nexus between a substance and one of its attributes is not exemplification. The attribute is thought to be *in* the substance. That makes inherence a suitable name for this nexus.

(1) There are two kinds of things;[33] some are physical; some, mental. *Realists₂* hold (1); *idealists* hold that all entities are mental. (2) Minds know physical things; the primary source of such knowledge is perception.[34] (1) without (2) is an empty husk. Realism₂ requires an assay of the knowing situation in general and of the perceiving situation in particular that bears out (2). Or, briefly, realism₂ stands and falls with a realistic₂ account of perception. Such an account must connect a mind with its intentions.

How does the classical schema account for perception? Assume that I perceive a tree. Both I and the tree are substances, one mental, one physical. When perceiving the tree, I abstract the tree's nature and make it temporarily my own. However crudely, that is the gist of the classical abstraction theory. For all we need to know, a nature is a character. Characters being universals, it is possible that while I perceive the tree, one universal, the tree's nature, inheres in two substances, my own and the tree's. Thus, in the perceiving situation the two substances, perceiver and perceived, literally share something. They are connected. The classical abstraction theory of perception is realistic₂. It is also compatible with the following formula: (I) *A mind knows only what is in it*. For the tree's nature, while a mind perceives it, is an attribute of this mind. Thus it is "in" it. Nor is there in the classical schema any other way to account for knowing. That illustrates how the ontological ground plan determines the account of the knowledge situation. Epistemology so-called is indeed merely the ontology of that situation.

In the late sixteenth and the early seventeenth centuries the abstraction theory fell under the double onslaught of the new science and the revived skeptical arguments. Thus a realistic₂ account of perception was no longer available. That was a great revolution. Call it, however inaccurately, the Cartesian revolution. But few revolutions, if any, are so thorough that they do not either wittingly or unwittingly preserve

[33] I say things rather than entities because the subsistents are neither physical nor mental.

[34] We can here safely disregard a mind's knowledge of minds, his own and others'.

some ideas which are compatible only with those they have destroyed. The Cartesian revolution preserved (I). Yet the only realistic₂ account of perception compatible with (I) is the abstraction theory which this very revolution destroyed. This, I submit, is the deepest root of that trend toward idealism which has proved irresistible ever since and which structurally is irresistible as long as wittingly or unwittingly one accepts (I). That is not to say, however, that the trend has not been resisted. Most resisters took "the way of ideas."

The physical object, so this gambit opens, is indeed not in the perceiver's mind. What is in his mind are ideas. These ideas, though, resemble, are *similar* to, the physical objects of which they are the ideas. That is how through the latter we know the former. The skeptic merely asked two questions. *If all you know is ideas,* how do you know that there are physical objects of which they are the ideas? And, even granted that there is one, how do you know that its idea is similar to it? Those who took the way of ideas had no answer. Upon their gambit, the mind and its intention have fallen apart, are no longer connected. The way of ideas leads to idealism or, for those who can stomach it, materialism. The only way out is to break the stranglehold of (I).

Historically, it would be foolish indeed to underestimate the impact of the revived skeptical arguments. Structurally, compared with (I), they are shallow. To see why that is so, or, if you please, to see what I mean by this deliberately strong way of putting the point, return for a moment to the two skeptical objections as they are stated in the last paragraph. The italicized phrase, "if all you know are ideas," is only one half of the shared premiss that makes them unanswerable. The other half is (I): and if all you know is in your mind. That shows what I mean. Structurally (I) is indeed the deepest root of that post-Cartesian trend toward idealism that has still to be stopped.

Speaking of skepticism, I might as well mention another attempted way out. This gambit assays the perceiver and the physical intention as things, perceiving as a relation jointly exemplified by them. Perception is fallible, what it presents as existing does not always exist. (That is the modest sound core of skepticism.) But, then, what does not exist, or exists only in the mode of possibility, cannot exemplify a relation. So the gambit collapses. The only way to keep it alive is to introduce such noncommonsensical things as propositions and construe perceiving as a relation connecting the mind with this sort of thing. For propositions, we remember, exist irrespective of whether or not the corresponding fact does. That is indeed the major structural reason why some philosophers introduced this noncommonsensical sort of thing. Those who do not countenance it cannot take this way out.

I turn to Stenius.

He devotes but a single page (p. 113) to his own thoughts on thought. The page is the key to the book. So I shall venture to state what it barely hints or merely suggests. But let us first agree to call the two members of each of the pairs of an isomorphism *similar* if and only if the isomorphism is internal and complete. Two fields connected by such an isomorphism obviously are similar in a sense in which two fields connected by an ordinary isomorphism, i.e., one which is either external or partial or both, are not similar. The use needs no special justification. Speaking as we ordinarily do, we all might use 'similar' in this way. Such uses, just because they need no special justification, sometimes provide cues to structural connections.

As Stenius and I use the word, (a) a *thought* is a mental entity and (b) two acts have the same intention if and only if they contain the "same" thought. (b) leaves two alternatives. (b1) A thought is a universal. In this case acts with the same intention literally share a constituent (and the quotation marks in (b) can be dropped). (b2) A thought is a momentary fact and two such facts are the "same" thought if and only if "they have something in common." In this case the thought individuates the act. Even in this case, though, an act must be more than its thought; otherwise its species could not be accounted for.

According to Stenius, a thought is a mental fact (b2).[35] Also, *a thought and its intention are similar*. The emphasis on their similarity dominates the book. The answer to the question what two mental facts "have in common" if they are the "same" thought is immediate. Being both similar to their common intention, they are also similar to each other.

Why should a thought and its intention be similar? If thoughts are facts, why won't an ordinary isomorphism do? If I have not been too clumsy, the answer should not come as a surprise. 'Similar' is the cue. *Our ideas are similar to what they are the ideas of.* Stenius' thesis is but the latest variant, and a most up-to-date variant it is, of that old gambit with which those who followed the way of ideas tried to provide a substitute for the connection between minds and their intentions that was lost when the abstraction theory fell. That is why I called that page the key to the book. It is of course also the reason why I find the mistake so extraordinarily illuminating. But, then, this mistake, the innovation or correction, concerns sentences, not thoughts. So we must check how things hang together.

---

[35] My gambit is (b1). See fn. 41.

Take perception. There is P, the fact perceived. There is $T(P)$, the thought intending P. There is $N(P)$, a fact caused by P in the body of the perceiver while he perceives P; and there is the sentence 'P'. Stenius clearly distinguishes between these four entities, P, $T(P)$, $N(P)$, 'P'. Nor does he blur the distinction between $T(P)$ and $T('P')$. As things now stand, alas, that alone makes him one of a distinguished minority. On the other hand, he seems to take it for granted[36] that the four entities are all similar among each other. That makes similarity the single idea behind his answers to the three questions with which I started. (1) 'P' can be made to represent P because the two are similar. (2) $T(P)$ and P are similar; that is the connection between a thought and the fact it intends. (3) 'P' can be used to express $T(P)$ because the two are similar. I should like to make two comments.

First. If (1) thoughts are facts and (2) similar to their intentions, then (3) all intentions are facts. I agree emphatically with (3). *Awareness is propositional.* I also believe that the insight is crucial. That makes it important to realize that while (1) follows from (2) and (3), it does not follow from (3) alone.

Second. Consider the following three propositions. (1) Conscious states[37] are mental facts. (2) Bodily and conscious states, e.g., a bodily state containing $N(P)$ and a conscious state containing $T(P)$, so correspond to each other that the "same" bodily state always goes with the "same" mental state. (3) $N(P)$ is similar to P. Or, less strongly, (3') $N(P)$ is isomorphic to P. The point I wish to make is that (1), (2), (3') do not jointly imply that $T(P)$ is a fact. Nor do (1), (2), (3) jointly imply that $T(P)$ is a fact similar to P. Stenius neither makes nor suggests either inference. Even so, the point may be worth making.

I turn to Wittgenstein.

The only passage in the *Tractatus* that deals interestingly and analytically even though most puzzlingly with mind is 5.542. To it I shall presently attend. Certain aphoristic passages toward the end, they have also been called "mystical," I shall not even cite. Some are solipsistic. In others the mind hovers outside the world. In the *Tractatus* world minds either (1) do not exist, or, less strongly, (2) their ontological status remains hopelessly blurred. I am prepared to assert (1). In the light of the philosophical behaviorism (materialism), or near-behaviorism, or behaviorism with a bad intellectual conscience, if you

---

[36] Here I state what Stenius barely hints or merely suggests.

[37] I say conscious states rather than acts because on the one hand some conscious states contain more than just one act while, on the other, the conscious state one is in when sensing something, even though a fact, does not contain an act. Sensing is an act, but this act is not a part of that state.

please, of the *Philosophical Investigations*, (1) is plausible, to say the least. For what really interests me, (2) will do. This weaker assertion needs no defense. Whether (1) or (2), the unresolved tension is unmistakable. The "mysticism" is merely its symptom.[38] The tension is caused by an intellectual impasse. What is this impasse? That is the question which really interests me.

Whether or not Wittgenstein ended as a materialist, with or without the saving grace of a bad intellectual conscience, he did not, I believe, start as one. Rather, *he thought of mind exactly as Stenius does*, in the classical empiricist pattern. If so, that key page of Stenius' clears up the fundamental blur. That makes it, not to be sure a correction, but a clarification as admirable as it is important. But, then, if Wittgenstein had these thoughts, why didn't he express them? If he saw the way, why didn't he take it? I do believe that the author of the *Tractatus* was, however chaotically, a great philosopher. That determines my answer. He at least felt that this way was an impasse. *Similarity, either in the classical style or à la Stenius, does not really connect minds with their intentions.* That is the impasse. Wittgenstein never found the way out. As long as one hasn't found it, the only alternatives are either idealism or materialism or, alas, the agony of unresolved intellectual tension.

Before turning to 5.542 we must recall the linguistic phenomenon of intentionality. Let 'P', 'Q', (a) ' $\ldots P \ldots$ ', (b) ' $\ldots Q \ldots$ ' be four sentences. (a) contains 'P'; (b) is obtained from (a) by replacing at least one occurrence of 'P' by 'Q'. The context is *extensional* if and only if, provided (c) 'P if and only if Q' represents a fact, (a) and (b) either both represent facts or both represent P-facts. Let now (d) 'the-thought-P' and (e) 'the-sentence-P' represent the thought which intends P and the sentence which represents P, respectively. In other words, (f) 'The-thought-P means (intends) P' and (g) 'The-sentence-P means (represents) P' both represent facts. In a systematically constructed language neither (d) nor (e) would contain 'P'. We acknowledge that by making 'P' in (d) and (e) unavailable for replacement, marking this unavailability by the hyphens. Replace now in (f) and (g) the single available occurrence of 'P' by 'Q'. The result is (f') 'The-thought-P means (intends) Q' and (g') 'The-sentence-P means (represents) Q'. There is a commonsensical use of 'means', call it the inten-

---

[38] Some philosophies are analytical; some, mystical. In some analytical philosophers mysticism so-called is a personality trait which under the strain of unresolved intellectual tensions at certain points appears in their philosophy. This I believe is Wittgenstein's case. If so, then one must not make too much of his so-called mysticism when discussing his philosophy.

tional use, upon which (f′) and (g′) both represent P-facts, not only if (c) represents a fact but even if (c) represents a necessary₂ fact. It follows that the contexts (f) and (g) are *intentional* (nonextensional). Notice, too, that if used as in (f) and (g), 'means' is synonymous with 'intends' and 'represents', respectively.

We are ready to look at 5.542:

> Es ist aber klar, dass "A glaubt, dass p", "A denkt p", "A sagt p" von der Form " 'p' sagt p" sind: Und hier handelt es sich nicht um eine Zuordnung von einer Tatsache und einem Gegenstand, sondern um die Zuordnung von Tatsachen durch Zuordnung ihrer Gegenstaende.

I shall make four comments. *First.* If it is asserted that '*A* believes *P*', '*A* thinks *P*', and so on, are synonymous with (h) ' '*P*' says *P*', then the species has once more been lost. *Second.* 'Says' in (h) is vague. Neither a thought nor a sentence literally says anything. The expression preceding 'says' in (h) represents either a thought or a sentence.[39] If it represents a thought, then 'says' stands for 'intends' and (h) is (f). If it represents a sentence, then 'says' stands for 'represents' and (h) is (g). If (h) is (g), then something mental in, say, '*A* believes *P*' has been replaced by something physical. That is, or would be, the decisive step toward materialism.[40] *Third.* A language is extensional if and only if all its contexts are extensional. There is no doubt whatsoever that, according to the *Tractatus*, everything that can be said at all can be said in an extensional language. Both (f) and (g) are intentional. So therefore is (h). It follows that (h) cannot really be said. Hence, we cannot really say that A believes something, thinks something, and so on. Mind, like logical form, is ineffable. Logical form is nothing. Does it follow that mind is nothing? It is all very confused and confusing. I would not argue that anything follows from anything in that confusion. But it can be argued, I think, that the later materialism or near-materialism has something to do with this very confusion. *Fourth.* The second sentence of 5.542, after the colon, supports what has been said about Stenius' clarification. Stenius' idea, the classical empiricist idea, is there, implicitly if you insist, yet unmistakably. Thus, if Wittgenstein did not make it more explicit, he probably had his reasons.

In Stenius' world there are thoughts which are unequivocally mental. In his world therefore, as in mine, there are minds. The agreement is basic. In his world a thought is a fact similar to its intention; in mine

---

[39] If it represents a Sentence, then (h) is a blurred mixture of (f) and (g).

[40] Believing and thinking are acts; saying is not an act. The parallel listing of the three shows that the later materialism is here foreshadowed, to say the least.

it is a simple character connected with its intention by a fundamental tie that subsists. The disagrement is hardly less weighty.[41] To argue it out would require another paper as long as this one, which is long enough as it is. All I shall do therefore is once more identify the issues. That requires two paragraphs about my own philosophy of mind.

I assay an act as an individual exemplifying two simple nonrelational characters. An act thus is a fact. The individual in it, like all others, is momentary and bare. One of the two characters is the act's species; the other, its thought. The fundamental tie connecting the latter with its intention I call the intentional or meaning nexus. In language it is represented by 'means' as used in (f) and (g).[42] The two characters account for the act's species and intention. The sole function of the individual, as of all individuals, is to individuate. Thus the three dimensions of an act are all accounted for. Nor can I think of a simpler way to do the job.

For this to be to the left of that, that must be there. A universal thing (e.g., to-the-left-of) cannot be exemplified by a thing (or fact) that exists only in the mode of possibility. 'P or Q', on the other hand, represents a fact even if one of the complexes represented by 'P' and 'Q' is a P-fact. A fundamental tie (e.g., or) can combine a fact (or thing) and a P-fact into a fact. That is another striking difference between subsistents on the one hand and things or facts on the other. Remember now the modest sound core of skepticism. (f), 'The-thought-P means P', does not imply 'P'. In each case of mistaken belief or memory, or of erroneous perception, the-thought-P exists; (f) represents a fact; 'P', a P-fact. Hence, if there is an entity connecting thoughts with their intentions, it cannot be a thing, must be a subsistent. But, then, must there be such an entity? Since I merely promised to identify the issues, I shall say no more than that I know no other way of keeping minds and their intentions from falling apart.

Stenius, we saw, has two basic ideas. (S) Sentence and fact are similar; that is how the former manages to represent the latter. (T) Thought and fact are similar; that is how the former manages to mean the latter. I rejected (S), yet called it an answer since what I believe to be the right answer can be obtained from it by two "corrections." The three subsistents I call individuality, universality, and exemplification exist. For atomic facts, to which I limited the argument, that is the first correction. It removes the intellectual motive for requiring similarity.

[41] See fn. 35.

[42] The use in (f) is primary, the one in (g) secondary, just as 'true' and 'false' apply primarily to thoughts, only secondarily to the sentences representing their intentions as well as to the acts (e.g., beliefs) containing them.

The second correction replaces this requirement by the weaker one of an ordinary isomorphism.

Is (T) an answer in the sense in which (S) is one? If I am right, one correction is indispensable. The subsistent I call the intentional tie exists. As with (S), that removes the intellectual motive for requiring similarity rather than merely an ordinary isomorphism. Clearly, this correction and the first correction of (S) have the same root. All subsistents exist. That spots one of the two basic disagreements between Stenius and myself. For exemplification at least, I have here argued my side.

If the intentional tie exists, must thoughts be simple characters rather than facts isomorphic to their intentions? If, as I hold, a thought is a simple, then of course the intentional tie connects it with the fact it intends. But if, as Stenius holds, a thought is a fact, why shouldn't the intentional tie connect each constituent of the fact the thought means with one constituent of the thought itself? That spots the other basic disagreement between Stenius and myself. This one I said I wouldn't argue. So I conclude with a question. If one recognizes that the intentional tie exists, what intellectual motive could he possibly have for insisting on even an ordinary ismorphism between thought and fact?

Synthetic a priori[1]

E VERY true sentence represents a truth or fact. This is the broad use of 'fact'. A true sentence is either analytic or synthetic. An analytic sentence represents a formal fact. Upon the narrow use, which I shall follow, only nonformal facts are facts. That is, only synthetic true sentences represent facts. Many philosophers have tried to establish a dichotomy among facts. The traditional labels are synthetic *a priori* and synthetic *a posteriori*. The idea is that the truths called *a priori* are in some sense intermediate between formal truths, which are facts only in the broader sense, and those which are "merely" *a posteriori*. I shall express this idea by calling the *a priori* kind or subclass a core of the class of all facts.

Which truths belong to this core? Two answers are extreme. One makes *a priori* truths into formal truths. The other makes all truths, or at least all general truths, *a priori*. I dismiss both extremes. The claims that remain still differ; yet they overlap. The several subclasses, each of which some have claimed to be the core, have a common core. I shall attend only to this common core, save words by dropping 'common'.

(1) (Middle) *e* is higher (in pitch) than (middle) *c*. (2) Everything that is colored is extended. (3) Peter is blond. (4) All dogs are carnivorous. Clearly, (1) and (2) belong to the core; equally clearly, (3) and (4) do not. Granted that there is a difference between the two pairs, it may yet, as one says, be one of degree. The falsehood of a sentence, or group of sentences, deductively implies the falsehood of some others. For each true sentence there is, therefore, a subclass of all true sentences such that, if the sentence were false, all members of the sub-

---

[1] I have benefited from discussions with E. B. Allaire and Professor Ivar Segelberg of the University of Göteborg. Both have prodded me on the bare particular. My Swedish friend has also helped me through his ingenious defense of the perfect particular and his concern with the synethetic *a priori*. See also Allaire's "Bare Particulars," *Philosophical Studies*, 14, 1963, 1–8.

class would be false. Call one truth more fundamental than another if the subclass corresponding to the sentence representing it is in some specifiable sense larger than the subclass corresponding to the sentence which represents the other. To say that the truths some philosophers call *a priori* are "merely" more fundamental than those they call *a posteriori* is to say that the difference in question is "merely" one of degree. Those who disagree must propose a criterion. That is the problem of the synthetic *a priori*.

What sort of criterion is acceptable? Let F_1 be a fact. A mind's intending F_1, i.e., thinking of it, either believing or disbelieving it, being more or less certain of it, and so on, is another fact, F_2. While F_1 is a constituent of F_2, the latter also has other constituents, i.e., constituents which are neither F_1 nor constituents of F_1. Call F_2 a knowledge situation. A criterion will be unacceptable if, applied to F_1, it mentions any constituent of any knowledge situation into which F_1 may or may not enter as a constituent, which is not also a constituent of F_1. Positively, one may state this requirement by saying that the problem is ontological; negatively, by saying that to violate it is to fall into the error of psychologism.

"A truth belongs to the core if and only if the evidence for it is not increased by the number of its instances." That is one of the criteria proposed. Since it applies only to generalities, it applies only to (2) and (4), not to (1) and (3). At least, it does not obviously apply to (1) and (3). But let that pass. The point is that what is meant by 'increasing evidence' could as well be expressed by 'enhancing certainty' or by 'strengthening belief'. The criterion is psychologistic. So are most criteria that have been proposed. I say *most* rather than *all* only because I do not want to dismiss the idealistic systems, or, for that matter, Kant's, as mere variants of psychologism. But there is a connection. My now believing that all dogs are carnivorous (F_2) is a mental fact; their being carnivorous (F_1) is not. Commonsensically, the distinction between the two kinds of fact, mental and nonmental, is very sharp. Idealists, by blurring this distinction, also blunt that between F_1 and F_2. Or, at least, they are in danger of blunting it. That is the connection.

What one calls the solution of a problem is always or almost always only the last of several steps. Yet there are differences. In some cases the last step is the most difficult. In some others the preparatory steps require the great effort; the last is easy. As for effort, so for importance. In some cases some of the earlier steps are of much greater intrinsic interest than the last. The problem of the synthetic *a priori* has never bothered me. Nor do I now judge it to be of great intrinsic interest.

Yet I shall at the end propose a criterion which (if I am right) solves the problem. What happened was that, when I finally saw the connection between two other questions or problems, which I do judge to be very important, I found not only the answers to both of them but also, as an easy last step, that criterion. One of the two questions concerns a crucial point in the ontology of space; the other, bare particulars. That accounts for two major preparatory steps in the argument which officially is the burden of this essay. Perfect particulars and elementarism account for two others. In the first step we shall attend to the distinction between internal and external relations.

While Peter loves Mary, they jointly exemplify the relation of loving. Four and two jointly exemplify the relation of being larger (between numbers). This is the broad use of 'relation'. As I now use it, loving is a relation, being larger (between numbers) is not. Loving and larger are both entities. But loving is a character (universal) and characters are things. Being larger (between numbers) is a subsistent. Things and subsistents are in several respects profoundly different from each other. From these differences the broad use of 'relation' diverts the attention. One may preserve it, of course, and, as is often done, distinguish between descriptive (loving) and logical (being larger) relations. As it happens, not I think by chance, all those who do that either explicitly or implicitly deny that what they call a logical relation has any ontological status whatsoever. That alone strongly recommends the narrow use I now follow. I shall call a relation only what some others call a descriptive relation.

Many philosophers have tried to establish a dichotomy among relations. One kind they called *internal*; the other, *external*. Quite a few divisions have been proposed. The subclasses they yield overlap. Being higher (in pitch), for instance, as far as I know, is an internal relation in all these divisions. Thus, not surprisingly, there is again a common core. But I am not prepared to argue that the criterion I am about to state explicates *the* idea. Perhaps it does, perhaps it doesn't. Perhaps there is no common idea. However that may be, my criterion explicates *one* idea of internal relation which (I believe) is important although (or should I say because?) we shall see that by this criterion there are no internal relations.

The criterion is ontological. Assume that α and β stand in the relation ρ. Relations obtain between things. If α and β are facts, ρ is a pseudorelation. Nothing will be lost if we ignore pseudorelations, assume that α and β are things. What are the constituents of the fact $\rho(\alpha, \beta)$? Or, rather, since α, β, and their constituents obviously are among them: What, if any, are the *additional* constituents of this fact?

Should there be none, I shall say that the relation needs no (additional) ontological ground. If there are some, they may either (a) all be subsistents or (b) at least one is a thing. Accordingly, ρ is either (a) a subsistent or (b) a thing. (a) If ρ were a subsistent, it would be a fundamental tie. Such ties can occur between entities which are mere possibilities. A relation cannot be exemplified by such entities. That is just one of the several profound differences between things and subsistents. Hence, ρ cannot be a subsistent. (b) The thing ρ, which is of course a (relational) character, tied to α and β by relational exemplification, is the ontological ground of the relation obtaining between them. Relational exemplification, which is a subsistent, is a further additional constituent of the fact. No harm will be done if, together with all other such constituents, we ignore it. Thus, a relation either needs no (additional) ontological ground or its ground is a "third" thing. *A relation is internal if and only if it needs no (additional) ontological ground.* That is the criterion.

Sameness and diversity need no ontological ground. Everything else does. Hence, the ontological ground of an internal relation must lie "in" one or both of the two entities related, in the sense in which an entity's constituents and only they lie "in" it. As philosophers have used 'nature', an entity's *nature* is "in" it. "An internal relation between two entities is grounded in their natures." That is the classical formula. But, then, what is a nature? The use undoubtedly is philosophical; thus it needs explication. Moreover, there are several philosophical uses of 'nature', and their explications are anything but simple. But there is also a minimal use whose explication is not at all difficult, i.e., there is a necessary condition satisfied by any entity that has ever been said to have a nature. The difference between two entities (of the same ontological kind) is either qualitative or numerical; if it is qualitative, the entity can be recognized as such; if it is "merely" numerical, the entity cannot be so recognized. That is the commonsensical idea. An entity has a nature if and only if it is qualitatively different from all others (of the same ontological kind). That is the condition. I shall not use 'nature' in any other sense.

Some philosophers, including the great Leibniz, said that there are no relations. What they meant, I believe, was that all relations are internal. This latter view has been held by quite a few, very explicitly. Some others, including myself, hold that all relations are external. So I shall make it my next business to show, by means of an example, that there are, upon my criterion, no internal relations. The example, to be fair, ought to be simple; it ought to belong to the common core; the entities related ought to be recognizable as such, i.e., in the minimal sense, have natures. (1), e being higher than c, satisfies all these conditions. Nor could anyone reasonably object if I modify (1), assuming 'higher' to be an abbreviation for 'higher-by-a-third' (and neglecting the difference between the two kinds of musical thirds). I shall also assume that pitches are things. In my world (ontology) they are. At this point some might object. Let them for a short while hold their peace.

Consider (c, e), (d, f), (e, g), and so on. Each of these ordered pairs exemplifies the relation. Take (c, e). If the relation is internal, there are three possibilities. Its ground is either (a) one entity which is a constituent of one of the two pitches; or (b) one entity which is a constituent of both pitches; or (c) two entities, one a constituent of one of the two pitches, the other a constituent of the other. (a) Assume the entity to be a constituent of c. Then the pair (c, f) should also exemplify the relation. Yet it doesn't. f is the fourth of c. (b) In view of the first pair, the entity is a constituent of c and of e; in view of the second pair, a constituent of d and f; and so on. Hence any pair of pitches should exemplify the relations. (One could also argue that in this case the relation would be symmetrical, which it isn't.) That leaves (c). A thing is simple if and only if no other thing is a constituent of it. Assuming that the two entities which are the ground of the relation are things, that leaves two possibilities. (c1) Pitches are simple things. (In my world they are.) Then the two things which are the ground of the relation as exemplified by the first pair must be c and e themselves. But c and e are not constituents of d and f, respectively. (c2) If pitches are complex, then one of the two things which are the ground, call it the lower, is a constituent of the lower pitch; the other, call it the higher, a constituent of the higher pitch in each pair. Thus, in view of the pair (c, e), the lower thing is a constituent of c; in view of the pair (d, f), it is also a constituent of d. As for the lower thing, so for the higher. It is a constituent of both e and f. Hence c and f should also exemplify the relation, which they do not. I conclude that there are no internal relations.

This type of argument is of course familiar. Even so, two comments should help to appraise it. *One.* Remember the objector I asked to hold his peace when assuming that pitches are things. If you examine the argument, you will see that no use is made of the assumption—except that in my world the dichotomy simple-complex does not even make sense for subsistents while, on the other hand, even simple things have constituents which are subsistents; e.g., in the case of individuals, individuality and existence. *Two.* Could not the two constituents mentioned in (c) be two subsistents jointly "exemplifying" a "subsistent (logical!) relation"? That possibility has been excluded by another assumption, namely, that the two constituents are things. To anyone who objects to this assumption I make a gift of that possibility. For he must surely be a "nominalist" who, even though he cannot stomach universals and exemplification among things, does countenance them among subsistents. Everyone else, if faced with this sort of "nominalistic" world, will reach for Occam's razor.

D_1. All relations are internal. D_2. All relations are external. Call D_1 and D_2 the strong doctrines of internal and external relations, respectively. D_1, we saw, is dialectically untenable. One refutes it by showing that no relation can be internal. D_2 follows. It does not follow that one may comfortably settle down with D_2 without mastering its dialectic. The critics of D_2 press many questions. One among these is (I believe) the structural root of all the others. The critics hold it to be unanswerable. This is the one question I shall try to answer.

Pitches have natures. Otherwise the example I used to refute D_1 would not have been fair. Being equally fair to D_2 requires that in the example used to defend D_2 the two things claimed to be externally related have no natures. Are there such things? The question leads rather quickly to another, which is the one, supposedly unanswerable, which I undertook to answer.

In some ontologies, call them Scotist, all simple things are characters. All characters have natures. In a Scotist world, therefore, there are no things which have no natures. In a nonscotist world some things are individuals. All individuals are simple. But the individuals of most nonscotist ontologies, including all classical ones, have natures. In such a world, therefore, there is again no thing without a nature. The classical entity without a nature is, of course, Aristotelian matter. Structurally, the problem we must eventually face and which no serious philosophy can dodge is indeed the one Aristotle first tried to solve when he invented his notion of matter. A *bare particular* is an individual without a nature. It is, as one says, a mere individuator and cannot be recognized as such. Some recent ontologies share two features. Their individuals are more or less explicitly bare particulars; their characters all enjoy the same ontological status; there being no difference between properties and relations except the obvious one, namely, the number of entities required to exemplify either the one or the other. I say more or less explicitly because none of these ontologies has fully faced the dialectic of the bare particular. Nor is any of them free of the taint of nominalism. That is why I did not say that all their characters are things but merely that they all enjoy the same ontological status. My ontology is very explicit in both respects. Its characters are things; its individuals are bare particulars.

Every individual exemplifies at least one character; there is no character which is not at least once exemplified. That is the *Principle of Exemplification*. It states a categorial feature of my world. Since only very few philosophers rejected it, I shall take it for granted, even though Plato was one of those few. From this principle in conjunction with the classical formula from which I took my cue, namely, that an internal relation has its ground in the natures of the things related, it follows immediately that all relations (and properties!) exemplified by bare particulars are external. For, bare particulars having no natures, what would an internal relation between any two of them be grounded in? It does not follow that in a world with bare particulars all relations are external (D_2). Relations among characters, e.g., higher among pitches, might still be internal. That is one reason I chose my first example as I did. Even so, if there are bare particulars then D_1, the strong doctrine of internal relations, is false. All one needs to do, therefore, in order to show that it is false is to present a relation between two bare particulars.

Suppose someone asks me what c is. I strike the right key, strike some others, strike the first again, tell him that c is what has been presented to him on the first and last occasion but on none of the others. There are some complications; e.g., not only a pitch but also a loudness may have been presented twice. None of these complications is very serious; they are all familiar; and they are beside the point. So I shall not worry them once more, assume that the questioner is satisfied. In my ontology, what is presented on each of these two occasions is a fact, namely, a particular exemplifying a pitch, a loudness, and so on. The pitch is one; the particulars are two. Suppose now that the questioner asks me to direct his attention to the particular in the way I just directed it to a pitch. Particulars, or, at least, this sort of particular being momentary, they cannot be presented twice. The questioner appreciates the point but insists that what he was in fact presented with on each of the two occasions is a pitch, a loudness, perhaps some other qualities, and nothing else. (That shows the appeal of Scotism!) Thus he keeps asking me what a bare particular is, demanding that his attention be directed to one. This is the question the critics of D_2 hold to be unanswerable. So far the defenders have not known how to answer it. Eventually I shall propose an answer.

(Let it be said once and for all that even if the question were unanswerable, it would not follow that there are no bare particulars. Should they turn out to be dialectically indispensable, an argument could be made for "postulating" their existence. The proper place for such postulation, though, is in science and in science only. Thus it is much, much better not to have to make the argument.)

Suppose I had answered that the particular is the tone, i.e., the thing that "has" this pitch, that loudness, and so on. The questioner recalls that my particulars are bare and is amazed. You hold, then, he asks, that a tone is a tone only because it happens to exemplify a pitch but wouldn't be one if it happened to exemplify a color or a smell. I agree, and, delighted that he understands so well, add that what in such discourse one ought to mean by 'tone' is indeed a complex character exemplified by those and only those bare particulars which exemplify a pitch, a loudness, and so on. He, though, listens no longer. For by now he is convinced that the notion of a bare particular is not commonsensical. Nothing is gained by glossing things over; better for once to heed the advice of the French: *reculer pour mieux sauter*. The way we ordinarily speak, e.g., the way I just used 'tone', is stacked against the bare particular, makes it doubtful whether the notion is commonsensical. Does the doubt spread to the notion of external relations? To show that it doesn't, I introduce the second example.

Take two small pieces of paper, call them spots. Each has a color (hue) and a shape. Ignore whatever other properties it has. Let us agree to use 'shape' and the shape words, 'round (circular)', 'square', 'triangular', and so on, not of contours but of areas and so that, say, two circles of different size have different shapes. One of the spots is red and round; the other, green and square. Put them on the table before you so that the red spot is to the left of the green one, then shift them around so that the first is above the second, to the right of it, and so on. There is nothing "in" either spot in which to ground any of these (successive) relations between them. Common sense agrees, even insists. The way we ordinarily speak supports this bit of common sense. We say, or may say, that the spots are (successively) at different places, some of which are to the left of some others, and so on. Spatial relations, we see, do for D_2 what relations among simple characters such as pitches do for D_1. The former provide *prima facie* plausible evidence that at least some relations are external; the latter, that at least some are internal.

Two comments will show where we stand; two more, in structural history, should add perspective.

1. Using 'spot' as I earlier used 'tone', I spoke, as we ordinarily do, as if the spatial relation obtained between the two spots. If, as I hold, there is a bare particular "in" each spot, then the relation obtains between them. Or, at least, that is in this case the structurally obvious way to assay the situation. But, then, had I now so assayed it, I would have prejudged the question which is presumably unanswerable. There is no need for doing that at this point. The *prima facie* plausible evi-

dence provided by the spatial relation between the two spots is not at all affected by what the ontological assay of a spot may or may not yield. At worst, the connection might turn out to be a pseudorelation. But it would still be an external pseudorelation.

2. A spot's being at a place must have an ontological ground. The connection between the crucial question about particulars and some others in the ontology of space is being impressed upon us. I shall indeed soon turn to the latter.

3. In some ontologies such "ordinary" characters as colors and shapes are not the only characters "in" the spot. There is still another constituent, or class of such, of the kind Scotus calls *haecceitates* and which I like to call coordinate qualities. Two spots agreeing in all non-relational "ordinary" characters are two and not one because the co-ordinate qualities in them, one in each, are two and not one. As far as I know, that is in a Scotist world the only way of solving the problem of individuation. As to relations, there are two possibilities. They may be either internal or external relations between coordinate qualities. Making them internal, you obtain Leibniz's assay of space. If you make them internal, then there is something "in" the spot which, together with something else "in" the other spot, is the ground for the one spot being to the left of the other. But even if you make them external, the ground for the spot's being at this rather than at another place is still "in" the spot. That is why these assays of space are repugnant to common sense. As to 'place', some philosophers have used it so that the spot's "place" is not "in" it. That is indeed one of the two differences between coordinate qualities and "places." The other is that while coordinate qualities are characters, "places" have been thought of as individuals. I, of course, used 'place' without any ontological commitment whatsoever, merely taking advantage of a locution to make the point that if the spatial relations were not commonsensical examples of external relations, ordinary language would not contain the locution.

4. To one not familiar with the refutation of D_1 the two examples may suggest that there are internal as well as external relations, the former all between simple characters, the latter all spatial. (As for space, so for time. I shall, however, up to the very end ignore time.) Turn now to Kant. 'Concept' is one of the most mischievously slippery words in the philosophical vocabulary. My concept of something is of course in my mind. Horse and green are not. That is the only clear use of the word. Yet we have been subtly conditioned to use the word so that horse and green are also concepts. That is why in philosophy I do not use it at all. Kant uses it, of course. Green and horse, he tells us, are discursive concepts (*Begriffe*). These are the only real concepts. The

spatial ones, being merely limitations (*Einschraenkungen*) of the single representation (*Vorstellung*) of space, are not really concepts, just as space itself is not a concept but an intuition (*Anschauung*). Accordingly, while a discursive concept subsumes *under* itself many representations, the "manifold in space," e.g., this being to the left of that, is merely a limitation of, or, rather, *in* a single representation. As it is put in this jargon, we cannot "think" a point without thinking it in its relations to all others. After a fashion, that makes all spatial relations internal. We see what went on. In the tradition to which Kant belongs all relations are internal. Commonsensically, the spatial ones are external. The jargon drowns that bit of common sense. Structurally, I believe, this is the reason why transcendental aesthetics is split off from transcendental analytics. The reason we are given is that while in intuition the mind is passive, in conception it is active. I am not impressed. In the system space as well as the discursive concepts are contributions of the mind; the only thing not contributed by it is sensation (*Empfindung*). And whenever the mind contributes anything it is active in the sense which is relevant in the system.

Presently I shall turn to space. First, though, I shall use what has been said so far to give a twist to the dialectic of the perfect particular. Perhaps that is a digression. But it can be done so easily and fits so well that it seems justified. It also yields a point that will come in handy.

Consider two spots of the same color (hue), say, red. To assay them so that a single entity, red, is a constituent of both spots is to make red a character (universal). This character is the ontological ground of the respect (color) in which the two spots agree. If you make characters things you are a realist; otherwise, a nominalist. Characters are not localized; the example shows what that means. "What exists is localized." If one is dominated by this pattern he will reject characters. Thus he must find another ontological ground for the respect in which the two spots agree. Some hold that this ground is provided by two entities, red_1 and red_2, one in each spot. That is the doctrine of *perfect particulars*. Obviously, it conforms to the localization pattern. Its proponents also hold, either explicitly or implicitly, that perfect particulars are simple things. The perfect particulars in the example are, of course, red_1 and red_2.

Even though a perfect particular be simple, any expression purporting to represent it must have two parts, one indexical, one adjectival. The indexical part is needed because (presumably) the entity does the job which in other ontologies is done by bare particulars; the adjectival part, because (presumably) it does the job which in other ontologies is done by characters. The crucial difference between a perfect and a bare particular is indeed that the former does and the latter does not have a nature; the crucial difference between perfect particulars and characters is that the former are and the latter are not localized. The purpose the entity is meant to serve is transparent. Things bare as well as things not localized are to become expendable. I shall next show that the perfect particular cannot do either job.

Take three perfect particulars, red_1, red_2, $blue_7$. The first two share something which neither of them shares with the third. The dead-end nominalism which does not even see that this something must be ontologically grounded we may safely dismiss. The sophisticated defenders of the perfect particular place that ground in a single relation of (exact) similarity jointly exemplified by red_1 and red_2 but not by either red_1 and $blue_7$ or red_2 and $blue_7$. Thus they do not really get rid of universals. They merely replace the class of all nonrelational characters by a single relational one, (exact) similarity. All this is familiar. Nor is it difficult to assign a structural motive to the preference for a single relational character over a class of nonrelational ones. That, though, is not the line I want to pursue.

The relation of (exact) similarity is either (a) external or (b) internal. (a) A relation, we know, is external if and only if, negatively, the ground for two things exemplifying it lies wholly outside these two things, and, positively, if it lies wholly in a third thing, namely, the relation itself and its being tied by (relational) exemplification to the two others. It follows that there is nothing in either red_1 or red_2 which the adjectival part of the expressions purporting to represent them could represent. That part is, therefore, merely an arbitrary name of one of the subclasses of the exhaustive and nonoverlapping division which the relation called (exact) similarity produces in the class of all perfect particulars. I say arbitrary, and not of course just in the sense in which every name is arbitrary, because, although each member of a subclass is "similar" to all other members and to no member of any other subclass, there is, in spite of the relation's misleading name, nothing "in" red_1 and red_2 which makes them similar. That shows that if the relation is external, the perfect particular is in all but name bare. (b) If the relation of (exact) similarity is internal then its ground lies "in" red_1 and red_2. These two entities are simple. Thus the ground is red_1 and red_2 themselves. But the relation is symmetrical, which it couldn't be if red_1 and red_2 were two things and not just one. That shows that if the relation is internal the perfect particular is in all but name a character and the problem of individuation is left unsolved. I conclude that there are no perfect particulars; or, if you insist, if there were any, they couldn't do the job they are supposed to do. That is the twist I wanted to give to the dialectic. Now for the point that will come in handy.

In some ontologies there are perfect particulars as well as substances; the former inhere in the latter; the latter are individuals though of course not bare. Upon the most important philosophical use of 'individual', an individual cannot either inhere in or be exemplified by anything else. In this respect the perfect particulars of those worlds differ from individuals. But the difference makes no difference for the point. So we may safely ignore it.

Let L_1 and L_2 be two schemata, of the kind called artificial languages, constructed and interpreted by the same rules. A primitive predicate represents a simple character. That is one such rule. 'x' marks the places at which the primitive signs representing individuals stand. That is another. L_1 contains the primitive predicate 'sim' and 'a', purporting to represent (exact) similarity and red$_1$, respectively; L_2, the primitive predicate 'red' representing red; L_2 does not contain either 'sim' or 'a'; L_1 doesn't contain 'red'. Suppose, finally, that both L_1 and L_2 are extensional. No schema representing mental entities can be; but the point does not depend on that; thus, if anything, the supposition strengthens the argument. Introduce now into L_1 the definitional schema

(D_1) '$RED(x)$'   for   '$sim(a, x) \lor (x = a)$';

let P_1 be a sentence of L_1 containing 'RED'; P_2, the sentence one could obtain from P_1, if L_1 contained 'red', by substituting 'red' for 'RED'. Everyone knows that '$P_1 \equiv P_2$' could be used as if it were analytic. I shall express this by saying that "formally" there is no difference between an ontology with perfect particulars and a single relational character of (exact) similarity on the one hand, and, on the other, an ontology with bare particulars and a class of simple nonrelational characters.

'Formal' has been put to several philosophical uses. The one just marked by double quotes stems from mathematics. There it causes no trouble. In philosophy it may and has become a source of error. "Since there is no formal difference between the two ontologies, there is none; the question which of the two is right is a pseudoquestion (meaningless)." The sentence between the double quotes exhibits both source and nature of the error. Its name is formalism. Formalism is an error as fatal as psychologism. That is the point. To reject formalism is one thing; to deny that artificial languages (formalisms) can be put to good philosophical use is quite another thing. Two comments will show that I mean that.

1. L_1 reflects the attempt to avoid nonrelational characters. 'RED',

being a nonrelational predicate expression, represents such a character. This is just another of the rules by which both schemata are built. Does that mean that on this ground alone the attempt has failed? Far from so. (D₁) shows that, being defined, the character represented by '*RED*' is complex. "What exists is simple." Either consciously or unconsciously some philosophers are dominated by this pattern. Such a one, while rejecting '*red*', may yet countenance '*RED*'.

2. The definition in L₂ which corresponds to (D₁) is

(D₂)   '$sim(x, y)$'   for   '$(\exists f)\,[f(x) \cdot f(y)]$'.

The definiens contains no sign that represents a thing. That makes the entity represented by '*sim*' a subsistent of the kind some call a "logical relation." Some of the predicate expressions in the range of the bound variable represent subsistents of the kind some call "logical properties," including that of being identical with itself, which makes any two individuals "similar." That trivializes '*sim*', as defined by (D₂). If, on the other hand, one says that two hues are similar, he does not use 'similar' trivially. (Remember that we agreed to let '*red*' stand for a single hue rather than, as usually, for a range of such.) In its nontrivial use, 'similar' no doubt represents, however succinctly, a complex relational structure. The formalism not only reflects the distinction between these two uses of 'similar' but also very effectively draws attention to it. If one misses it, he is in danger of doing what the more sophisticated champions of the perfect particular did. He may mistake a trivial subsistent for a relation which is not there.[2]

Some of the world's features are spatial. Some facts, call them spatial, have some of these features. Rome being south of Milan is such a fact; being south is its spatial feature. Everyone knows what these features are. In this sense everyone knows what space is. The ontological assay of a spatial fact must yield at least one entity which is the ground of its spatial feature. There is thus a class of entities, call them spatial, such that a fact is spatial if and only if its assay yields at least one member of the class. An inventory of all spatial entities, or, rather, as usual, of all kinds of such entities answers the ontological question: What is space? It could not be answered, or, for that matter, it could not even be asked unless everyone knew what space is. (That is the point of Augustine's aphorism about time.)

[2] A bare particular exemplifies more than one property. Hence, even if you called two of them similar if and only if they exemplify the same simple property, similarity would not yield a class division. But one could replace the several primitive predicates by several primitive relations of "similarity (similar in a certain respect)." The two languages will again be formally equivalent.

We cannot and need not begin at the beginning. I take it for granted that the spatial entities do not merely subsist but are things. Things are either individuals or characters. Characters are either properties or relations; and they are either simple or complex. That makes for quite a few possibilities. Are all simple spatial things individuals? Are they all relations? Either properties or relations? Either individuals or properties? And so on. Each of the so-called theories of space propounds one of these alternatives. Since the one clear and important use of 'theory' occurs in science, I would rather avoid the word, speak instead of the several ontological assays of space that have been proposed. But it may be best to compromise. So I shall speak of the several *views of space*. These views have been classified in several ways. Each classification consists of, or, at least, starts from a dichotomy. Some of these classifications are helpful. But it is dangerous, to say the least, if in different classifications the same labels are attached to different dichotomies. Yet this is what happened. Everyone tells us that a view is either *absolute* or *relative* (nonabsolute). Distinguishing the several ways in which the two words may and (I believe) have been used in this context is as good an approach as any, if not perhaps the best of all, to the issues themselves.

If all "things" now ceased to exist, would space be left? The view of those who answer negatively is *relative*$_1$. Those answering affirmatively hold the *absolute*$_1$ or, as it is also called, the container view. The use of 'thing' in this traditional question clearly is not the one I make of the word in ontology. For, if it were, since all spatial entities are things, the answer would be trivially negative. Yet the container view is anything but trivial. There is thus an ambiguity that must be eliminated. Remember the small pieces of colored paper, we called them spots, which were shifted around on a table. Suppose that the "things" mentioned in the traditional question are all spots (and, if you please, that space is two-dimensional). Making this supposition, we shall lose nothing that matters for our purpose while, on the other hand, we can now so restate the question that the ambiguity disappears. If all spots now ceased to exist, would space be left? (In other words, we retain the ontological use of 'thing', have found a way of getting along without the one marked by double quotes.) Now we can see what is and what is not at stake.

What is not at stake is the assay of the spots themselves. All the relativist$_1$ is committed to is the view that all spatial entities are either things "in" the spots or relations among such things. The absolutist$_1$ is merely committed to holding that at least *some* spatial entities are neither things "in" the spots nor relations among such things. Or, as

I shall say for the moment, an absolutist$_1$ must hold that there are space-things. The most interesting kind of absolutism$_1$ is the view that *all* spatial things are space-things. Since there are three kinds of things, there are still some alternatives left. The most interesting among them is the view that at least some space-things are individuals. As some philosophers have used the word, these space-individuals are "places." If there are such entities then a spot's "occupying" a "place" must have an ontological ground. That is one obvious weakness of this view. But we need not dwell on it. For, once more, I take something for granted, dismiss all kinds of absolutism$_1$ out of hand. The alternatives to which I turn are all relativistic$_1$.

In a nonscotist world there is an individual "in" each spot. Is this individual a spatial thing? Depending on whether your answer is affirmative or negative, you are an *absolutist$_2$* or a *relativist$_2$*. Unfortunately the question that produces the dichotomy is not a good question. In a world of bare particulars it does not even make sense. That is indeed one of the major points of the essay. Of this more presently. For the time being, we shall be well advised not to scrutinize the question too closely. For it provides us with an access not only to the dialectics of the space issue but also to one of the fundamental gambits on which all issues hang.

Why should one care whether or not the individual "in" the spot is spatial? "Only what is independent exists. (The more independent an entity is, the higher is its ontological status.)" The pattern is familiar. There are quite a few philosophical uses of 'dependent' and 'independent'. The pattern shows their ontological import. In a world of bare particulars there is no structural reason not to accept the Principle of Exemplification as a categorial truth. That makes individuals and characters equally dependent$_1$[3] on each other. But the individuals of the classical ontologies are not bare. In these ontologies only individuals exist "independently." Their characters exist only "dependently." The idea is that while characters need individuals to inhere in, the latter can or could somehow manage without the former. I say can or could and I say somehow because the idea is irremediably vague. Its root is anthropomorphic. The individual "creates" its characters. Yet, vague as this idea is, it helps us to understand why one may care. Space, or at least some of it, exists "independently" if and only if the individuals "in" the spots are spatial; it exists only "dependently" if and only if they are not spatial. That is why the issue of absolutism$_2$ versus rela-

---

[3] In this essay only two of the philosophical uses of 'independent' play a role. That makes it convenient to represent them by 'independent$_1$' and 'independent$_2$', disregarding other notations occurring elsewhere in this book.

tivism$_2$ has been so sensitive for so long, and, also, why absolutism$_1$ and absolutism$_2$ have not always been clearly distinguished. (Leibniz was a relativist$_2$. The view he so vigorously opposed was, I believe, absolutism$_2$. His opponent, Newton, was an absolutist$_1$.)

Relativism$_2$ is the view that all simple spatial things are either properties or relations. Are they all properties or are some of them relations? If all relations are internal then no spatial thing is a relation. If the spatial relations are external then it is plausible, to say the least, that some of them are simple. The issue, we see, is part and parcel of the issue of relations. So we need not pursue it.

Remember those peculiar spatial properties I called coordinate qualities, hereness, thereness, and so on. The Scotists need them to solve the problem of individuation. That is why I also called them *haecceitates*. If there are such properties then they are simple; or at least some of them are simple. Are there such properties? Depending on whether your answer is affirmative or negative you are an *absolutist$_3$* or a *relativist$_3$*. There are no coordinate qualities. We are neither presented with them nor dialectically forced to "postulate" them. Absolutism$_3$ is wrong. (Leibniz, though not a Scotist, was an absolutist$_3$.)

Round is a shape; triangular is another. If the wording startles you, think of color. We say that green is a color. Shape is a kind of spatial property. Some shapes are simple. When presented with a triangular spot, I am presented with the simple property triangular. That is not to say that 'triangular' always represents a simple. As carpenters and geometricians often use the word, the property it represents is complex. I merely insist that *some* shape words have two uses. The best labels are probably *phenomenological* and *geometrical*. Used phenomenologically, the word represents a simple. When it is used geometrically, the property represented is complex. (Remember that we agreed to use the space words so that they represent contours, not shapes, and that, say, two circular areas of different size also differ in shape. Thus there is a phenomenological use of 'triangular' in which it represents neither a shape nor, since there are many sorts of triangles, a kind of shape but, rather, a kind of kind of shape. But it is merely pedantic to speak more accurately than the context requires.)

Geometry, i.e., the Euclidean calculus is an axiomatic system. Call it the schema. With the appropriate idealizations it can be interpreted into space. The interpretation is very successful. Because of its success a certain way of thinking, call it the schematic way, has become very deeply ingrained in all of us. That makes it difficult to see space as it is, phenomenologically (ontologically). Our vision is blocked by the schema. Yet, space is one thing, the schema is another. Space is in the world; the schema is nowhere. In the schema there are points, lines, areas, and so on. In the several axiomatizations 'point', 'line', 'area', and so on, may or may not be undefined. In the schematic way of thinking the single element or building stone of space (!) is the extensionless point of the schema (!). A line becomes a class of points; an area, another such class; and a class is a line rather than an area because its members stand in certain relations to each other. I speak, vaguely, of elements or building stones rather than of simples. The vagueness is deliberate. The schematic way itself is irremediably vague, if only because in space there are no extensionless points. The extensionless points of the schema are interpreted into certain series of spots. (That is the gist of the method of extensive abstraction.) That there are such series is an idealizing assumption.

Some shapes are simple and all simple spatial properties (of the first type) are shapes. To me that has become obvious. Those who have not freed themselves of the schematic way will probably object. Or, at least, they will be puzzled. The cause of their trouble is that they see the schema, not space. If the schema were space and if the schematic way were not as vague as it is, there would indeed be only one simple spatial property (of the first type), namely, that of being an extensionless point. All other simple spatial characters would be relations. (Historically, I surmise, the unpalatability of coordinate qualities (absolutism$_3$) has cast a shadow on the very idea that some spatial properties are simple. Thus the quest for these entities has been neglected. Leibniz did slay absolutism$_1$. But that is not to say that the acceptance of absolutism$_3$, which was the view he proposed, has ever been both wide and articulate. That is just one of the many ironies of history.)

In my world there are neither space-things nor coordinate qualities. That makes my view relative$_1$ as well as relative$_3$. Whether or not I am also a relativist$_2$ depends on whether or not the individuals which exemplify shapes are themselves spatial. That takes us back to the bare particular and the question which supposedly is unanswerable.

Remember the questioner who, when presented with middle c, insisted that all the entities presented to him were properties. Suppose he gives me another chance, asks me to direct his attention to the bare particular "in" the spot. I first acquaint him with my use of 'shape', then tell him that the bare particular is the spot's area. He grants that this time I direct his attention to an entity which is presented to him and that, therefore, if this entity were a bare particular I would, in the case of spots, have answered the "unanswerable" question. Then he offers two arguments. The first purports to show that the entity is not bare; the second, that it is not an individual.

"Being a certain area is a character. The entity to which you directed my attention is this character. Thus it is not bare. If it were, how would I know that it is an area and not, say, a tone." This is the first argument. I answer as follows. I know that the entity is an area because it is round. Or, rather, to be an area is to be an entity that has a shape. Otherwise I would not know what 'area' meant. (When in our first exchange I made this point about 'tone' he broke off. This time he lets me go on.) Assume that you are presented with two spots. If they agree in all nonrelational characters, including shape, they will also agree in the character you claim the entity is. How then would you know that they are two and not one? The questioner has no answer.

"Call the areas bounded by the inner and the outer of two concentric circles a and b, respectively. a is a part of b. $(P(a, b))$. Individuals are simple. What is simple has no parts. Hence b is not an individual." That is the second argument. I answer as follows. 'Part' has many uses; some are literal; some, metaphorical. A thing is simple if and only if it has no constituent which is a thing. As I use 'constituent' in ontology, a constituent of an entity is not a part of it in the sense in which a is a part of b nor in any other literal sense of the word. Since all individuals are simple, the only complex things are complex characters. Stone is such a character; hard, a constituent of it. Yet, clearly, hard is not a part of stone in the sense in which a is a part of b. P, on the other hand, is a simple spatial relation between areas just as higher is a simple relation between pitches (or tones). In this respect there is no difference between '$P(a, b)$' and 'e higher than c'. So I ask the questioner whether that makes either pitch a constituent of the other. He agrees, of course, that it doesn't but points out that there is a difference. If I am right, P is of the first type, while 'higher' is of the second. Now it is my turn to agree. I add, though, that I cannot see what difference this difference makes. If he remains unconvinced, I can do no more than try to release his block. What may block him is the way of thinking which the success of the schema has so deeply ingrained in us.

The schema produces not just one block or likely block, but two. In the schematic way of thinking an area is a class of points which stand in certain relations to each other. If this were so, then areas would indeed be complex. More precisely (whatever that means once one has taken the schematic way) area would be a complex character. That may make it hard to see that areas are simple. This is one likely block. In the schematic way, a and b "are" two classes of points, the former being included in the latter. Class inclusion is one of the literal meanings of 'part'. It is also a subsistent, of the kind some call "logical relations." That may make it hard to see that P is a relation, i.e., a thing of the kind some call "descriptive relations." This is the other likely block.

The spot's area is not only round, it also is red. I take it, then, that the bare particular "in" the spot is its area. At this point, for reasons which are about to transpire, I discard 'area'. The two reasons I used it up to now are that it is suggestive and that either 'individual' or 'bare particular' would have verbally prejudged the case. In geometry 'area' has many uses with which of course I have no quarrel. But we have learned to be wary of geometry in the ontology (phenomenology) of space.

Absolutism$_1$ and absolutism$_3$ are rightly discredited. Nor are the three absolutisms always clearly distinguished. Thus one may try to discredit my answer to the "unanswerable" question by pointing out that it commits me to "absolutism." If particulars are spatial things, then I am indeed an absolutist$_2$. Are they spatial things? (Since I consider as yet only those particulars which are constituents of spots, I suppress the qualifying clause: "in" the spot.)

There are two kinds of reasons, one psychological, one verbal, why particulars may *seem* to be spatial things. In the first and the second of the four comments which follow I shall show that two such reasons, one of each kind, which are at least as good as any other I can think of, are really bad reasons. In the third and the fourth comment I shall give two reasons why, even if particulars were spatial things, I would not be an "absolutist" in any sense in which "absolutism" is rightly discredited.

First. Let a be a particular; b, c, and so on, parts of it. When presented with a fact of which a is a constituent, one more often than not becomes very quickly and more or less clearly aware of (is being presented with) quite a number of other facts such as $P(a, b)$, b being contiguous to c, and so on. P and contiguous are spatial relations. These facts, therefore, are all spatial facts. Clearly, this is not a good reason for a itself being a spatial thing. (I call this bad reason psychological rather than phenomenological because the laws by which presentations succeed each other are psychological.)

Second. Call a word a space word if and only if, when used phenomenologically, it represents a simple spatial thing. 'Area' has geometrical uses. Clearly that is not a good reason for its being a space word. The illusion that it is one has two sources; one is purely verbal; the other is the schema. 'Area' obviously is a predicate. Hence, if it were a space word, area would be a character. Thus it would be either of the first or of a higher type. Round is of the first type; shape, of the second. Round, which is *a* shape, is "in" the spot, shape is not. Nor can I think of any other property of a higher type which is "in" it. Yet the spot's area undoubtedly is "in" it. I conclude that area is not a higher-type character. If one holds that it is of the first type then I turn the tables on him, ask him to direct my attention to the individual that exemplifies the spot's area. This question is unanswerable. Your only way out is to become a Scotist. Then you will need coordinate qualities.[4]

Third. The individuals of my world are bare; the Principle of Exemplification is a categorial truth; individuals and characters are equally dependent$_1$ on each other; neither can "manage" without the other. In other words, one of the traditional philosophical uses of 'dependent-independent' (as in "Only individuals exist independently, characters only dependently") does not even make sense. Nor does therefore the formula, which as we saw discredited absolutism$_2$, that space exists only dependently if and only if individuals are not spatial things. True, if the entities "in" the spots which I claim are individuals were spatial things, then my view of space would be absolute$_2$. But, since the formula makes no sense, why should that be discreditable?

Fourth. Each individual exemplifies at least one character. That is one half of the Principle of Exemplification. At least one of the char-

---

[4] Notice that 'area' does not behave like 'shape'. One can say that round is a shape but not that it is an area. One could of course construe 'area' as the (impredicatively) complex property (A) of having a property which is a shape, in analogy to 'colored' and, if 'extension' is used instead of 'area', to 'extended'. In a world otherwise like ours but without time and minds, every individual has the property A. That is not to say, though, that even in this truncated world to be an individual would mean to be an A. In an improved language, we know, 'individual' cannot even occur without futility. 'A' can be defined in such a language. That is not to say that in speaking about the truncated world it would have any ordinary use. But the possibility of defining it, jointly with the truth of '$(x)A(x)$', explicates the aphorism that in that truncated world space is the *principium individuationis*, just as space and time are in ours.

Instead of 'area' one could use either '(spatial) extension' or 'piece of space'. From the former we better keep away until time is brought in. Use of the latter would have strengthened the suspicion of "absolutism." To dispel the suspicion, one merely has to point out that the phrase is metaphorical. There is, as one says, no Space with capital S.

In our world not all individuals are areas (extensions). That makes 'extended' a very convenient synonym for 'having a shape'.

acters an individual exemplifies is a property. That is a most reasonable refinement of this half.[5] Since among (simple) spatial things there are properties as well as relations, the Principle, even if so refined, does not exclude the possibility that the characters some individuals exemplify are all spatial. The view that there are some individuals of this strange sort is a kind of "absolutism." If these strange individuals were themselves spatial things, it would be a strange variant of absolutism₁. There are of course no such individuals. Yet one may feel that unless a view excludes this possibility it smacks of "absolutism." So we may be asked to exclude it. When one philosopher is asked by another to "exclude a possibility," he is not only asked to acknowledge a certain truth but also expected to show that in his way of thinking this truth lies rather "deep."[6] If one counts black, white, and the greys as colors, then it is of course true that what is extended is colored (and conversely). It is also, we shall see, an *a priori* truth. Such truths lie "deep." This particular one excludes the possibility which smacks of "absolutism."

Let us take stock. Formally, the purpose of this essay is to solve the problem of the *a priori*. Once the preparatory steps required have been taken, one sees that neither the solution nor the problem itself is either difficult or very important. Some of the steps are both. What has been said about internal relations, bare particulars, and space covers three of the four steps required. Some comments about elementarism will cover the last.

Are all simple characters of the first type? The affirmative answer is *elementarism*. If one does not make other mistakes then his answer to other philosophical questions will not depend on whether or not he is an elementarist. Thus the issue is not important. Probably that is the most important thing to be said about elementarism.[7] Yet, since philosophers do make mistakes, it will help if we connect it with the issues at hand.

Remember the first example. (1) *e* is higher than *c*. Phenomenally higher is simple. *Prima facie*, therefore, in view of (1), elementarism seems wrong. I say *prima facie* and I say seems because, if in an improved language 'higher' (and all other such predicates) can be represented by a predicative expression (i.e., as one says, by a defined

---

[5] H. Hochberg, "Elementarism, Independence, and Ontology," *Philosophical Studies*, 12, 1961, 36–43.

[6] To say that a truth lies deep is to speak metaphorically, of course. The metaphor will be unpacked in the first concluding remark.

[7] See "Elementarism," *Journal of Philosophy and Phenomenological Research*, 18, 1957, 107–14 (reprinted in *Meaning and Existence*).

predicate) containing no primitive of a higher type, then elementarism nevertheless is right.

This is the place where an earlier digression comes in handy. Remember the two artificial languages L_1 and L_2. Let L_1 contain a class of primitive predicates of the first type as well as one of the second type, 'hg^2', which have been made to represent the pitches and higher, as used in (1), respectively. L_2 is like L_1 except that instead of 'hg^2' it contains a first-order predicate, 'hg^1', which is so interpreted that '$hg^1(a, b)$' is true if and only if a and b both exemplify pitches such that the one exemplified by a is higher than the one exemplified by b. Add to L_1 the definition

(D₃)   '$HG^1(x, y)$'   for   '$(\exists f)(\exists g)[hg^2(f, g) \cdot f(x) \cdot g(y)]$';

add to L_2 the definition

(D₄)   '$HG^2(f, g)$'   for   '$(x)(y)[f(x) \cdot g(y) \supset hg^1(x, y)] \cdot (\exists x)f(x) \cdot (\exists x)g(x)$'.

L_1 and L_2 are formally equivalent.[8] A formalist, therefore, will dismiss as meaningless the question whether elementarism is right or wrong.[9] I merely said that if one makes no other mistakes it is not important. Since the mistakes philosophers make are often interesting, the following question may be and in fact is of interest. Which motives may lead one to embrace either elementarism or nonelementarism?

The dead-end nominalists tell us that characters do not exist. The more sophisticated nominalists try to depress their ontological status. In these attempts, wittingly or unwittingly, they are often guided by two patterns. By the localization pattern, what exists is localized in

---

[8] Some may wish to argue that this time the equivalence is merely "factual," or, even, that L_1 and L_2 are not equivalent at all because (1) the proof that two individuals exemplify hg^1 if and only if they also exemplify two pitches requires the premiss that two properties exemplify higher if and only if they are pitches; and, (2) this premiss introduces the simple second-type character pitch.

$Ad(1)$. The premiss, we shall see, is an *a priori* truth. That is why one may not notice that it must also be stated in L_1, where it becomes the closure of

$$hg^2(f, g) \lor hg^2(g, f) \equiv pitch^2(f) \cdot pitch^2(g) \cdot \sim (f = g)$$

$Ad(2)$. If in L_2 one defines

'$PITCH^2(f)$' for '$(x)(y)[f(x) \cdot e(y) \supset (hg^1(x, y) \lor hg^1(y, x) \lor x = y)] \cdot (\exists x)f(x)$',

where e of course represents a pitch, then the closure of

$$hg^1(x, y) \equiv (\exists f)(\exists g)[f(x) \cdot g(y) \cdot PITCH^2(f) \cdot PITCH^2(g) \cdot \sim (f = g)]$$

will do as premiss. Thus the argument is fallacious.

[9] Twenty years ago, since the logical positivists were my first teachers, I myself dismissed it on this ground. See "Remarks concerning the Epistemology of Scientific Empiricism," *Philosophy of Science*, 9, 1942, 283–93.

space and time. No character is so localized, of course. Yet there is a difference. If I may use a metaphor which needs no unpacking, higher-type characters are even less localized than those of the first type. By the simplicity pattern what exists is simple. That makes nominalism a potent motive to incline one toward elementarism.

We often say that this tone is higher than that. We also say that e is higher than c. Tones are individuals. On the other hand, a tone is what has a pitch. There is also the *a priori* truth that if one individual is higher than another then they are both tones. Some may wish to argue that the (phenomenally) simple relation sometimes presented to us is hg^2. I do not engage in this sort of argument. But I can see that it may incline one toward nonelementarism.

In L_1 (1) becomes (1') $hg^2(e, c)$; in L_2 it becomes (1'') $(x)(y)[e(x) \cdot c(y) \supset hg^1(x, y)]$. (1') is atomic; (1'') is a synthetic generality. (1) belongs to what I called the common core of truths that were claimed to be *a priori*. Such truths supposedly are more "certain" than "mere" synthetic generalities. This provides a very potent motive for rejecting elementarism. Those who believe that it also provides a good reason commit the error of psychologism. To say the same thing differently, the use of 'certain' which is marked by double quotes is philosophical. In one such use, to be certain is to be an atomic fact; in another, to be certain is to be *a priori*. The argument on which the supposedly good reason rests thus suffers from a *quaternio terminorum*. Notice, finally, that just as (1) belongs to the common core of *a priori* truths, being higher in pitch belongs to the common core of supposedly internal relations.

Speaking nonelementaristically not only makes it easier to state the solution of the *a priori* problem, it also makes the connections of this solution with the various strands of the traditional dialectic more perspicuous. These are two appreciable advantages, if only, characteristically if I am right, with respect to an issue which like the elementarism issue is not very important. In view of these two advantages I shall henceforth speak nonelementaristically. But, then, advantages of speaking nonelementaristically are one thing, reasons for choosing between elementarism and nonelementarism are another thing. I see no need for a choice. (This strengthens my conviction that elusive phenomenological details such as those on which the choice depends[10] never make a dialectical difference.)

I once presented in a lecture the idea of the solution which I am about to propose. In the discussion a distinguished colleague asked me whether "my" *a priori* was a "real" *a priori* such as, say, Kant's. I

---

[10] Is the simple relation with which we are sometimes presented hg^1 or hg^2?

readily assured him that it was nothing of the sort. The difference has been explained in the introduction of this essay. Yet it may help if with a twist I explain it once more. Some synthetic truths (facts) are felt to lie "deeper" than some others. They are those called *a priori*. The proponents of the "real" *a priori* account for that felt difference by so assaying these privileged facts that they alone contain an ingredient (I avoid 'constituent') which is a contribution of the minds that know them. Or, since anyone who puts "in" the act (mind) what belongs "in" the intention is either an idealist or on the way to idealism, perhaps I had better say that this spurious ingredient is a contribution which minds make to these facts alone. This is the idea of the "real" *a priori*. I ask myself whether there is in those privileged facts themselves something which distinguishes them structurally and not merely as a matter of degree from all others. The solution I propose is therefore quite different. The problem obviously is the same.

Each truth of the common core belongs to one of six kinds. The following list contains examples of each:

(A) Round is a shape. Green is a color. e is a pitch. Of two pitches one is higher than the other; only a pitch is higher than anything else.

(B) e is higher than c. (This shade of) brown is darker than (that shade of) yellow.

(C) If the first of three pitches is higher than the second and the second is higher than the third, then the first is higher than the third. (Higher is transitive.)

(D_1) What has pitch has loudness and conversely. (Pitch and loudness depend$_2$[11] on each other.) What has shape has color and conversely. (What is extended is colored and conversely. Color and shape depend$_2$ on each other.)

(D_2) Nothing (no tone) has two pitches. Nothing (no area) has two shapes. Nothing (no area) has all over two colors.

(E) If the first of three things (areas) is a part of the second and the second is a part of the third, then the first is a part of the third. (P is transitive.)

By the idea that produces this classification there is still another class and there is something to be learned from the fact that (as far as I know) the truths of this seventh class have never been called *a priori*. First, though, I must state the idea.

The simple properties of the first type fall into several classes such that all the members and only the members of a certain class exemplify

---

[11] This explicates one philosophical use of 'dependent'. For its importance, see E. B. Allaire, "Berkeley's Idealism," *Theoria*, 29, 1963.

a certain simple property of the second type, e.g., shape. In this sense
the second-type property constitutes the class. In some cases at least
the class is also constituted by a simple relation of the second type, e.g.,
higher. The psychologists call these classes modalities. Since in philosophy that word is preempted, let us call them *dimensions*.

The truths of (A) are those and only those constituting the several
dimensions. Some of them are atomic; some are general. A simple relation obtaining between two (or more) members of a dimension is an
atomic fact. (B) is the class of all such facts. The truths of (C) are all
general. They are all those and only those which connect the properties of a single dimension with the simple relations between them. The
truths of (D$_1$) are the general truths by which the members of two
dimensions depend$_2$ on each other. The truths of (D$_2$) are those and
only those by which the members of one or two dimensions exclude
each other. The last two classes are labeled with the same letter because they have long provided the most popular examples of *a priori*
truths. The class (E) corresponds to (C). The reason for setting it apart
is that the spatial relations "in" the facts of (E) are the only relations
of the first type that are mentioned in the list.

Taken together, these six characterizations are the idea of the classification. They are all structural. Nor is the sum of the six classes an
arbitrary collection. There is a sense of 'simple' in which the facts in
the sum are the simplest we know. I also understand what one means
when he says that *we* are more certain *of* these facts than we are of any
other. One may reasonably doubt that what he says is true. That,
though, is unimportant as long as psychologism is kept out by the two
little words which are italicized.

Let once more a and b be two areas such that $P(a, b)$. The seventh
class, the one which has been overlooked, contains such spatial (and
temporal) atomic facts as $P(a, b)$. The only difference between this
class and (B), which contains $hg^2(e, c)$, is one of type. Our confidence
in the idea of the classification will be strengthened if we can find a
likely reason why this seventh class has been overlooked. When seeing
a and b I am (sometimes) presented with $P(a, b)$. When hearing two
tones, one an e, one a c, I am of course not presented with all such
pairs. Express this difference by saying that while one may be "wholly
presented" with $P(a, b)$, one is never so presented with $hg^2(e, c)$. One
may easily take for granted that what is "wholly presented" is as "certain" as an *a priori* truth. And what one takes for granted he easily
overlooks.[12]

[12] The double quotes around 'certain' mark again the connection with psychologism. For the connections between elementarism, nominalism, and the philosophical uses of 'wholly presented' see the essay on "Elementarism" cited in fn. 7.

Some of the truths in the list are atomic; some are general. What is the difference between one of the latter and a general truth which is *a posteriori?* Dogs being carnivorous is general and does not belong to the common core. That makes it an example. But the usual examples are too complicated. It will be better to invent one that is as simple as one can make it. Suppose that what is round is also red. Round is a shape; red is a color. The general fact that color and shape depend$_2$ on each other is *a priori*. The (fictitious) fact that whatever has a certain shape (round) also has a certain color (red) is general as well as *a posteriori*. As for dependence$_2$ (D_1) so for exclusion (D_2). Just consider the (fictitious) fact that nothing is both yellow and triangular. That shows the difference. Nor is it chance that there are no truths which are general, *a posteriori*, and as simple as these examples. Otherwise those which are *a priori* wouldn't be the simplest truths we know.[13]

To say that an entity is *in space* is to use a metaphor as inconspicuous as it is convenient. An entity is in space if and only if it stands in spatial relations to others. It follows that only individuals are in space. All areas are in space. Areas also have shapes. Tones do not. Yet they are spatially localized. Are they in space? If you can make that a good question, you will discover that the answer depends on some of those phenomenological details and subtleties which dialectically make no difference. That makes it safe to suppose that in the truncated world without time and minds which we have so far considered all particulars are in space without depriving ourselves of the musical examples which because of their simplicity are so attractive. Or, to use the traditional phrase, in the truncated world the *principium individuationis* is space and nothing else.

A spot is a bare particular exemplifying two simple properties. In this respect spots and acts are alike. In the case of the spot the properties are a shape and a color.[14] In the case of the act they are a species

---

[13] A little reflection will show that if the three claims I am about to make are justified and the seventh class is included in the classification then all atomic facts are *a priori*.

[14] That supposes that the spot is one color all over. No harm is done if in this context we "schematize" by ignoring this complication, just as we ignore all other properties which the individuals may or may not exemplify. Philosophy, being dialectical, always schematizes. That is why those who get lost in phenomenological details and subtleties so often do so badly in philosophy.

This is as good a place as any for mentioning another detail or complication lest some be puzzled. The transitivity of pitch appears in the list, under (C), as an *a priori* truth even though, because of the so-called threshold phenomena, it is literally a falsehood! The details which at this point the schema neglects are in their different aspects the proper concern of scientists and mathematical logicians.

(perceiving, believing, and so on) and a thought. When the questioner asked me to direct his attention to the bare particular "in" the spot, I directed it to the spot's area, i.e., to the entity which has a shape. Had he asked me to do the same thing for an act, I would have directed him to the entity "in" it which has a duration. A particular is *in time* if and only if it has a duration. That unpacks another inconspicuous and convenient metaphor. The bare particulars "in" acts are in time but not in space. In the truncated world, the bare particulars "in" the spots are in space but not in time. In our world they are in space and time.

'Duration' corresponds to 'shape'. The bare particulars "in" spots I also called areas. This use of 'area', we know, is phenomenological, not geometrical. Yet there is nothing startling about it. It is, as one now says, an ordinary use. The bare particulars "in" acts I call awarenesses. This use of 'awareness' is technical. As things now stand, I would improve my case if I could produce a word that corresponds to 'area' as 'duration' corresponds to 'shape'. As it happens, there is no such word. Ordinary language seems to be against me. Yet I can do even better. Instead of 'area' I could have used '(spatial) extension'. To have a shape is to be a (spatial) extension. To have a duration is to be a (temporal) extension. (There is, of course, a chronometric use of 'duration' which *mutatis mutandis* requires the same clarifications as the geometrical use of 'area'.) We do use a single word, 'extension', to speak of particulars irrespective of whether they are in space and time or in time only! Or we use the word with one of the two qualifying adjectives, 'spatial' and 'temporal', depending on the characters the particular we talk about exemplifies. As it happens, ordinary language really is on my side. (Some may be impressed. Or they should be impressed. I am not.)

Considering time and minds makes new examples available. We can enlarge the list. Shape and color constitute two dimensions. Thought and species constitute two others. Remembering being a species goes into (A); the transitivity of later goes into (E). The dependence$_2$ of thought and species, or, as one says, the intentionality of mind becomes an *a priori* truth in (D$_1$). Nothing being both a thought and spatially extended goes into (D$_2$).

I now make three claims. Each truth of the common core belongs to one of the six classes. Or, equivalently, each such truth fits one of the six characterizations which are the idea of the classification. This is the *first claim*. (I have made it once before. But it bears repeating.) If this claim is justified then the problem of the *a priori* is solved. The relations "in" the facts of the first five classes are all those and only those which belong to the common core of relations which were held to be internal. This is the *second claim*. The particulars we have so far considered are all either in space and time or in time only. Briefly, they are all extensions. The *third claim* is that all particulars are extensions.

Is the first claim justified? The enlarged list supports it impressively. I, for one, cannot think of a truth in the common core that does not fit into one of the six pigeonholes. That, though, doesn't prove the claim. The only way of literally proving it is to start a huge historical investigation, compile a complete list of all truths in the common core and show that one of the six characterizations applies to each of them. That is hardly practical. Nor, if it were, is it the sort of thing I would do. As for the first claim so for the second. One would have to compile another complete list and check it against the first.

Is the third claim justified? I, for one, cannot even think of an individual (of our world) that is not an extension. Again, that does not prove the claim. What, though, does it mean to "prove" a claim of this sort? How would one go about "proving" it? But one can, and I shall, do something else. I shall show that the three claims dialectically support each other.

Unless the first claim is justified the second cannot even be made. If they are both justified, then the common core of relations which were held to be internal contains those and only those of (at least) second type which are mentioned in the list. Hence, even though there are no internal relations, those in the common core do have something in common. We not only understand why there was a problem of internal relations; we have completely unraveled its connection with that of the *a priori*. That shows how, even though the second depends on the first, the two claims dialectically support each other.

In our world the *principium individuationis* is space and time and nothing else. All individuals are extensions. This is the third claim. In our world space and time are uniquely pervasive. That is indeed one of its most striking features. Without it, the container view of space and time would never have seemed plausible to anyone. Because of it, in spite of some fundamental differences[15] between space and time, philosophers have always put the two together. By the Principle of Exemplification, every simple character is exemplified. Hence, of whatever type the character may be, there is a "descent" from it which leads to individuals. That shows how in view of that striking feature the third claim and the Principle of Exemplification dialectically support each other. The Principle, though, is more fundamental than

[15] See the essays on Leibniz and on time in *Meaning and Existence*.

either claim or feature. That makes the claim the root of the feature and a structural reason for putting time and space together.

If the first and the second claim are justified, then the only simple relations of the first type are the spatial and temporal ones between bare particulars. All other simple relations are of (at least) second type. This is, or would be, another structural reason for putting space and time together. Nor is that all. The spatial and temporal relations, we saw, are not only the simplest examples but quite probably also the commonsensical source of the philosophical idea of external relations, just as the simple relations of the second type, higher, darker, and so on, provide not only the most plausible examples but quite probably also the commonsensical source of the very idea of internal relations. Thus, if all three claims are justified, then we have completely unraveled the connections between the ontology of space and time on the one hand and the three problems of internal relations, of bare particulars, and the *a priori* on the other. That shows how all three claims dialectically support each other.

The two structural reasons for putting space and time together are also reasons for setting them apart from everything else. The second, all simple first-type relations being either spatial or temporal, also explains why in the grammar of philosophical uses the two pairs 'extensive-intensive' and 'external-internal' are sometimes interchangeable. Kant surely set time and space apart. Remember his distinction between *Einschraenkungen* and *discursive Begriffe*. He also tells us that while the spatial and temporal "magnitudes (*Groessen*)" are "extensive," all others are "intensive." What he meant by these two words remains obscure. We see what one could reasonably make them mean.

Now for some concluding remarks.

Some truths were said to lie deeper than some others. The metaphor must be unpacked. The Principle of Exemplification was called a categorial truth. The opening paragraph contains a classification of all truths. A truth is either analytic or synthetic. A synthetic truth is either *a priori* or *a posteriori* (contingent). To which of these three classes do categorial truths belong? As 'deep' has been used and as (I believe) most philosophers have used it, analytic truths lie deeper than those which are *a priori;* the latter in turn lie deeper than those which are *a posteriori*. That unpacks the metaphor. A categorial truth clearly is not contingent. Since "analytic" and "synthetic" are essentially mathematical (combinatorial) notions, one must in explicating them make use of an improved language. In such a language *a priori* and analytic truths can be stated. Categorial truths cannot (without futility) even be stated in it. Nor is that surprising. The distinction between what is analytic and what is synthetic and the very possibility of the distinction itself depends on what the categorial truths are. That puts all the latter on a fourth level, which is the deepest of all.[16]

Is what is said about time in this essay compatible with what is said elsewhere[17] in this book? I believe that it is. But I shall not pursue the matter.

We may have stumbled upon a fundamental difference between space and time. If "two" particulars (areas) coincide in space, as one says, then they are one and not two. If two awarenesses, e.g., one of mine and one of yours, are exactly simultaneous, i.e., as one says, if they coincide in time, they are still two particulars and not one.

Philosophers have long speculated that time and mind depend$_2$ on each other. The later Husserl even tells us that they "constitute" each other. Awarenesses are in time but not in space. Being particulars, they are also bare. What is bare is neither mental or nonmental. Yet, awarenesses are the only particulars which exemplify the simple characters which are mental. If one accepts the Principle of Exemplification then he may express this by saying that if there were no time there would be no minds. That explicates one half of the speculative proposition. The other half is at the root of idealism.

---

[16] These are bare hints, of course. Several aspects of this issue are in considerable detail discussed at several places in this book. The cliché in the opening paragraph will (I hope) be excused as an expository device.

[17] I refer to the essay on "Duration and the Specious Present."

Realistic Postscript[1]

Bisogna cercare una cosa sola per trovarne molte.
Pavese

THE realism-idealism issue has been the cross of modern philosophy. The efforts that went into it since Descartes are out of proportion. Their fruits are scant and bitter. Other issues were neglected, beclouded, distorted. With not a few the preoccupation became a block. The intellectual torment it caused to many more is appalling. Of this torment I have had my share.

Structurally, whatever they may have said, the logical positivists, my first teachers, are all either phenomenalists or materialists. None of them saw another alternative. Neither, therefore, when I began to philosophize, did I. So I chose what I thought and after a fashion still think the lesser evil, phenomenalism. Yet I was restive. Eventually I broke away, recognized that there are acts and proposed an assay of them which, in its main outlines, I still think adequate. Structurally, that made me a realist. But my ontology was still cluttered with phenomenalist dross. Every distinction and every argument I have presented since then has made the realism a bit more explicit, got rid of a bit of the dross. In this essay I propose to present some further distinctions and some further arguments which should resolve some of the perplexities of classical realism to which I have as yet not attended and, at the same time, get rid of the last bit of dross.

The way to the solution of a philosophical problem leads, we know, through the explication of the philosophical uses of some key words. Once explicated, such a use is no longer philosophical. In this way we come to distinguish among several ordinary uses of a single word. The

[1] This essay could not have been written without the encouragement and help I received in many discussions with Edwin B. Allaire. Reinhardt Grossmann also has contributed by steadily nudging me toward realism during the last few years.

ordinary man, though he uses the word, is not aware of the distinctions. Can he grasp them when they are pointed out to him? Obviously, he will not appreciate them, even if he can grasp them, unless he himself has suffered philosophical torment, in which case he is not the man I am talking about. The question, therefore, is not whether he can appreciate the distinctions but, rather, whether he can grasp them. With one crucial exception the answer is Yes. (The ordinary man I am talking about is of course the proverbial man on the street. But the phrase sticks in my throat.)

Common sense has a soft fringe and a hard core. The soft fringe is science. The hard core is what we attend to when we adopt the phenomenological attitude. If that makes me a phenomenologist and my realism phenomenological, then I accept the label, though only after having reminded the dispensers of labels that one of the longest essays in this book dissects the errors which drove the founder of the phenomenological movement to idealism.

Attending to the hard core, we sometimes find ourselves in situations which cannot be accurately described without one of the several commonsensical (ordinary) uses of a key word. An ordinary man never finds himself in a situation of this sort; or, again, he is not the man I am talking about. This one particular use he will therefore not grasp, even if it is pointed out to him. We may of course try to instruct him how to attend to the hard core. But the attempt may fail. This is the exception. It makes a difference for what the ordinary man on the one hand and the philosopher on the other can do about the meaning of a key word. That is why it is crucial.

Ask an ordinary man what a word he uses means. What will happen depends on the word. If you pick 'is', all you can reasonably expect is puzzlement. If it belongs to one of two very large classes of words, you will receive, or at least you may reasonably expect to receive, an answer. 'Horse' belongs to one of the two classes, 'green' to the other. Depending on the class to which the word you picked belongs, the answer you will receive is of one of two kinds. If the word belongs to the 'horse'-class, the answer is, however roughly, a definition. If it belongs to the 'green'-class, all you will get and all you can reasonably expect is examples.[2]

If a word has several ordinary uses, one may be a 'green'-use; the others, 'horse'-uses. A use of a key word may be recognizable as a

---

[2] 'Green is a color' is neither a definition nor mentions examples. Yet it is a likely answer. Oxford philosophers may think that this is an objection. I leave it to them to resolve or rejoice in.

'horse'-use if and only if one knows how to attend to the hard core. That is the difference between what an ordinary man and we can do about the meaning of a key word. It is crucial because there are cases where one cannot spot an insidiously elusive philosophical use without first having discovered and distinguished from others that 'green'-use we make of it only when attempting to describe accurately some feature of the hard core. An example will help.

For an ordinary man 'mental' and 'nonmental' are 'green'-words. If you ask him what they mean, what you will get and all you can reasonably expect to get is examples. He will tell you that the tree in front of him is nonmental while his seeing it is mental; that yesterday's sunrise is nonmental while your remembering it now is mental; and so on. Ask him, then, whether the dragon which at this very moment you imagine is mental or nonmental. Or ask him the same question about the spot Lady Macbeth cursed. You may or may not give him a moment's pause. In either case you will be told that the dragon and the spot are both mental. (The actual words may be that they are both merely in the head.) If there is that pause, you are catching the moment of transition from an ordinary to an insidiously elusive philosophical use of 'mental' and 'nonmental'. This particular philosophical use is at the root of some of the perplexities in which the classical realists bogged down. To ferret it out, one must recognize it as a 'horse'-use, which in turn cannot be done without first anchoring the 'green'-use of the two words in the hard core. But I am getting ahead of my story.

What exists? What reason do we have to believe of anything that it exists? The first question leads into ontology; the second, into epistemology. Ontology is primary; epistemology is but the ontology of the knowing situation. That is the gist of my ontologism. Epistemologism reverses the order of precedence. The point has been made more than once in this book. The reason for making it again is that the three hundred years of anguished preoccupation with the realism-idealism issue coincide with the reign of epistemologism. Why this is so you will, if I am right, understand completely after you have read this essay. But it may help you to read it if I now try to state the connection in one paragraph.

The things we perceive are nonmental. Some of them are real, some aren't. Perception, that is, is sometimes erroneous. At the time of Descartes, the new science and, not unconnected with it, the resurgence of skepticism, had made perceptual error a major problem, if not the major problem, of philosophy. Such concern is the mark of epistemologism. By that time, the Aristotelian-Thomistic assay of perception, which is realistic in structure, had collapsed, partly because it could not account for perceptual error. Yet the Aristotelian-Thomistic formula by which a mind can only know what is "in" it had not lost its power.[3] Assume now that in this ambience one uses 'mental', 'real', and 'exist' so that (1) to be "in" the mind and to be mental is one and the same thing, and (2) what is nonmental and not real does not exist. Such a one will easily be led to wonder how he can know that anything nonmental exists, and, eventually, to deny that it exists. That shows how the realism-idealism issue arose as well as why the three centuries during which it had such a baleful fascination coincide with the reign of epistemologism.

The next paragraph gets again ahead of the story. But it, too, may help you to read it.

Concerning (1), I shall argue that with the hard-core use of 'mental' and the one clear use of 'being in the mind', being mental and being in the mind are two and not one. Concerning (2), I shall argue that with the hard-core use of 'nonmental' and the one clear use of 'real', to be real and to be nonmental are two and not one. To make either (1) or (2) true thus required some very special uses. Going unrecognized, these special uses became the philosophical uses at the roots of the perplexities with which I am here concerned.

The traditional dialectic of the realism-idealism issue is a tangle of ontological and epistemological questions. That may make you suspect that my emphatic ontologism prevents me from doing justice to the issue. It may again help if, in a paragraph, I try to allay the suspicion. That will be the last preparatory remark.

"You insist on ontology being primary. I take this to mean that in systematically expounding your philosophy you begin with what you call general ontology, then proceed to what you claim is the ontology of our world. Why should I accept this claim?" Suppose that one who harbors that suspicion asks me this question. I answer with a comparison. There is in the game of chess a sense of 'winning' in which the last and only the last move is *the* winning move. This move, though, must be preceded by many others. A philosopher's ontology is like the preceding moves; his epistemology (ontology of the knowing situation), like the winning move. If his last move does not win, you have indeed no reason to accept the claims he makes for his ontology. Since our issue is a tangle of both kinds of questions, which I believe is a major cause of its sorry state, the successive distinctions and arguments of this essay will be of both kinds, some ontological, some epistemological.

[3] This is explained at several places in this book and implicit in several others. But see p. 264.

As it happens, the very first distinction I shall make, concerning the phenomenological uses of 'mental' and 'nonmental', will be introduced by an epistemological question: What reason do I have to believe of anything that it exists? But I shall not bother to say of each step to which of the two kinds it belongs. As long as one knows what he is doing and does not improperly mix the two, no harm will come to him.

The key words of the realism-idealism issue are *'mental'*, *'nonmental'*, *'real'*, *'dependent'* in such expressions as 'mind-dependent' and 'independent of mind(s)', and, of course, in view of the ontological involvement, *'exist'*. 'Physical' and 'phenomenal' occur as synonyms or would-be synonyms of 'nonmental' and 'mental', respectively. Until much later I shall avoid them both. About 'exist' much has been said in this book. But it will be well to recall, very concisely, six points which will play a role.

1. 'Exist' is a 'green'-word for everyone, ordinary man and philosopher alike. Notice that I speak of a 'green'-word, not of a 'green'-use. That leads to the next point. 2. 'Exist' is univocal. When I read in a philosophical book that there are several kinds of exist*ing*, I am tempted to put it aside. If I don't, it is because I hope that reading on I shall discover that what is so unfortunately expressed is the proposition that there are several kinds of exist*ents*. If this hope is disappointed then I know that I could not possibly understand the book. So I put it aside. 3. The philosopher's concern is only with the most general kinds of existents. These are the ontological modes, categories, subcategories. 4. In my world there are quite a few ontological kinds. There are subsistents and simple things. The latter are either individuals, which are bare particulars, or universals. There are complexes. And so on. There are also two modes, actuality and possibility. (The modes will play a role in this essay. 'Actual' I haven't used before. But the proper contradictory of 'possible' is of course 'actual', not 'real'.) 5. All the philosophical uses of 'exist' are narrower than the univocal commonsensical one. That fits with the second point. To use 'exist' philosophically is to adopt unwittingly what I call a pattern, i.e., a sentence one does not allow to be falsified. By one such pattern, only individuals exist; by another, only simples; by a third, only facts. And so on.

6. An ontological kind is "in" the entity to which the latter belongs. A thing's individuality or universality, for instance, is a subsistent which is "in" it. What is "in" an entity is, as one says, "internal" or "intrinsic" to it. Both these words have been used philosophically. So I shall avoid them. A tree's color is "in" it; its distance from another tree is not; nor is color itself. What is not "in" a thing is, as one says, "external" or "extrinsic" to it. I shall again avoid these two words, for

the same reason as before, use 'contextual' instead. *A classification based on contextual criteria does not yield ontological distinctions.* That is of the very essence of ontology.

The only primary reason I have to believe of anything that it exists is that it is presented to me.[4] The first two of the following five comments unpack the formula. The third introduces an assumption that will simplify the exposition. The last two not only show the import of the formula; they also will, once more, run ahead of the story in order to make it easier to follow.

1. Seeing footprints in the sand, I believe that someone walked there. The primary reason for the belief is my seeing the footprints. That unpacks 'primary'.

2. To be presented (to me) is the same as to be the intention, or "in" the intention, of an act (of mine). The act's species makes no difference. It may be direct (immediate) acquaintance, or perceiving, or believing, or disbelieving, or any other. That unpacks 'presented'.

3. Speaking of the reasons *I* have rather than of those *we* have provides an opportunity for introducing the assumption that will simplify the exposition. I believe that the group of philosophical questions I set out to answer in this essay can and must be answered without ever mentioning another group of such questions, namely, those concerning our knowledge of other minds. The later Husserl[5] and his followers hold that this belief is false. If, as I shall suppose, it is true, then I shall neither prejudge nor distort anything but merely disentangle the two groups of questions by assuming, as I shall, that the intention of an act (of mine) contains a constituent which is mental if and only if its species is direct acquaintance. The assumption is contrary to fact, of course, but it merely keeps out what can and must be kept out.

4. If we accept the formula, are we not dialectically forced also to accept its converse, i.e., that whatever is presented exists? I believe that we are. But I also have another reason, which is as weighty as any, for accepting the converse. No realistic ontology, we know, is adequate unless it provides an ontological ground for the connection between a thought ($\ulcorner P \urcorner$) and its intention (P). In my world, the connection is the intentional tie (M) in $\ulcorner P \urcorner MP$. Since M and $\ulcorner P \urcorner MP$ both exist, the former as a subsistent, the latter as a formal fact, the connection is

---

[4] This is what Descartes' *Cogito* has long meant to me. In a recent essay parts of which I greatly admire, Jaakko Hintikka argued that it meant this also to Descartes. See his *"Cogito, Ergo Sum;* Inference or Performance?" *The Philosophical Review,* 71, 1962, 3–32. See also fn. 37.

[5] I refer to the strange idea that our knowledge of rocks, trees, chairs, and so on, structurally depends on that of other minds. See p. 222.

grounded. But I do not see how $\ulcorner P \urcorner MP$ could exist unless P has some ontological status. That is the second reason for accepting the converse.

5. If all intentions are to exist, how about those of (the thoughts in) false beliefs and false memories, which, as one says, do not "exist"? How about perceptual error? The double quotes around 'exist' mark the philosophical use that limits existence to the actual. In my world, we know, the intention of, say, a false belief is a possibility (p-fact) and as such has ontological status (exists), even though it is neither actual nor, as we shall see, real. In all cases but one (and those which depend on it) the mode of possibility provides the way out of the difficulties the realists encountered in assigning, as I believe they must, some ontological status to the intentions of all acts. The recalcitrant case, as we shall see, is perceptual error of the kind called existential. In the traditional dialectic it looms very large. The classical realists were more anguished by the arguments drawn from it than by any others. I have as yet not attended to the recalcitrant case. In this essay I shall. (Psychologists may attribute the delay to a reaction against the classical realists' frenzy.)

What is mental, what nonmental? The right answer is the one that keeps one out of philosophical trouble. To find it, one must attend to the hard core. There, we shall see, the dichotomy mental-nonmental "corresponds" to another. Yet they are two and not one. Nor does one depend on the other. Unless a philosopher grasps that firmly he gets into trouble. It should make it easier for you to keep these two dichotomies apart if I first direct your attention to the second. That requires that you recall the schema of the act and, from the opening essay (p. 27), how and why I use 'conscious state'.

The several species, perceiving, believing, doubting, and so on, are simple characters. Hence, if I know them at all, I also know them from each other. To ask how or why makes no more sense than to ask how or why I know red from green. Sameness and difference are primary. Similarly, it makes no more sense to ask how I know that a character is a species than to ask how I know that green is a color and square is not. 'Remembering is a species' is exactly like 'green is a color'. Both are synthetic *a priori*. As for species so for thoughts. To ask how I know that a simple character is a thought makes no more sense than to ask how I know that round is a shape. Remember what has been said in the preceding essay about the dimensions. Thought and species are two dimensions; and it is a synthetic *a priori* truth that every individual exemplifying a member of one of these two dimensions also exemplifies a member of the other. (These individuals I call awarenesses.)

Schematically,[6] a conscious state is an act, e.g., *a* perceiving, i.e., an awareness that exemplifies perceiving and a thought. But it is a conscious state only by virtue of a second act whose intention it is.[7] The second act is not "in" the conscious state. Yet this second act can and often does itself become a second conscious state through what psychologists call a shift in set. Every act by virtue of which another act is a conscious state is *a* direct (immediate) acquaintance. Direct acquaintance is as unmistakably a species different from all other species as green is a color different from all other colors.

When I perceive something, my conscious state is an act of perceiving. Yet "my attention centers" on the intention of the act. As for perceiving so for all other species. The expression between the double quotes is a metaphor. I know no better way of directing attention to what I am trying to express. Husserl expresses it by saying that we "live in" the intentions of our acts. That, too, is a metaphor.

Direct acquaintance is not just a species among species; it has a "flavor" that sets it apart from all others. That is again a metaphor. A comparison may help. Black, white, and the several greys have a flavor that sets them apart from all other colors. (Hence the familiar use of 'color' that excludes them.) If the comparison does not help, recall the metaphor of the *"liséré"* Proust uses in the passage that is the epigraph of the opening essay. The two metaphors may illuminate each other. When my conscious state is a perceiving, I "am" this perceiving. When it is a direct acquaintance, I "am" this direct acquaintance. In this respect there is no difference. The difference is that when my conscious state is a perceiving, there is between me, i.e., the act which I "am," and its intention that *liséré* which is not there when I "am" a direct acquaintance. Philosophers, speaking about these matters, have used four adjectives. One species is said to yield acquaintance which is "direct" or "immediate." All others yield only "indirect" or "mediate" acquaintance with the intentions of the acts whose species they are. Direct acquaintance, then, is one thing. All other species, the several kinds of indirect acquaintance, are another thing. This is the dichotomy to which I wanted to call attention first.

In establishing the dichotomy direct-indirect no reference has been made either to the differences, if any, among the intentions of the dif-

---

[6] I say schematically because dialectically it makes no difference whether or not a conscious state also contains sense data. Nor is there any reason why one conscious state shouldn't contain several acts or be what the classical psychologists call a fusion of them. See also fn. 26.

[7] More precisely, it is the intention of the thought in the act. But I shall permit myself this contraction.

ferent kinds of acts or to anything else except the species themselves and their "flavors." That makes it an ontological distinction among species. Call now an act's intention direct (indirect) if its species is direct (indirect). That saves words and does no harm as long as it is kept in mind that this classification of intentions, being contextual, is not, like the dichotomy between the two kinds of acquaintance, onto-logical. There is, however, a dichotomy among intentions, based on what is "in" them and hence ontological, that is coextensive with the contextual classification.

The dichotomy mental-nonmental is primarily one among simple characters. An individual, being bare, obviously is neither mental nor nonmental. Nor, even more obviously, is a subsistent. *Thoughts and the several species are mental; all other simple characters* (of the first type) *are nonmental.* This is one way of stabilizing the hard-core use of 'mental'. Another way is to call thought and species themselves the two mental dimensions. The first way puts mental and nonmental in the second type; the second, in the third. The difference makes no dif-ference whatsoever.

With the sole exception of the temporal characters, no individual exemplifies two simple characters of the first type one of which is mental while the other is nonmental. Nor am I acquainted with any simple character of the second type exemplified by both mental and nonmental characters of the first type; and so on. This is due to a re-markable pattern of dependences and exclusions (p. 295), all of which are synthetic *a priori*.

I have said that the hard-core use of 'mental' is a 'green'-use. In other words, I believe that mental itself is a simple character. Perhaps you disagree; propose to define 'being mental' as 'being either a thought or a species'; believe that I am reifying a "flavor" produced by that remarkable pattern of dependences and exclusions. Again, the disagree-ment makes no difference whatsoever as long as you agree that I have succeeded in calling attention to the hard-core use of 'mental' and 'nonmental'; that this use can never get us into philosophical trouble; and that the dichotomy it represents is ontological.

All uses of 'mental' and 'nonmental' share a feature that gives no trouble and which it will therefore be safe for us to preserve. A complex is called mental if and only if all the simple characters "in" it, if they are of the first type, are either temporal or mental; or, if they are of the second type, are exemplified only by mental characters; and so on. A complex is called nonmental if and only if all the simple characters "in" it, if they are of the first type, are nonmental; or, if they are of the second type, are exemplified only by nonmental characters; and so on. This is the derivative use of 'mental' and 'nonmental'. All other complexes may be called mixed. Mixed intentions we may safely ignore. That is the import of the assumption by which we disentangled the realism-idealism issue from that of our knowledge of other minds (and, as we now see, also from the mind-body problem). If we keep that in mind and adopt the derivative use then we can state the "correspondence" between the dichotomies mental-nonmental and direct-indirect very perspicuously.

A species (acquaintance) is either direct or indirect. An act's intention is either mental or nonmental. These are the two ontological dichotomies. An act's intention is mental if and only if its species is direct acquaintance; it is nonmental if and only if the act's species is indirect. That is how the two dichotomies "correspond" to each other. Close as the correspondence is, we have seen that the two dichotomies are equally fundamental, so that neither of the two depends on the other. To appreciate how important that is, suppose that mental-nonmental depends on direct-indirect. This is the one of the two possible dependencies which, if one is not accurate, may seem plausible. In this case, a distinction within the "seen" would depend on one between kinds of "seeing." That blurs the distinction between "seeing" and the "seen." One who blurs this distinction is, we know, on the way to idealism. That is why I have been so emphatic, almost prolix.

The phenomenalists hold that we acquire the "idea of external existence" from the "coherence" of what I, though not they, call the intentions of our several acts. Presently we shall hear much more of this coherence. For the moment I merely avail myself, for a limited purpose, of what everyone who will read this book knows.

I hold that when I am presented with a nonmental intention, i.e., when I "am" an act which is not a direct acquaintance, then I am *eo ipso* presented with the "idea of external existence." For this "idea" is nothing but the "idea" of the nonmental. Or, perhaps, it is Proust's *liséré*. The difference makes no difference. In other words, 'external existent' is not the name of an ontological kind. Or, if you prefer it that way, it is merely a synonym of 'nonmental'. Hence, even if *per absurdum* my Self exhausted itself in a single act and this act were, say, a doubting or a disbelieving—I deliberately pile absurdity upon absurdity—I could yet have the "idea of external existence" without, as the phenomenalists hold, having to acquire it from a plurality of conscious states. That alone shows the realistic impact of grounding the dichotomy mental-nonmental in the hard core. It also frees the notion of coherence for the use I shall presently make of it by relieving it of a burden which it cannot bear.

"Some things are mental; some, nonmental. (Things of both kinds exist.)" This is a familiar statement of the classical realists' claim. If one construes the two key words in it with their hard-core use and recognizes that a certain proposition is a hard-core truth, the statement itself becomes such a truth. Why, then, call it a claim? Why argue for it? The answer is that the classical realists understood neither the hard-core use of 'mental' nor the proposition in question.[8] The latter is the converse of the one from which we started. "If anything is presented (to me), so is its existence." If one doubts that this is a truth of the hard core, let him ask himself how he knows what 'exist' means.[9] Why the classical realists failed to grasp this truth we understand already. There are the difficulties they could not overcome because they did not recognize that possibilities exist. There is also the recalcitrant case, perceptual error of the kind called existential.

We just saw that unless the two key words in a familiar statement of the classical realists' claim are used in a special way, the statement is a hard-core truth rather than anything to be worried about and argued for or against. We could of course explore that special use directly, but it will pay if we proceed indirectly.

The controversy is about stones, trees, chairs, and so on. We must first agree on a suitable name for their kind. 'Thing' I so often use technically that it is preempted; even 'ordinary thing' does not recommend itself. 'Physical object' and 'perceptual object' I want to avoid because we shall need them later. I think it will be best if we agree to call stones, trees, chairs, and so on, *ordinary objects*.

"Ordinary objects are real." This is another familiar statement of the claim. It rings in the third key word, 'real'. The idealists deny that ordinary objects are real. Everything depends on how the two sides use 'real'.

An entity is real if and only if it is actual, i.e., not merely a possibility, and, in case it is not mental, mind-independent. That explicates how both sides use 'real'. I, too, shall use it this way. The materialists, we shall see, use it differently. As far as the idealists are concerned, the explication is a bit schematic. Yet it does justice to the analytic center of their claim and the speculative accretions do not interest me at all.

---

[8] From what I know about him, Meinong, for all his tenacity and all his profundity, is no exception.

[9] This is one of the main points of Essay Three.

The explication makes all actual mental entities real.[10] 'Mind-independent' is the last of the four key words. We must answer three questions. What does it mean for an entity to be mind-independent? What reason do we have to believe that there are such entities? If there are any, are ordinary objects among them? The answers depend on how one ontologically assays ordinary objects and the situations in which he perceives them. Since ontology is primary this is as it ought to be.

A substance is a simple individual, is a continuant, and has a nature. Or, rather, this is the "idea" of substance. Its several parts are irreconcilable with each other.[11] In my world there are therefore no substances. The structurally consistent alternative to them is bare individuals. The particulars of my world are bare individuals; but they are momentary,[12] not continuants. The reason is that we cannot recognize particulars as such.[13] That may seem to exclude continuants on epistemological grounds; yet it really doesn't. Epistemology asks how we *can* know what we *do* know. Ontology accounts for what in fact we do know. Since we do not recognize particulars as such, we do not in fact know continuants (in the relevant sense).[14] That virtually determines my assay of ordinary objects. An ordinary object is a temporal succession of particulars each of which exemplifies certain nonmental (nonrelational) properties and stands in certain nonmental relations to every other. ('Temporal succession' merely refers suggestively to the temporal ones among these relations.) That makes table, even schematically, a very complex character. Beyond the schema we cannot and need not go.[15]

A perceiving is an act among acts. Perceiving is a single species. 'Perceiving' has three uses; we shall distinguish them by subscripts. Since perceiving, like all species, is a simple character, the distinctions

[10] Upon the broad use of 'realism' and 'idealism', materialism is a variety of realism; phenomenalism, one of idealism. I stay here with the narrow use. See fn. 32.

[11] For an argument in support, see the Leibniz-essay in *Meaning and Existence*.

[12] The dialectic of moments, instants, and the specious present we can here safely ignore. See, however, Essay Five.

[13] This is one of the major burdens of Essay Nine.

[14] For all we know, some physical entities may be continuants. See the concluding essay of *Meaning and Existence*. Concerning the notion of physical entities, see Essay Six and below.

[15] For some relevant features of the schema see the essay on Logical Atomism in *Meaning and Existence*. In that essay the particulars of the schema are still sensa. Very significantly, that makes no difference whatsoever except in the one respect which is being considered in the present essay. See below.

are contextual, not ontological. That is so important that I want to emphasize it by stating succinctly what these distinctions are before describing them in detail. The intention of a perceiving$_1$ is narrower than that of a perceiving$_2$. A perceiving$_3$ is the last of a series of perceivings$_2$.

Every time I look up from my desk I perceive a table. These are all perceivings$_2$. Take one of them. The thought "in" it is the-thought-that-this-is-a-table. ($^\Gamma$This is a table^1; briefly: $^\Gamma P^1$). $^\Gamma P^1$ is simple. Its simplicity accounts for a striking feature. All thoughts are simple.[16] In the case of perception, some philosophers sensitive to the feature insist that what I am presented with is the table and nothing else. They are right, of course; but the way they express themselves easily leads to the misunderstanding that the intention (P) of the thought $(^\Gamma P^1)$ is itself simple. We know that all awareness is propositional; hence, no intention is simple. That is why I rather express what these philosophers try to express by insisting that the intention in question is the fact[17] represented by 'This is a table'. How shall we assay this intention? It will pay if we postpone the answer for a moment.

When I perceive$_2$ the table, my "attention does not center" on any of the particulars "in" it that may or may not on this occasion be presented to me. This is but a third way of expressing, by means of a metaphor already familiar, what the philosophers just mentioned insist upon. But we all are, when perceiving$_2$, capable of shifting to another act whose intention is the fact of some particular (or particulars) exemplifying some properties (and relations). These particulars are all "in" the table; and they are all simultaneous with the awareness, i.e., with the particular "in" the (second) act. The species of the latter is again perceiving. Its intention, accordingly, presents me with the "idea of external existence." Yet it is characteristically "narrower" than that of the preceding perceiving$_2$. An act with such an intention I call a perceiving$_1$. Psychologists call the shift in question a shift of set. In painters it is supposed to be a professional habit. The impressionists made it the corner stone of their technique. To us it provides a cue for assaying the intentions of perceivings$_2$.

Return to the example. How are we to assay its intention (P), i.e., the fact represented by 'This is a table'? Let 'Mp' be the sentence representing the fact that would have been presented to me if the act had been a perceiving$_1$ instead of a perceiving$_2$. Let 'a_1, . . . , 'a_n' stand for

[16] For the dialectic that springs from this feature see in particular the first section of Essay Seven.

[17] Or possibility (p-fact). We are as yet not concerned with this distinction.

the particulars "in" it and, whenever it helps, write '$Mp(a_1, \ldots, a_n)$' instead of 'Mp'. The letter 'M' in 'Mp' is to remind us that the fact is molecular. The letter 'p' is to recall 'part'. For I assay P (This is a table), which is the intention of the perceiving$_2$ with which we are concerned, as a conjunction of two (part) facts. One is Mp; the other I call Op. That makes 'P' an abbreviation for '$Mp \cdot Op$'. The letter 'O' is to remind us that 'Op' contains operators. Op, the *operator part* of P, is very complex indeed. Fortunately we need no details. The idea is easily grasped. 'Op' schematically states that there are all the particulars which must be there, that these particulars have all the properties they must have, and that they stand in all the relations in which they must stand, among themselves and to the particulars in the *molecular part*, if the latter is to be "in" a table. One may indicate this complexity by expanding 'Op' into '$[\alpha]Op(a_1, \ldots, a_n, \alpha)$', where the bracket stands not for one but for many operators, some existential, some general; and the Greek letter serves to avoid commitment to either number or type of the bound variables.[18]

Details, I said, don't matter. One, though, must be singled out. For the statement that a certain particular, one of those which as I just put it must be there, is in fact there, or that it exemplifies a certain character, to become deducible from 'Op', some synthetic *a priori* truths (facts) about the relevant dimensions, particularly about space and time, must be included among the parts of Op. That may well be one of the sources of the need, felt by so many philosophers, for setting apart the truths they call synthetic *a priori*. Thereby hangs another point too good to be missed. Some now believe, very strangely, that synthetic *a priori* truths are "linguistic." Nothing being both red and green (all over) is one such truth. Everything red being extended is another. Neither is molecular. That spots a likely source of the strange belief. Those holding it not only are sure that there are no sensings but also fail to distinguish[19] between sensing and perceiving$_1$. Thus they miss, or ignore, all molecular intentions.

Even the most fleeting glimpse I have of I know not what is a perceiving. One perceives when he dreams or hallucinates; otherwise he would not be dreaming or hallucinating. We all make perceptual errors; may have mistaken for round a tower that is square. We have all been victims of cleverly devised illusions; may have mistaken a dummy for a

---

[18] Write now '$Table (x_1, \ldots, x_n)$' for '$Mp(x_1, \ldots, x_n)$. $[\alpha]Op(x, \ldots, x_n, \alpha)$' and you have the predicate which (in this case) represents the complex character table. For this as well as some related details, see the essay cited in fn. 15.

[19] The distinction will of course be made below.

man. In this sense, all perceiving is problematic. *In principle, it forever remains so.* Practically, when we check a perceiving, we are much less likely to be, or remain, deceived. One checks a perceiving by making it the first of a series of perceivings, all of the same ordinary object (if there is one). I walk toward and then around the tower; I touch the dummy; and so on. When I am satisfied, I stop and the series breaks off. Its last member I call a checked perceiving or perceiving₃. That makes 'perceiving₃' what some now call an achievement verb. There is no harm in the label as long as it does not cause one to ignore the two other kinds or not to recognize that the species is the same in all three. Perceiving₃ involves remembering. We may safely ignore this circumstance. Again, one cannot neatly separate perceiving₃ from the "coherence" which is our next topic. But, again, nothing will be lost, and, the traditional dialectic being what it is, something will be gained by proceeding as I do.

We are ready for the three questions. What does it mean for an entity to be mind-independent? What reason do I have to believe that there are such entities? If there are any, are ordinary objects among them?

An entity is mind-independent if and only if it exists while it is not in the intention of an act (of mine). That explicates how both sides to the classical controversy use 'mind-independent'. I, too, shall use it this way. 'While' is temporal. What exists while it is presented is in time. At this point I draw on my ontology. The only entities literally in time are (momentary) particulars. That allows for a rephrasing, without substantial loss, of the last two questions. What reason do I have to believe that a particular not presented to me exists? What reason do I have to believe that there are all the particulars not mentioned in 'Mp' which, according to 'Op', must be there if the table I perceived is to be mind-independent? We need not, we see, bother with the rephrased second question. If we can find the reason asked for in the rephrased third, we have also found the one asked for in the second, except for one pedantry which it will be best to dispose of right now, Taken literally, the explication implies that $a_1, \ldots, a_n$, the particulars in Mp, are not mind-independent, simply because they are presented (to me). If you noticed that, modify the explication so that they, too, become mind-independent provided only that we can find the reason asked for in the rephrased third question.

(One pedantry brings to mind another. G. E. Moore often makes much of the distinction between good and bad reasons. Sometimes he has a good reason for that. I here always speak of reasons. I mean good reasons, of course. Presently I shall in a long footnote give some plausible structural reasons why the good reason I am about to give in answer to the rephrased third question seems bad to some. For the moment, keep in mind that, given the relevant uses, if this reason is a good reason, then we have also found a good reason for believing that ordinary objects are real.)

The only reason I have to believe that ordinary objects are real is coherence. That means three things. (1) '*Op*', we remember, deductively implies statements to the effect that there are certain particulars exemplifying certain characters which were not presented to me when I perceived the table. Whenever I am in a position to perceive such a particular I do in fact perceive it. More precisely, I perceive it in a very large proportion of all cases provided the original perceiving was a perceiving$_3$. (2) There is a huge body of generalities (laws) about the changes ordinary objects undergo in their properties and relations to each other. None of these laws mentions anything mental. In a very large proportion of the cases in which either we do not perceive the particulars which according to (1) we expect to perceive or the particulars we do perceive do not exemplify the characters which we expect them to exemplify, these laws "explain" the discrepancy. When I last saw these leaves they were green; now they are yellow; fall has arrived. (3) The remaining cases in which we do not perceive what according to (1) and (2) we ought to perceive as well as the cases in which our perceivings$_2$ deceive us are "explained" by another large body of laws. These laws do mention mental things. The stick partially immersed in water seems bent. We know that it is straight. If waking from a dream I remember it, I know that it was a dream.

To separate sharply (2) from (1) is no more important than so to separate from each other the notions of perceiving$_3$ and coherence. Another distinction is most important. The laws mentioned in (3) are one thing; the job of ontologically assaying perceptual error, dreaming, and so on, is quite another thing. To believe that those laws do this job is the crudest kind of scientism.

Do our perceivings in fact cohere without residue? If they have so far, could they not cease to cohere from now on? The answer is familiar. *In principle, coherence, like perception, is forever open or problematic.* This is their very nature.[20]

---

[20] Or, what amounts to the same, perception and coherence share the characteristic feature of *induction*. There is, of course, a sense of 'problematic' in which induction is not problematic at all. Neither, therefore, are perception and coherence. Some nevertheless reject the above analysis because of this feature. G. E. Moore, for instance, asserts that '*P*' follows *deductively* from either 'I perceive that *P*' or 'I know that *P*' (though not from either 'I judge that *P*' or 'I believe

My perceivings of the table cohere. The table is real. The spot I saw on my blotter while having an afterimage is not real. I had an hallucination, saw a ghost. The ghost is not real. What has been said explicates this use of 'real'. The key idea is coherence. That makes the notion contextual. Hence, *real is not an ontological kind.* (In speaking about ordinary objects I shall use 'real' in no other way.)

Characters are either mental or nonmental; particulars, being bare, are neither. Yet, as it has been convenient to call a particular an *awareness* in order to indicate its being "in" a mental fact, so it will help

---

that P'). If my assay of the act is adequate, then Moore is radically wrong. If you substitute in '$\phi(a) \cdot {}^\ulcorner P^1\urcorner(a) \supset P$' the name of a species for 'ϕ', the resulting sentence will be synthetic in all cases, including those of 'perceiving' and, *if it be a species*, of 'knowing'. What is analytic is, rather, "$^\ulcorner P^1\urcorner MP$', and this irrespective of any species, which is not even mentioned in it, and of whether 'P' is true or false.

If you use 'real' as I do and accept my assay of P, then, *if what Moore asserts were true*, the table I perceived would be real (mind-independent) on the sole ground that I perceived it. Clearly, this is a short-cut to realism. It is true, although not analytic, that what we perceive is nonmental. But the (actual) nonmental does not, we shall see, coincide with the real. The realistic urge behind the short-cut is only too transparent.

Knowing is not a species. Believing, on the other hand, is not a single species but a series of such. The series is produced by the relational character *more-certain-than*. The higher in the series a believing is, the more inclined we are to call it a knowing. But there is a complication. Just as there is perceiving$_2$ and perceiving$_3$, i.e., checked perceiving$_2$, so there is believing and checked believing. The complication is that when one says he knows something he implies not only that he believes it with a high degree of certainty but also that he has checked the belief in a manner appropriate to it, while, on the other hand, we also hold beliefs with very high degrees of certainty without having checked them.

The only reason Moore gives for his assertion is that it merely makes explicit the way 'perceiving' and 'knowing' are used. As to 'perceiving', I have my doubts. As to 'knowing', I have no doubt whatsoever. We all say such things as "How could he have known it if it isn't the case?" It does not follow that the sentence (or sentences, if you include 'perceiving') which Moore asserts to be analytic are analytic. Checked beliefs, like checked perceptions, are very reliable. This more than suffices to account for the use. That creates the following situation. Moore's assertion and my assay of the act contradict each other. His assertion rests on no more than a certain use. My assay rests on the hard core. Also, the use in question is easily accounted for in a manner consistent with my assay of the act. The situation shows how dangerous it is to introduce uses as reasons into philosophical arguments. Those who now agree with Moore on what he asserts about knowing and perceiving and also accept his reason for it, no doubt satisfy their realistic urges. So, we saw, did Moore, although he did not, as these latter-day disciples, either miss or prejudge virtually all the distinctions and analyses which are the heart of the realism-idealism issue. But, then, most of his arguments were better than theirs, which are *all* from use.

to have a word for the particulars "in" nonmental facts. Let us call them *external particulars*. The expression will remind us that each non-mental intention presents us with the "idea of external existence." Let us also agree to call external particulars and molecular nonmental facts real if and only if they are "in" real ordinary objects. (This is but a slight and most natural extension of the above use of 'real'.) Are all external particulars real? In order to anwer we must assay perceptual error. To this task I now turn.

Take a perceiving; let its intention be P.[21] Perceptual error occurs if and only if 'P' is false. 'P' is an abbreviation of '$Mp \cdot Op$'. The conjunction is false if and only if at least one of its terms is false. That provides us with a schema for the cases which must be considered and the comments which must be made.

First Case. I perceived a coin. For some reason I reached for it. Touching it and weighing it in my hand, I discovered that it was a cardboard imitation of the kind used in games. I also saw that the imitation of the visual appearance of a coin was very accurate. In other words, the 'Mp' of the original perceiving is true; its 'Op' is false.

First Comment. If 'Op' is false, Op is a mere possibility. The conjunction of two entities at least one of which is a possibility is itself merely a possibility. Possibilities, though, have ontological status. P exists. (The same holds *mutatis mutandis* in the other cases.)

Second Comment. There are now quite a few who would object to my saying I saw a coin, would insist that what I saw merely looked like a coin or seemed to be one.[22] Those who would make this objection either confuse or tend to confuse the task of ontologically assaying perception with the quite different and most tedious one of accurately describing the relevant uses of 'looking', 'seeming', and 'appearing'. What is the ontological ground of looking, seeming, appearing? The mere question suffices to spot the confusion.

Second Case. I perceive₂ an oval coin. Surprised that there should be such a thing, I reach for it, examine it, perceive₃ it to be round. The 'Op' of the original perceiving₂ is false. How about its 'Mp'? Let a be the particular (area) "in" it that was presented to me. 'a is round', I have now reason to believe, is true; 'a is oval', false. The latter is a conjunction term of 'Mp'. That makes Mp, too, a mere possibility. But *the external particular in Mp is real.*

Third Comment. Some believe, mistakenly, that the particular pre-

---

[21] No harm will be done if I continue to use 'P', 'Mp', 'Op' even though the examples will be different.

[22] For the ground of this objection see fn. 20.

sented "in" Mp when I perceive a round coin is in fact often oval. Probably they have been misled by a familiar bit of science. The irrelevance of science at this point is obvious. But there is also a dialectical blur, or apparent difficulty, which is easily cleared up. Having shifted from a perceiving₂ of a round coin to a perceiving₁, one sometimes is presented with an area that is oval. The spurious difficulty arises when one fails to realize that the intentions of the two acts are two and not one. Turn back to the statement on p. 314 which introduces the notion of Mp and you will read: Let 'Mp' be the sentence representing the fact that *would have been* presented *if* the act *had been* a perceiving₁ instead of a perceiving₂.

Fourth Comment. Perceiving a coin, I think and perhaps say: "This, though it looks oval, since it is a coin, is round." The sentence represents the intention of an act (of mine) which is not a perceiving. This act—of judgment, as one says—is the last of a series. The first of the series is an instance of the second case. The series may be run through very quickly. We often recognize "immediately" a familiar object even though we are "fleetingly" aware of its unusual color due to an unusual illumination. If you take that to be a single act of perceiving, you will be in trouble; for, 'Mp' ('a is green') is false, yet 'P' ('This is my blue easy chair') is true. Since recognition was "immediate," you may wonder. Was there really a series? How many members did it have? What were they? Did they fuse? One who worries about the answers to these questions will get lost in what I call the wrong kind of phenomenology because, as I have repeatedly insisted in this book, it is dialectically irrelevant and a philosopher must therefore know how to keep away from it.

Third Case. Suppose I saw a ghost. Let a be the particular (area) presented to me. Assume, schematically, that 'a is white' exhausts 'Mp'. The operator part of 'P' is again false. In this respect the three cases are alike. In two others they differ. 1. In the first two cases, the particulars "in" Mp are all real. In this case, *the external particular in Mp is not real.* 2. Since all particulars are "momentary," we cannot "check" any.[23] Yet, if a particular is real, we can check the ordinary object "in" which it is. If we do that, coherence provides us with the only reasons we could possibly have for believing that a certain particular not presented to us exemplifies certain characters. Since in the first two cases the particulars in Mp are all real, we had reasons for believing that the 'Mp' of the first case was true; that of the second case, false. For

---

[23] For the significance of such "checking," also in connection with the now fashionable idea of a criterion, see Essay Eleven, p. 238.

the 'Mp' of the third case we have no *such* reason for believing either that it is true or that it is false. Presently we shall see that there is an*other* reason for counting it as true.

The first two cases cover schematically all the perceptual errors of the kind called qualitative. In assaying them there is only one hurdle to overcome. One must recognize that possibilities exist. The third case covers schematically all the perceptual errors of the kind called existential. This is the recalcitrant case, the one which undid the classical realists (and to which I have as yet not attended). In assaying it adequately a second hurdle has to be overcome.[24] One must recognize that *some external particulars are not real*. The classical realists identified the external with the real, either because they did not make all the distinctions required or because they did not make them correctly. So they were undone.

The resistance against recognizing the *critical particulars* for what they are must have been very great. Its source is not hard to spot. On the one hand, these particulars are not mind-independent; on the other hand, they are external, i.e., they are "in" nonmental facts. That has an appearance of paradox which is a plausible source of the resistance. Notice that I called the critical particulars "not mind-independent" rather than "mind-dependent." As we use 'mind-independent', it stands for the one clear notion that goes by this name. But there are several ways in which entities may depend, or be thought to depend, on a mind. The thing to do, therefore, is to describe accurately and distinguish from all others the way in which a critical particular depends on the act which intends it. Then the appearance of paradox will disappear.

1. A classical substance "creates" its attributes. The created "depends" on its creator. An act (mind) may be thought to create its intentions. That makes the latter depend on the former. Since this use of 'create' is irremediably anthropomorphic, this notion of dependence remains blurred. I mention it nevertheless because, according to the idealists, a mind creates its intentions. An idealist thus need not deny that nonmental entities exist. He merely claims that, since they are mind-dependent, they are not real.

2a. Let 'A' and 'B' be the descriptions of two temporal cross sections (momentary states), at times t_1 and t_2 respectively, of a system that undergoes a process. Both A and B are facts, of course. B being the system's state at t_2 follows deductively from the law of the process in

[24] This is not to imply that the classical realists all overcame the first hurdle. Hardly any did.

conjunction with the premiss that A is its state at t_1. That makes the earlier of the two states a "cause" of the later; the later, an "effect" of the earlier.[25] An effect "depends" on its cause. Process laws are synthetic generalities.

2b. There are also cross-section laws; for instance, the laws connecting features within a cross section of a process; hence the name. The Pythagorean theorem is such a law. The synthetic *a priori* truth that everything colored is extended is another. The (parallelistic) connection between a conscious and a bodily state is a third. The facts in an instance of a cross-section law "depend" on each other. Cross-section laws, too, are synthetic generalities.

3. Let A and B be two facts such that '$A \supset B$' is a formal truth (analytic). 'A' logically implies 'B'. B "depends logically" on A. Process and cross-section laws being synthetic, neither 2a nor 2b are logical dependences. That makes it convenient to lump them together as two kinds of causal dependence (in a broad sense of 'causal').

Let now 'A' be an abbreviation of '$perceiving(b) \cdot \ulcorner B \urcorner (b)$'. The fact A is an act of perceiving; b, the awareness "in" it; B, its intention. The only connection between the two facts A and B is the formal fact $\ulcorner B \urcorner M B$. Hence, even if you identify the act (A) with the thought ($\ulcorner B \urcorner$) "in" it, the connection is not one of either logical or causal dependence. Since '$\ulcorner B \urcorner M B$' is analytic, B does not causally depend on A, even though, as in 2b, the awareness b is simultaneous with the particulars in B. Since '$\ulcorner B \urcorner M B$', even though it is analytic, is not a conditional, B cannot be deduced from either A or $\ulcorner B \urcorner$. Hence, B does not logically depend on A. The connection, we see, is *sui generis*.

Let B stand for 'a is white'. If a is real, there is no good reason for calling the connection a dependence of B on A. If anything, the occurrence of A depends causally, among other things, on B. If, however, a is the particular presented to me when I saw the ghost, then, if the act, i.e., my perceiving the ghost, did not exist, neither would a. This is a good reason for calling a as well as the fact of its being white mind-dependent. Only, this is a fourth kind of dependence which is unique in that it obtains only between *some* acts and their intentions. Also, it is in a certain sense mutual, as in 2b.

External particulars which are not real are mind-dependent.[26] Unless

---

[25] For a detailed analysis of the notions that appear in 2a and 2b, see the second chapter of *Philosophy of Science*.

[26] Suppose I imagine a dragon. Or suppose I have a memory image of a mermaid in Lake Michigan. In either case I am presented with critical particulars (i.e. particulars which are external but not real). Nor is there any good reason to believe that the particulars I am presented with in a true memory accompanied

some acts existed, they would not exist. There being such particulars is part of the intentional nature of mind. To see that there is nothing paradoxical about this one merely has to recognize the dependence for what it is. Then one will not be tempted to say of *any* act either that it creates its intention or that the latter either causally or logically depends on it.

A sentence represents a fact or a possibility (*p*-fact) depending on whether it is true or false, respectively. If you noticed that I just called the entity which in the case of the ghost is represented by '*a* is white' a fact, then you probably also remembered that I promised to give a reason why, in the absence of reasons from coherence, this sentence should be counted as true. This reason is negative, as it were. Since *a* is mind-dependent, i.e., since it would not exist unless it were presented, it is plausible, to say the least, that it does exemplify the characters with which it is presented. If you don't think this is a good reason, I shall merely say that, if you agree with the way in which I am resolving the classical dialectic in this essay, then it does not matter at all whether the Mp of the ghost case is a fact or a possibility. The reason I nevertheless try to convince you that one may at least plausibly hold it to be a fact is that this plausibility does matter, is indeed, as we shall see, of crucial importance in connection with the

---

by an image are "in" the ordinary object I remember. The conscious states which we "are" when we make a perceptual error of the kind called existential are not, we see, the only conscious states in which we are presented with critical particulars. As philosophers have used 'image', the conscious states of this sort are those in which we are presented with an "image." The word is dangerous, but it is also suggestive.

The adequate assay of perceptual errors of the kind called existential provides us with schemata for so assaying all conscious states in which we are presented with critical particulars that we can answer all the dialectical questions that have been asked about them. This is all that matters. Take a conscious state which is a fusion of three acts; one an act of remembering; one an act of perceiving "in" whose intention are critical particulars; the third an act of believing that the intentions of the first two resemble each other. I have little doubt that this fusion will do as a schema for rememberings accompanied by an image; and I have no doubt whatsoever that if it shouldn't, we have the means to construct another that will. Is the perceiving in this schema a perceiving$_1$ or a perceiving$_2$? Dialectically, what does it matter? If you are fascinated by such details you are in danger of getting lost in the wrong kind of phenomenology.

If there are sense data, of which more anon, then there are still other possibilities. In the above schema for rememberings accompanied by images, for instance, the perceiving could be replaced by sense data. Even the conscious state which I "am" when perceiving something could be a fusion of an act of perceiving with sense data. And so on.

so-called "infallibility of sense data" which is one of the pivots of the classical dialectic we must resolve.

The critical particulars are external and not real. A particular is external if and only if it exemplifies nonmental characters. It is not real if and only if it is not "in" a real ordinary object. Both criteria are contextual. The critical particulars are therefore not an ontological subkind (of the kind particular). Occam's razor is primarily a weapon against redundant ontological kinds. Yet, the resistance against the critical particulars is so strong that one should know how to defend them against attempts to excise them with the razor. I shall next examine one likely attempt.

A critic argues as follow: "First you made possibilities exist, which was bad enough. Now you insist that there are particulars of the kind you call critical, which crowds your world still more (although not, I grant, your categories). Why don't you at least make those particulars possibilities?" I answer that, as I explicate the ontological use of 'possible', a possible entity is essentially a complex. Take sentences, which of course represent complexes. To say that what a false sentence represents is an entity in the mode of possibility is merely another way of saying that its being well-formed has an ontological ground. So explicated, the ontological use of 'possible' makes sheer nonsense out of the expression 'possible particular'. Nor can I think of any explication that doesn't. But assume, for the sake of the argument, that there is one. Then actual and possible would be two ontological (sub-)kinds of particulars. Hence, there would have to be two subsistents such that whenever I am presented with a particular I am *eo ipso* presented with one and only one of these two subsistents. All I can say and all I need say is that I have never been presented with either. At this point the critic, who is eager to use the razor on something, tries to strike a bargain. If I permit him to excise the mode of possibility, he will let me have the critical particulars and permit me to make every well-formed sentence represent an actuality. I reject his proposal; refer him for my reasons to Essay Seven. Their gist is that the only way of doing what he proposes without being overcome by immediate dialectical disaster is Frege's.

Ordinary objects exist independently of the minds which may or may not perceive them. If you don't believe this truism you are mad. Believing it does not make you a realist. A realist is a philosopher who propounds an ontology which perspicuously reflects the truism. An ontology cannot be adequate unless it can be defended against all dialectical challenges. The recalcitrant case presents a challenge to the realist. If he fails to meet it, he may be driven to idealism. If he cannot stomach idealism, he must choose phenomenalism. (I ignore for the time being materialism, which is the only remaining alternative sufficiently articulate structurally as well as important historically to deserve serious consideration.) To the phenomenalist perception, including the recalcitrant case, causes no trouble. We must understand accurately why this is so.

The time has come to talk about sense data. Are there such entities? The question is controversial. I have long sided with those who take the affirmative. Nor do I now see any cogent reason to change sides. That, though, is entirely beside the point. The point, which I have not grasped accurately until recently even though fortunately I have sensed it for quite some time, is, rather, that *dialectically it makes no difference whatsoever whether or not there are sense data.* If one can show that, one can dismiss the question. Since I hope to show it, I put the question aside, start from another. *If* there are entities of the kind philosophers call sense data, *what* are they?

Everyone can make the shift from perceiving$_2$ to perceiving$_1$. Having made it, he is no longer presented with an ordinary object but with a molecular fact simultaneous with the awareness intending it. (This is an abbreviated way of speaking. Literally, no fact is in time; only the particulars "in" it are. Nor does either an act or the awareness "in" it literally intend anything; only thoughts do. But no harm will be done.) The molecular fact intended by a perceiving$_1$ (of mine) still presents the "idea of external existence." There is the *liséré* between it and the act which I "am." Or, to say the same thing still differently, this conscious state is what it is by virtue of the act of perceiving$_1$ which is "in" it. Whatever else may or may not be "in" it, the molecular fact, its intention, certainly is not.

To claim that there are sense data is to claim that, just as we can shift from perceiving$_2$ to perceiving$_1$, we can make a second shift, in the same direction, as it were, from perceiving$_1$. If you have made this shift, there is no longer an act "in" the conscious state which you "are." If the intention from which you shifted is Mp, call this conscious state $\overline{Mp}$. $\overline{Mp}$ is exactly like Mp. Only, the *liséré* has disappeared$_2$! This conscious state $\overline{Mp}$ is a sense datum.[27] One radical difference between such conscious states and all others is that there is no act "in" them. In

---

[27] This is not to say that all philosophers who use the expression use it consistently as it is here explicated. This is a very major source of trouble. Even G. E. Moore uses it so ambiguously that sometimes it stands on the same page once for an entity which is in the mind, once for one which isn't. The cause of this ambiguity, which is so unusual with him, is of course his overpowering urge toward that adequate realism at which, alas, he never arrived. See also fn. 50.

another respect they are like all others. A fact, we remember, is a conscious state only by virtue of a direct awareness which intends it but is not "in" it. A direct awareness which intends a sense datum is called a sensing. The criterion is contextual. Hence, sensing is not a species. When I am, as one says, sensing something, I "am" not the sensing but what I sense. This is only another way of stating the radical difference. But it is of course very easy to shift from a sense datum to a direct awareness of the sensing that makes it a conscious state.

There is still another radical difference between an $\overline{Mp}$ and all other conscious states. Call a fact intentional if and only if there is a thought "in" it. (The appropriateness of the word is, I trust, obvious.) All acts are intentional; all nonmental facts, nonintentional. So far I have proceeded as if all the atomic facts "in" a conscious state were intentional. Now we see that this is so only if there are no sense data. *Sense data are nonintentional facts "in" conscious states.*

The real does not coincide with the nonmental. The distinction proved crucial. We achieved it by starting from, and holding fast to, the hard-core meanings of 'mental' and 'nonmental'. Now we are ready for a second distinction of equal import. Are sense data mental? If we stay with the hard-core use, as of course we shall, the immediate answer is No. Those answering Yes get into trouble because they have without noticing it abandoned the hard-core use. Yet they try to express something which is important. I shall first provide ourselves with a safe way of expressing it, then show that it is important.

(1) An entity is *"in the mind"* if and only if it is "in" a state of consciousness. (2) An entity is "in the mind" if and only if it is the intention of a direct awareness which, depending on its intention, may or may not be a sensing. If you make (1) the explication of this use of 'in the mind', (2) becomes a very fundamental truth. If you make (2) the explication, (1) becomes the truth. I shall make no other use of 'in the mind'. Those who call sense data mental try to express that they are in minds. Speaking as accurately as one must if the classical dialectic is to be resolved, one sees that a *sense datum is a nonmental fact which is in a mind*. Every accurate terminology leads to some such clashes with the covertly philosophical way we often speak. To apologize for them is as foolish as it is for a soldier to be ashamed of his battle scars.

The entities in our minds are those which correspond parallelistically to brain states. They are never mentioned in the physical and biological sciences. They are those which interest the psychologist, who calls them "subjective." This is indeed the one clear use of 'subjective' I know. This not only shows the importance of the notion of being in a mind; it also shows how easily the notion is confused with that of being mental.

Are there sense data? To ask this question, we now see, is to ask another. Can we make the shift from perceiving₁ to (as one says) sensing which I mentioned when explaining *what* sense data are *if* there are any? Or, if you believe that you can make the shift, is it as clear and distinct as it would have to be if your Yes is to be completely unproblematic? The answer depends on phenomenological subtleties which belong to the wrong kind of phenomenology. Hence, if I am right about these subtleties, the answer is dialectically as irrelevant as that huge catalogue of all the subtleties of all ordinary uses which is now being dreamt of by the worshipers of the *Oxford English Dictionary*.

Are there sense data? In this century (and, alas, in my own thought) the question has been so important that I undertook here to demonstrate its dialectical irrelevance. To have shown that it belongs to a certain kind of questions, although encouraging, is not yet the demonstration itself but at best only its first step. Presently I shall take the others. Let us first attend to a historical situation.

With the rise of what now at Oxford passes for philosophy the battle against sense data grew fiercer and fiercer. Why all this sound? Why all this fury? The answer is as simple as it is ironic. Those who now attack sense data are all more or less explicit materialists. That is, they deny, more or less covertly, with or without bad intellectual conscience, that there are minds (conscious states). Sense data, we saw, are indeed problematic in that they are perhaps never as clearly and distinctly presented to us as are, on countless occasions, rocks, chairs, trees, and so on, which are all ordinary objects, as well as rememberings, perceivings, thinkings, and so on, which are all acts. Acts, that is, are not in the least problematic, whether or not sense data are. And if there are acts, there are minds. Why, then, have those who recently attacked mind by attacking sense data been so successful? Why have the defenders of sense data been so timid, even though they had at least the good sense to hang on to mind by hanging on to sense data? Once more, the answer is simple and ironic. The attackers and the defenders had both lost the act. That left them only the choice between (covert) materialism and (covert) phenomenalism. The attackers chose the former; the defenders, the latter. As a man grows older, if he believes that he has slowly been learning a few things, he becomes less and less certain even of what he believes to have learned well. Of this historical diagnosis, though, I am as certain as the child was when it exclaimed that the emperor wore no clothes.

As we agreed to use 'external', sense data being nonmental facts, the particulars in them are external. Yet they are in minds, or, to bring

out the potential verbal clash for once, they are "internal to minds."
You see again that when I asked you to agree on how to use certain
words, I ignored, quite deliberately, the complications due to sense
data. The adjective in 'external particular' was to remind us that the
intentions "in" which these particulars occur present us with the "idea
of external existence." Sense data don't present us with it. That makes
the clash so awkward that we must do something about it. Considering the way philosophers speak, the best thing to do is to introduce a
new word. That will kill two birds with one stone by explicating the
relevant use of the new word as well as spotting the verbal sources of
certain confusions. Call a thing (particular or simple character) *phenomenal* if and only if it is in a mind, i.e., to repeat, if it is "in" a
conscious state.[28] Call a fact phenomenal if and only if all the simples in
it are phenomenal. Now we can without danger of confusion say such
things as that the particulars "in" sense data are phenomenal (and
external); that the (external) particulars in the intentions of all indirect acquaintance are nonphenomenal; that if there are no sense
data,[29] then all external particulars are nonphenomenal; that acts are
intentional phenomenal facts; sense data, nonintentional phenomenal
facts; and so on. The criterion for being a phenomenal entity is contextual. Hence, *phenomenal is not an ontological category.* That alone
shows that 'phenomenal' and 'mental' do not stand for the same. Yet
philosophers have used the two words as if they did.[30]

What is a mind (Self)? Whenever there is a mind, there is a temporal
series of conscious states which are in certain ways connected among
themselves as well as (parallelistically) with a body. E.g., some are
memories of some others. Conversely, whenever there is such a series,
there is a mind. That much is obvious. If it weren't, I wouldn't know
what 'mind' means. Are a mind and the series which belongs to it two
or are they one? Since there are no substances in my world, I agree
with those who hold that they are one. But it makes no difference for
what follows if we are wrong.

There are countless ordinary objects such that the particulars "in"

[28] Some philosophers use 'experience' as I use 'conscious state'. But the word
has been batted about so irresponsibly that, since it is expendable, I avoid it.

[29] I ignore, as throughout this essay, certain phenomenal things and facts
which the classical psychologists from James Mill to Wundt, taking their cue
from the phenomenalists, called *affective*. These facts are "like sense data"; most
importantly, they are molecular and nonintentional. See fn. 33.

[30] If so much "mere terminology" bores or even irritates you, let me remind
you that to build, check, and recheck in this way a terminology that starts
from the hard core is to track down the blurs and ambiguities which lead to the
philosophical uses.

them which are simultaneous with my writing this line are not "in" the intention of any act and therefore, *a fortiori*, not in any mind.[31] If all minds now ceased to exist, ordinary objects would not cease to exist. There were such objects before any minds existed. *Ordinary objects are not phenomenal entities.* The table I now perceive, for instance, is not in my mind. Nor is it in any other.

All phenomenalists claim that *all things are phenomenal.* Hence, they must consistently deny that ordinary objects exist. That distinguishes them from the idealists who, we saw, need only claim that, being mind-dependent, ordinary objects, though existents, are not real.[32] *Typically,* phenomenalists also claim that *there are no intentional entities,* or, equivalently, that all phenomenal facts are either sense data or "like sense data."[33] Both claims are absurd. Each suffices to dismiss phenomenalism. But it will pay if we first attend to three questions. How do phenomenalists assay the conscious state I "am" when perceiving a table? How do they account for the "idea of external existence"? How do they assay perceptual error?

First. The phenomenalists and the classical psychologists who took their cue from them all rely on analytic introspection. To introspect a conscious state analytically is not to inspect it but, rather, to produce under a special set a series of other such states. The idea is that the original state is uniquely determined by the series, and that, being so determined, it is a fusion of states exactly like those in the series and of *nothing else.* If you state this idea as of course a typical phenomenalist wouldn't, in terms of intentions, replacing the original state by the intention of an original act, the series by the intentions of a series of acts, then, taken as a structural possibility the idea is not at all unreasonable. Yet it cannot be realized.

Take my perceiving the table. Its intention, we know, is $Mp \cdot Op$. That makes $\overline{Mp}$ the obvious candidate for the first member of the series. $\overline{Mp}$, you remember, is exactly like Mp except that it is a phenomenal fact. Unfortunately $\overline{Mp}$ does not uniquely determine the

---

[31] I put it this way, in terms of particulars, partly because of the old gambit that those countless objects are at this very moment intended by a thought of mine. The intention of ⌜There are tables⌝ is $(\exists x_1) \ldots (\exists x_n) \, Table \, (x_1, \ldots, x_n)$ and contains no particulars! See fn. 18.

[32] That this way of drawing the line between idealists and phenomenalists also makes sense historically is shown by the case of Berkeley, whom it puts with the idealists, since for him an ordinary object is a cluster of universals which, though it exists, depends on a substantial mind to exemplify it. See E. B. Allaire, "Berkeley's Idealism," *Theoria*, 29, 1963, 1–16.

[33] See fn. 29.

original state. If it did, what would be the difference between my perceiving the table on the one hand and my thinking of it, in case the thought is accompanied by an image on the other? The many futile attempts at overcoming the difficulty all lie between two extremes. At one extreme, one adds to $\overline{Mp}$ a huge class of other sense data, which the mind supposedly produces by association, including all those, past, present, and future, that might be caused or might have been caused by the table. This is the absurd "solution" of James Mill. At the other extreme, one adds to $\overline{Mp}$ a series of alleged phenomenal entities which, whatever they may be called, structurally are like $\overline{Op}$. Psychologists may want to call some of them expectations. The trouble with this "solution" is that sense data are essentially molecular facts. Thus, even if there were such entities, they would not be "like sense data" but, if anything, like acts.[34]

Second. When perceiving something, I "am" the perceiving. When sensing something, I "am" not the sensing but the sensed. Sense data (if there are any) are not perceived. When perceiving either the table or the ghost, I am presented with the "idea of external existence." Yet the table is real; the ghost is not. To be real (mind-independent) and to present (if presented at all) the "idea of external existence" are two and not one. This is one of the crucial distinctions we have achieved. Phenomenalists cannot make it, must compound the two notions into a single one, which therefore remains blurred. In the next paragraph, 'idea of external existence' stands for this compound.

If the intentions of my perceivings cohere, so do the sense data which, if the phenomenalists were right, these perceivings would be. The inadequacy of the phenomenalists' assay of perceiving does not, we see, prevent them from utilizing the notion of coherence. They do in fact take full advantage of it, which permits them to explain how we come by the "idea of external existence."[35] To say that this table is an external existent (or, synonymously for them, that it is real or mind-independent) is, according to them, to say no more nor less than that the sense data which, as we would say, are caused by the table, cohere. Hence, if our perceivings did not cohere we would not, according to the phenomenalists, have the "idea of external existence." Contrast that with what has been said earlier (p. 311).

Third. We know the two hurdles the realist has to overcome in his

---

[34] All this is very succinct, selective, and allusive. There is of course much more to be said, some of which is quite interesting as well as instructive. But why flog dead horses? For some details, see the essay on "The Problem of Relations in Classical Psychology" in *The Metaphysics of Logical Positivism.*

[35] I do not ask the embarrassing question what a sense-data assay of the "idea" itself would be like.

assay of perceptual error. There is the real particular exemplifying one character (e.g., round) which is presented as exemplifying another (e.g., oval). This was our second case. There is also the (nonphenomenal) external particular which is not real. This critical particular, though, may plausibly be believed to exemplify the characters it is presented as exemplifying. Or, if you prefer it that way, neither the belief that it does exemplify them nor the belief that it doesn't will ever conflict with beliefs based on coherence (p. 323). This was our third case, the recalcitrant one.

The phenomenalist in his assay of perceptual error encounters no hurdles. *For one*, he believes that all the particulars presented to him are in the mind; hence none can be critical. (In a world without acts nothing could be literally "presented." It would therefore be more accurate to say that a phenomenalist would hold this belief if he could consistently speak of anything being presented to him. But I shall continue to take advantage of the word.) *For another*, the phenomenalist has no reason to believe that any particular does not exemplify the characters it is presented as exemplifying. In the third case that follows from what has been said about the critical particulars. In the second case, one merely has to remember that the psychological laws (clause (3), p. 317) which enter into the notion of coherence explain why our sense data are what they are or, as one says, why they are what they seem.

A sense datum is indeed what it seems (is presented as). Many consider that as much a part of the notion of a sense datum as its being in a mind. This is the famous *infallibility of sense data*. I have no quarrel with the notion, merely add two comments. 1. If being infallible is made part of the notion, then of course sense data are infallible. Necessarily so, as one says, but also trivially so. The only question that remains is whether there are sense data. As I introduced the notion, infallibility is not a part of it. 2. To say that sense data, as I introduced the notion, are in fact infallible is, we just saw, but another way of saying that our perceivings cohere. And coherence we know to be a fact which, however sweeping and reliable it may be, partakes in principle of the openness of induction.

I am about ready for a comment in structural history which, however, will be more convincing if we first glance at a world in which there are not only sense data but also acts. This is the world of the atypical phenomenalist. Acts and sense data are the two kinds of fact "in" the intentions of direct awareness.[36] This, though, is not the only feature

[36] That ignores the great binder of the mental and the nonmental, time. An awareness and a particular in a sense datum being simultaneous is a phenomenal fact. But no harm will be done.

they share. Acts, too, are infallible in exactly the same sense in which sense data are! Coherence sometimes leads us to believe that we perceived erroneously or remembered falsely. But the perceiving itself and the remembering itself can always be accommodated in the pattern which coherence imposes upon the world of the atypical phenomenalist.

"Perception is fallible." The formula can stand for the skeptical critique of perception whose revival heralded the Cartesian revolution. "A mind can only know what is in it." The survival of this Aristotelian-Thomistic formula was a major cause of the drift away from realism, toward either idealism or phenomenalism, which began at the time of the revolution. Acts and sense data are in the mind. Acts and sense data are infallible. Phenomenalism, including atypical phenomenalism,[37] satisfies the intellectual needs represented by the two formulae. Structurally, that accounts for two of its major strengths. Historically, it stands to reason that these two major strengths of phenomenalism are also among the major causes of its rise.

The time from the Cartesian revolution to the present is also, alas, the age of epistemologism. Phenomenalism has a third feature which in that age became its third major strength and therefore, plausibly, the third major cause of its rise. Aphoristically and a bit paradoxically, it can be stated in one sentence: *The phenomenalists discovered the right ontological assay of ordinary objects.* We must next unpack the aphorism.

(1) An ordinary object is a temporal succession of particulars each of which exemplifies certain nonmental properties and stands in certain nonmental relations to all others. That makes 'table' a very complex character (p. 313). (2) The intention of my perceiving the table is $Mp \cdot Op$. (3) There are no substances nor even continuants. (4) The right assay of causation is Humean in style. (1) is the right assay of ordinary objects. (1) and (2) entail each other. The structural connections between any two of these four propositions are very close. We need not on this occasion inquire what entails what. That these propositions are true is of course not argued but assumed in this essay. But it should perhaps be said that I call an assay *the* right one only if I believe that it is the only one compatible with an adequate ontology.

[37] As I read Descartes, the hard-core base from which he tried to arrive at realism was indeed atypical phenomenalism. That is why he couldn't be certain that an entity existed unless it was presented to him in immediate awareness and why, therefore, since his concern was, classically, with acts and not at all with sense data, which are a later discovery, he fastened on a species, *cogitare.* The inference from *cogitare* to *ens cogitans* is a different matter. It rests on the old ontology of substance and attribute which only the later British critique showed not to be the "truth of reason" for which Descartes still mistook it. But I do not pretend to be a scholar. That is why I said: "as I read Descartes." See also fn. 4.

Return to the phenomenalists. Nothing will be lost if we let them all be represented by those who propose $\overline{Mp \cdot Op}$ as the assay of the act which I "am" when perceiving the table. As an assay of the act that is hopelessly wrong. But one merely has to remove the bars in order to obtain the right assay of its intention. So we must ask: What does it mean either to add or to remove the bars? If 'a' stands for a particular, '$\bar{a}$' stands for one that is phenomenal. If 'f_1' stands for a color, '$\bar{f}_1(\bar{a})$' stands for a phenomenal fact.[38] '$\overline{S}$' is obtained from 'S' by putting bars over all names[39] in it. If one removes the bars from '$\overline{Mp \cdot Op}$', one therefore merely drops the claim that ordinary objects are phenomenal entities. Everything else, as far as these objects are concerned, remains unchanged. *Structurally*, that unpacks the aphorism. In their peculiar way, the phenomenalists did discover the right assay of ordinary objects.

Historically, the credit for the discovery does not belong to the phenomenalists alone but, rather, to the succession from Locke to Hume, the movement of thought known as British Empiricism. But there are three reasons why the synecdoche does not go beyond what may pass in an aphorism. For one, the whole movement is under the spell of the formula that a mind can only know what is in it. For another, Locke's critique of such "abstract" entities (ideas) as substance and of the alleged truths of reason in which they occur could not but spread to powers (causes). Nor, thirdly, did anyone understand that there can be acts in a world without powers.[40] These three reasons make typical phenomenalism the inevitable consummation of the movement.

'Empiricism' is now used so broadly and so vaguely, so often merely honorifically or ideologically, that the word has lost all its savor. Originally, it stood for two important ideas, a specific thesis and an attitude. The *empiricist thesis* asserts that all our knowledge of ordinary objects comes to us through the senses. The *empiricist attitude* demands that all "abstract" entities as well as the alleged truths of reason in which they occur be securely grounded in what is presented to us.

---

[38] As you see, it would not be necessary to put the bar over the names of universals. This is the strongest structural reason against there being sense data. But it is far from cogent. If you wonder what sense it makes to speak of structural reasons in matters of fact, I shall remind you that the "facts" of the wrong kind of phenomenology are peculiarly elusive.

[39] I.e., about the marks representing either particulars or simple characters. That presupposes that 'S' contains no defined descriptive terms. The connectives and operators are constituents of the world's form. Phenomenal-nonphenomenal is a dichotomy among the world's things.

[40] The argument for this compatibility is one of the major burdens of Essay One.

The thesis and the attitude are the two cornerstones of every epistemology worthy of the name. During the reign of epistemologism their
combined strength was at least as great, if not greater, than that of any
other force which shaped the classical dialectic. Thomas, I take it,
upheld the empiricist thesis. So did Leibniz. *Nihil est in intellectu quod
non prius fuerit in sensu.* The famous qualification, *nisi intellectus ipse,*
merely safeguards the act. Yet the men in the British succession were
the only ones to embrace vigorously both thesis and attitude. Recalling
the close connections among the propositions (1), (2), (3), (4), you will
see that the phenomenalists' assay of ordinary objects involves them
both. That makes the peculiar "rightness" of this assay their third
major strength.

Are there sense data? I promised to demonstrate that dialectically it
makes no difference whether the answer is Yes or No. If you have for-
gotten that promise, let me remind you of it. If you haven't, perhaps
you still wait for the demonstration. In case you do, let me present you
with three propositions which, if true, jointly are this demonstration.
The first is obvious. The other two I believe to have demonstrated.
First. In case there are no sense data, phenomenalism is sheer nonsense. Second. In case there are sense data, it is absurdly false; atypical
phenomenalism because ordinary objects are not phenomenal entities;
typical phenomenalism also because there are acts. Third. In either
case, the phenomenalist assay of ordinary objects becomes the right
one if the particulars it mentions are taken to be nonphenomenal entities. The first two propositions are the destructive part of the demonstration; the third is the constructive part.

Are ordinary objects phenomenal entities? Some tell us that we must
not ask the question. Nor must we ask whether there are sense data.
Both questions are "metaphysical" and therefore "meaningless." The
right question to ask instead is: Can one in principle talk about ordinary objects in a sense-data language? The answer, we are told, is Yes.
This "linguistic" defense of sense data against the recent attacks by the
ordinary-language philosophers surely is the weakest and meekest of
all. One can and one must explicate the relevant use of 'phenomenal'
and 'sense data'. Then both questions—Are ordinary objects phenomenal entities? Are there sense data?—become factual. The only
thing peculiar about the second is the peculiar elusiveness of the wrong
kind of phenomenology. The linguistic defense, we see, is not only
weak and meek; it is completely futile. Yet there is an idea behind it.

A schema is an ideal language if and only if (1) everything can in
principle be said *in* it, and (2) all philosophical problems can be solved
by talking commonsensically *about* it. Both (1) and (2) are familiar;
both need unpacking; but we need not unpack them once more. I

merely restate them in a way that suits the immediate purpose. (1′) There is a "coordination" of a certain kind between certain sentences of the language we actually speak on the one hand and the formulae of the schema into which these sentences are said to be "transcribed" on the other. (2′) The schema perspicuously reflects an adequate ontology.

In a schema that contains such expressions as '$Mp \cdot Op$' everything about ordinary objects can in principle be said. Thus it *partially* satisfies (1). Such a schema is called a *sense-data language* if and only if (a) it contains no names for mental characters (species and thoughts) and neither 'M' nor the corners ($^\ulcorner \ldots ^\urcorner$); and, (b) its names all stand for phenomenal entities. To restate (b), making use of an earlier device, the bars have been added to the names in the schema. But, then, either adding or removing the bars obviously does not affect the possibility of a "coordination" of the kind mentioned in (1′). That shows the peculiar way in which everything about ordinary objects can be said in a sense-data language. Not surprisingly this peculiar way corresponds exactly to the peculiar way in which the phenomenalists' assay of ordinary objects is right. A sense-data language also *partially* satisfies (2). One can by talking commonsensically about it solve many philosophical problems. Many, but not all. To see that at a glance, switch from (2) to (2′). In the ontology the schema perspicuously represents there are neither acts nor nonphenomenal particulars.

The last paragraph merely restates in the "linguistic way" what we knew already. Yet this recourse to artificial languages serves two purposes. For one, ironically, it shows that if one wants to demonstrate the complete futility of the "linguistic" defense of sense data, one merely has to state it, *correctly*, in the "linguistic way." For another, it provides the cue for attending to some unfinished business.

The schema which until now I claimed to be the ideal language reflects perspicuously the ontology of atypical phenomenalism.[41] That makes

---

[41] Or, to say the same thing differently, I insisted for the names of the ideal schema on the *Principle of Direct Acquaintance*. The principle implicit in this essay is one of *Presentation*. Making it explicit is hardly worth the trouble. Another point, though, deserves unpacking (or, more accurately, rehearsing).

Since the obeisance I have paid to the incomplete schema has been a rather empty gesture for quite some time, it did no harm. But, then, the emptiness of this ritual was not just a piece of good luck. Or, if it was, there is a lesson in it. The fundamental dualism is intentional-nonintentional. Compared with it, the dualism between what is and what is not in minds is shallow. That is the way the lesson is put in the opening essay. Within minds "in" which there are acts, sense data are an adequate model of what is not in any mind. That is the way the lesson is put in Essay Six. *Structurally one is a realist if one knows how to assay the act.* That is the way the same point is made, concisely, in the second paragraph of this essay.

it adequate in all respects but one. Hence it is incomplete and cannot be the ideal language. I now complete it by adding to it names for non-phenomenal particulars. Whether or not names for phenomenal particulars which are not awarenesses (i.e., for particulars in sense data) are retained makes no dialectical difference. Thus I get rid of that last piece of phenomenalist dross which is mentioned in the second paragraph of this essay. I also understand now, in retrospect, why this last step took so long. One cannot make it unless he has first purged his thought from the last taint of epistemologism. For one who comes from where I started this is very difficult.[42]

Unlike idealism and phenomenalism, *materialism*, the last of the four classical ontologies, is not only absurd but also very dull. Yet, since we have assembled all the tools and since it will not take long, we might as well render materialism a service by distinguishing what is absurd in it from what *very probably* is true. We shall be rewarded by a clear view of an instructive similarity between idealism and phenomenalism on the one hand and what passes *wrongly* for two variants of an ontological position on the other.

Phenomenalists claim that ordinary objects do not exist. Idealists merely claim that these objects, though existents, since they are mind-dependent, are not real. Materialists$_1$ claim that minds (conscious states) do not exist. Materialists$_2$ merely claim that minds, though existents, since they are body-dependent, are not real. Or, rather, this is how they would put their claim if they understood the significant use of the key words. In this case, their use of 'real' would be a mirror image of ours. In this mirror, materialism$_1$ corresponds to phenomenalism; materialism$_2$, to idealism.

Materialism$_1$ (metaphysical materialism) is an absurd ontology. Materialism$_2$ (scientific materialism) is not really an ontological position but merely the best scientific truth available. Science is not ontology. (That is why, in the paragraph which precedes the last, 'wrongly' is italicized.) In a familiar sense, no scientific truth is more than very probable, least of all one as sweeping as the truth in question which, because of its sweep, I would rather call a frame of reference. (That is why, in the same paragraph, 'very probably' is italicized.) Yet, we have no good reason to doubt this frame of reference. Philosophers who

---

[42] There are now many among us who have come by their ontologism very easily. Mostly they derive it from the later Husserl. Tomorrow they shall perhaps derive it from the later Wittgenstein. Such ontologism, alas, is merely the battle cry of the latest rebellion against dialectical discipline in general and epistemological discipline in particular. Looking at this spectacle, I remember with a very warm feeling the debt of gratitude which I owe to the logical positivists.

pin their hopes on its collapse are merely quixotic. Good philosophers take the world as they find it.

The word 'real' which I used, deliberately of course, promotes the illusion that the claim of scientific materialism is ontological. Without that word, the claim is simply that minds depend on bodies. That is what both common sense and its long arm, science, tell us. The dependence is of the kind 2b, parallelistic. There is of course much more to be said. This is the dialectic of the mind-body problem, which requires and deserves a book of its own.[43]

Materialism$_1$ and phenomenalism are mirror images of each other. How could one who insists on taking the "linguistic way" express this feature? The answer is again instructive. Just as in principle one can say everything about ordinary objects in a sense-data language, so one can, *if parallelism is true*, in principle say everything about minds in what the logical positivists call a thing language, i.e., in a schema without names for phenomenal entities. Smith perceives a table. He is in this conscious state if and only if his body exemplifies a very complex property which, being nonphenomenal, can be represented by an equally complex predicative expression of the thing language.[44] *'Being in the (bodily) state-of-perceiving-a-table'* may be introduced into this language as a definitional abbreviation for that predicative expression. Having provided yourself with a sufficiency of such definitions, you can *after a fashion* say everything about minds in a thing language, just as one can say everything about ordinary objects in a sense-data language. Yet there are two differences. That is why I say after a fashion.

First. The phenomenalist can in his way say everything about ordinary objects because he discovered (what I believe is) the right assay of them. Whether or not this assay is in fact right is an *ontological* question. The materialist can in his way say everything about minds because (as I believe) parallelism is true. Whether or not parallelism is in fact true is a *scientific* question. Second. The phenomenalist, having introduced his definitions,[45] can in the sense-data language say 'This is a table'. After the materialist has introduced his definitions, he cannot

---

[43] A very large part of this dialectic belongs to the philosophy of psychology about which I have already said many things. Some of these things I can now say more simply; some others, more accurately; still others should be added. Perhaps I shall be able to undertake this task.

[44] Very probably, the (perceptual) thing language must for this purpose be supplemented by that of physics. This, though, makes no difference for the argument. For the distinction perceptual-physical, see the next paragraphs.

[45] See fn. 18.

in the thing language say 'Smith perceives a table' but merely 'Smith's body is in the state-of-perceiving-a-table', where the hyphens indicate that there are no substitutions *salva veritate* for any of the words in the phrase. If this were not so, one could transcribe an intentional context into an extensional language.[46]

These two differences alone will convince any philosopher that dialectically materialism is very dull. That is why, if faced with the unhappy choice between phenomenalism and materialism, as I was when I started, he will choose phenomenalism. Materialism, alas, is a philosophy for nonphilosophers. That is why scientism has undone so many.

We are ready for the last turn of the dialectical screw. It starts from the distinction between *perceptual* and *physical* objects. Until now I deliberately avoided both words. To be an ordinary object and to be a perceptual object is one and the same. Science (physics) *replaces* the perceptual object by the physical object. This is a long story. It is told in Essay Six. So I merely recall its gist.

The table I perceive is colored. The physical table lost its color at the time of Descartes.[47] This, though, was only the beginning. By now, as I understand the quantum theory,[48] there is not even space in "physical reality." To find out what physical reality is like is the scientists' business. Our concern is merely with their use of 'real' and its derivatives.

Science *replaces* the perceptual object by the physical object. To appreciate the import of the italicized prefix, introduce 'reconstruct'. Science reconstructs the perceptual object. One cannot replace or reconstruct what is not there. According to the phenomenalists, the perceptual object, which is not there, is a construction out of sense data. According to the "positivistic" analysis of physical theory, the physical object is a construction out of perceptual objects. If you accept both views, phenomenalism and the "positivistic" analysis of physical theory, then the physical object, too, is merely a construction out of sense data and not, as I hold, a reconstruction of the perceptual object. That explains the affinity between those two views.

[46] See Reinhardt Grossmann, "Propositional Attitudes," *The Philosophical Quarterly*, 10, 1960, 301–12; also the essay on "Sameness, Meaning, and Identity" in *Meaning and Existence* and May Brodbeck, "Meaning and Action," *Philosophy of Science*, 30, 1963.

[47] The historical (causal) connection between the rise of science, that of epistemologism, and the Cartesian revolution is plausible, to say the least.

[48] I.e., there is no physical space if the entities of quantum mechanics are taken to be physical reality. About this feature of the scientists' use of 'real', see "The Logic of Quanta," reprinted in H. Feigl and May Brodbeck, *Readings in the Philosophy of Science* (Appleton Century Crofts, 1953).

Perceptual objects present us with the two ideas of external existence and reality (mind-independence).[49] *Only because we are thus provided with these two ideas, can we combine them with that of the physical object.* Scientists use 'real' as if to be real, to be an existent not in a mind, and to be a physical entity were one and the same. Within science, the ambiguity does no harm. In ontology it leads to disaster.

We do not know physical objects in the sense in which we know perceptual ones. The gap is as unbridgeable as that between that mythical entity, the "percept" of representative realism, and the entity it allegedly "represents." It is indeed the fatal weakness of representative realism that it displaces this gap between the perceptual and the physical object, puts it between the mind and the perceptual object, and then tinkers with the latter in order to resolve the dialectic of perception. Just think of G. E. Moore who considered, seriously even though reluctantly, such "Pickwickian" possibilities as the coin being a bundle of sense data,[50] round, oval, and so on, from which the perceiving mind selects one. This kind of tinkering is the business of science, not of philosophy. The proper place for it is the gap, which is in the nature of things, between the perceptual and the physical object rather than the alleged gap between a mind and what it perceives.

For the scientist there is nothing not in minds which is literally the color of the perceptual object. As for colors, so for all nonmental characters. That makes the perceptual object "mind-dependent" in what, where and when I grew up, they called *das Weltbild der Wissenschaft.* This "picture" is not an ontology. *Ontology is phenomenological. The rest is merely science. Such is the nature and such are the limits of human knowledge.*

We can of course think of physical entities. Such thoughts may be accompanied by "images" of all kinds. Yet they remain peculiarly "abstract." For instance, we are never presented with a physical entity in a manner allowing us to name it. Nor is that the only striking peculiarity of such thought. *Inaccurately,* one may express them all by saying that there is no intentional tie between a physical entity and the

[49] This is not to deny what we know to be of strategic importance, that a single act of indirect awareness presents us with the "idea of external existence." But, then, perceptual objects are of course very prominent among those which do present us with this idea.

[50] These are of course the passages in which Moore's "sense data" are not in minds, which merely increases the confusion even though it also shows his sound distrust of representative realism. See fn. 27. The rejection of representative realism is, quite probably, the sound core of the ordinary-language philosophers' attack on sense data. If so, why don't they say so? Representative realism and the existence of sense data do not, in spite of the historical connections, entail each other. And philosophy, I submit, is still the dialectical art of distinction.

thought which intends it. Imagine now an ontologist who, while not a materialist₁, is yet so preoccupied with science that in his world all things are either phenomenal or physical. In such a world, we just saw by means of a deliberate inaccuracy, the intentional tie is easily lost sight of. If this tie is lost (and the Aristotelian-Thomistic assay of perception seems no longer viable), then, we know, realism is lost. Our ontologist will eventually become either an idealist or a phenomenalist or, if he has the stomach for it, a materialist.

At the time of the Cartesian revolution, when the trend toward epistemologism and away from realism began, philosophy found itself in the situation of the ontologist whom I just asked you to imagine. Dialectically that closes the circle. Such closure is encouraging. The cross of the realism-idealism issue may be lifted off our shoulders. The reign of epistemologism may be drawing to a close.

Ontology, I said, is phenomenological. The rest is merely science. Such is the nature and such are the limits of human knowledge. I do not want these sentences to be misunderstood. There is now a rising wave of talk about the *Lebenswelt*. What is true in this talk is not philosophical; what is philosophical in it is not true; the bulk of it is a mixture, *à la française*, of ignorance, antiscience, and mediocre literature. Today it is supported by the spurious authority of the later Husserl, tomorrow perhaps by the equally spurious one of the later Wittgenstein. Any similarity between this sort of talk and the sentences I do not want to be misunderstood is purely incidental, just as I did not endorse either scientism or philosophical behaviorism or any other kind of materialism when I gave science its due. Philosophy, I also said, takes the world as it finds it. The most likely present threat to first philosophy is an unholy alliance among those who now propound these two opposite kinds of error. But, then, first philosophy, the fundamental dialectic, never attracted any but the happy few. Thus its position has always been precarious. There is no more cause for alarm than usual.

Having said that much, I shall say one more thing in order to forestall another misunderstanding. The largest group of contemporary philosophers who stand against that likely threat are the heirs of Thomas and Aristotle. With them I share the realism and the recognition of the act. Yet, fundamental as these two agreements are, they are but two islands in a sea of disagreement. *Der Starke ist am maechtigsten allein.*

AUTHOR'S NOTE

The papers previously published appeared as follows:

I   (a) "Dell'Atto" in *Rivista di Filosofia*, 51, 1960, 3–51.
    (b) "Acts" in *The Indian Journal of Philosophy*, 2, 1960, 1–30 and 96–117.

II   "Ineffability, Ontology, and Method" in *The Philosophical Review*, 69, 1960, 18–40.

III   "Generality and Existence" in *Theoria*, 28, 1962, 1–26.

IV   as the first of two essays under the joined title "Meaning and Ontology" in *Inquiry*, 5, 1962, 116–42.

V   "Duration and the Specious Present" in *Philosophy of Science*, 27, 1960, 39–47.

VI   "Physics and Ontology" in *Philosophy of Science*, 28, 1961, 1–14.

VII   "Alternative Ontologiche" in *Giornale Critico della Filosofia Italiana*, 17, 1963.

VIII   as the second of two essays under the joined title "Meaning and Ontology" in *Inquiry*, 5, 1962, 116–42.

IX   "Strawson's Ontology" in *The Journal of Philosophy*, 57, 1960, 601–22.

X   "The Ontology of Edmund Husserl" in *Methodos*, 12, 1960, 359–92.

XI   "La Gloria e la Miseria di Ludwig Wittgenstein" in *Rivista di Filosofia*, 52, 1961, 387–406.

XII   "Stenius on the *Tractatus*" in *Theoria*, 29, 1963, 176–204.

Index

Acquaintance: direct, 5, 11, 14, 29, 37, 38, 41, 118, 219–20, 227, 307, 309, 326, 331; and sensing, 5, 11, 27, 37, 40–41, 110; principle of, 14, 15, 16, 19, 38, 40, 41, 45–46, 110, 217–18, 335n; with acts, 28, 29, 36, 38, 40, 110, 238, 309; and perception, 40–41, 110–11, 113, 118, 217, 227, 309; explicated, 110, 309; and causality, 115; and existents, 218; and mental, 307; indirect, 309–10. *See also* Presented

Acts, mental, Essay I 3–44; species of, 4–5, 31–32, 35–36, 93, 126, 134, 136, 163, 208, 234–35, 263, 298, 308–10, 318n, 326; and content, 5, 12, 34; intentions of, 11, 16, 19–20, 22–23, 26, 30, 33, 93–95, 126–28, 234–36, 263, 267–71, 323; analysis of, 12, 18, 20, 24, 31–33, 93–95, 126–28, 134, 136, 208, 234–36, 263, 270; and science, 22, 25; and relations, 24–26, 31, 34, 39, 95, 163–64, 169–70, 265; and substances, 24, 34, 235; Aristotelian account of, 26, 34, 235, 263–65, 304–5, 340; and conscious states, 27–29, 35–36, 38–44, 214, 267, 308–9, 325–26; presented, 28, 29, 36, 38, 40, 110, 119, 327; and time, 29–30, 105, 238; and realism, 35, 126, 163, 264, 302, 307, 318n, 335n, 340; and judgments, 136, 138–45; and logic, 152–53; and Husserl, 193, 194, 205, 209–14, 240–41, 301, 309. *See also* Intentional nexus; Intentions of acts

Actuality, 306, 308, 313

Adequation of thought, 130–31, 149

Affective elements, 219n, 222, 328n

Allaire, E. B., viii, 98n, 112n, 145n, 162n, 191, 203n, 230n, 233n, 243, 272n, 295n, 302n, 329n

Analyticity: and world's form, 10, 53, 56–57, 113, 135, 136, 157n, 228; commonsense core of, 33; and definitions, 80, 113, 183; and quasirelations, 116; and necessity, 251, 255–56; and *a priori* truth, 272, 300–1. *See also* Form; Truth

Aquinas, Thomas, 26, 34, 61, 119n, 126, 133, 165, 235, 304–5, 340

Aristotle, 23, 26, 34, 115, 119n, 125, 126, 133, 149, 150, 151, 152, 156, 181, 188, 207, 213, 235, 277, 304–5, 340

Arithmetic, 84, 97, 106, 239

Atoms. *See* Particles of physics

Augustine, 284

Awareness, awarenesses: as propositional, 12, 35, 127, 130, 140, 223, 267, 314; ingredients of acts, 24, 31, 34, 36, 134, 136, 308; are individuals, 24, 31, 44, 134, 214, 238, 298, 301, 308; characters exemplified by, 31–32, 34, 42; and time, 44, 105, 238; as phenomenal, 117–19, 208; and identity, 148. *See also* Acquaintance; Acts

Begriffsschrift, 134, 137, 146

Behaviorism, 27, 152, 191, 237, 238, 267, 336–37, 340

Berkeley, G., 42, 131, 329n

Bradley, F. H., and exemplification

88; represents, 49–50, 51–54, 61–63, 81–82; vs. "things," 51, 52–53, 54, 99, 111; uses of term, 51, 52, 54, 56, 80, 111, 228, 283; presented, 52, 56, 62, 65, 230, 240; and picture theory, 54–55, 255–63; and simplicity, 80–82, 96, 112; and thought, 157, 235–36, 240. *See also* Logical

Formalism, 19, 172, 283, 293

Frege, G., Essay VII 124–57; his ontology, 61, 136n, 138–49, 259; and facts, 61, 136n, 141–42, 146–48, 250, 259; and implicit definitions, 116; his *Begriffsschrift*, Essay VII 124–57 *passim;* and nominalism, 124, 140, 250; and idealism, 124–25, 145, 148–49, 153; and realism, 125, 135n, 139, 149; and subsistents, 130, 140, 249–50; his "senses," 135n, 139–40, 142–45, 154, 163, 324; and thoughts, 135n, 138–39, 142, 154, 155; and intentionality, 135n; and psychologism, 138, 142n, 154; and judgment, 138–39, 144, 154; and True, 139–43, 145–48, 164, 250, 259; his functions, 139, 142, 145, 147, 154–55, 189, 190, 250, 259; his semantics, 143,146, 155; and identity, 144n, 146, 147n; his logic, 151–52, 155; and Wittgenstein, 230, 257, 259

Fundamental ties: and complexes, 81, 129, 134, 244–63; notion explicated, 87, 159, 197, 229, 244; of exemplification, 87, 134, 160, 161, 199, 230, 245, 253–55, 275; of intentional meaning, 95, 208–10, 234–36, 270–71; connectives as, 96, 198–99, 246; structure world, 134, 141; and functions, 139, 141, 250; and substances, 166; in Moore, 166, 169; in Husserl, 202–5, 210; in Wittgenstein, 230, 244–63; and possibilities, 275. *See also* Connectives; Exemplification; Intentional nexus; Subsistence

Gegenstand, 139

Gellner, E., 171

Generality, Essay III 64–84; and quantifiers, 66–70, 78–80; subsists, 67, 70, 75; represented, 70, 81–82;

presented, 70, 71, 75; not a "thing," 70, 71–72, 75; and definition, 78–80, 81–82

Gentile, G., 13

Goodman, N., 160n, 186, 187

Grossmann, R., viii, 4, 5, 12n, 50n, 98n, 125, 147n, 198n, 204n, 243, 302n, 338n

Hahn, H., 243

Hegel, G. W. F., 222

Hintikka, J., 307n

Hobbes, T., 29

Hochberg, H., viii, 38n, 98n, 158n, 159, 162, 292n

Holism, 111, 114, 116, 239

Hume, D.: and causality, 23, 35, 117, 332; on mind, 132, 201

Husserl, E., Essay X 193–224; and subsistents, 130, 198, 240, 249; *Logische Untersuchungen*, 130, 193n, 194, 199, 202–16 *passim*, 220, 240; and basic ties, 160n, 202–5, 210; *Ideen*, 193n, 199, 211–24 *passim*, 241; and mental acts, 193, 194, 205, 209–14, 301, 309; and idealism, 193, 194, 199, 208, 213, 214, 216, 217–24, 241; and realism, 193, 194, 199, 240, 307; and nominalism, 194, 203, 215, 217; and relations, 194, 205–8, 210, 217, 224, 240; *Erfahrung und Urteil*, 216; mentioned, 239, 336n, 340

Hypostatization: of form, 51, 81, 88; of thought, 135n, 139, 142, 145n, 163; of truth, 139, 143, 148, 149, 155

Idealism, 7, 9, 13, 19, 23, 25, 35, 128, 235, 302–40 *passim;* commonsense core of, 20, 22, 42; and time, 104; and Frege, 124–25, 145, 148–49; vs. realism, 125, 126, 130–31, 156, 229, 264–65, 307, 312; vs. materialism, 126, 336; and phenomenalism, 132, 194, 218, 329, 336; objective, 148, 149, 153, 173; and reism, 149, 159; and judgment, 153–54, 321; of Husserl, 193, 194, 208, 213, 216; and truth, 229, 239, 273, 295; and language, 238, 239

Ideal language: and philosophical method, 6, 7–8, 46, 83–84, 88, 92–93,

25, 32–34, 40, 92n, 93–95, 115, 116n,
119, 135, 152, 208–9, 219, 235, 268–
71, 307; of sentences, 60, 61; "same",
80, 95–97; and reference, 85–86, 89,
114, 237, 268; and ontology, 85–97
passim; contextual, 94n; meanings
of, 94, 237; logical, 96; and logic, 152,
235, 268–69; and verification, 237;
238; and use, 237, 239. *See also* Intentional nexus
Measurement, 106
Mechanics: Newtonian, 113, 121;
quantum, 122, 338
Meinong, A., 25, 50n, 312n
Memory, 5, 36
Mental: use of term, 11, 21, 26, 31, 35,
44, 148, 304; and phenomenal, 11,
30, 35, 208, 223, 306; and phenomenology, 20, 28, 29, 36–38, 39, 306,
308, 310; entities, 31, 44, 118, 126,
135, 208, 214, 234, 266, 310; vs. nonmental, 126, 128, 273, 304–5, 308,
310, 326; and acquaintance, 307;
complexes, 310–11. *See also* Acts
Merleau-Ponty, M., 222n
Mill, James, 328n, 330
Mind: analysis of, Essay I 3–44 *passim,*
252–53, 328; ontological status of, 5,
18, 31, 44, 156, 219, 226, 234–36; and
meaning, 10, 20, 22, 23, 25, 32–34,
40, 92n, 93–95, 115, 116n, 119, 135,
152, 208–9, 219, 235, 268–71, 307;
and body, 20–22, 121n, 234–36, 267,
328, 337; and substance, 24, 31, 213,
235, 240, 321, 328; Aristotelian-
Thomistic account of, 26, 34, 126,
156, 213, 235, 304–5, 332; what is
"in" it, 26, 34, 156, 235, 264, 265,
305, 326–27, 329, 332, 333, 339; and
time, 44, 104, 208, 222, 238, 310, 328;
activity of, 149, 153, 159, 213, 223–
24, 240, 241, 281, 295, 321, 323; and
world's form, 157, 235–36, 240; and
rules, 252, 257; independent of, 313,
316, 321, 339; dependent on, 322–
23, 339; intentionality of, 323. *See
also* Acts
Models in physics, 121–23
Monism, 196, 197
Moore, G. E., Essay VIII 158–70; and
propositions, 3, 163, 169; and sense

data, 15, 20, 29, 325n, 339; and
common sense, 15, 178; and mental
acts, 16, 72, 194, 211, 318n; and
realism, 24, 159, 166, 167, 223, 317–
18n, 339n; and existence, 74–75,
164–65, 167, 169; his ontology,
Essay VIII 158–70; *Principia Ethica,*
158, 159, 162; *Some Main Problems
of Philosophy,* 159, 165, 169; and
nominalism, 163, 169; and simples,
169; mentioned, 239, 316

Nakhnikian, G., 77n
Name: and exemplification, 8, 48, 231;
explication of, 9, 46, 75–76, 146, 227,
247; and simple, 9, 32, 46, 58, 61, 65,
76, 81, 91, 146, 148, 227; and categories, 49, 81, 146n, 179, 231; and
descriptive signs, 53, 65, 228; and
sentences, 59, 60, 61; and existence,
75–76, 146, 227–28; "proper", 93,
179, 187; and the presented, 104,
227; and identity, 144n, 146, 147;
and communication, 179, 187, 237–
38
Natures, 23, 115, 117, 165, 166, 206–7,
213, 275, 277–80
Necessary truth, 189, 204–5, 213, 232–
33, 251, 255–56, 269; and intel-
legibility, 204–5, 219
Negation, 60–62, 79–80, 137n
Newton, I., 113, 121, 123, 287
Nominalism: explicated, 9, 47, 75, 133,
196, 246, 262, 281; and localization,
110, 114, 219, 281, 293–94; and
Frege, 124, 140, 250; and psychologism, 133, 194; and Aristotle, 150;
and subsistents, 150, 277; and
Moore, 163, 169; and Husserl, 194,
203, 215; and common names, 215

Occam's razor, 277, 324
Ontological status: of exemplification,
8, 49–56, 81–82, 86–88, 134, 179,
197–99, 200, 245–63; of form, 10,
51–54, 56, 59, 63, 81, 90, 111, 140,
228–33, 256–57; explicated, 56, 65,
72, 84, 86, 195, 227, 232, 244, 306–7;
of existence, 75, 84; of integers, 84;
of logic, 84, 151; of complexes, 90,
246; of possibility, 90, 94, 306; rep-